i

SUNDANCING AT ROSEBUD AND PINE RIDGE

SUNDANCING AT ROSEBUD AND PINE RIDGE

Thomas E. Mails

Published by
The Center for Western Studies—
an historical research and archival agency
of Augustana College, Sioux Falls,
South Dakota

ISBN: Regular edition 0-931170-01-X
ISBN: Leather bound edition 0-931170-05-2
Library of Congress Catalog Card Number: 78-55075
Copyright 1978 by Thomas E. Mails
Published by The Center for Western Studies
  All rights reserved including the right of
  reproduction in whole or in part
Prepared and printed by Graphic Publishing Co., Inc.
  Lake Mills, Iowa

CONTENTS

I	Prelude To The Sun Dance: Where The Past Still Lives In The Present—Thomas E. Mails	1
II	Terminology And Sources—Thomas E. Mails	15
III	Sioux History: Tetons, Oglalas, Brules—Thomas E. Mails	27
IV	The Vow And The Sun Dance Pledgers Of 1974—Thomas E. Mails	43
	The Sun Dance Intercessor—Eagle Feather	45
	The Sun Dance Pledgers of 1974—Eagle Feather	47
V	The Vision Quest—Thomas E. Mails	61
VI	Jesse White Lance, And The Sun Dance Of August, 1956—Eagle Feather	69
VII	Preparations For The Sun Dance of 1974—Eagle Feather	75
	The Problems Of Putting On A Sun Dance—Thomas E. Mails	78
VIII	Preparations For The Sun Dance Of 1975—Thomas E. Mails	81
IX	The Sweatlodge And The Sacred Rite of Purification—Eagle Feather	87
	Stones—Thomas E. Mails	95
	The Number of Sweatlodges—Thomas E. Mails	95
	The Yuwipi—Thomas E. Mails	95
X	The Mystery Circle And The Sacred Pipe—Thomas E. Mails	97
	Building The Dancing Lodge—James O. Dorsey and George Bushotter	104
	The Shelter—Frances Densmore	104
XI	The Mystery Circle Altar—Thomas E. Mails	111
	The Altar—Frances Densmore	112
XII	The Preparations Tipi—Thomas E. Mails	115
	Tent Of Preparation—James O. Dorsey and George Bushotter	116
XIII	The Sacred Tree Of 1974—Eagle Feather	119
	The Sacred Tree Of 1975—Thomas E. Mails	125
	The Sacred Tree—James O. Dorsey and George Bushotter	127
	The Sacred Tree—Frances Densmore	129
XIV	The Sun Dance Costume and Body Paint—Thomas E. Mails	135
	Body Paint—Fools Crow	138
	Decoration Of Candidates—James O. Dorsey and George Bushotter	139
	Costume And Body Paint—Frances Densmore	139
XV	Sun Gazing and Dancing—Eagle Feather	143
	The Sun Dance Step And Music—Thomas E. Mails	154
	Capt. Bourke On The Sun Dance—James O. Dorsey	156

	Forms Of Torture And Ear Piercing— Frances Densmore	163
	Puberty Ceremony At The Sun Dance— James O. Dorsey	167
	The Conclusion Of The Sun Dance— Thomas E. Mails	168
XVI	The Rosebud Sun Dance Of July 3-6, 1975— Thomas E. Mails	169
XVII	The Pine Ridge Sun Dance—Fools Crow	197
	The Traditional Sun Dance of July 26-29, 1975— Thomas E. Mails	219
XVIII	Postlude To The Sun Dance—Thomas E. Mails	227
	Footnotes	235
	Bibliography	236
	Pictorial Record Of The Rosebud Sioux Sundances Of 1974 And 1975	237

List of Original Oil Paintings by Thomas E. Mails

Ponca Sun Dancer in typical plains costume of the 1870s	53
Traditional powwow dancer Ellis Head	54
The Spirit Keeper and Jerry Dragg invoking the Sun	55
Sun Dancers in traditional costumes at Rosebud in 1928	56
Orrie Farrell	105
The piercing	106
George Eagle Elk and Titus	107
The healing ceremony	108
The piercing of Robert Blackfeather	157
Pulling back on the rope	158
Gilbert Yellow Hawk	159
Going forward to touch the Sun Pole	160

To all those
who dance
each year
that the people
might live.

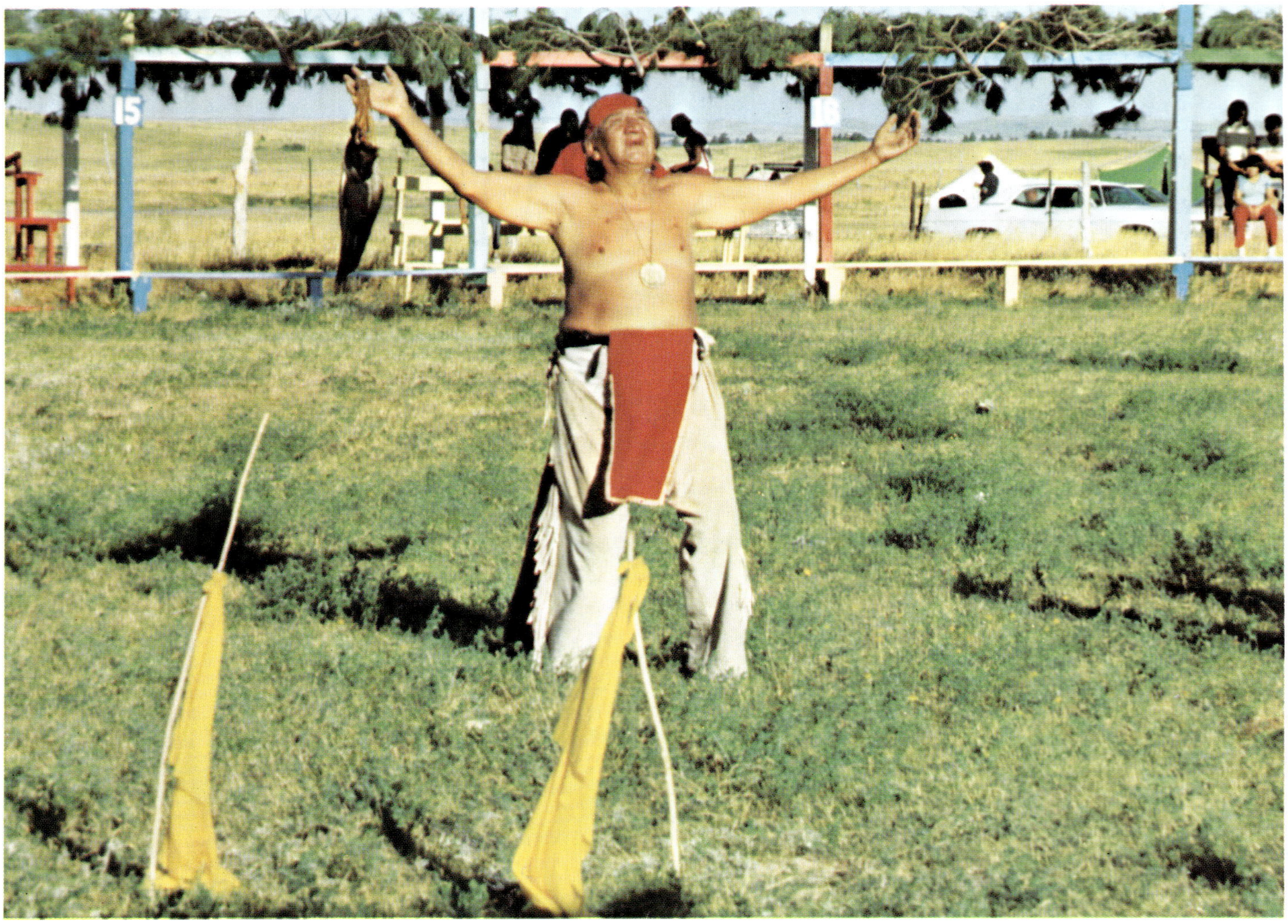

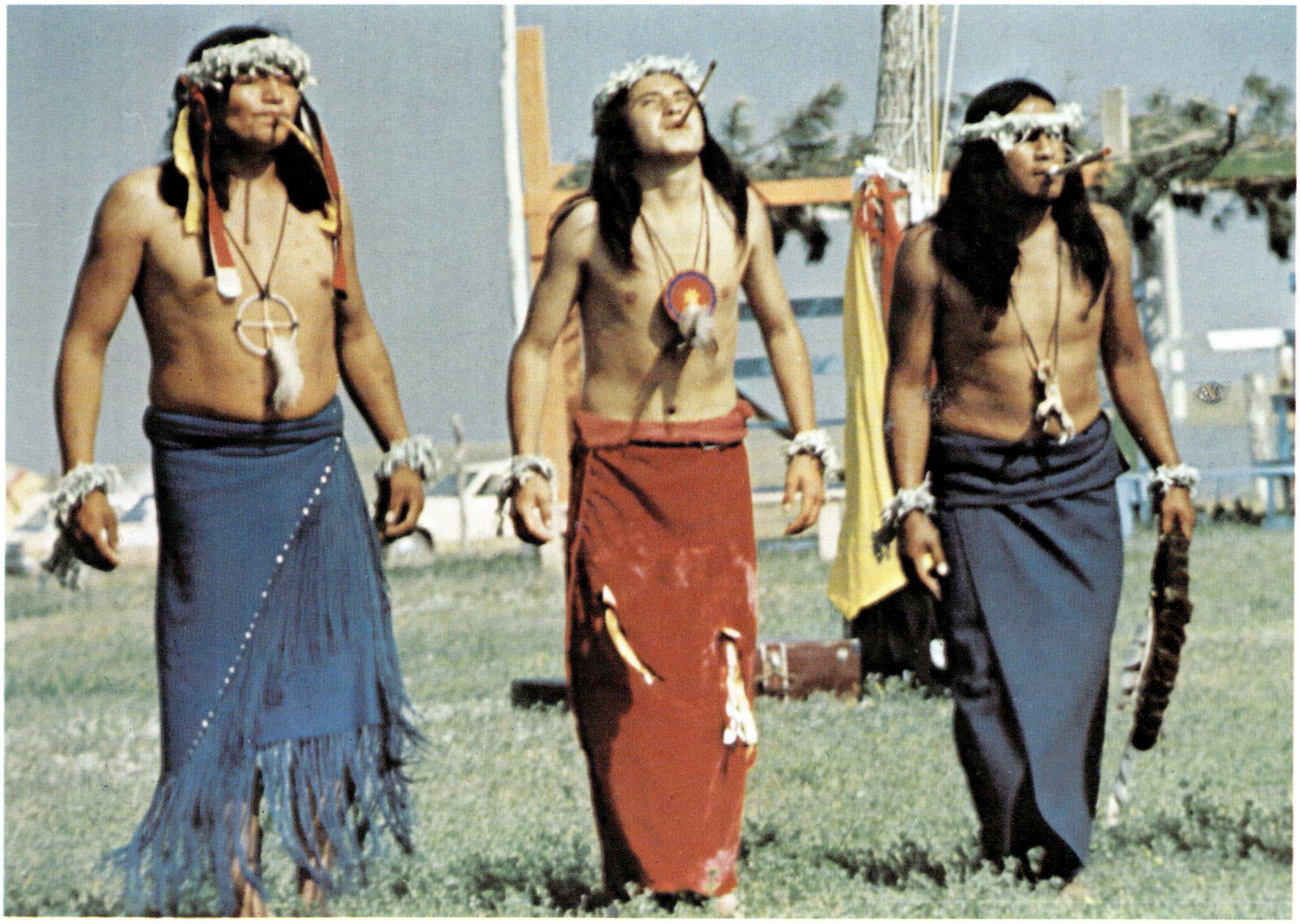

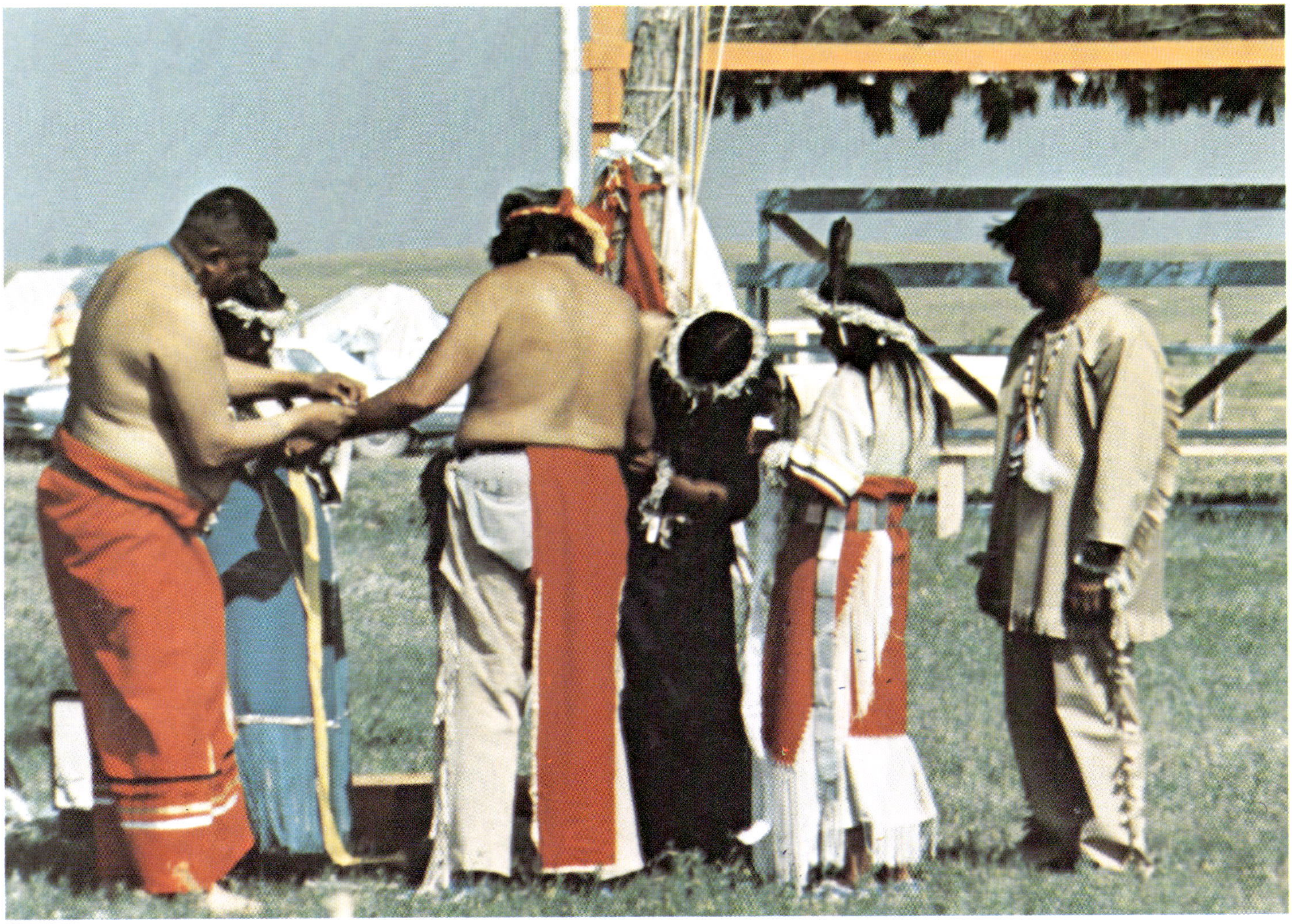

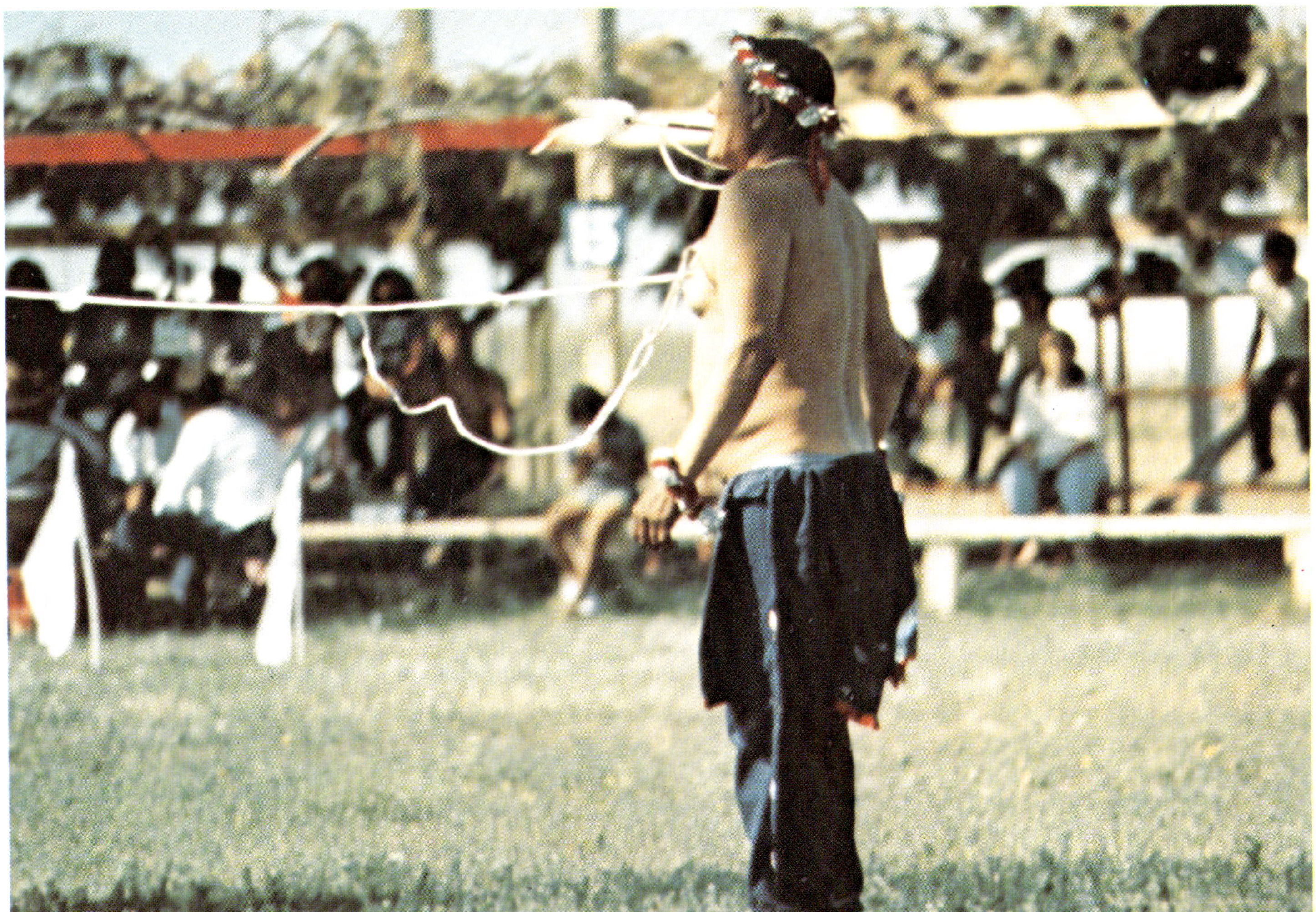
15

1
Prelude To The Sun Dance: Where The Past Still Lives In the Present

THOMAS E. MAILS

We left Pierre early and were not many miles on our way that Saturday morning in July, 1974, when Arthur said what was already on my mind: "It's beautiful." At 6:00 A.M., the South Dakota wheat and hay fields were assuredly in fine fettle, a rich, mellow combination of apple-green and burnished gold under a deep blue sky.

Still, the endless rolling hills were not so spectacular as the Rocky Mountains of Colorado, nor so colorful as the red rock canyons of Arizona. No one would rate them among the scenic wonders of America. Mile after mile they looked the same.

"I never feel so aware of God as when I am here," he went on. That moved us closer to why he had said "beautiful." Arthur was Arthur Mahoney, a ballet master who had spent most of his life in cities. It was not hard to understand why the vast expanse of earth and sky would speak to him in such a special way.

But there was something more profound than that involved in his selection of the term. Arthur had been close to the native inhabitants of South Dakota for many years, and as I had, he had fallen in love with the Sioux.

This very morning we were on our way to the Rosebud Reservation, the home of the Brule, to share with them one of the annual celebrations of their great religious drama, the Sun Dance, which they speak of as "bringing down the sun power."

To be at a Sun Dance is a remarkable experience, one that is as much a part of today as it was of yesterday. It is a link with the engrossing past of an exceptional people, and for many of the Sioux it is the core of their present life as well.

When Arthur said, "It's beautiful," what he really meant was that every part of what we were moving into at that moment was magnificent and enchanting: the land, the air, their inhabitants above our heads and at our feet, the promise of what we were to see at Rosebud—each was an important part of the experience ahead.

Oh, we were neither unaware of the squalor we would see, nor of the frightful damages done to the people themselves by a century of reservation life. Nor were we naive about the human shortcomings we would find, nor of the occasional inartistic aspects of the modern dance. To say that one has fallen in love with the Sioux is not to say that all Sioux are lovable. Yet even these aspects remained beautiful because we knew that the word can also apply to forms of survival in the face of seemingly hopeless odds. When a gifted people are given no place in the present, they dream of the past, they

scheme for the future, and for the moment they dance the dances that have sustained their people for generations. They dance resolutely, persistently, passionately, and for a while at least the participants rise above the earth and the odds. The outside world is still there. The sun comes up and glares. The ground turns steadily warmer and warmer, and the heat rises up from it in shimmering and stifling tentacles to grasp at those who presume to walk and dance upon it. But at the Sun Dance ground it is neither resisted nor noticed. The Sioux are free and proud again in mind and body. The thoughts are good thoughts, and a desire for harmony reigns. The forbidding and the foreboding melt away for a time, and that is beautiful—at least to those who care about such things.

George Bird Grinnell pointed out an important consequence of the dance, saying that "the sacred influences extend through the entire camp and last throughout the ceremony," making the occasion "one particularly favorable for the performance of any spiritual and sacred operations of which prayer is especially a part."[1] He suggests that awesome forces for good can be loosed at a Sun Dance, which also means that its influence will expand and remain when the dance is over. The Sun Dance effects change.

All this is firmly in the mind of the Traditional Sioux whenever a Sun Dance is held, and it was in our minds, too, as we journeyed on.

In writing about the Sun Dance one is tempted to begin with a vivid description of the absorbing, flesh-piercing ritual. But to do so is a tragic mistake, for in focusing everything upon a single, albeit sensational, fraction of an entire and splendid religious ceremony, the overall significance of the four-day event is missed, and it is inevitable that the rest of the Sun Dance will be ignored and misunderstood—even by some Indians.

That is indeed a tragedy, because the Sun Dance is a profound celebration of thanksgiving, growth, prayer, and sacrifice. It is full of significance, full of power, and full of drama, for the Sioux and for all mankind.

It was the failure of the United States Government reservation agents to recognize this truth that caused them, beginning in 1881, to issue a series of foolish edicts banning the performance of the Sun Dance. As Frances Densmore said, "It is probable that no Indian ceremony has been misinterpreted so widely and so persistently as the Sun Dance."

Although the publicly held dances did not cease immediately thereafter, they weren't to survive uncontested and in their old way for long. Agent James McLaughlin believed that he had put an end to them at Standing Rock in the summer of 1882. Agent William A. Swan made the Cheyenne River Sioux call off their Sun Dance in 1883.[2] Agent V. T. McGillycuddy permitted the Pine Ridge Sioux to hold a last Sun Dance in 1883. Then, on April 10, 1883, the Commissioner of Indian Affairs issued a set of rules he hoped would stifle forever the "demoralizing and barbarous" customs of the Sioux. Henceforth it would be against the law to hold feasts and dances, and in particular, the Sun Dance. In 1904, the Department of Interior issued a law prohibiting its performance.[3]

Taking these actions as a whole and at surface value, one would gather that the Sun Dances did come to a disheartening end. Many sympathetic researchers have in fact assumed this, and have gone on to lament the ruinous woes that consequently descended upon the Sioux. I agree only in part. The woes came, but not because the Sun Dances were concluded. When, for example, Robert Utley states that the dance at Pine Ridge in 1883 was "the last held anywhere on the Great Sioux Reservation,"[4] my evidence tells me that he is wrong.

Some of the Pine Ridge and Rosebud Reservation country is like the famous Black Hills of South Dakota. It is studded with dark green spruce trees, and etched with beautiful stone formations.

4

Before explaining precisely why he is in error, though, we should first consider the reasons for the issuance of the edicts.

In his book, *My Friend, the Indian,* published in 1910, McLaughlin reveals the state of mind of those at the turn of the century who thought they were putting a fit end to the ritual:

> In 1880 he writes, "I was offered the agency at Standing Rock. The place was an important one from the fact that many of the Indians had been out as hostiles, and they required treatment by a man who knew the Sioux. It was the fall of the following year before I moved to Standing Rock.
>
> The sun-dance was the most baneful of the old-time practices of the Sioux people. It was not, as is generally supposed, a function to test the personal courage of the candidates for place among the warriors. That was merely an incident of the ceremony. It was held for the purpose of propitiating by personal sacrifice the Great Spirit, and placating the pernicious spirits of the earth. It was an obligation purely, the persons taking part desiring to show that they were willing to submit to personal suffering in the hope that the community would be blessed in the harvest, or in any undertaking in which they were about to engage. The sun-dance pole, which was usually about twelve inches in diameter at the base and twenty feet in length, was selected with much ceremony. After being carefully prepared, the larger end was set in the ground a sufficient depth to give it firmness. Throughout the preliminaries the medicine men fasted and prayed, and during the dance the ears of children were pierced.
>
> While the ceremony was in progress, and the candidates were suspended by lariats run through the muscles of their breasts or back, from a cross-bar situated near the top of the pole, the prayers and dancing went on without interruption, the selected singers chanting in weird and mournful strains. The men fastened to the pole made good their self-immolation by staring continually at the sun, in consequence of which their eyes invariably became terribly inflamed. Some of the lookers-on would plead with the candidates that they be cut down, to which they would not consent. On the contrary, they whistled continuously to show that they were not affected by their sufferings. Other candidates for the sacrifice had buffalo-heads attached to their bodies by lariats with skewers through their back muscles, and ran around jumping and dancing until the weight of the drag broke the flesh away.
>
> Among the Sioux, the sun-dance invariably continued three consecutive days, the test of courage and endurance being reserved for the last day. The lacerated wounds received no attention in the way of dressing or being cared for until the dance ended at sundown on the third day. At one of such dances, which I attended in 1872, a young man had raw-hide thongs run through the muscles of his back, the thongs being attached to a cross near the top of the sundance pole, and another young man was fastened to the pole by thongs through the muscles of his breast. Both remained with their feet barely touching the ground, swaying back and forth for an hour or more before being released by the sorely tried flesh giving away.
>
> Before leaving Devils Lake, I put a stop to a sun-dance, and believe that it has never been practiced there since. Learning that there was such a ceremony in progress at Wood

But most of the land is like that near the Rosebud Fairground. It is quite flat, and well populated with prairie dogs and rattlesnakes. Cattle and horses graze there, but it is not good for farming.

Lake, about ten miles east of Fort Totten, I took with me J. E. Kennedy, agency clerk, and Tawacihomini, an Indian policeman, and went to the scene of the dance. The Indians were in the midst of this barbarous ceremony when we broke through their ring and stopped the affair. It was good evidence of their subjection that they stopped without protest when ordered to desist, an outcome that would not have been possible a few years previous, when such an attempt would doubtless have resulted seriously to the sacrilegious interloper."[5]

McLaughlin was self-deluded. He was hardly "a man who knew the Sioux"—unless, of course, he meant that he was a man who knew how to devastate a people by taking from them the things that mattered most. It was this same James McLaughlin who ordered the bungled arrest which led to the death of Sitting Bull.

Fredrick W. Hodge has written that "the Sun Dance was not only the greatest ceremony of the Plains tribes, but was a condition of their existence."[6] Numerous anthropologists have agreed with him. Therefore, Robert Utley is close to correct when he writes that the Sioux "were forced to surrender a large group of customs on which the old life was focused. During the following decade (1880-1890) the white man cut the very heart out of the only life they knew."[7]

Yet it must be emphasized again that the Sun Dance should not be lumped in with the surrendered customs until a distinction in terminology is made between "concluded" and "affected." Hodge's phrase, "a condition of their existence," gives us the key. People do not give up, under any circumstances, that which their life depends upon. In fact, adversity increases practice of it, especially if it is a religious matter. The Sioux gave up neither the Sun Dance nor its torture aspect.[8]

What did happen when the agents issued their edicts was that changes occurred in the location and the nature of the dance, even though it was performed as close to the old way as circumstances would permit. It could be said that the dance "went underground."

We shouldn't blame the agents and others for not knowing this. Even such supposedly informed men as Sioux Chief Standing Bear were deceived into thinking that performance of the dance had ceased. "It was," he wrote, "about the middle of the summer of 1879 that I saw the last great Sun Dance of the Sioux. The Brules were holding the dance about six miles southwest of Rosebud Agency, on the place where old Chief Two Strikes band now have their allotments."[9] And then Standing Bear inadvertently explains why he didn't know better. "As I started for Carlisle Indian School in the fall of 1879, I cannot say whether this was the last dance held or not."[10]

Indeed it was not, and I have already mentioned the dances which were either held or attempted on the reservations in 1881, 1882, and 1883. In addition, the photographer John A. Anderson took pictures of a Sun Dance at Rosebud which he dates 1910.[11] In his comments he notes that instead of being pierced, the five main participants used ropes passing under arms and around their backs.

These, however, were only the known dances. Far more Sun Dances were being held than most people imagined, a fact which in itself proves that there is nothing malicious about the intent of the dance. It is not a stimulus to rebellion but, when done in the traditional way, is rather a springboard to peace and unity.

My strongest evidence for disputing the claims that the dance was discontinued after 1883 and not resumed until permission was granted for the public ceremonies of 1928 at Rosebud and 1929 at

Consecrating the Mystery Circle at Rosebud in 1928.

Pine Ridge comes from the esteemed Frank Fools Crow, the eighty-seven-year-old Ceremonial Chief of the Teton Sioux. He has been a practicing holy man at Pine Ridge since 1913, and the principal Sun Dance Intercessor since 1929.

Declaring that I knew the Sioux consider the holding of the Sun Dance vital to their well-being, and adding that I just couldn't believe that either the dance or the piercing were ever terminated, I questioned Fools Crow about it at Martin, South Dakota, in June, 1975.

He replied that at Pine Ridge the dances were held nearly every year in one of two ways: as semipublic Sun Dances without piercing, done quietly with no fanfare and with the occasional knowledge of the Agency officials, but no interference from them; or as secret Sun Dances with piercing, performed back in the hills and including audiences. Harry Paige confirms this by mentioning that "there are still a few old-timers who bear the scars of *sub rosa* dances held in remote sections of the reservation from time to time."[12]

Whenever secret piercings took place, extraordinary precautions were taken to avoid discovery by Agency officials and Indian policemen.

A sacred tree, with the attached rawhide images of man and buffalo, and the cherry branch bundle, was set up in a clearing in a remote area, and it remained there for four days. The tree was cut short so as not to attract attention. As a further camouflage, no shade was built around the Mystery Circle for the spectators.

Aside from these precautions, the traditional format for the Sun Dance was followed. The pledgers danced each day for four days from sunrise to sundown. At sundown they returned to their homes and pretended that nothing out of the ordinary was going on. The next morning they sneaked back and resumed the dancing. The piercing took place on the fourth morning.

A few White spectators were present at some of these secret dances. They were sympathetic and knew the severe penalties if the Sioux were caught, so they did not report these occurrences and kept the secrets of their Indian friends.

The Sioux Sun Dance has thus been held continuously since its origin with the White Buffalo Maiden, and it gives every evidence of going on for as long as the people last.

Actually, one ought to wonder why the Government sought to ban the Sun Dance in the first place.

Certain friends of mine who are holy men think they know the reason, and told me, as recently as this past summer, that the dance was banned because the White authorities thought it was done "to put a curse on the Whites." The reports of the agents in 1881 bear this out. There is no question but that they believed the Sun Dances, for which thousands of Sioux and other Indian people assembled, were potential hotbeds for inflaming an already discontented and hostile people. One can easily understand and sympathize with such fears. The disastrous Custer affair on the Little Big Horn was only five years old and still a vivid memory. The Ghost Dance, which took warlike overtones among the Sioux, was already being performed elsewhere and, moving from tribe to tribe, was approaching Sioux country. In reinforcement of the Agency anxieties, it reached the peak of its frenzy among the Sioux in the middle of 1890.

But there were other reasons, perhaps more important than fear of another Sioux uprising, for the attempt to ban the Sun Dance. The first was rooted in the untenable belief that because a materialistic society is economically stronger and makes greater progress in some ways than a spiritualistic one, the materialistic society is superior in all ways and all realms, the religious and the cultural, as well as the practical. One society is plainly civilized, the other is plainly heathen. Therefore, the dominant system sees no reason to listen to the subordinate one. After 1881, it was a firmly established opinion that the subjugated Indians had nothing worthwhile to say. Regrettably, and at considerable, although perhaps unrecognized, cost to everyone concerned, that is still close to the case a century later.

A second reason for misunderstanding and thus fearing the dance was more subtle. It had to do with myopia. George Bird Grinnell was concerned about this when he wrote about the Cheyenne Indians in 1923. In considering the torture aspect of the Sun Dance—actually called the Medicine Lodge by the Cheyenne—he said that "to the civilized eye the acts [of torture] were so striking that they obscured the real ceremony, which has thus always been misunderstood." Continuing on, he wrote:

"Civilized man usually assigns to primitive people under his observation those motives and modes of reasoning that he himself would employ under like circumstances, but often the motives of the savage and his reasoning may be wholly different from those of civilized man, and he may be governed by impulses that the latter would not at all understand. The difficulty of getting at the basic motive for any act by the old-time Indians is very great, and years of association, study, and inquiry may be needed to discover the real facts in such connection.

"It was the practice of the primitive Indian, when he found himself in situations of difficulty or danger, to promise to sacrifice to the great powers, in case these powers would help him, something that was very precious; and what can be more precious than a man's own body and blood? Such sacrifices are confined to no race, creed, or sect. From earliest times this has been a means of invoking the help of the powers that rule the universe. The parallel between Old Testament sacrifices and those of the Indians is close. Analogous offerings are made by Christians today.

"All these things have to do with long ago, and are no longer performed in public, though, as I shall show farther on, young men who desired to offer this sacrifice to the powers have done so within the last few years. The strongly religious character of the Indian, and his simplicity, tend to keep alive in him these notions which in others we call primitive, but which we regard as wholly natural if they are found in sacred books in which we believe." [13]

Part of the problem, then, was that Agency officials made no attempt to appreciate the intent of the Sioux in performing the Sun Dance. When the concepts of the conquered did not fit the views of the conquerors, they took for granted that the subjugated people were wrong. They saw only what was done, and how, but never asked why. The only resource was to stamp the "pagan" ritual out. That was best for all concerned. This was the steadfast position of Anglos who thought of themselves as the only true believers in God.

A third reason for misjudging the Sun Dance was that a number of skeptics sought to evaluate, explain, and judge the religious practices of a people whose entire lives were faith-centered. It should be evident by now that this is an impossibility, yet the atheist and agnostic in America continues today the bicentennial-old practice of believing that he can, from outside the faith, present a fair and accurate portrayal of what a wholly religious people truly amount to.

Religions are in such instances always derided, and frequently relegated to primitive superstition and paganism. If an opinion as to how the Indians feel about this is desired, it should be asked of the traditional Sioux holy men. I have, and their response to being judged by nonbelievers brings forth, to say the least, a withering blast of condemnation.

Therefore, I would like to repeat what I have written in other books: that while I fully respect the right of any person to express an opinion, the reader is entitled to know plainly whence the author speaks. How else can the opinion be judged? [14] It is only fair that whenever anyone speaks or writes about the religious practices of the Indian peoples, the opinions expressed should be prefaced with a statement as to the writer's own religious view. The rest of what is said can then be weighed in that light.

I am a practicing Christian, and I have profound respect for the Indian religions. I have, as a consequence, been able to achieve excellent rapport with several noted Sioux holy men, and they have given me every assistance in bringing this inside account of the Sun Dance into being.

The obvious alternative to the problems posed by the three approaches just mentioned is first to look at the Sun Dance as fully as is possible, and then attempt to evaluate it from the Indian's point of view.

The Sioux announcers repeat over and over again as the pledgers dance: "This is our religion, this is our religion, this is our religion." [15]

I confess that when I first heard this chant, I was puzzled. Were the announcers, I wondered, saying that the Sun Dance alone was their religion? That couldn't be, since the Sioux perform numerous other ceremonies. Finally the meaning dawned on me. The Sun Dance performance, at one point or another during the four days,

includes every aspect of the Sioux religion. Everything spiritual they do on a year-round basis is represented within the single ceremony. That is what makes the Sun Dance so great and so special. Therefore, if a person goes to a Sun Dance with this understanding and watches carefully, he will see revealed before his eyes the essence of the Sioux religion as practiced from the time of the White Buffalo Maiden until now. Some things may be emphasized more than others, but nothing is left out.

The Sun Dances of olden times were magnificent events. For two weeks during the summer of most years the entire Sioux band would gather in a splendid encampment to renew friendships, to reorganize the societies, to bolster political ties and stability, to plan for the future, and to join in their religion, the Sun Dance.

Under reservation strictures, the pattern was curbed and changed drastically. From 1883 to 1920, the Sun Dance with torture went underground, and the only public celebrations consisted of fairs held on the Fourth of July and at harvest time in the fall. Semisecret Sun Dances without piercing were held in the twenties, and from 1928 through the thirties were conducted openly. In the forties, interest in the Sun Dance lagged somewhat, while powwows and fairs took over the limelight. Some returning Sioux World War II veterans had to go to the Cheyenne to find Sun Dances to share in. In the late fifties, enthusiasm for the Sun Dance revived, and the public piercing was begun by the Traditionalists. But the influential liberals either disdained it or sought to use the dance as an opportunity to advance social and political interests.

Ethel Nurge has served as editor for a book containing a number of articles which sum up the consequences in stating that while the Sun Dance was held among the Oglalas at Pine Ridge each year in early August, the real attraction that drew the crowds was the social dancing held in the afternoons and evenings. In addition, the authors say that even these purely social aspects were being avoided by the liberal "mixed-bloods," who accordingly were "neither present nor missed," and a distinction is drawn between the "true believers," who participated in the religious observance, and the tribal council people who advertised the dance as a reenactment. "Yet all differences were put aside as the social dancing got underway."

In these accounts, mention is made of "one significant revival" which took place in 1959, when self-torture was performed, and it is noted that the piercing has continued since then, with more and more men undergoing it. "However," they add, "under the sponsorship of the Oglala Tribal Council, which presents it as a tourist attraction, it [the Sun Dance] has deteriorated to the point where it is little more than an unsuccessful sideshow—a flesh carnival, if you will—in which the audience is invited to watch the spectacle of self-inflicted pain."

Finally, it is pointed out how "the conservatives [Traditionalists] consider this a mockery" of the old ways and want to take over direction of the dance for themselves, keeping it separate from the powwow. The conclusion is that if they do "it will be a major achievement."[16]

Nurge's first-rate book, *The Modern Sioux,* was published in 1970, which means that her data probably terminated in 1968 or 1969. And, in considering the Sun Dance, she mentions two factors which need further development. Over the past six years since her book was written, several important things have become clear regarding the Sun Dance.

One is that the traditional ways and traditional leaders have been stronger than most people thought, and are gaining strength with every passing day—so much so that if things continue as they are,

10

the political power on the Sioux reservations may soon shift to them.

Another is that because of reservation developments, the traditional faith has remained the cohesive cultural and moral force of the people in spite of the adoption of, or accommodation to, non-Indian ways.

Traditionalism is more prevalent now than it has been for sixty years, and it is the repository of whatever hope there is for the people. None of this should be surprising. Liberalism, as exemplified by tribal councils, has led to serious divisions and disintegration, while purpose, spirituality, morality, ethics, and insight are the basic fiber of Traditionalism. If reverence, a sense of well-being, and direction are to be found today, it will be within Traditionalism or not at all.

It is the Traditionalist who senses that the Sioux, and for that matter all Indians in America, can, by a return to as many as possible of the old methods and qualities, emerge at last as a vital part and power of modern life. Therefore, stung by what the apathetic trends have been doing to their precious Sun Dance, the Traditionalists have begun a systematic drive to upgrade it and rid it of any appendages which degrade or cheapen it.

Now the Sun Dance powwows must either be traditional dancing, and thus more reverent in tone, or else be held in another place. Any activities or actions which might be interpreted as "commercial" are severely criticized and shunned, as are the people who promote or engage in them.

Drinking liquor at or coming drunk to a Sun Dance, at Rosebud at least, is taboo; those who do so are severely reprimanded and removed from the premises. Some posters advertising a Sun Dance will say in bold type: "No Alcohol or Drugs," or "No Alcoholic Beverages Permitted."

Posters also emphasize the spiritual and traditional nature of the dances. Cameras and tape recorders may be expressly forbidden.

Some signs extend a special welcome to all Spiritual and Traditional Leaders. A poster for the Sun Dance at Crow Dog's, which took place from July 29 to August 4, 1974, and was performed in memory of "brothers" who had died, carried the line, "3 Days of Purification by All Sacred Things." Something like *eighty* pledgers took part in that dance.

The poster for the 1974 dance at the Rosebud Fairground emphasized the flesh offering and healing ceremonies, the honoring ceremonies, and a "Prayer Offering for the Spiritual Bringing Together of All Nationalities." There were also to be social dances every afternoon and evening, but the people came to support the Sun Dance, not social things, and little took place in the way of social dancing.

The need for change on the Sioux reservations is urgent. As several young men who were at the most recent Wounded Knee confrontation told me, and they meant it, "We would rather be dead than go on living as we, and our parents and grandparents, have during the last century."

So the stress today is upon tradition and, because of its central place in Indian culture, tradition in the Sun Dance particularly.

By July, 1974, Sinte Gleska College at Rosebud and the Medicine Men and Associates were already planning to "put up" a jointly sponsored and truly traditional Sun Dance in the summer of 1975. Unfortunately, lack of cohesion, or drive, or something else caused their planning and scheduling to drag on through the winter and almost until July, 1975, before anything concrete was established. There were delays in setting dates, choosing a coordinator,

a site, and an Intercessor. Pledgers did not make early vows, and long before the dance was over it could be clearly seen that the best of intentions do not replace careful planning. In this instance tradition was handled poorly, at times not even honored, and in the end some Traditionalists were left wondering whether *Wakan-Tanka* (God) did not chastise the participants for it.

Finally, in the first week of July, posters were printed advertising a "Traditional Lakota Sun Dance" to be held half a mile west of St. Francis, South Dakota, on July 26-29. This would be followed by a "Thanksgiving Powwow" from July 30 to August 2. Hopes were high, and intentions were certainly the very best. The college people would capture it on film, and for the first time in years a pure Sun Dance would be held. The implication was clear. Things would be done right at last, certainly better than had been done elsewhere, and in consequence the people would benefit greatly.

The record of this dance is set forth in Chapter 17 and will serve several purposes. It will show both victory and pathos. It will show how far the revival has come and how far it still has to go. The Intercessors who lead their own Sun Dances elsewhere will derive particular comfort from the account, for if this "Traditional Sun Dance" was indeed traditional, so is theirs. With few exceptions it simply duplicated that which others were already doing, and perhaps doing better.

At the same time, the very fact that a uniquely traditional Dance was attempted may be taken as a strong indication of the present state of mind of the college people and the medicine men. It points up their firm desire to bring the Sun Dance back to a point as identical with the performances of yesterday as is possible. Whether the people belong also to Christian churches or not, *the Sun Dance is their religion*, and they mean to celebrate it as purely and as closely to the divine command given through White Buffalo Maiden as it can be done in today's world. Its holiness, its reverence, its fervency, and its power will be observed as completely as God intended they should be.

Based on the observable data it is possible to predict that the sacred Sun Dance will grow and prosper in that manner, rather than revert to a "flesh carnival" or a "mockery."

I have personal knowledge of at least five Sun Dances which were held on the Rosebud Reservation during the summer of 1975, and there may have been more. Add to them an undetermined number held at Pine Ridge—although the killing of FBI men there in June did affect the holding of such dances—and those which must have been put on at other Sioux reservations, and finally the total picture begins to emerge. More than 120 men underwent torture on the Rosebud Reservation, and the import is plain. It will not be sit-ins at the Bureau of Indian Affairs in Washington or sieges at Wounded Knee which will gather and direct the power for most reservation Sioux. It will be Sun Dances; it will be sacrifices, healings, visions, and purification. And, at the very least, it will be soul-stirring for all of us to see what eventually comes of it.

So far, what has been said about the powwow tends to place it in an unfavorable light. Actually, I'm afraid that I'd find it hard to muster really negative thoughts about the powwows in their relationship to the Sun Dances. I'll admit that I agree with those who feel it might be best to hold them away from the Sun Dance grounds, since to do otherwise detracts from the intimacy and the reverent atmosphere of the dance. Yet I hasten to add that I do not consider a powwow irreverent—not by any means. It is only that I prefer the Sun Dance Mystery Circle to remain quiet between the hours of Sun Dancing so that one's mind stays centered on the prayers, the pow-

Ellis Head, the classic traditional pow-wow dancer, wears the porcupine-tail roach with two eagle feathers symbolizing two warriors returning from a hunting or war party.

ers, and the hopes which are always so vibrant and alive there. The best evidence of my feelings about dancing circles per se is the fact that in August of 1974 I purchased the topsoil for the new ceremonial ground at Lower Brule, knowing that it would be used far more for powwows than for Sun Dances. Whenever I think back on the honors dance and star blanket they gave me at a nighttime powwow, it is with warm thoughts of Indian feet pounding in concert with throbbing drums on soil I supplied.

I can also recall with the greatest pleasure an afternoon preceding that, when at a powwow held in Mission, South Dakota, on July 14, 1974, the several thousand Sioux assembled there gave me the rare privilege of being the first white man at Rosebud (insofar as those directing the dance were aware) to carry the American flag and lead, along with Ellis Head, who carried the Sioux nation flag, the grand entry parade of dancers. It was there that in an honor song I was given my Sioux name, *Waokiye*, which means, "One Who Helps."

So I could hardly think badly about powwows, even if I were not aware of the more important purposes they serve. Those who go to them in such great numbers today are doing so with a whole new attitude about things Indian. The people are happy. The costumes are absolutely splendid, and the dancing is impressive. Among the Sioux at least, the traditional dance style is rapidly gaining favor, and I have twice seen the entire dance arena cleared spontaneously for the elder, such as Henry Crow Dog, who performs so regally in the traditional style.

The agency town of Rosebud as viewed from the north. The large building to the right is the government hospital.

Another view from the north reveals mostly Bureau of Indian Affairs housing for employees. In the midst of the heavy growth of trees at the top left is the tree which served as the Sacred Tree for the Sun Dance of 1975.

II
Terminology and Sources

THOMAS E. MAILS

As soon as one touches upon the Sun Dance of the Sioux Indians, one begins to use terms and titles which will be meaningless to those who are not familiar with the ceremony. Therefore, I think it wise to begin with a series of explanations.

The Sun Dance ceremony is performed in a large circle called either the *Mystery Circle* or the *Mystery Hoop*.

In the exact center of the Mystery Circle is a tree called either the *Sacred Tree* or the *Sun Pole*.

Just west of the tree is an *Altar*, which consists of a pipe rack and a buffalo skull.

At the east, west, north, and south points of the circle perimeter, *Flags* are placed in pairs to establish the cardinal directions and the limits of the circle.

An arbor is built around the entire circumference of the circle to provide a sheltered area for the spectators. This is called the *Shade* or *Shade Arbor*. Its main entrance is at the east.

In addition to the Mystery Circle, there are one or more *Sweatlodges* in which the participants are purified during the ceremony. Each one has a small fire pit in which the rocks for the sweatbathing ceremonies are heated. This is called the *Old Man Four Generations Fireplace*.

Near the sweatlodge there is a tipi in which the participants dress and the ceremonial items are kept. This is called the *Tipi of Preparation* or the *Preparations Tipi*.

All of the people directly involved in the dance have titles:

The one who conducts the dance is known as the *Intercessor*, since he serves as a go-between or channel through which communication is carried on with Almighty God and his delegated powers. The Intercessor is always a holy or a medicine man.

Assisting him are other *Holy Men* or *Medicine Men*. The terms are not synonymous. A medicine man is a doctor who practices healing. He is not necessarily a priest as well. If he is both, then he is more properly called a holy man. Thus, the holy man is a prophet and spiritual counselor in addition to being a healer. The distinction may seem fine, but it is an important one to the present-day Indians. Whenever I am not certain as to the proper designation for a specific individual, I refer to him as a medicine man.

Every Sun Dance has a lead dancer who is experienced and knows how to do the ceremony. He is called either the *Dance Leader* or *Leader of the Dancers*, and he is first in line whenever the dancers assemble. He is easily identified in another way, too, since the Intercessor walks beside him and holds on to his sage wristband as the line dancers moves from one place to another within the Mystery Circle.

Each dancer carries his own pipe in the ceremony, and presents it at the prescribed time to a medicine man whose title is *Keeper of the Pipes* or *Receiver of the Pipes*. This man also has charge of the ceremonial paraphernalia, including the buffalo skull.

A man or woman superintends the sweatlodge fire pit, opens and closes the lodge door, and passes in the rocks, pipe, and water as they are needed while the purification ritual is in progress. He or she is called the *Custodian*.

Those who make vows to take part in the dance are called *Pledgers* or *Candidates*. The same title is applied to men and women, and is appropriate whether they are pierced or not.

Those who beat the drum and sing while the ceremony is in progress are called *Singers*.

A woman is sometimes asked to sit with the pledgers to comfort them while they are pierced. She may receive this additional honor when she is chosen *Mother of the Year*.

A person might also be involved in the Sun Dance as part of a Spirit Keeping ritual. This is an ancient custom by which the soul of a deceased person is "kept" for as long as a year before it is released to go to heaven. The person filling this role is known as the *Keeper of the Spirit* or *Soul*.

Piercing is the process whereby an awl or knife is thrust under and through the skin or flesh of the chest, and a stick or eagle claw is then pushed through the holes. This in turn is tied to a rope whose other end is secured to the Sacred Tree. The pledger then pulls back on the rope until the skin gives away and the stick or the claw breaks free.

Flesh Offerings are small bits of skin, perhaps a quarter of an inch square, which are cut as sacrificial thank offerings from various parts of the body—usually the arms.

The Sun Dance as it is performed by the Sioux today is a four-day ceremony. It is customarily held in July or August, but even that time is not an absolute anymore. Writers sometimes refer to it as an eight-day event, and even as a twelve-day ritual. Such designations would apply only to the old days when either one or two four-day periods of preparatory events preceded the time of the Sun Dance proper.

Old-timers are mystified when I ask them the duration of the Sun Dance. They hold up four fingers and seem unable to comprehend why anyone would think of it as lasting any longer than that. Four is, of course, the prime sacred number of the Sioux. They believe that the Great Spirit has caused everything in the world to be arranged in fours, such as, for example, four directions, four divisions of time, four parts in plants, four periods of human life. Therefore mankind achieves harmony and completeness by ordering all of his ceremonies and activities in terms of this sacred number.

I will make extensive use of the terms *tradition*, *traditional*, and *Traditionalists*. *Tradition* and *traditional* refer to the historic way in which something was done during known history of the nation up until A.D. 1890. Traditionalists are those conservative Indians who live as closely as possible in accordance with the old ways of their people. They strive to keep and even expand the ancient customs. There are three groupings of people on the Sioux reservations today: Traditionalists or conservatives—who are usually full-bloods; American Indian Movement members or activists—who are tradition-oriented; and the liberals—who consist for the most part of the politically oriented mixed-bloods who are closely allied with Federal Government offices such as the BIA.

In the modern Sioux mind, the terms *Wakan-Tanka*, Great Mystery; *Tunkasila* (Tunkashila), (Great) Grandfather; God-Head,

Great Mystery, Great Spirit, Almighty God, and God are interchangeable and synonymous. Buechel's Lakota-English Dictionary defines these as follows: God, n.p. Wakan-Tanka: Tunkasila—the Supreme Being.[1]

The antiquity of the Sun Dance as it is practiced on the Plains has been the subject of considerable debate. Some contemporary Sioux date it as far back as A.D. 1685. Non-Indian anthropologists give it a more recent origin, ranging anywhere from 1750 to 1800.

About twenty Plains tribes made the Sun Dance their most important religious festival.[2] Each had its own name for the ritual, and not all had torture rites as a part of the ceremony. The Arapaho, Cheyenne, and the Teton Sioux seem to have developed the most complex and significant Sun Dances, and these, until a few books concerning the dances of other Indian nations came out recently, have been the most widely known.

Which of the nations performed the finest old-time Sun Dance?

Several Sioux have echoed the sentiments of Standing Bear, who states: "I have read many descriptions of this dance, and I have been to different tribes which claimed they did the 'real thing,' but there is a great difference in their dances from the Sun Dance of the Sioux." Then he goes on to claim that the Sun Dance "started many years before Christopher Columbus drifted to these shores." I question both his claim regarding the antiquity of the dance and his rating of the Sioux performance, especially in the light of what is known today about the finely detailed celebrations of the Arapaho, Cheyenne, and Blackfoot. But that the Teton Sioux do rate high there is no doubt.

The changes which came with White domination altered continually the way in which the Sun Dance was performed. Over a period of less than twenty years its theme and thrust shifted from associations with the hunt and war complex to that of the survival of the culture within severe confines. It remained for some Indian nations the vital core of their answer to life's problems and needs,[3] while others phased it out and before the turn of the century were practicing the Sun Dance no more. It is still performed today, however, by the Sioux, the Arapaho, the Cheyenne, the Utes, and the Shoshone—though not necessarily on an annual basis. The Crow and the Blackfoot tribes are said to do the Sun Dance regularly, but I have no detailed information about them.

While many articles have been written about the Sioux Sun Dance, thorough accounts of the rite are few in number, and no one has given a really detailed and helpful account of any Sioux Sun Dance held since 1883. The best of the older narratives are by Black Elk, James O. Dorsey, and Frances Densmore.

In 1947-48, Black Elk, an Oglala holy man, gave Joseph Epes Brown a full description of the origin of the Sun Dance, including all the details of how the first dance was to be done.[4] The excellent thing about this account is that Black Elk places great emphasis upon the spiritual aspects that non-Indian authors usually overlook.

In 1890, James O. Dorsey was able to translate and publish an essay on the Sun Dance which was written in the Teton dialect by George Bushotter, a Teton. This is a very good explanation of the ceremony of the late eighteen hundreds and of the preparations for it.[5]

The most comprehensive details of the dance were collected by Frances Densmore, who made a study of it among the Teton and Yanktonai Sioux on the Standing Rock Reservation in 1911. Fifteen of her primary informants had had firsthand experience in the dance, and forty other eyewitnesses were interviewed.[6] Enough selected information from each of the Dorsey and Densmore public domain sources will be quoted herein to make comparisons possible between the Sun Dance as it is done today and the way it was done a century ago.

My concentrated studies concerning the Native Americans of the Great Plains began in 1962 and have been carried on continuously since that time, with their religion being an area of particular interest. Over the ensuing years, and especially during the past three, I have had the good fortune to become more than close friends with several Traditional Sioux holy men, medicine men and leaders whose experience and stature in ceremonial matters rank at the top of the finest available on the Sioux reservations of North and South Dakota. Three of these men—Dallas Chief Eagle; Frank Fools Crow, the Ceremonial Chief of the Teton Sioux; and Chief Eagle Feather—are my primary sources for the information contained in this book. Some of this material is unique because it deals at length with the contemporary dance, and because to my knowledge no other living Sioux holy men who have served as Intercessors for countless Sun Dances in this century have ever before given the inside and comprehensive details of what they do and how they interpret the various parts of the dance. Understandably, my gratitude to them is beyond measure.

In addition to the information supplied here by important performers of the dance, other Indian participants, and general research, my account is based upon four witnessed Rosebud Sun Dances: one held at the Fairground July 11-14, 1974, one held at the Fairground July 3-6, 1975, one held in an area near St. Francis July 26-29, 1975, and one held at Rosebud July 1-4, 1976.

Dallas Bordeaux, whose Indian name is Chief Eagle, is fifty years old, a Brule, and presently lives at Mission, South Dakota. He was the Community Action Program Director for the Rosebud Reservation and is now Assistant to the Tribal Chairman. He has served as the coordinator for several Sun Dances, usually knows all of the participants personally, and has been a critical student of the Sun Dance for many years. His popular book, *Winter Count*, published in 1967, contains a thorough account of the Sun Dance as it was being done in the late nineteenth century. His source material for it was gathered from Sioux elders. We are very close friends and have spent countless hours together discussing the Sioux way of life. Some of his thoughts on the Sun Dance are included here.

To my knowledge, Dallas has not been pierced in a Sun Dance, but he has vision quested, attended *Yuwipi* ceremonies, and been in the sweatlodge. He commands great respect among his people, and Frank Fools Crow considers Dallas to be his spiritual son. The high title, Chief of the Teton Sioux, was conferred upon him in a special ceremony in October, 1967. He is a delightful, fun-loving, sensitive, sincere, and brilliant man, assuredly one of the finest translators and interpreters around today.

Dallas exhibits a trait commonly found among the Sioux. He is a devout Roman Catholic and at the same time holds firmly to the traditional religious ways of his people. The older contemporary Indians are not in the least troubled by this, for they are convinced that true Christians and true Sioux Traditionalists worship the same Supreme Being.[7]

Frank Fools Crow lives near Kyle, South Dakota, on the Pine Ridge Reservation. As I mentioned earlier, he is the Ceremonial Chief of the Teton Sioux. This means that he is the highest-ranking chief among the Teton Sioux today and is recognized as such by all Traditionalists, excepting a couple of envious medicine men. He is another of my principal informants.

Frank was born sometime between 1890 and 1892, and has been

The costumes of Sioux pledgers who Sun Danced in 1928. Some held loose sage in their hands, and others sage or otter skin covered hoops.

Some pledgers wore eagle feather war bonnets, and carried staffs strung with eagle tail feathers.

On thongs around their necks were sun or sunflower symbols. The curved split-feathers worn on the head were an indication that the bearer was a buffalo dreamer. The head wreaths were sage, the wristbands were rabbit skin.

a Sun Dance Intercessor at Pine Ridge, Rosebud, and other reservations since 1929. It is obvious that he would not have been selected to fill this high position had he not merited it. So for over forty-six years he has served as a Principal Leader for the ceremony, despite the fact that he has never been pierced.

He has received some mild criticism for this, although he regularly gives flesh offerings from his forehead, arms, and feet at the dances. But Frank explains his lack of piercing as being the result of a vision in which he was given explicit instructions concerning what he should and should not do. Most Sioux understand, and pay no attention to the critics. In July, 1975, Frank Fools Crow was chosen from among nominations submitted by tribal councils from throughout the country and named "Indian of the Year" by the Indian members of the All-America Indian Days board of directors.[8]

Hardly a publication concerning the Plains nations appears nowadays which does not mention Fools Crow. In September, 1975, he led a delegation of fifty Lakota Indians to Washington in hopes of meeting with President Ford. The Chief Executive did meet with him, and also assigned his assistant, Theodore Marrs, to record everything Fools Crow said. *Wassaja*, a national newspaper of Indian America, devoted the entire front page of its October issue to coverage of the trip, including pictures of Fools Crow and recapitulation of his historic prayer before the United States Senate. In his book, *The Death of the Great Spirit,* published in 1971, Earl Shorris describes a Sun Dance at Pine Ridge in which Fools Crow served as Intercessor.[9] Vinson Brown, in *Voices of Earth and Sky,* published in 1974, devotes one full chapter and parts of several others to descriptions of Fools Crow as the exceptional holy man he is.[10]

Fools Crow and I became acquainted in August, 1974, at the Lower Brule Reservation, South Dakota. Since that time a deep friendship has flourished. We have spent many days and nights together, and I have completed for publication the enthralling story of his life.[11]

While still a young man, he was taught how to conduct the Sun Dance and the *Yuwipi* ceremony by a holy man named Stirrup, and from his earliest childhood he has been a careful observer of the ceremony. The Traditional Sioux venerate him for his ceremonial understandings and moral life. As one quite properly called a holy man, his blessing is essential for all important gatherings at most, if not all, reservations, and his presence is acknowledged in special ways whenever he appears. I find him to be the most extraordinary holy man I've ever known. As another Sioux friend put it, "To be in Fools Crow's presence is a spiritual experience."

I should insert here that Fools Crow is not alone in not being pierced. Most Sioux men have not undergone the torture in this century, and most have not made flesh offerings. Even the venerable Standing Bear admits that while he always wanted to be brave, "I do not think I could ever have finished one of these Sun Dances."[12]

Bill Schweigman, whose Sioux name is Chief Eagle Feather, was the Intercessor for Sun Dances held in July, 1974, July, 1975, and July, 1976. He is sixty-three years of age. According to several Indian sources, he is the only mixed-blood holy man on the Rosebud and Pine Ridge reservations. Yet considering the number of mixed marriages there have been over the years, I find this hard to believe. Nevertheless, I'll accept it until I know for certain otherwise.

His title, "Chief," comes from his having been ordained a Chief of the Sioux Nation Sun Dance Association in 1960. This is an incorporated organization of accepted holy men, medicine men, tribal leaders, and medicine men trainees. He is also a *Yuwipi* man—one who leads that traditional ceremony.

Further on, Eagle Feather will tell his own story of his fascinating life, so I need not dwell upon it here. I might add that he is a controversial figure, yet no one has ever told me that he conducts a Sun Dance, or any other ceremony, improperly. My experiences on the Pine Ridge and Rosebud reservations indicate that Eagle Feather is little different from a number of Sioux when he seeks financial help.

I receive numerous requests for such aid whenever I am present, and they continue to approach me by mail and telephone. I've had requests for ceremonial costs, childbirth expenses, funeral expenses, hospital costs, wood for the winter, for moving houses, for building houses, food, buffalo hides, skulls and meat, for clothing, gasoline, and for any number of "loans" that could never be returned. One should not go to the reservations as a friend unprepared to face the same requests, and if one can help, do so. Anyone who sees with his own eyes how the people are forced to live at Pine Ridge and Rosebud will know that there is no place in the world where such assistance is needed more.

Personally I feel that the people to whom I contribute are returning more than they are getting in the way of faithful friendship and dependable information. They make my knowledge and books and paintings possible. So why shouldn't I, and every other western writer, artist, or anthropologist, do everything we can to help them?

Eagle Feather is similar to all Sioux medicine men; the only difference is in technique. He exhibits an aggressive and outspoken manner. He is self-assured and direct. At the same time, these are the very qualities which make him an effective Intercessor. Sun Dances need rigid control and what cannot be faulted is Eagle Feather's experience in the Sun Dance, which enables him to achieve this. The views stated here are his own, and not intended to represent those of all medicine men.

He says that he learned all he knows from Frank Fools Crow. This is not entirely the case, since he has participated in several Sun Dances conducted by other holy men. Furthermore, there are some differences between the way Fools Crow conducts a dance and Eagle Feather's own way. Several of his ideas are unique. For example, his view of Red Power is by no means the commonly held one. He sees it in terms of the blood, while most think of it ideologically.

Since 1956, Eagle Feather has participated in twenty-eight Sun Dances, and when he was pierced in July, 1974, it was his twenty-fifth time. He knows every detail of the ceremony. In fact, it is difficult to find a record of a dance held since 1960 that does not mention his presence. John Anderson lists him as a participant who pierced at Pine Ridge in 1961, 1965, and 1966. "Billy Schweigman [Eagle Feather] was a key figure because of his Sun Dancing the past thirteen years but declared publicly that he was retiring."[13] Obviously, though, Schweigman did not retire, and it is the commonest thing in the world, when someone wants to have a Sun Dance, to sooner or later ask for his assistance. If he does not serve as the Intercessor, he helps in other ways, such as giving advice, piercing, and healing. I doubt that there is anyone living, save Fools Crow, with a more thorough knowledge of the modern Sun Dance than Eagle Feather.

I was introduced to him by Dallas Chief Eagle at the Sun Dance in July, 1974. He was occupied with conducting the dance at the time, and I became so busy soon after that that we were not able to talk much. About all that we did was make arrangements for me to take photographs and to make notes—for educational purposes.

In August of that same year I went to the Lower Brule Reservation. On the way there I stopped to see Dallas at Rosebud, and one evening we drove down to St. Francis to visit with Eagle Feather. While we were at his house, we talked about the Sun Dance. It was then that Eagle Feather learned the depth of my interest in the great ceremony, and he invited me to come by on my way back from Lower Brule for more discussion and a sweatbath.

Being a diabetic, and knowing how blazing hot sweatlodges are, my first inclination was to say no. But Eagle Feather revealed that he, too, was a diabetic and, as it turned out, was taking three times as much insulin as I. Besides that, he had had twelve heart attacks, several of which were severe enough to require hospitalization. Yet he used the sweatlodge every day and sometimes twice a day.

What could I say? I just stared at him dumbfounded for a moment, and the deal was on.

I returned to St. Francis on the morning of August 12. At 10:30 A.M., Eagle Feather, his wife Hazel, and I went into the sweatlodge. It was then that I really began to get the feel of what kind of man he was.

The structure Eagle Feather uses for bathing is a permanent one, located just a short distance east of his home. The huge stone fire pit for heating the rocks is built into the side of a hill, and the canvas-coverd lodge sits like an upside-down cup on a flat area about ten feet east of it. Average-sized, about four feet high and less than ten feet in diameter, the lodge would seat six comfortably and eight uncomfortably. Its entrance faces west, and the structure is secluded and protected from the wind; an excellent place for Eagle Feather to conduct his curing, prayer, and purification ceremonies.

I was more than eager to see the interior, and I was not disappointed. We sat on a mat of outdoor carpeting which circled the perimeter of the lodge. As I looked up at the domed ceiling I saw that it was literally festooned with brightly wrapped offerings of every kind. In fact, it looked for all the world like a decorated Christmas tree.

But the import of it all! I knew that every tiny bundle tied up there in its red, yellow, black, blue, or green package was a sacrificial offering, holding tobacco, or herbs, or flesh, or something else important. Each one marked a time of devout prayer and ceremony in the lodge, and together they gave the lodge a feeling of overwhelming significance.

The lodge had had much use. I stress this because it is a measure of Eagle Feather's sincerity about what he does, and it tells us whether or not we can assume that *Wakan-Tanka*, God, would be willing to work through him in the sweatlodge and in the Sun Dance Mystery Circle.

The prayers and the ceremony were superb. By the time the sweatlodge was over, Eagle Feather, Hazel, and I were well on our way to becoming good friends. During the next few months we corresponded by letter and telephone. On occasion I had an opportunity to help them with problems that came up.

Every now and then we discussed our deep and abiding interest in the Sioux Sun Dance, and during the winter of 1974-1975, Eagle Feather invited me to come and stay long enough when the dance was held in 1975 to be in on both the preparations and the four-day ritual itself. It was a generous offer and a golden opportunity—one that anyone who is interested in the Plains Indians and their lore would give the proverbial arm and leg to have.

Furthermore, the privilege included the freedom to sketch and to photograph with both still and movie cameras. No price was set. We did skirt the issue, but it was left to me to decide what I would do to help them put on the dance. Eagle Feather did know that I had contributed substantial amounts to the Sun Dance of 1974, and,

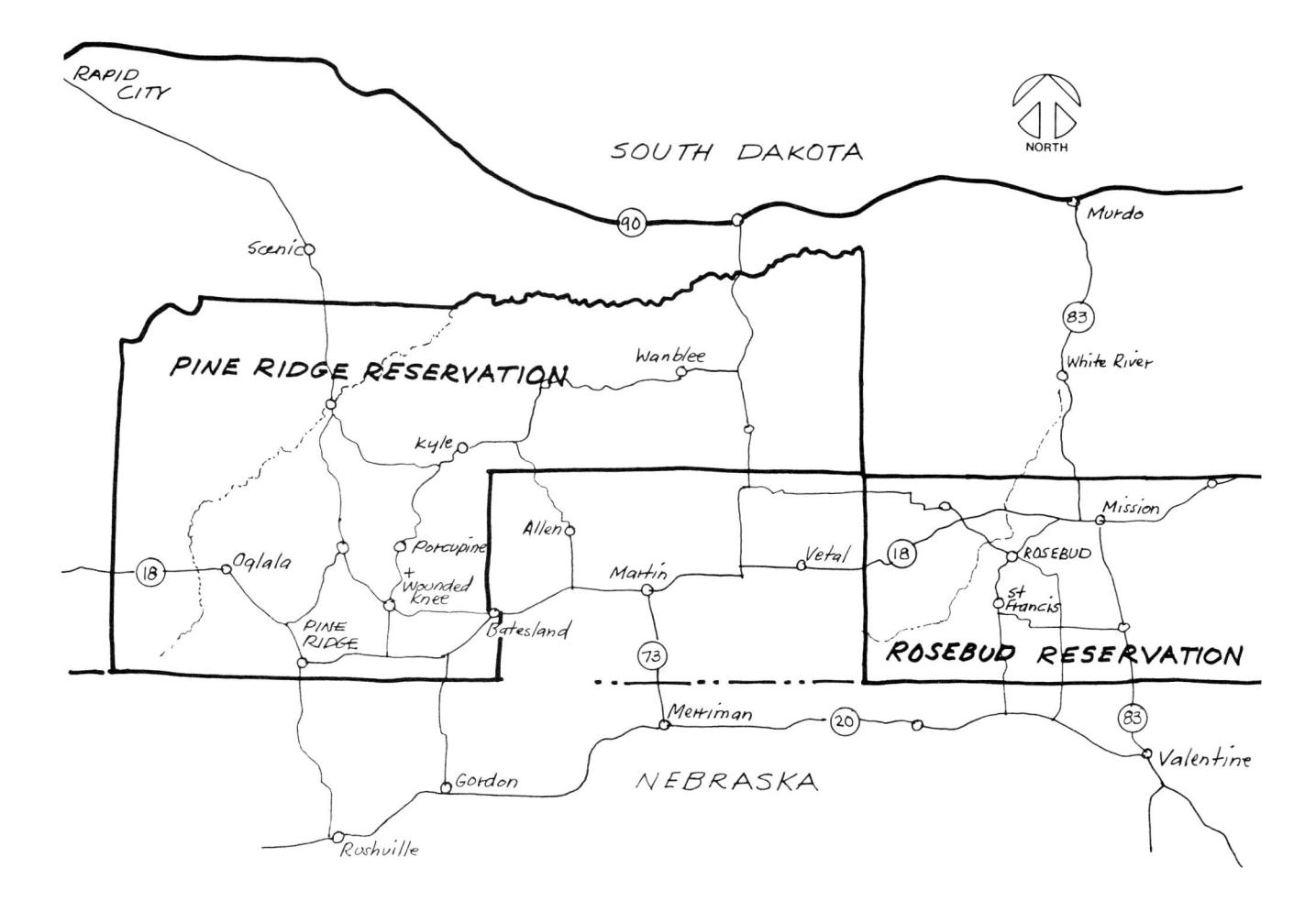

Map of Pine Ridge and Rosebud Reservations.

during the same summer, to the Mission Powwow, and that I had purchased the sod for the Lower Brule Trade Fair ceremonial ground. So he at least had high hopes. Would anyone blame him for that, considering the financial problems involved in putting on a dance? I surely didn't. Special contributions would only be a fair exchange on my part, and I was delighted at the prospect. I decided that I would contribute three cattle, and funds for extra foodstuffs and publicity costs.

I'm glad that I did so, for the 1975 dance became a milestone event in my life. In some ways my gift made Eagle Feather's load easier, too, because for once in his life he could go into a dance not needing to wonder where the funds were coming from—and when. I'll admit that I didn't mind when he said later on, "I couldn't have made it without you."

It would be satisfying to be able to say that this account is a modern-day first, that no one else has had such an opportunity to study the contemporary dance at such close quarters. Yet I find at regular intervals that just when you think you are alone in a discovery, someone else has either been there before or is in the midst of doing the same thing. So I make no such claims, and I wish others wouldn't either. Not long ago, for instance, I read that a certain artist had stated that he was the "first" to be invited by the Oglala Sioux to do a series of studies on the Sun Dance at Pine Ridge. Little did he know that at the very moment he was settling down with camera and watercolors there, I was doing the identical thing in even more detail at Rosebud, and would soon be at work on the biography of the principal Sun Dance Intercessor at Pine Ridge. I don't know what other people are collecting in the way of Sun Dance material right now, but with the interest there is, it is safe to assume that someone is busy doing something! One word of caution, though: The situation on the Pine Ridge and Rosebud reservations is highly volatile today, and they are not healthy places to be. Murders occur monthly and senseless beatings are a daily event. Indians claim that there were over 18 murders on the Pine Ridge Reservation in the first eight months of 1975. Whites are well advised to go there with utmost caution, and *not* with cameras. In the concluding chapter I will explain why conditions are as they are today, but I think that even at this point the reader can appreciate why I am doubly grateful for what I already have. I hope others will be, too.

Information was coming my way, in preparation for the dance of 1975, that would exceed my fondest expectations. Eagle Feather had decided that he could depend upon me to produce a faithful and reverent account of the Sun Dance. He therefore offered to supplement my personal materials with a full description of what preceded a typical dance, using the 1974 dance I had seen as the example and what went on during it from the holy man's point of view. We would then round out his basic information, which would be provided on tapes, with personal conversations and my further observations of his next dance, to be held in July, 1975.

If, then, this part of what I offer has been or is being duplicated elsewhere, I am not aware of it. And I believe it is at this moment the most comprehensive and personal narrative available of a modern Sioux Sun Dance as it is done on the Rosebud and Pine Ridge reservations.

Eagle Feather's profound wish is to preserve the details of the great dance as he and his contemporaries do it. He is worried, and has often said so, about its future. The same thing applies to Frank Fools Crow, and for the identical reasons.

Eagle Feather's information was delivered to me in English, but it was necessary to edit the tape recordings extensively. I trust the reasons for doing this will be understood and appreciated. It is never a simple thing to dictate continuously, as Eagle Feather did for long periods of time. Clarity is lacking. Rambling occurs. Sentence structure is ignored, and repetition is frequent. Dates can be confused, and even contradictions crop up now and then.

In addition, I, as I said earlier, had to supplement the tapes with material gathered from him in personal conversations, by telephone, by letter, and by observation. Nevertheless, it is my devout hope that in all of my editing I have not violated his account in any way.

Since my material has been compiled from several sources and includes my personal observations, the problem was deciding how to present it in an orderly, lucid fashion, clearly maintaining the identity of each contributor. After wrestling with the alternatives for some time, I decided to present under their names the contributions of my living authorities, then to set forth under my name my own observations, and finally to add enough material from the aforementioned early sources to make comparisons possible between the modern and the ancient Sun Dances.

I should emphasize that none of this information is of a confidential nature, and none of it reveals anything which cannot be seen and learned by visitors attending Sun Dances today. We are not dealing with secrets here, although the Traditional Sioux always speak of any part of the Sun Dance with the greatest reverence and care, and expect others to do the same. While some things about the Sun Dance are not made public by the holy men and medicine men, and some things which I have learned are too personal and private to be published, there is enough that can be learned and reported to make it more than worthwhile.

I have already referred to the three men who made the greatest contributions to my Sun Dance account. But there were others who gave added insights that contribute greatly to the whole. Therefore, I thank these Indian friends for the insights they have so generously shared with me over the past three years: Hazel Schweigman, Kate Fools Crow, Evelyn Staub, Joe Staub, Charles Ross, Everett Lonehill, Melvin Spotted Elk, Eugene Crow Good Voices, George Eagle Elk, Pete Catches, Robert Stead, Robert Blackfeather, Orrie Farrell, Gerry Dragg, Reuben Fire Thunder, Gilbert Yellow Hawk, Albert Stands, Lorenzo Hodgekiss, Titus Smith, and Kermit Bear Shield.

There are others I must mention, those close friends who helped by encouragement and ideas, and who shared in the work: Arthur Mahoney, Jim Wentzy, Gregg and Barbara Pietz, Lisa Gray, Roy Dale Sanders, and my daughter Allison, who has assisted me now with five books on the life and customs of the Indian nations. Unless otherwise credited, photographs are by the author.

Old time Sioux Sun Dance pledgers divided into individual groups. Here, all of the groups face the sun as they dance, blow on their whistles, and pray. In Eagle Feather's contemporary dances the groups face the Tree and go forward four times to touch it. Fools Crow identified the two men at the left as brothers named Pulling Rope and Mountain Sheep, and the woman as Mrs. Mountain Sheep. He added that, "They are all gone now."

A closer view shows that Mountain Sheep has a rawhide effigy of a horse attached to his wristband. Each pledger carries a sage hoop, and the woman holds also one of the directional flags.

In a photograph by John A. Anderson, entitled, Sun Dance, 1910, the pledgers, who were not permitted to pierce publicly at the time, had the ropes looped around their bodies just under the arms. It could not have been a satisfactory way to do the sacrificial part of the dance.

III
Sioux History: Tetons, Oglalas, Brules

THOMAS E. MAILS

Those not already acquainted with Sioux history will find it helpful to know something about the intriguing past of this illustrious nation, and particularly about the Teton, two of whose subdivisions, the Brule and the Oglala, are the people whose Sun Dance is treated in particular here.

Present-day scholars believe that the history of the Sioux began in North Carolina, where they were a sedentary people. Sometime around the fifteen hundreds they began to migrate toward the Northwest, in the general direction of the Great Lakes.

The Sioux are the largest division of the Siouan family. According to Chippewa tradition the name *Nadowe-ss-iw-eg*, "Lesser Snakes," later corrupted by the French to "Sioux", was first applied to a body of Indians living on an island somewhere east of Detroit, Michigan.

Dakota, Nakota, and Lakota are the names used by the Sioux themselves, in the Santee, Yankton, and Teton dialects respectively. Each of the names means, literally, "friends" or "allies." Dorsey, in his classification of the Siouan languages, divides the Dakota group into four dialects: Teton, Santee, Yankton, and Assiniboine. The Assiniboines, however, constitute a separate tribe. The term "Dakota" is popularly but incorrectly applied to all the Sioux, because non-Indians contacted the Santee first and erroneously applied their name to the rest of the Sioux. The close linguistic relation of the divisions—the differences being largely dialectic—indicates that they are branches of an original group.

By the end of the sixteenth century they were residing in the upper reaches of the Mississippi River in what is present-day Minnesota. From 1700 to 1750, the Tetons and Yanktons were engaged in wars with the Mandans, Arikaras, Hidatsas, Omahas, and Poncas for control of the eastern Dakotas. When, after 1750, these tribes progressively abandoned land to them, the Yankton and part of the Teton remained there while the rest of the Tetons moved far beyond the west bank of the Missouri and on to the Great Plains. At the time of Major Stephen H. Long's scientific expedition in 1825, the bands were still located in these respective areas.

From the time of French fur trader Pierre Charles LeSueur's visit in 1700, recorded history reveals that the Dakotas became an important factor in the development of the Northwest. Once they had begun to move, continued progress westward was in reaction chiefly to the persistent attacks on them by the Chippewas, who received firearms from the French, while they themselves were forced to rely almost wholly on bows and arrows.

Lieutenant Gorrell, an English officer, gave evidence of the Sioux problem in this regard as late as 1763: "This day, 12 warriors of the Sioux came here [Green Bay, Wisconsin]. It is certainly the greatest nation of Indians ever yet found. Not above 2,000 of them were ever armed with fire-arms, the rest depending entirely on bows and arrows and darts, which they use with more skill than any other Indian nation in North America. They can shoot the wildest and largest beasts in the woods at 70 to 100 yards. They are remarkable for their dancing; the other nations take the fashion from them."

He goes on to mention that the Sioux were always at war with the Chippewas. When the French dominion ended, the Dakotas at once entered into friendly relations with the English. It is probable that the erection of trading posts on Lake Pepin enticed them from their old residence on the Rum River and Mille Lacs, for it was in this section that Captain Jonathan Carver of the Provincial Troops in America found those of the eastern group in 1766. He says: "Near the river St. Croix reside three bands of the Naudewessie Indians, called the River bands. This nation is composed at present, of 11 bands. They were originally 12, but the Assinipoiles [Assiniboines] some years ago revolting, and separating themselves from the others, there remain only 11. Those I met here are termed the River bands, because they chiefly dwell near the banks of this river. The other eight are generally distinguished by the title, Naudewessies of the Plains, and inhabit a country that lies more to the west. The names of the former are Nehogatawonahs, the Mawtawbauntowahs, and Shahsweentowahs."

Around 1775, epidemics reduced the once-powerful Arikaras to about five thousand people, and at about this same time the Sioux obtained enough firearms and horses to overcome them and begin a tremendous era of expansion westward, during which the Teton Sioux became one of the most powerful Indian nations in the United States. Interestingly enough, it was during this period that the Sun Dance as we now know it came into being.

From 1775 to 1825, the Oglalas were engaged in simultaneous wars with the Cheyenne, Arapaho, Kiowa, Crow, Ute, and Shoshone for control of the Black Hills region and beyond. Other Sioux were battling other Indian nations for their territories.

At the close of the eighteen twenties, the Sioux had established control of a huge area which included a large part of the Dakotas, northern Nebraska, southeastern Montana, eastern Wyoming, and the northwestern tip of Colorado.

During an investigation by Congress in 1824 of the claim by Carver's heirs to a supposed grant of land (including the site of St. Paul) made to Carver by the Sioux, General Leavenworth stated that the Dakotas had informed him that the Sioux of the Plains had never owned any land east of the Mississippi.

During the Revolution and the War of 1812, the Dakotas allied themselves with the English. There was, however, one chief who sided with the United States in 1812; this was Tohami, known to the English as Rising Moose, a chief of the Mdewakantons, who joined the Americans at St. Louis, where he was commissioned by General Clark.

By a treaty of July, 1815, the first period of peace between the Dakotas and the United States was established, and by a treaty of August, 1825, the boundary lines between them and the various tribes in the northwest were defined. The first conflicts between the Sioux and the United States took place during the years 1825-1850, when westward expansion caused immigrants to travel a route through the Sioux territory. In 1854, an unfortunate incident concerning a stray cow resulted in the Lieutenant Gattan Battle, in

The Sacred Tree for the same dance. Unlike the modern Tree, some of the offering cloths are mounted like banners on long poles, and the bundle of cherry branches at the top of the photograph was either not tied on crossways, or slipped into its present position.

which the Brule destroyed the lieutenant's entire command. In retaliation, General Harney punished an innocent Sioux camp.

In treaties made in 1837 and 1851, the Santees gave up millions of acres of their land in return for promises of payments which were poorly administered and led the eastern Sioux into continual debt and starvation.

The most serious outbreak of the Sioux in reaction against the Whites occurred in Minnesota under Little Crow and the Santees in 1862, when about 700 White settlers and 100 soldiers were killed by the Indians; but the entire Dakota group never participated unitedly in any of the modern wars or outbreaks. The bands engaged in the uprising just mentioned were the Mdewakantons, Wahpekutes, Wahpetons, and Sissetons.

In the end they were defeated by superior forces. A total of 303 men were sentenced to hang, but the list was later cut to 38. It was enough, however, to put an end to the once-powerful eastern Sioux.

Although this revolt was put down and the Sioux were compelled for a time to submit to the terms offered them, a spirit of unrest continued to prevail. In 1866, the Bozeman Trail was commenced. This trail, a shortcut to gold country, sliced through the very heart of Sioux territory. When forts were built there to protect the route, a series of inconclusive wars erupted. In the Treaty (Agreement) of 1868, the Sioux agreed to relinquish to the United States all their territory south of the Niobrara River, west of longitude 104 degrees and north of latitude 46 degrees, and promised they would retire to a large reservation in southwest South Dakota before January 1, 1876. Finally, when it appeared that they might not win the battles in a hurry, the United States adopted a "peace policy," and duped the Sioux into signing the infamous Treaty (Agreement) of 1868, wherein the Indians entrapped themselves by unwittingly agreeing to live on a number of smaller reservations.

With the discovery of gold in the Black Hills in 1874, the rush of miners occasioned another famous battle. This was led by such well-known warriors as Crazy Horse, Spotted Tail, Rain-in-the-Face, Red Cloud, American Horse, Gall, Sitting Bull, and Crow King, and was rendered famous by the eradication of Major General George A. Custer and five companies of cavalry on the Little Bighorn, June 25, 1876. It was the finest hour for the Sioux, but at the same time it signaled the end of their freedom. Under constant pressure after that from the United States military forces, the subdivisions were one by one brought in and placed on reservations under strict control. The late eighteen hundreds became a period of bitter readjustment and decline, and the final uprising of the Sioux during the Ghost Dance excitement of 1890-1891 was subdued by Colonel Forsyth and the Seventh Cavalry at Wounded Knee, South Dakota, on December 29, 1890. An avoidable, lopsided, and tragic battle there resulted in at least 153 Sioux men, women, and children killed and 51 wounded. The Sioux only think of it as a massacre. It was a grim and appalling moment, made worse by the fact it was entirely unnecessary. But it did the job. Resistance collapsed once and for all, and the reservation period really began in earnest.

The Sioux are universally conceded to be among the highest types, physically, mentally, and probably morally of any of the western tribes. Their bravery has never been questioned by the Whites or Indians in general, and they conquered and drove out every rival except the Chippewas.

Socially, the Sioux originally consisted of a large number of local groups or bands, and although there was a certain tendency to encourage marriage outside the bands, these divisions were not true gentes, remembered blood relationship being the only bar to marriage. In a summary view of their way of life, personal fitness and popularity determined leadership more than heredity, and where descent played any part it was usually from father to son. The authority of any civil or camp chief was limited by the council and the warrior societies, without whose agreement and support little or nothing could be accomplished. War parties and horse raids were usually recruited by individuals who had acquired reputations as successful leaders. Holy men and medicine men conducted ceremonial dances and rites, and did healing. The Sun Dance was their religion. The buffalo was the staff of life. The tipi and domestic life was supervised by the women. Polygamy was expedient, and common. Remains of the dead were usually, though not invariably, placed on scaffolds or given tree burials. The Sioux were and are a deeply religious people, and produced superb arts and crafts which were spiritually influenced.

Some of the best early descriptions of them were given by the artist-author George Catlin, who was among them in the early eighteen thirties, and by Francis Parkman, Jr., who stayed with the Oglalas and Brules during the summer of 1846. Parkman gave excellent critical descriptions of all aspects of their life.[1]

Early explorers usually separated the Sioux into an Eastern or

Forest, and a Western or Prairie, division. A more complete and accurate classification, one which is also recognized by the people themselves, is the following:

(1) *Mdewakantons;* (2) *Wahpetons;* (3) *Wahpekutes;* (4) *Sissetons;* (5) *Yanktons;* (6) *Yanktonais;* (7) *Tetons;* each of which is again subdivided into bands and sub-bands. These seven main divisions are often identified as "the seven council fires." The first four names together constitute the *Isanyatis,* Santees or eastern division, of which the *Mdewakantons* appear to be the original nucleus, and they speak one dialect. Their home was in Minnesota prior to the outbreak of 1862. The middle division Yanktons and Yanktonais—the latter subdivided into (a) Upper and (b) Hunkpatinas or Lower—held the middle territory between Lake Traverse and the Missouri River in East Dakota, and together spoke one dialect, from which the Assiniboine was an offshoot. The great Teton or western division with its seven tribal subdivisions—the *Sicangus* or Upper and Lower Brules, *Oglalas, Itazipco* or Sans Arcs, *Sihasapas* or Blackfoot, *Miniconjous, Oohenonpas* or Two Kettles, *Hunkpapas,* and comprising together more than half the nation—held the whole tribal territory west of the Missouri and spoke one dialect, Lakota.

In 1925, the total number of Sioux was set at 24,000. In 1975, it was approximately 42,000.

THE TETON SIOUX

Teton is a contraction of *Titon-wan*, "dwellers on the prairie." The Teton Sioux are the western and principal division of the Dakota or Sioux, including all the bands formerly ranging west of the Missouri River and now living on reservations in South Dakota and North Dakota. The tribes officially recognized are: Oglala of Pine Ridge Agency; Brule of Rosebud and Lower Brule agencies; Blackfoot; Miniconjou; Hunkpapa; Sans Arc and Two Kettle of Cheyenne River Agency. Their history is interwoven with that of the other Dakotas. They were first met by Father Louis Hennepin in 1680, "20 or 30 leagues above the Falls of St. Anthony in Minnesota, probably in Sauk Rapids, on the Mississippi River about seventy miles above Minneapolis." He placed them in the neighborhood of Mille Lacs, far to the east of their later home in the Dakotas.

Lahonton also numbers them among the tribes on the Upper Mississippi, which reinforces the conclusion that at least a part of the Tetons formerly lived in the prairie region, near the Upper Mississippi, though the main body may have been near Upper Minnesota River. LeSueur, in 1700, included the Teton among the western Sioux who lived between the Upper Mississippi and the Missouri. On a map of Del'Isle, dated 1701, Lake Traverse is seen to be surrounded by villages of wandering Tetons. Pachot located them 120 miles west of the Falls of St. Anthony in 1722. In 1766, Carver met at least a segment of them at the extreme west point of his journey up the Minnesota River, about 200 miles from its mouth.

According to Doane Robinson, the younger Henry came upon Teton Sioux in 1800 on the Upper Missouri, where Lewis and Clark encountered them a few years later. Their divisions given at this time were as follows: Tetons of the Burnt Woods (Brule), about 300 men, who roved on both sides of the Missouri, White, and Teton rivers; Tetons Okandandas (Oglalas), 150 men, who inhabited both sides of the Missouri below Cheyenne River; Teton Minnekineazzos, about 250 men, on both sides of the Missouri above the Cheyenne

River; Teton Saones, about 300 men, living on both sides of the Missouri below Beaver Creek.

Governor Ramsey placed them in an area ranging from the Cannonball River to the Niobrara River.

In 1815, the Tetons entered into a peace treaty with the United States at Portage des Sioux, Missouri. This was confirmed by a treaty of June 22, 1825, at Fort Lookout, South Dakota. It was warriors of this group who defeated Lieutenant Grattan and his party at Fort Laramie, Wyoming, in 1854; none, however, took part in the Minnesota uprising of 1862.

In 1865, a commission concluded treaties with each of the several divisions of the group allowing for a right of way through their territory. By the Treaty of 1868 the Teton agreed to give up their free range and go on a huge reservation which included all of South Dakota west of the Missouri River. Under chiefs Red Cloud and Crazy Horse, and with the assistance of Sitting Bull, they were the principals in all the Indian wars and outbreaks of the northern plains, notably in 1864, 1876, and 1890.

At Fort Laramie in 1868, a treaty was made which set aside the "Great Sioux Reservation" for the western Dakota. But under continuous pressure, in 1882 and 1883 the western bands surrendered the Great Sioux Reservation—a matter still being contested today—and in 1889, they accepted six smaller and separate reservations: Pine Ridge, Rosebud, Standing Rock, Cheyenne River, Crow Creek, and Lower Brule. Settlement on these followed the Dawes Allotment Act, which became law in 1887. Today there are nine Sioux reservations in South Dakota. In addition to the six previously mentioned, there are the Sisseton, Yankton, and Flandreau. Part of the Standing Rock Reservation is in North Dakota. The Devils Lake Reservation there is Sioux, and two Siouan tribes, the

Another photograph by Anderson of what is said to be the same Sun Dance shows people adding prayer offering cloths to the Sacred Tree. . . .

32

Mandans and Hidatsas, live on the Fort Berthold Reservation in North Dakota.

Governor Ramsey characterized the Tetons as a large, finely formed, tall and vigorous people, hardy, indomitable, and restless warriors, daring horsemen and skillful hunters, possessing in perfection "all the Indian virtues of bravery, cunning, treachery and hospitality," loyal to one another and ready foes to all others.

Doane Robinson quotes Neil as saying: "They are the plundering Arabs of America, and have of late years been a terror to the emigrants to the Pacific coast." According to Lewis and Clark, the policing of a Teton village in the early eighteen hundreds was delegated to two or three officers and their society followers, who were named by the camp chief for the purpose of preserving order till the camp chief appointed their successors. These were always on the watch to keep tranquillity during the day and guard the camp at night. The short duration of their office, usually one year, was compensated by its authority, their power being supreme, "and in the supression of disturbance no resistance to them was tolerated." This was a custom which was followed until the societies phased out and were replaced by Indian policemen in the reservation period.

The Teton is the most populous and important of the Dakota divisions, constituting more than half of the whole nation. Lewis and Clark estimated its membership at 1,000 men in 1804, about 4,000 persons in all, which was probably much less than the true number. In 1842 the Indian Bureau estimated the total number at 12,000; Governor Alexander Ramsey of Minnesota Territory said, in 1849, that there were more than 6,000; The Reverend Stephen R. Riggs, an ethnologist, guessed fewer than 12,500 in 1851. The Indian Bureau in 1861 gave their total as 8,900. It is probable that all of these estimates were below rather than above the real numbers, as in 1890 the total Teton population was said to be 16,426, and in 1909 the number, including Yanktonai bands at Standing Rock agency, North Dakota, had increased to 18,098. In addition, about 100 of the former refugees were still in Canada.[2]

THE OGLALA SIOUX

Oglala means "to scatter one's own," or, "sprinkling unto oneself or one's own."[3] It is the principal division of the Teton Sioux. The early history of the Oglalas is completely obscured; their modern history recounts incessant wars with other tribes and the Whites. The first recorded notice of them is that of Lewis and Clark, who in 1806 found them living above the Brule Sioux on the Missouri River, between the Cheyenne and Bad Rivers, in present-day South Dakota, and numbering an estimated 150 or 200 men. In 1825 they inhabited both banks of the Bad River, from the Missouri to the Black Hills. They were then friendly with the Whites and at peace with the Cheyennes, but enemies to all other tribes except those of their own nation. They were estimated now at 1,500 persons, of whom 300 were warriors.

Their general rendezvous in 1825 was at the mouth of Bad River, where there was a trading establishment for their accommodation. By 1850, they were roaming the plains between the north and south forks of the Platte River, and west of the Black Hills. In 1862 they occupied the country extending northeast from Fort Laramie, at the mouth of the Laramie River, on North Platte River, including the Black Hills and the source of Bad River, and reaching to the fork of the Cheyenne, and ranged as far west as the head of Grand River.

Father Pierre-Jean De Smet, the well-known Roman Catholic missionary of the eighteen forties, says: "The worst among the hostile bands are the Blackfeet, the Oglalas, the Unkpapas and Santees."

The Oglalas participated in the defeat of Lieutenant Grattan and his men at Fort Laramie in 1854. From 1865 on, they and other restless tribes of western Sioux were the terror of the frontier, constantly attacking emigrant trains on the plains and boats on the rivers, fighting soldiers, and harassing the forts and way stations for several years, under the leadership of Sitting Bull and Crazy Horse.

The invasion of the Black Hills by gold seekers led to the famous battle of June, 1876, in which Custer and his command were wiped out. For several months before that stragglers from other tribes had been flocking to Sitting Bull's standard, so that, according to the best estimates, there were at the Battle of the Little Bighorn 2,500 to 3,000 Indian warriors. The victors were soon thereafter defeated by General Miles, and while some fled to Canada, Crazy Horse and more than 2,000 followers surrendered at Red Cloud and Spotted Tail agencies in the following May. These different groups were composed in large part of Oglalas, of whom most probably surrended with Crazy Horse.

The Oglalas entered into a treaty of peace with the United States at the mouth of the Teton (Bad) River, South Dakota, on July 5, 1825. Another treaty was signed at Fort Sully, South Dakota, on October 28, 1865, prescribing relations which would be maintained with the United States and with other tribes. An important treaty with the Oglalas and others was made at Fort Laramie, Wyoming, on April 29, 1868, in which they agreed to cease fighting and which defined the limits of their tribal lands. An agreement confirming the Treaty of 1868 was concluded at Red Cloud Agency, Nebraska, on September 26, 1876. It was signed on behalf of the Oglalas by Red Cloud and other principal men of the tribe.

In 1906, the Oglalas were officially reported to number 6,727, all at Pine Ridge Agency, South Dakota. Today that number is something over 13,000.

THE BRULE SIOUX

The Brule derived their present day name from the French translation of Sichangzus, "burnt thighs," their own ancient name being of indefinite origin. They are the second-largest division of the Teton, and they were mentioned by Lewis and Clark in 1804 as the Tetons of the Burnt Woods, numbering about 300 men, "who rove on both sides of the Missouri, White, and Teton Rivers."

In 1806, they were on the east side of the Missouri in an area reaching from the mouth of the White to the Teton River. Ethnologist F. V. Hayden described the country inhabited by them in 1856 as being on the headwaters of the White and Niobrara, extending down these rivers for about half their length, the Teton River forming the north limit. He also says that they were for a number of years headed by a chief named Ma-ka-to-za-za, who was very friendly to the Whites and who, "by uniformly good management and just government kept his people in order, regulated their hunts and usually avoided placing them in starving situations incident to bands led by less judicious chiefs."

They were good hunters, usually well clothed and supplied with meat, and had comfortable lodges and a large number of horses. The men varied their occupations by hunting buffalo, catching wild horses, and making horse raid or war expeditions either against the

Arikaras, then residing on the Platte, or the Pawnees, lower down on that river.

Every summer, trips were made by the young warriors into the Platte and Arkansas country to capture the wild horses which abounded there at that time. After emigrants to California and Oregon began to pass through the Sioux country, the Brules, whose villages were closest to the trail, suffered more from diseases introduced by the intruders than any other division of the tribe. The Treaty of April 29, 1868, between the Sioux bands and the Government, was in a large degree brought about through the efforts of Swift Bear, a Brule chief. Nevertheless, it was about this time or shortly after that a band of Brules took part in the attack on Major Forsyth, on the Republican River.

Hayden gives 150 as the number of their lodges in 1856, which would only be 750 people. In 1890 the Upper Brules on Rosebud Reservation, South Dakota, numbered 3,245; the Lower Brules at Crowneck and the Lower Brule Agency, South Dakota, 1,026. The present number of Brules at Rosebud is about 8,500.

. . . while women are busy at the left of the Tree cooking food in a skin or paunch suspended from four sticks. No cooking is done in the Mystery Circle today.

RESERVATION LIFE

As the Indians of the Upper Missouri entered into treaties with the United States Government, agents were appointed to supervise the distribution of goods to the various tribes in compliance with treaty obligations. Gradually, as the Indians were more restricted in their range and their ability to live from the hunt, they became more dependent on the United States for subsistence. Thus the role of the agent broadened. Permanent agencies were established, often providing a farmer and a blacksmith to help the Indians learn the new way of life, as it was the Government's policy to make farmers of all Indians—in effect, to suppress and alter the life-way and culture. Agencies were set up at trading posts as a matter of convenience, and often military posts were established at the same places. Christian missions usually located near the agencies, and next came schools, conducted by the missionaries at first, and later taken over by the Government. Some of the local Indians were trained as police and judges, and courts of Indian offences were established. With the passing of time, medical care and other services were provided. Homes were built for employees, a few stores and restaurants went up, and Indian families built their cabins nearby. Thus evolved the typical agency town.

So far as administration is concerned, the states have until recently had little to do with Indian affairs. At the first Congress of the United States in 1789, Indian affairs were placed under the supervision of the Secretary of War. The chief problems at that time were keeping the peace along the frontier, where many of the Indians had been pushed, and regulating trade with the Indians. Superintendents, directly responsible to the Secretary of War, were appointed and had somewhat the role of ambassadors in their large areas of jurisdiction. In 1824 the Bureau of Indian Affairs was created. The office of Commissioner of Indian Affairs was not established until 1832; an act of Congress in 1834 reorganized the Bureau of Indian Affairs along modern lines. By this time a great many Indians tribes had been overtaken by the advancing frontier, creating a variety of administrative problems. In 1849 the Bureau was transferred from the War Department to the Department of Interior, where it has remained.

The Office of Indian Affairs is in Washington, D.C. At its head is a Commissioner of Indian Affairs, appointed by the Secretary of the Interior. There are eleven area offices, each with a director in charge. The North Dakota agencies are under the area office in Aberdeen, South Dakota, along with all the South Dakota and Nebraska agencies.

Each agency has a superintendent in charge, and under his supervision are the following divisions and branches: a division of administration, with an Administrative Officer at its head, includes a branch of finance, of buildings and utilities, and of property; the division of resources includes branches of extension, of land, of soil conservation, of forestry and grazing, of roads, and of credit; the third division, community services, includes the branches of education, health, law and order, welfare, and placement. The agency positions are filled through Civil Service examinations.

The Indian people of North Dakota are, on the average, very poor in comparison with their White neighbors. Their incomes as of 1976 are generally low, less than $2,500 a year for a family, and are derived from leasing their land to White farmers and ranchers, from their own farming and ranching, and from day labor, often temporary or seasonal. A large percentage of able-bodied Indians are unemployed much of the time. Depending on the season, unemployment ranges from 40 to an awesome 80 percent of the employable people. Many own no land, and others who do own land prefer to lease it out rather than to attempt the expense and risk of beginning their own farming or ranching enterprises. With some loans available from tribal funds, and with some encouragement from the regular federal farm assistance programs, more Indians in recent years have attempted to farm and ranch on their own. Local employment is extremely hard to find, especially if one lacks specialized training; for the Indian the problem is further complicated by race prejudice on the part of narrow-minded employers. Moreover, the nearest cities are 100 miles away, and the Indians lack adequate transportation.

Now and then something happens to give a false impression of wealth, but except for a few individuals, the gloomy economic picture has not changed.

Poverty has been acute for most of the Sioux for nearly a hundred years. The amount of workable land originally set aside for the people was miserably inadequate, so many of the Indians obtained land off the reservations under homestead provisions and other terms, and others received allotments on reservations in Montana. Resources are still insufficient, but the people manage to retain a great deal of pride and independence, supporting themselves when it is at all possible. The largest part of their income has been from agriculture; other sources are sale of wood, wages—largely for work in the potato and beet fields—and land leases. Some emergency relief has always been necessary, usually in winter; this comes partly from federal appropriations through the Indian Service, but more through the Social Security Act, in which the state and federal governments cooperate. A few manufacturing plants employ a relatively small number of the local Indians on some Sioux reservations.

One of the recent trends in federal administration is the placement program, in which state employment agencies cooperate. The object is to encourage Indians to leave the reservations and to engage in industrial work in distant cities where they can become assimilated into the White communities. If given an opportunity and judged on their own merits, Indians are found to be fully up to the standards of non-Indian society. This has been demonstrated on a large scale by their performance in war industries and military service, and on a smaller scale by the accomplishments of individual Indians in many other fields of endeavor. Nevertheless, it is unfortunately true that considerable prejudice toward Indians still exists in the immediate vicinity of reservations, and some prejudice exists in urban areas as well. So the placement program tries to locate Indian workers in jobs where they have a chance to succeed, and to locate the families to communities where they will be judged by the same standards as anyone else, and not as members of a substandard or conquered race.

No Indians today are receiving any annuities or other direct payments from the Government. The only direct benefits are in the form of emergency relief where state funds are not provided as for other citizens. The Federal Government does continue to render several services to Indians. Most of these services began in fulfillment of treaty stipulations; since the Indians had not been made self-supporting or been assimilated by the time of treaty expiration, the services were continued through "gratuity appropriations" of Congress, often helped by income from invested tribal funds.

One of the major functions of the Indian Service is to help the Indians manage trust lands. The fact that lands held in trust by the Federal Government are not taxable by state or local governments is the chief reason why states and counties do not render Indians the services they give their other citizens. It is often overlooked that millions of landless White people pay no land taxes, and that Indians do pay taxes other than on land.

Education is today the largest item in the budgets of most reservations. This includes supplies, construction and upkeep of buildings, salaries of teachers and administrators, and operation of school buses and dormitories. The next largest item is health. There are several Federal Indian hospitals in the states of North and South Dakota, and where these are too distant, contracts are made with local hosptitals. Maintenance of roads on the reservations is the third-largest expense. Since much of the land on reservations is "alienated," that is, no longer held in trust by the Federal Govern-

Hazel Schweigman

ment, it is taxable by local governments, and therefore the state and county share the responsibility for building and maintaining the roads.

Before 1924, individual Indians had received United States citizenship by meeting certain stipulations. In that year an act of Congress gave citizenship to all Indians born in the United States. Although the Fifteenth Amendment would seem to guarantee the vote to Indians, there are still states which discriminate against them in this matter on the excuse of taxation. North and South Dakota make no such discrimination.

During the history of the United States the Congress has enacted almost 4,500 laws (including treaties) with specific application to the Indians. This unwieldly mass of legislation, often overlapping that of the state and local governments, has caused much difficulty and required much compromising on the part of the various levels of government. In the matter of maintaining law and order, this uncertainty has often led to acute trouble and still constitutes one of the most serious problems in Indian communities.

Liquor and the Indian have been a serious problem since colonial times. The first federal action on this question was taken at the request of President Jefferson in 1802. The Act of July 23, 1892, as amended in 1938, prohibited the sale or gift of any intoxicating liquor to any Indian who has trust land or over whom the Federal Government exercises any form of guardianship. The legislation was designed to protect Indians from unscrupulous White men who would use liquor to obtain furs, land, or other concessions; use of liquor was especially demoralizing at a time when native ideals were crumbling and had not been replaced by new knowledge and standards.

The difficulty of enforcing prohibition anywhere is well known, and it is also common knowledge that an Indian who wants liquor can usually find a white man who will take the slight risk of obtaining it for him—either for friendship's sake or for a small fee. Recognizing that specific legislation of this sort is discriminatory, Congress in 1953 amended the existing law so that Indians may obtain liquor except where it is prohibited to them by state laws or tribal ordinances.

The Federal Govenment has often, and with some justification, been accused of despotic, paternalistic administration of Indian affairs, even though over the years many changes have been made to try to bring the handling of Indian affairs into touch with current needs. The changes made during the first term of Franklin Delano Roosevelt, with Harold L. Ickes as Secretary of the Interior and John Collier as Commissioner of Indian Affairs, were of far-reaching consequence. In 1934, Congress passed the Wheeler-Howard (Indian Reorganization) Act, which gave the various tribes the right to organize tribal councils with a very substantial amount of power in reservation affairs. At Pine Ridge and Rosebud this has not always worked out well. A concerted effort was made to decentralize administration, adapting the policy of each agency to local conditions, and to encourage coordination between federal agencies and state and local governments. Other policies stressed under the Collier administration were the increased use of day schools in place of boarding schools, use of natural resources by the Indians themselves with emphasis on conservation, increased employment of Indians in the Indian service, and the protection of the Indian's cultural heritage.

All of the Sioux reservations now have tribal business councils of some kind; these do not have the social prestige of an old-time council of chiefs, but rather function more as a board of directors for a corporation. Many Indians from both local and distant reservations

Titus Smith

hold positions in agencies; several of the superintendents have been Indians. Tribal land, acquired with federal aid, can be used by Indians for a nominal sum. If the land is leased, the rent goes into a tribal fund. Funds have been set up for loans to Indians who want to start farming or ranching. The Indian Division of the CCC in the nineteen thirties provided many youths with both employment and training. Arts and crafts shops were set up to give instruction and to market the products.

Not all of these innovations were successful. In fact, some were disastrous, and it may be difficult for the casual observer to notice any real change in the conditions of the Sioux Indians over the past fifty years. Fools Crow believes that the Sioux were virtually programmed to death, but it is clear that the "Indian New Deal" did revive in the Indian an interest in managing his own affairs and a desire to advance, which is being fulfilled in many cases.

Until Congress prohibited the use of federal funds for sectarian education, the Indian Bureau often farmed out the job of education to various religious bodies. At present there are large parochial schools on the reservations, but the majority of Indian children attend government schools. The instruction follows the state course of study, and is generally comparable in quality, including active extracurricular programs. In addition to the reservation boarding and day schools, there are schools especially for children from broken homes and those who cannot make arrangements to attend the reservation schools. In some areas it has been found practical for the agencies to contract with public schools for education of Indian children. This is a further step toward assimilation, which is generally considered by the Indian Bureau to be the solution of the "Indian problem." A number of Dakota Indian young people are studying in colleges and universities. Rosebud has a small college of its own. Such education is financed both privately and with loans available from tribal funds.

The current trend is for the Federal Government to prepare to terminate its administration of Indian affairs, reservation by reservation. This is by no means desired by all Indians or as easy to do as it might seem. The social, economic, and legal difficulties are numerous and intricate. If the transfer is to take place, and to work, the state and local governments must be willing to cooperate. Turning the Indian out, if indeed it is ever done, will require a great deal of time, patience, and good will on the part of the several levels of Government involved, on the part of the neighboring White community, and on the part of the Indians themselves.

The Government and the churches no longer follow their old policy of trying to suppress every manifestation of native culture. They have recognized the fact that self-respect and pride in one's own traditions will not hold a people back, as was formerly feared, but will rather encourage progress. It is often observed that Indians who are leaders in traditional customs are also among the more successful citizens. Families who have been working in distant cities participate with renewed enthusiasm in tribal functions when they visit the reservation, and gather for the same purpose in the cities.

Native dances, both sacred and secular, are now held whenever anyone wishes to sponsor them; men in service are often honored with a dance upon their return. Patriotism for the United States is mingled with ancient patterns of honoring warriors when Indians gather on national patriotic holidays. Sun Dances are being held, *Yuwipi* men are at work, spiritkeeping is practiced, puberty rites are celebrated, old people still tell the ancient stories, the native languages are spoken in hundreds of homes. Horsemanship is a prized skill among boys and young men. Hospitality and generosity are

Sun Dance pledgers at Pine Ridge in 1929. Fools Crow identified them, left to right, as White Bull, Little White Man and Two Sticks. Their hoops were wrapped with mink or otter, the wrist and ankle bands were rabbit skin. Little White Man was an Elk Dreamer, and the horns worn on his head were wrapped with mink or otter. Two Sticks was a Buffalo Dreamer, and the curved split feathers on his head simulated buffalo horns.

still thought of as prime virtues, and the "give away" is still practiced on appropriate occasions.

A century under the White man's domination has not destroyed the life-way and spirit of the Sioux Indians, and their art and living traditions continue to enrich the lives of all mankind.

Old time Sioux pledgers wearing otter skin collars. Their whistles are made of the wingbone of an eagle, wound with braided porcupine quills, and are tipped with a downy white eagle feather. The mouthpiece is wrapped with fresh sage.

IV
The Vow And The Sun Dance Pledgers Of 1974

THOMAS E. MAILS

The great Sioux Sun Dances of early times had their origin in fervent vows sent heavenward by individuals during times of extreme crises. Desperate people declared that in return for the Great Spirit's help they would seek a vision, undergo solemn purification ceremonies, and do the Sun Dance—making at that time whatever physical sacrifices were necessary to the fulfillment of the vow.

The pledger's initial vow did not always include the extent of the sacrifices he would make. Extenuating circumstances might not permit that. So the full terms were established as soon as possible after the emergency was over. Once that was completed, it was just a matter of setting the schedules and getting it done.

Some of the early researchers were fortunate enough to obtain brief accounts of the circumstances under which Sun Dance vows were made. From these we learn that in most instances the promises were associated with a desire for revenge, with the carrying out of a raid, or with a crisis during a battle. Other pledges had to do with healing and with economic concerns. But while some of the emergencies which brought about the vows of the early dance participants are known, little if anything has been recorded of the personal lives and concerns of pledgers living in the twentieth century; therefore, when Eagle Feather volunteered a capsule profile of himself and the other men and women who took part in the 1974 dance at Rosebud, I was delighted! We will be given here the rare privilege of knowing the background of the individuals, insights into their personalities, and their reasons for giving flesh offerings and piercing. Because of this we can become an intimate part of the absorbing dance accounts that follow.

Most of the people who participated in the 1974 ceremony at Rosebud were in the 1975 dance as well. Therefore, by the time the second ritual was over I knew a few of the pledgers personally and will add a few details and observations about them to Eagle Feather's account.

It is evident that the majority of the modern-day vows find their impetus in the devastating liquor problem which plagues the Sioux reservations. Moving steadily like a grim reaper, it destroys lives and homes with a vengeance awesome to see. It is, in the view of every medicine man and leader, a curse of incredible proportions. To make matters worse, the influx of cheap drugs is compounding the situation daily. Other reasons for present-day vows are ill-health and poverty. On occasion, too, it serves political expediency to take part in the dance.

Once you get to know them, you realize that the men and women who pledge each year have triumphed, with God's help, over situa-

Gilbert Yellow Hawk

tions so grim and yet so common as to stagger anyone not acquainted with the daily way of life on the Rosebud and Pine Ridge reservations. This fact will stand out more and more as we pass beyond the biographies and into the prayers made in the sweatlodge and in the Mystery Circle. When all of its details are known, the agony and the ecstasy of the Sun Dance become a monumental experience. We see the pain of ordinary living for a beleaguered people countered and triumphed over by the pain endured in the Mystery Hoop and at the Sacred Tree. Moreover, the benefits of the dance reach out to encompass all of the Sioux, all the Indians, and pass beyond them to the rest of mankind. It is a brave and a noble thing they do.

Thus, with a few exceptions, the names of those who participate in the dances can be reported with pride. In one or two instances only the initials of the pledger will be used. Usually, this is because family members are involved in the account. The Sioux will know the pledgers and their personal circumstances in any case, so the inclusion or absence of full names will not affect the story for them in any way. In fact, at some point during every modern dance at Rosebud, each pledger is given an opportunity to come to the microphone and tell the spectators why he is taking part in the ceremony. On these occasions it is common to include a confession of past sins, such as excessive drinking and other bad behavior. The details supplied in this account by Eagle Feather are therefore for the most part neither restricted nor private. Sun Dances are public events, and he is only repeating what is generally known.

Nothing so specific, and so personal, has been available since Frances Densmore published *Teton Sioux Music* in 1911. Through Eagle Feather's account the men and women dancing here will be real to us in a way they could not have been otherwise—real people with real problems and purposes, not mere statistics, and not imagined in any way.

THE SUN DANCE INTERCESSOR—Eagle Feather

Today is March 19, 1975. It is a beautiful spring day here at St. Francis. The sun is shining, the wind is calm, and the snow is all gone. Even some of the birds have returned. It is a good time to talk about the Sun Dance. First I'll make some comments about the people who participated in the 1974 Sun Dance, and then I'll describe what it takes to get us ready. I'm going to start out with myself, Chief Eagle Feather.

I want to tell you how I became involved in the Sun Dance. My grandfather was a German who emigrated to the United States from Hamburg, Germany, became a soldier, and settled at Fort Randall, which is a dam now. His name was Joseph Peter Schweigman. At the fort he met my grandmother, Millie Pino, a full-blooded Sioux. They got married and had four half-breed children, of which my father was one.

My mother was a full-blooded Sioux, a Brule. Her name was Annie Eagle Feather. She was born and raised here on the Rosebud Sioux Reservation.

I was born on July 10, 1914, in the town of Rosebud, on the Rosebud Creek. I attended school at the town of Rosebud for many years. My dad was chief of police of the Rosebud Indian Reservation. He died of cancer in 1922. When I was in the fourth grade, my mother married a man named John Good Elk. He was a fullblooded Sioux from St. Francis, so we moved here and I received some of my education at the town's Roman Catholic school. Hazel Flory and I were married in an Episcopal church in 1936. She is from the Crow Creek Reservation, and was born in Fort Thompson. She is fifty-nine years old now, and we have been living together thirty-nine years. Of this time we have practiced the Indian religion for the last twenty years. She has danced in the Sun Dance many times with me, and is a great helper. However, as of this evening, Hazel has been treated in the hospital for a kidney infection, and she has been in bed at home for almost two weeks. I am hoping that we can bring her out of this by our Indian belief and medicine. After we were married I made up my mind to become either an Episcopalian minister or a lay reader, and I began to study to be an Episcopal lay reader in the Sioux language. However, there were other things which weighed heavily on my mind, things having to do with the Sun Dance.

When Thomas Mails and I visited at the Sun Dance and in my house here at St. Francis, we talked about how I had lived in California, and how I was an electrician by trade. I had a very good job, earning as much as nine dollars an hour. Then, in 1963, I had a severe heart attack. I recovered from this attack but had a second one while I was working for the Menasco Manufacturing plant in Burbank. Even though the union did all they could for me, I was finally called into the office and told, "Bill, even though you are a good electrician, we have to let you go because of your heart condition. Our insurance company will not take care of you."

Although I went back to the Rosebud and Pine Ridge reservations for the annual Sun Dances, I continued to live in Palmdale, California, and received Unemployment Compensation until 1964. Then I got a letter from the Motor Vehicle Department at Sacramento requesting that I surrender my driver's license. So I said to my wife, "This is no place for us. Perhaps God doesn't want us to be here, maybe we better go back to our own reservation." I had sensed in my ceremonies that my guardian angels were telling me to move out of there. They seemed to be telling me to go home, go home, go home, and events were confirming this. So we packed up one morning and came home.

First we went to Pine Ridge and we tried to settle there, but every time I held a ceremony the angels kept urging me to go home to St. Francis on the Rosebud Reservation. Nevertheless, we next moved to Pierre, South Dakota, where I could find work, and had a beautiful home there. But the guardian angels wouldn't let us rest, and still said, "Go home." So we finally moved to my own reservation, the Rosebud, and we settled near the place where I used to live as a boy in St. Francis. And no guardian angel has ever ordered me out of here. The spirits and I have been getting along very good.

Many years ago, way back in 1931 and before my mother passed away, we had a *Yuwipi* ceremony at our house. At that time the holy man who conducted the ceremony told me, "Nephew, you are going to be a holy man within twenty-five years from now." I was surprised, yet gave it little thought until 1950, when I dreamed I had taken part in the Sun Dance and been pierced. Then, in 1951, I had another dream in which I was told that I was to partake in the Rosebud Sun Dance, and that I was going to be well known there. It was one of the most terrible dreams I have ever had and I couldn't get it out of my mind. I thought about it from 1952 to 1956, when I went to Rosebud to be in a Sun Dance I'll describe in detail later on.

In 1957, I was to have yet another dream and a vision, in which I learned that I was to go back to the Sioux, to remain with them on the reservation, and to bring the full Sun Dance, including piercing, back to life. Even then, I still didn't know that this dance was actually the core of my traditional religion. I just dreamed about the Sun Dance and got into participating in it without really knowing much about my Indian religion and culture. It wasn't an easy thing to do. I hated to leave the Episcopal Church because I had enjoyed learning to be a lay reader, and might even have become a minister. But by 1957 I couldn't resist the call to complete annual involvement anymore, and I did my second Sun Dance at Crow Dog's Paradise. And since then I have Sun Danced at least once every year.

In the summer of 1958, I went to the Pine Ridge Reservation, where public Sun Dances were being held every year without the piercing of the flesh. Since I had had a dream about piercing, I told the Intercessor, Frank Fools Crow, "You must pierce me because I dreamed that I was pierced."

Fools Crow is a man of about eitghty-two years old, and he is a great man. He replied, "Brother, I have never pierced a man."

But I told him, "You must pierce me. This is the will of God." So he agreed.

How very well I remember that time. In 1958, we had to get authorization from Washington, D.C., for the piercing. I wish I'd kept the letters. At one time they had them on file at the Pine Ridge Reservation Historical Center, and you might be able to find them there even now. Finally, Frank and I obtained permission from the Bureau of Indian Affairs and from the Pine Ridge Tribal Council, whose chairman gave us the necessary authorization to go ahead.

Yet to get it I had to file a statement agreeing that should there be any ill effect from the piercing of my flesh, the Public Health Service and the reservation officials would not be held responsible for my injury or death.

So I was pierced that year, and from then on I have been pierced every year through 1974, which makes me a real old-timer of the piercing of the flesh. It was in 1960, at Pine Ridge, that I was given the honor and the pleasure of being made a traditional chief of The Sioux Nation Sun Dance, Incorporated.

In spite of the predictions and dreams I am still amazed to think that my wife and I have come this far. That same year, in addition to my becoming a chief, I was made a holy man by Lame Deer and Chief Fools Crow. I have been a practicing medicine man since then, and Hazel has worked closely with me.

In the fall of 1973, my wife made a vow to Sun Dance if God would give her a good year with her children and great-grandchildren. Then a crisis hit us all in January, 1974, when our dear friend, Mrs. Yellow Hawk, had to undergo a major heart operation in Omaha, Nebraska. So during a ceremony we had that month, Hazel made yet another vow that she was going to participate in the Sun Dance and give flesh offerings, provided Mrs. Yellow Hawk got well. She came through the very serious operation on her heart, and Hazel thanked Almighty God at and through the 1974 Sun Dance.

During the prayers that were being offered at that ceremony I made a vow to pierce for the same reason, because we all wanted Mrs. Yellow Hawk to get well and come home. And she was there with us at the 1974 Sun Dance, even though she had an ugly scar on her left side which ran from the front of her chest clear to her backbone, where they had cut her open. Moreover, she has been healthy to this day, and she is living a wonderful life. We sincerely believe that *Tunkasila Wakantanka*, the Great Spirit, has helped her this far. And this is why the Sun Dance is being done every year, because such vows are made by the Sioux people.

THE SUN DANCE PLEDGERS OF 1974—Eagle Feather

Titus Smith, age eleven.

The 1974 Sun Dance marked the first time my grandson, Titus Smith, was pierced. His Indian name is His Swift Pipe and he is part Sioux and part Gros Ventre. Titus was born in Bell Gardens, Southern California, and he has been living with us ever since he was born. Hazel and I raised him. When he was just five years of age we had a Sun Dance in the little community of Spring Creek, which is located ten miles west of St. Francis, on the Little White River. On the first day of the dance I had another heart attack. They took me to the hospital and I didn't know anything for two days. Finally I came out of it, and I was laying peacefully in my second-floor hospital room on the afternoon of the day the Sun Dance ended in Spring Creek, when my wife came up and said, "Can you look out of the window?" And I said, "Yes," and I looked, and there below me stood my little grandson, Titus Smith.

They wouldn't let him inside the hospital because he was so young. But he looked up and saw me and shouted, "Hey, Grandpa, you chicken, I finished the Sun Dance for you." Amazingly, he had taken my place for the other three days and gone through the difficult dance. In some of the recent books which describe the Sioux Sun Dance, the little boy you will see in the Sun Dance photographs is Titus.

Titus has continued to vow and dance from that day, and the only

Fools Crow identified this photograph as that of an old time Sun Dance Intercessor leading the line of pledgers toward the Mystery Circle to begin the dance.

Albert Stands blows on his eagle wing-bone whistle and glides forward to present his pipe to the Keeper of the Pipes in 1974.

regret I have is that he knows nothing about the non-Indian religions. My hope is that in the near future God will enable me to help Titus in this respect, for he must also understand something of the White man's religions.

I should mention that there have been several Sun Dances at the Rosebud Fairground, but there was no piercing until 1974. That was the first one, and when Titus pierced he made history for himself in our traditional way. Actually, he wanted to pierce when he was only nine years old, but no one would pierce him. We tried everyone, asking all the old-timers that I had done Sun Dances with over a period of twenty-three years. Some refused without explanation, and others said, "I'm not pure enough to pierce the little man. I drink and I run around with women. I've done wrong and I'm a sinner. I can't pierce the little gentleman because so far his life is so pure that I'm not worthy to touch him that way."

So I've done a lot of praying and a lot of other things with Titus. I've spent long hours with him out in the prairies and out in the flats. The first time he vision quested was in 1974, and he did pretty well. He went to a place called *Follow the Woman Butte* and stayed out there for three days and three nights. And when he returned he said, "Grandpa, the only visitor I had was an old coyote." Of course, we do not pump anyone about their vision quests, and I can't tell you what the coyote said to him, but he came right up to Titus and talked to him. These are his sacred things. The vision quest is a person's own.

However, he did a lot of praying during the three days and three nights, and he told me about some of his prayers and thoughts. He said, "I prayed for many people. I prayed for the Indians, the Whites, the Chinese, the Japanese, and the Blacks. I prayed for them as I have learned to do from the past Sun Dances. And I sang up there, I sang some of the sacred songs. This year I want to learn more in school, and my hope is that a lot of people, including the non-Indians, will have a long and peaceful life." And he also hoped that during the coming winter the Indian people would not starve. He made many prayers. He prayed for his mother and father, for his little sister, and for all of the people he knew.

Since he made that first Sun Dance at Spring Creek, Titus has participated in the ritual every year, so you might say he's an old-timer. Someday the Great Spirit will enable us to make a medicine man out of him.

Albert Stands, age sixty-five.

Albert Stands is from Parmalee, South Dakota. His full name is Albert Stands on the Island. He is an uncle of mine, and has been a medicine man for many years. We have participated in twenty-three Sun Dance piercings together at the communities of Rosebud, Pine Ridge, and Wounded Knee. He is a medicine man, and his flesh offerings, prayers, and vows are made in thanksgiving for his success with the people he doctors with herbs. Albert sincerely believes in giving medicine herbs to patients during the twelve months between Sun Dances. Therefore he always makes the same vow. I have heard him make it, saying, "Because Almighty God blessed the people I gave herbs to and made them well, I promise, I vow again, to take part in the Sun Dance." So Albert participates in the Sun Dance every year to thank Almighty God for what He has done in answering the many prayers he has made for the people.

Albert served in the Second World War. He was in Germany and he fought against the Japanese. Although he does not speak English, speaking only the Lakota language, and in a very traditional way, he became a corporal. He is a very humble man. Albert is an enrolled member of the Rosebud Sioux tribe, and he has lived here all of his life.

George Eagle Elk, age seventy-nine.

George Eagle Elk is another of the other old-timers and was the oldest man to take part in the Sun Dance at Rosebud in 1974. He was in the First World War and served with the Rainbow Division. He has been a holy man ever since 1921 or so; as long as I can remember. His medicine work was bestowed upon him by his father, and he has practiced it faithfully. His father was named Jesse James Eagle Elk. I imagine he was registered under this name at Rosebud during the old hot time of Jesse James and his bunch.

George Eagle Elk has been a great man, a great leader and a great help in the practice of our Sioux religion and culture. He has a profound belief in Almighty God and in the peace pipe. And like Albert Stands, he makes prayers and a Sun Dance vow every year.

L. H., age sixteen.

L.H. was baptized as either a Lutheran or a Methodist. He is the product of two different Sioux communities. His father, C.H., is enrolled in the Cheyenne Indian Reservation at Eagle Butte, and his mother, B.O.H., is enrolled in the Crow Creek Indian Reservation.

His parents and his grandparents all became alcoholics, and since his grandmother is my wife's full sister, when he was fourteen years old he came to stay with us as our grandson.

He would come to the sweatlodge with us and chop wood, and in time I showed him how to place the rocks on the fireplace so they would heat properly. Finally he became interested and started going into the sweatlodge with us. Then about a year ago, in November, he came in, sat down, and prayed openly and beautifully. He said that his family had broken up, and that his brother and sister had been placed in foster homes. He told how his brother, C.H., who was only twelve years old, had broken into a liquor store in Pierre, South Dakota, and the police had him up on charges. He mentioned that his mother was being treated at the alcoholic center in Pierre, South Dakota, so there was no home, no place to go.

L.H. said, "Grandfather, I want you, and I need you. Therefore, I am going to vision quest this coming year, in the spring of 1974. And I am going to Sun Dance and I will pierce. For this I truly need your help, and I have made these promises and vows to you to obtain it."

He prayed this many times in the sweatlodge. I remember well how he would sit there with tears in his eyes and pray to Almighty God that his parents could be brought together.

So this is why L.H. danced the Sun Dance in July, 1974, and he has Sun Danced twice since then.

As I am taping tonight, the entire H. family is together and right here with us. The Great Spirit has answered the prayers of my grandson. L.H. himself is going to school in New York, but he will be coming home in the summer of 1975 because in some of his letters he has told us he has vowed to vision quest and to participate in the Sun Dance again, thanking the Great Spirit for all He has done for him.

Gilbert Yellow Hawk, age forty-two.

At one time Gilbert was a heavy drinker, and although he was baptized a Catholic and raised here in St. Francis as a Catholic, he became a nonbeliever. After his parents died, he drifted away into Nebraska and became an alcoholic. He lost his first wife, and then he came back here and married O.M. After they got married he came to my ceremonies. He prayed, and he discovered that he was supposed to be a medicine man. So we took him in for training, and three years ago I made him a medicine man. Last September, an-

Jerry Dragg

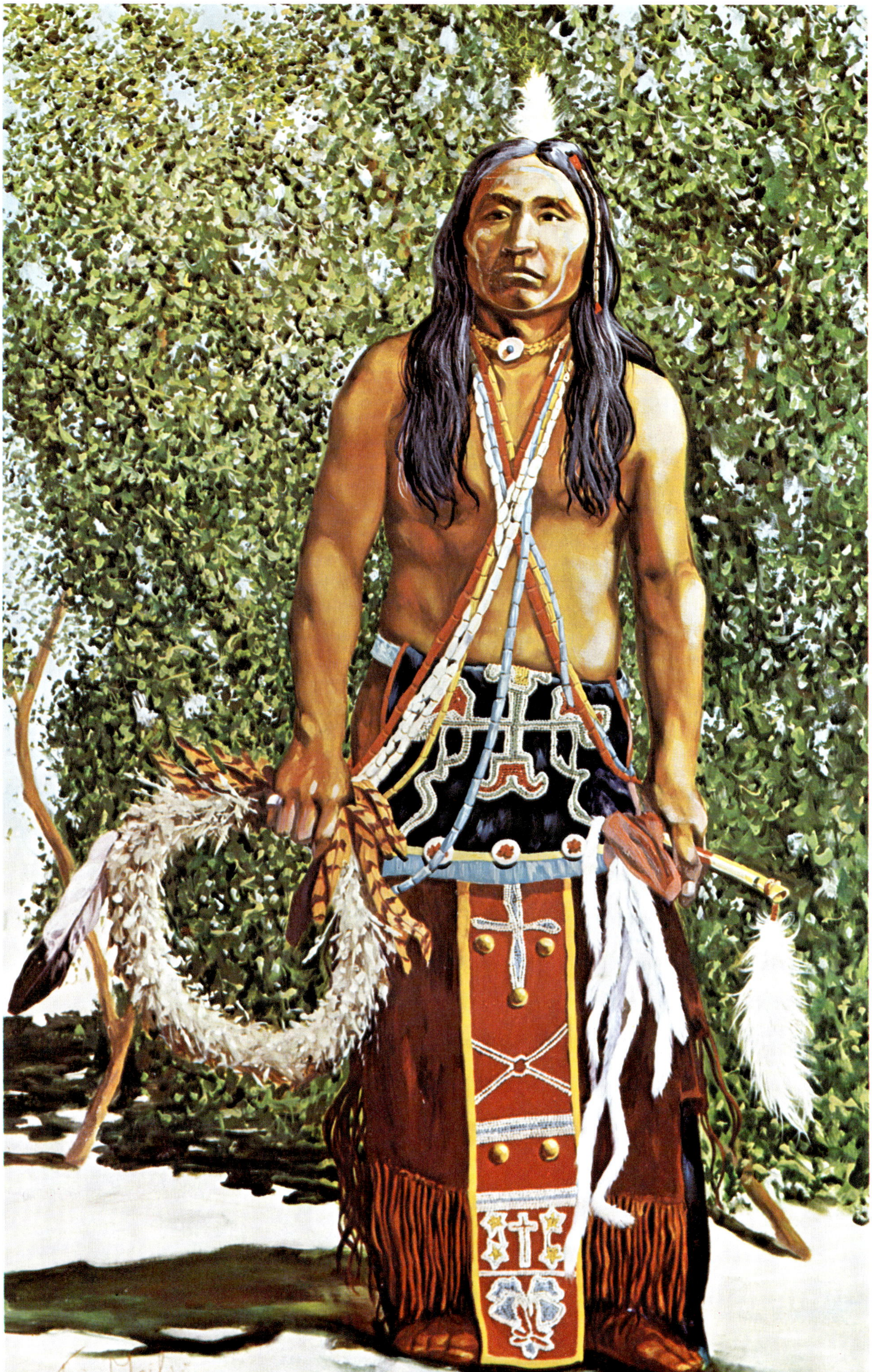

Previous page:
  Ponca Sun Dance in typical plains costume of the 1870s. Oil painting by author.

Top:
  Traditional powwow dancer Ellis Head. Oil painting by author.

Right:
  The Spirit Keeper and Jerry Dragg invoking the Sun. Oil painting by author.

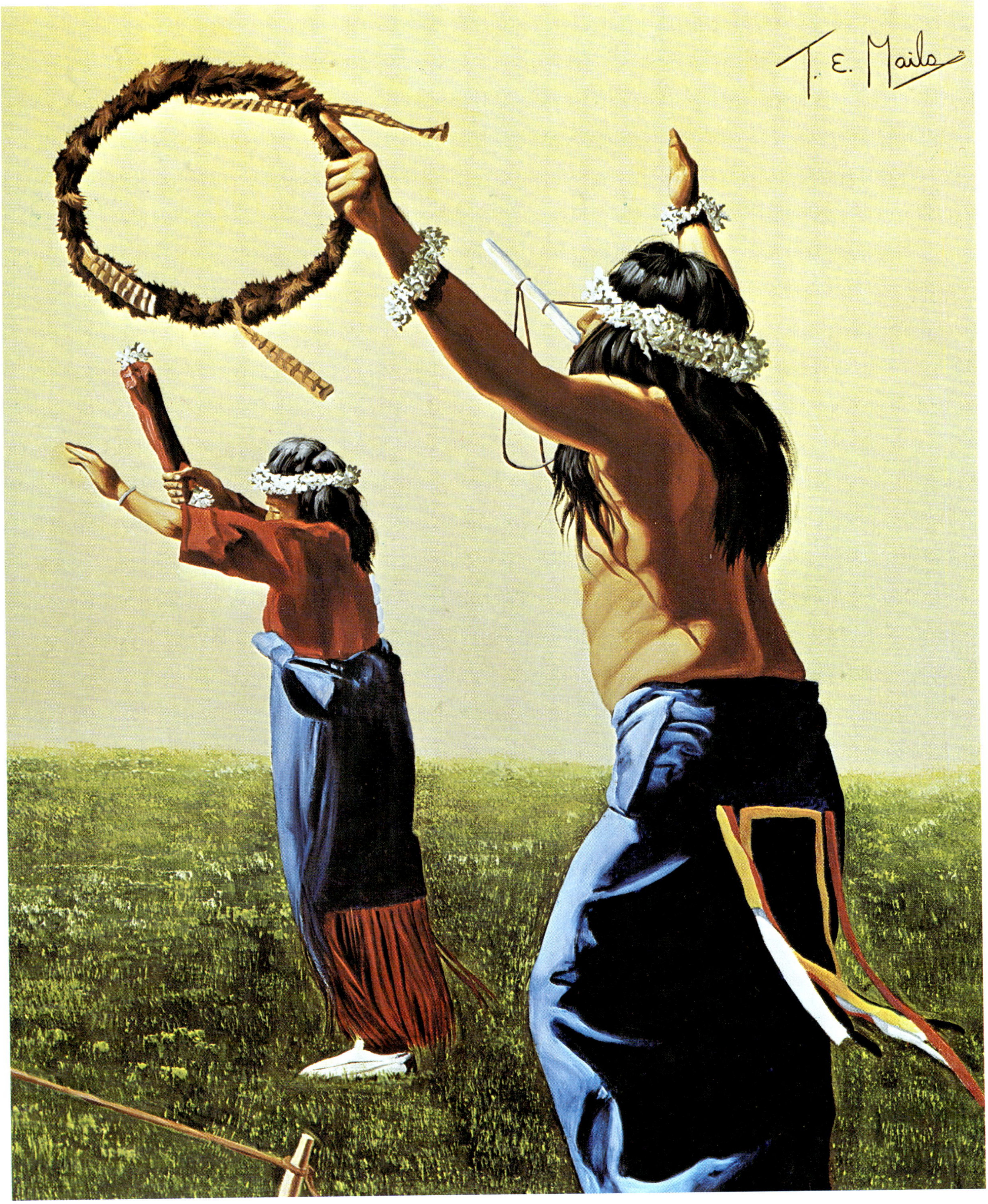
T. E. Mails

Sun Dancers in traditional costumes at Rosebud in 1928. Oil painting by author.

Orrie Farrell

other holy man by the name of Arthur One Feather and I ordained him as a *Yuwipi* Clan Ceremony medicine man.

In February, 1973, his wife had the very serious heart operation I mentioned earlier, and in one of my nighttime ceremonies, Gilbert vowed that if his wife came through the operation successfully, and if all his prayers were answered, he would vision quest and pierce in the Sun Dance, and everything has come out beautifully for him.

He is continuing his work as a medicine man, and he has quit drinking. We hope that he will quit forever now, and be what he has promised Almighty God he will be.

Orrie Farrell, age twenty-six.

Orrie is from the Standing Rock Reservation, the home of the famous Chief Sitting Bull. In 1973, his dad and mother and a brother were all very ill. So he prayed to Almighty God, asking for His help, and made his vow to do the Sun Dance in 1974. Orrie is not a holy man, Titus is not, L.H. is not, B.M. and Hazel are not. Orrie still hits the bottle now and then, but he has been through the Sun Dance with us three times.

Jerry Dragg, age twenty-five.

Jerry is another man who made a vow to pierce in 1974. He is from across the river, east of the Rosebud. He was born and raised at Wagner, South Dakota, on the Yankton Reservation. When he was married, which was four years ago, I performed his marriage in Yankton. His bride is a White girl by the name of Mary, from Winona, Minnesota. Their first little child was a little boy. His name was Jerry, Jr., and I performed the blessing for the boy. As time went on, Jerry, Sr., like so many other young men on the reservations, became a heavy drinker.

In 1973 he came to St. Francis and stayed with us, becoming very interested in the Sioux Indian religion. Shortly thereafter he made a vow to Almighty God that he would quit drinking and was going to participate in and carry on the traditional Indian religion. And he is doing a very good job of keeping his promises. He has been with us in the Sun Dance for two years now, and in addition has done a lot to help the Indian and non-Indian understand each other's religions. This is important, because whenever we make vows they must be made with faith and hope in Almighty God; and regardless of what nationality we are or what religious denomination we belong to, we are all to live as brothers and sisters.

Kermit Bear Shield.

Kermit Bear Shield is from the Wounded Knee Community on the Pine Ridge Reservation. He participated in the Second World War and was wounded and crippled. Because his health wasn't very good he made a vow in 1973 which I didn't learn about until the very time of the Sun Dance, but he said he needed help and his health back. So he made a vow to vision quest, and to do the sweatlodge and Sun Dance in 1974, and he did a beautiful job of it. I think he is a very great man.

Reuben Fire Thunder.

Reuben is from Kyle, South Dakota. He is an enrolled member of the Pine Ridge Reservation. Last year his little girl was very sick. She had cirrhosis of the liver and the doctor said she was going to die. However, she and her mother and dad had faith in Almighty God. So they talked to Him, prayed to Him, and the girl is well today. Because of this, Reuben made a vow a year ago that when his daughter got well he would do the Sun Dance. The first year I shared in a Sun Dance with him was 1974. However, he was in two of the Sun Dances I conducted then. I do not have too much information on him. I wish I had more.

Robert Black Feather.

Robert is from Canada, although he has lived on the Rosebud Reservation now and then. His father was Sioux and his mother was Spanish. He was a great man to watch in the Sun Dance because he was a real hard worker out there. He believes deeply in the Indian religion and puts great effort into it. I pierced him for the first time this year.

C.Q., age forty-three.

C.Q. was in the war in Korea and received a bad head injury. Now he has a metal plate in his head. He is a Sioux from the Rosebud Reservation, and he has watched many Sun Dances. He became a heavy drinker, and as a result his family broke up. So he decided to vision quest, and he did this with Titus Smith at *Follow the Woman Butte* five miles from St. Francis.

After he quested with his peace pipe and prayed, he came back and said, "I don't believe in the White man's religion anymore; I have found Almighty God in my own culture and in my own religion." We never pumped him about these things because God has given each of us minds and the right to choose whatever religion we see fit. So C.Q. vision quested and he pierced. He wanted to pierce both sides, but when it came to the moment of actual piercing he said, "Uncle Bill, it hurts, and I'll only pierce one side."

After the ceremony, something odd happened to him. I don't know what you'd call it, but he became what people sometimes describe as demon-possessed. About two months ago he turned entirely against religion of any kind. He said, "I don't believe in the White man's religion and I don't believe in the Indian's religion. There is no God. You people are foolish and crazy, praying to something you really don't know about."

He went to Minneapolis to where his brother lived and was so troubled that he shook all over and sweated. He didn't want to go anyplace anymore, and he refused to go into the sweatlodge or to pray with the pipe. Finally it got so bad that no one could do a thing for him.

Since he was born and baptized a Roman Catholic, the priest and other Catholics talked to him, and he just didn't seem to care about anything anymore. The only thing he had pleasant memories about was the time when he had had a wife and a good job in Eagle Butte, South Dakota. He had worked there with the Bureau of Indian Affairs for twenty-one years, and had only two or three years to go to draw a pension. But he began to drink day and night, eventually becoming an alcoholic and losing everything.

So when he came up here to Rosebud before the 1974 Sun Dance, we went into the sweatlodge with him and prayed with him. Finally he said, "I'm going to vision quest and I'm going to Sun Dance." Actually he didn't tell us about his troubles in so many words, but when prayers were being made and we were talking to the Great Spirit he said enough to describe his sad situation. He admitted that he once was a good man, but he was not anymore. So we talked with him, but maybe we didn't do all we should have for him. Perhaps we didn't even pray for him as we should have.

While he was in Minneapolis after this, a psychiatrist got hold of him. We had wanted to arrange something like that here, but there wasn't any available at the time. The worst part is that the psychiatrist said C.Q. had been a religious fanatic and was lost because of religion. Now, although C.Q. appears to have snapped out of it, he doesn't want anything to do with Indian or White religion. He claims he is going to live the way he thinks is best for himself.

B.M., age thirty-five.

B.M. wanted health and financial help for her father, who was ill. Her home was broken up, too, and she needed many things. So she vowed, Sun Danced, and made prayers. She is an enrolled member of the Rosebud Sioux Tribe, and lives in Spring Creek, South Dakota.

V
The Vision Quest

THOMAS E. MAILS

A number of Eagle Feather's brief biographies of the pledgers include references to their vision quests. For untold centuries, it has been the Sioux custom to vision quest. That is the traditional way of putting it. What it means is, it is the custom to seek, or to go in search of, a vision. Black Elk taught that visions take the viewer to literal places where things are and exist. The seeker must then find that place.[1]

The belief is that a person cannot be a success in any aspect of life without the Great Spirit's help. The way to obtain this assistance is through supernatural helpers whom God has created and empowered for this very purpose. The first contact with these helpers is made in a vision, and it is continued in dreams, subsequent visions, and as encounters take place with earthly counterparts of the visioned helper.

For instance, one might experience in his vision a giant wolf. Shortly thereafter, the seeker obtains some part of a wolf to be carried in his medicine bundle as a constant reminder of the experience; and from that moment on the wolf is in his consciousness in every prayer and ceremony. Moreover, when a real wolf appears as the man journeys, he holds a conversation with it in the absolute belief that it is his spiritual helper.

Such beliefs are as prevalent among Traditionalists today as they were years ago, and medicine men report frequent and important conversations with birds, animals, rocks, and the thunder beings who live in the clouds.

In prereservation times, the first vision quest for a budding warrior took place sometime between the ages of eleven and thirteen. The candidate usually sought the aid and guidance of a holy man in preparing for it, since mental and emotional conditioning were necessary prerequisites.

Then the holy man, sometimes accompanied by his friends as assistants, would take the boy to a remote and lonely place, far from the camp and interferences, and of such an awesome physical nature as to encourage visions. After purification in a sweatlodge, they would place him in a covered pit. Ideally, he would remain there for four days and nights, fasting and praying for a vision.

Sometimes the vision came, and sometimes it did not. If he failed, he tried again until he was successful. Marvelous things were seen and learned in visions about the present and the future. The candidate received guidance for his life's pattern, and often information which aided and directed his people.

Original visions might be expanded and clarified in dreams and in ceremonies such as the sweatlodge, the *Yuwipi*, and the Sun Dance. Indeed, vision seeking was part of the preparation of the pledger for fulfillment of the Sun Dance vow, and further visions

Social dancing took place within the Mystery Circle at the old time Sun Dances too. This one was held at Pine Ridge, South Dakota. Fools Crow thought that the man at the left wearing the full-tail bonnet might be himself.

Huge numbers of dancers in full regalia took part in the social dancing, and it was an exciting and awesome sight and sound for visitors to experience.

were sought through the prayers and suffering during the dance itself.

The vision-seeking practice remains a standard part of the Sun Dance ceremony today. Pledgers are expected to vision seek sometime prior to the day the four-day ceremony begins. Some men and women, and always those who live away from the Rosebud Reservation, vision quest on their own. Those who live on the Rosebud sometimes go in pairs to a well-known vision-seeking place—most often a hill—and remain there fasting and praying for four days and four nights. Now and then the stay is shorter because they are not able to stand the suffering.

Eagle Feather, his family, his relatives, and whatever friends wish to join them, go in a group to vision quest together. They have a favorite place for this where all of the facilities needed are in close conjuction: a fine stream, plenty of wood for fires, and several low but separated hills. They set up camp, and then they build a sweatlodge and the same kind of Old Man Four Generations fireplace as that used at the Sun Dance grounds. When this is ready, the pledgers, both men and women, undergo purification in the lodge, and then are placed in separate locations on the hills to begin their lonely vigil.

The arrangement of the individual fasting places is most interesting and inspiring. Long branches with the leaves left on are taken from cottonwood trees and stuck upright in the ground to make the four corners of a square approximately eight feet in width. Then bright cloth banners are tied to the trees in conformity to the Sun

The pledger as he begins his four days of fasting and vision seeking.

Dance directional colors: black for the west, red for the north, yellow for the east, and white for the south.

After this, strands of string are stretched horizontally between the trees like the ropes of a prize-fight ring, and to these strings are attached dozens of small colorful cloth packets containing tobacco, herbs, and flesh offerings. The number of strands varies from one to four, and the final result is a handsome enclosure in the middle of which the candidates sit.

They rest on a blanket or a buffalo robe and have another blanket with which they can wrap or cover themselves. The women wear dresses and moccasins. The men wear trousers but are barefooted, just as they will be in the Sun Dance. There is an eagle feather in the hair to call upon the power and qualities of that sacred bird, and also some sage to be used for purification.

Each pledger has a pipe and will use it to pray for Grandfather's blessings now and in the dance. Prayers will also be offered for the Sioux nation, and for the unity of all people. Toward one end of the square, usually that end where the red and black flags are, the Rosebud pledger erects a small pipe rack made from cherry branches. The pipe will rest on this rack when the candidate is not praying with it. The bowl will be on a bed of sage on the ground, and the stem will be leaned against the rack. At Pine Ridge there is no pipe rack, just a wooden dish containing meat and other items.

With reverence, sincerity, and good fortune, some time during the next four days and nights the vision will come. Not much of it will be told to others—it is too personal for that. The exception will be when the vision helper instructs the pledger to reveal more for the good of the nation.

While we were on our herb-gathering expedition on July 1, 1975, Eagle Feather told me some things about his own vision quests. He went to Holy Lodge Hill each year over a period of seven years extending from 1965 to 1972. Holy Lodge Hill is located a short distance northwest of the Rosebud Fairground, and it is a relatively small hill. Yet its cone-like shape stands high above the plain surrounding it. At the very top is a sandstone formation which, if you use your imagination, resembles the form of a man lying down.

Despite his persistence, Eagle Feather never received a vision there, although he did say that whenever he put his ear to the ground he heard regular thumps, like steady drumbeats. He doesn't know what it is, but he does expect one day to receive a vision in a most unusual way.

He ended his vision quests there when, in 1973, a county road was put in that passed close by the south side of the hill. The noise and activity made the silence required for effective vision questing impossible. But before he left that site, a strange thing happened. On the morning of the fourth day of the seventh year, Eagle Feather looked out across the plain to the south and saw a man walking across the fields toward the hill. When the figure came close enough, Eagle Feather saw it was Circle Elk, a well-known holy man.

Circle Elk was dressed in bibbed overalls, a brown suit coat, a yellow-white, flat-topped cowboy hat, and plain moccasins made out of canvas. He was close to ninety years old at the time, yet he climbed steadily up the steep side of Holy Lodge Hill and was not out of breath when he reached the top.

Once there, he told Eagle Feather that he knew he had been here to vision quest many times, and that he would one day learn the vision he sought through his body on the hill.

Eagle Feather has pondered this many times and has come to the conclusion that he will learn it only when he is buried there. So

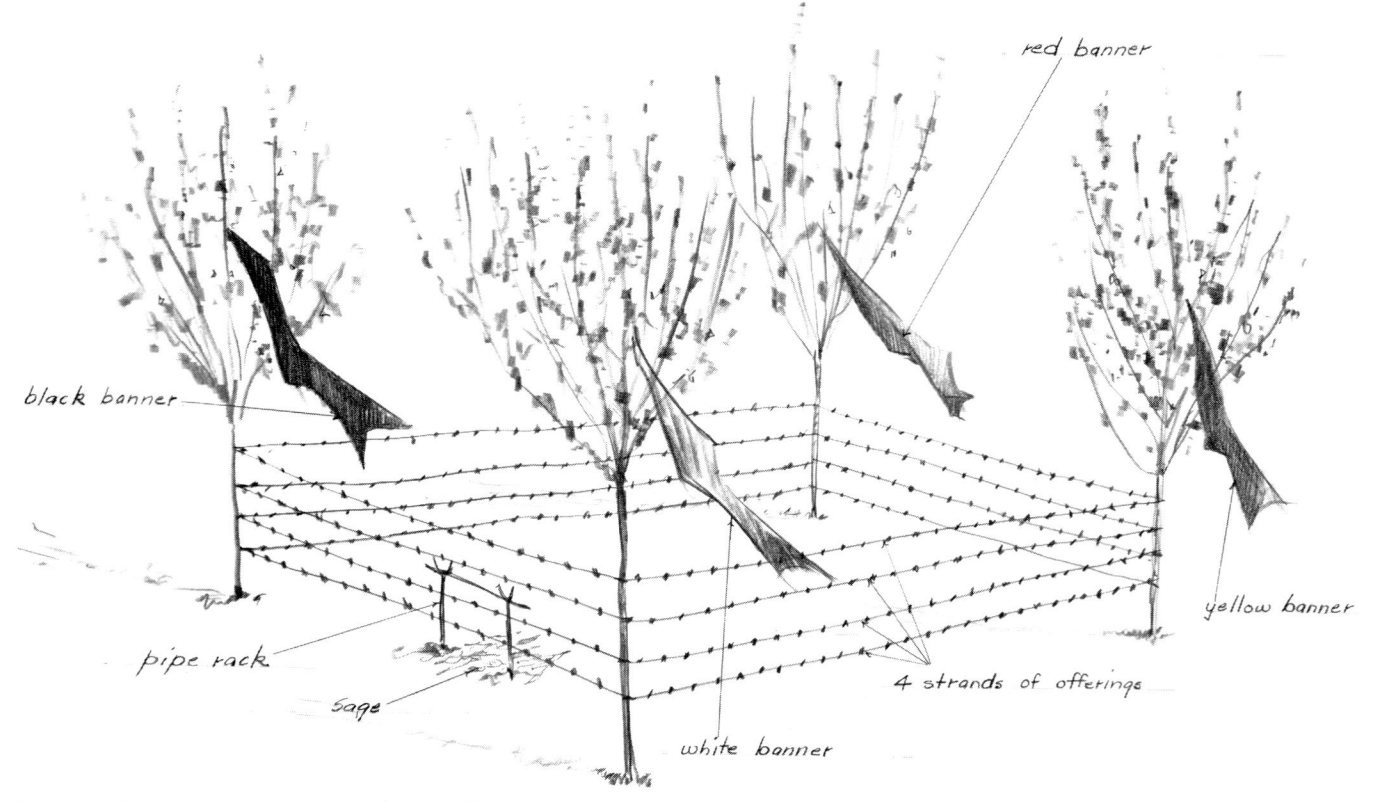

Diagram of the contemporary Vision Questing Place. Four small cottonwood trees mark the corners of an eight to ten foot square, and appended to them are cloth banners whose colors correspond to those used in the Sun Dance proper. From one to four offering strands may be used. The pipe rack is at the west-south end. The pledger sits in the center on a buffalo robe or a blanket.

The Vision Questing Place in 1975. The pledger is alone with his thoughts and prayers in a place that will accentuate his fasting and search for a vision.

Arrangement of the pledger's pipes on the Mole Hill at the Vision Questing Camp. At the top are the milk can containing water and the water bucket to be used for the sweatlodge purification ceremonies.

The relationship of the sweatlodge, the Mole Hill and the Old Man Four Generations fireplace at the Vision Questing Camp. The relationship is the same as that used at the Sun Dance site.

Excavating the Old Man Four Generations fireplace at the Vision Questing Site.

Contemplating the arrangement of the seven stones and the four lines which make up the face of the Old Man Four Generations fireplace at the Vision Questing Site.

Stacking the cottonwood in the Old Man Four Generations fireplace in preparation for the first purification ceremony at the Vision Questing Site.

he has told his medicine-man friends that when he dies he wants to be buried on top of Holy Lodge Hill. His instructions are that if he is brought there in a casket, he is to be taken out, wrapped in a buffalo robe or a blanket, tied with his Sun Dance ropes, which he has kept for this purpose, and buried that way. Only the medicine men are to bring him. No one else is to be present, not even his wife, Hazel.

In concluding this tale, Eagle Feather did not say where he seeks his visions now, although his account of the dance reveals that he does see them in the sweatlodge and during Sun Dances.

A holy man named Stirrup and two other men took Frank Fools Crow on his first vision quest in 1913. I saw the secluded hill on the Pine Ridge Reservation where it took place, and I thought it still a marvelous place for the purpose.

On this first occasion, Fools Crow was placed in a shallow pit, which was covered over with a buffalo hide. He remained there for four days and nights without food or water, and on the last night had his first vision.

Fools Crow made a number of subsequent vision quests over a period of many years at awesome Bear Butte in the Black Hills. He saw many wondrous visions during these quests, the most important of which he related to me for inclusion in his forthcoming biography.

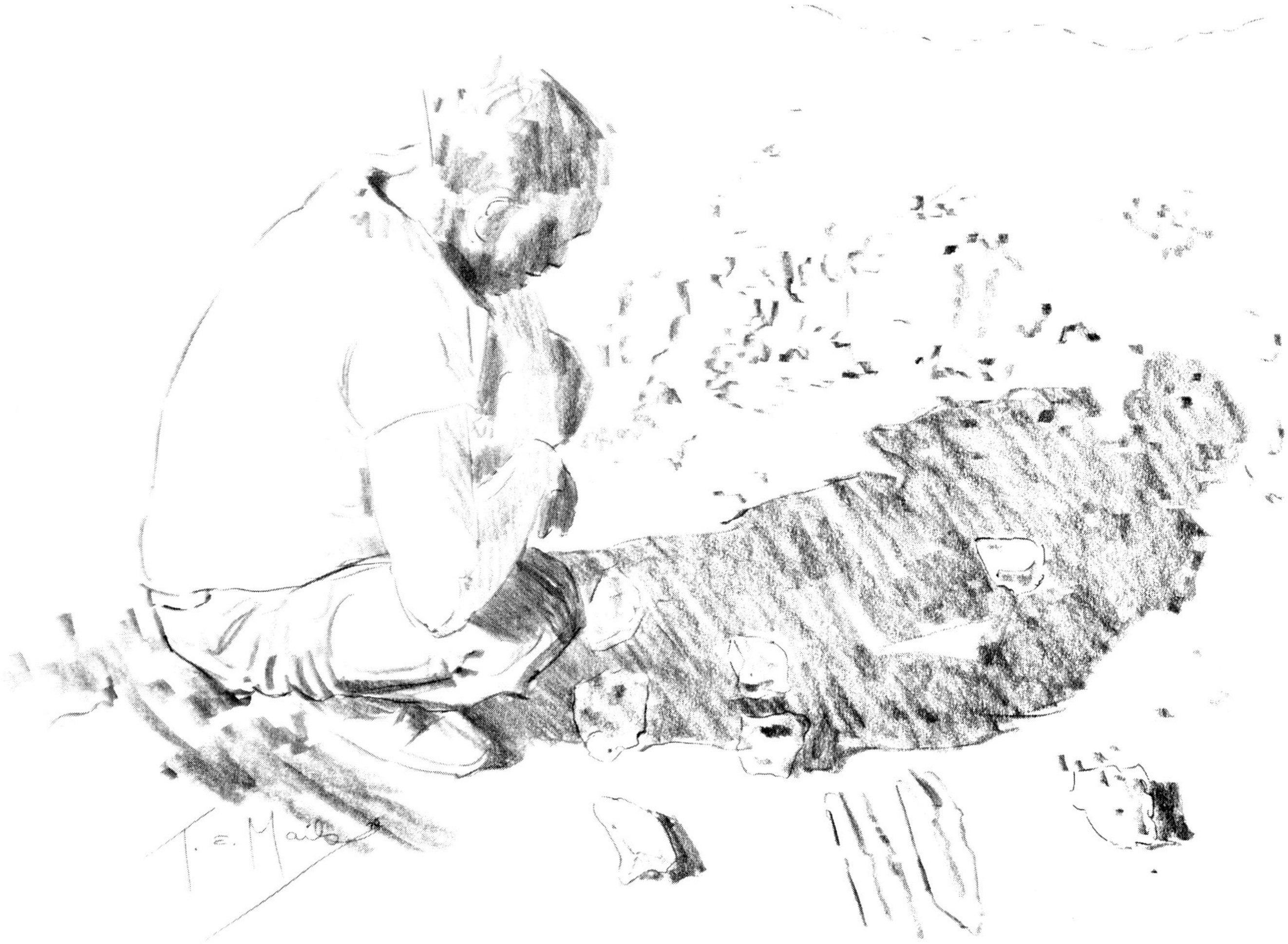
T. E. Mails

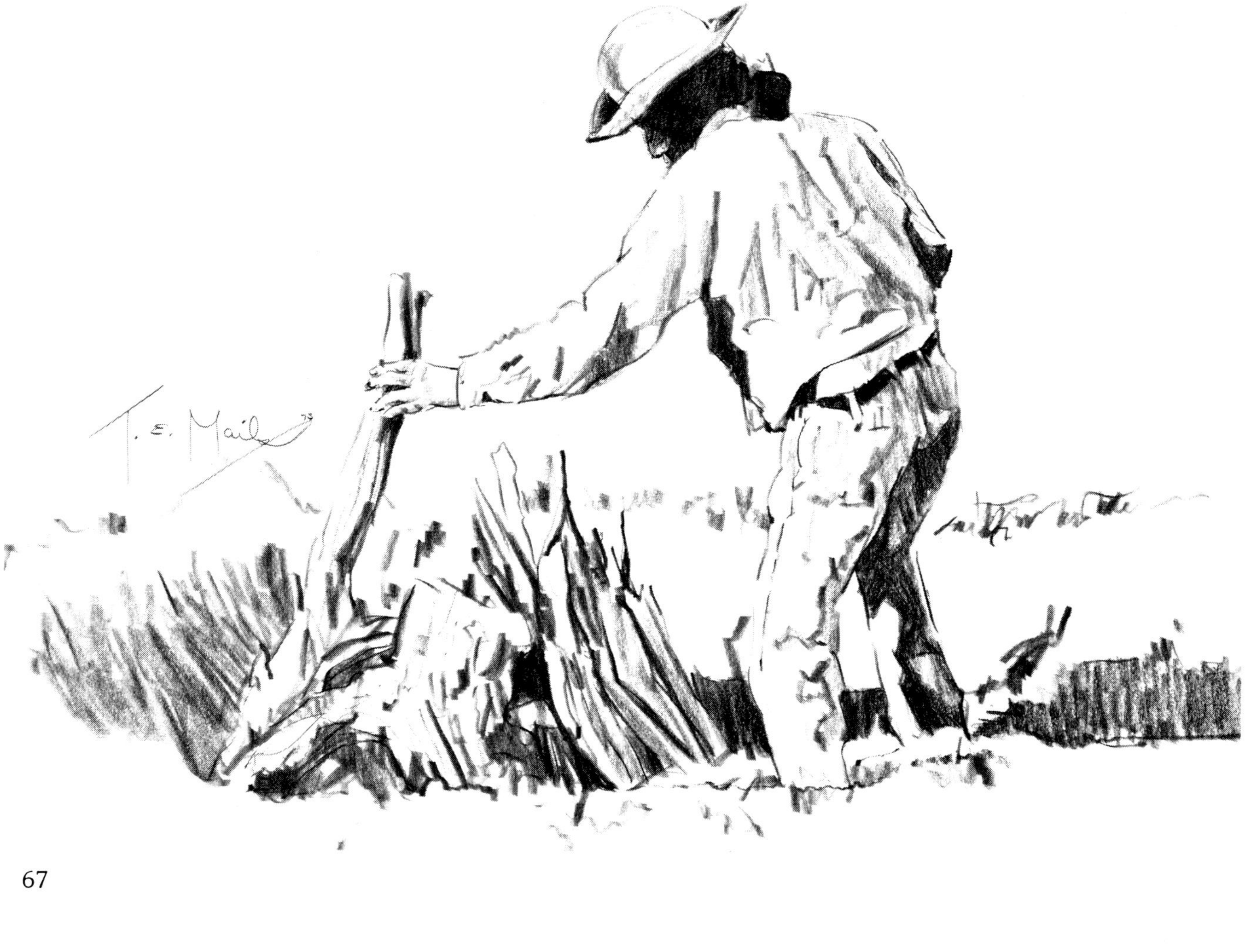
T. E. Mails

VI
Jesse White Lance, And The Sun Dance Of August, 1956

EAGLE FEATHER

During the years I went to school to learn how to be an electrician I also learned to live with the non-Indians to get along with them. So for the most part I had no fear about living in the outside world. But by 1956 I had to readjust my life with my own people, because I was getting into something portentous and different, back into my ancient Indian culture and religion.

In August, 1956, there was to be a Sun Dance at Frank Picket Pin's home, which is located on the Little White River, about seven miles west of Rosebud. By now I had made up my mind that I was going to participate in this dance, even though I knew nothing about the details of the ceremony.

So I went down to Frank's place and I inquired around. I told different ones there that I had come down to take part in the Sun Dance. So they told me what I had to have: a whistle made out of an eagle wingbone, and an eagle plume feather; I had to find the long single plume that is found only on a golden eagle. Once I obtained these they helped me get ready, and I participated in the Sun Dance there without piercing. There were three of us who danced: Henry Crow Dog, Leo Claremont, and myself. Each day for four days we danced from four o'clock in the morning until noon. The Intercessor, the person that conducted and directed the Sun Dance, was a man named Jesse White Lance. He was a medicine man and a member of the Rosebud Sioux Tribe. He was about seventy years old at the time, so he knew all of the old ways.

On the day before the first day of the dance, we cut down the Sacred Tree on the bank of the Little White River. Many people gathered there for the great event. Four girls that ranged in age from six to eight, whose names I do not remember, were taken to where the pole was. It was a cottonwood tree, about fifty feet tall, and its diameter at the base was about twelve inches.

The Peace Pipe and the braided sweet grass were brought by medicine men, and the sweet grass smoke was used to purify the Sacred Tree. The four little girls represented the four directions: the west, the north, the east, and the south. Each one took the axe in turn and hit the tree on the side she represented. Then the burning sweet grass was carried clockwise around the Tree and the Tree was cut down. Of course, there were also prayers being made with the Pipe, such as the prayer which stated that a stranger, the Tree, was going to go to a Mystery Circle, a Mystery Hoop, and be set in its center. Many prayers were offered to the Sacred Tree because it was especially holy. God has raised it up from the earth, transforming it from a bunch of roots into a beautiful tree, and now it would fulfill a holy purpose.

Then the Tree was hauled by men on foot to about half a mile from where the Sun Dance was to be held. Eight men, including the three of us that were going to dance, carried it butt first. Of course, our leader and medicine man, Jesse White Lance, was at the head of the procession, carrying the Peace Pipe that had been filled at the tree site and was being brought along to be buried under the foot of the Tree.

Jesse White Lance halted the procession four times on the way to the dance arena. Each time he did this, sage was spread on the ground as a bedding for the Tree, and the Tree was laid down. This was done to allow the men who carried it to rest, while the medicine man made prayers in Sioux with the Pipe to each of the four directions. His first plea was made to the west, whose color is black. He began by saying that the black is to the west, and it represents the loved ones who have passed away and made their last journey to the place Whites call the Happy Hunting Ground. His prayer included the deceased peoples of all times and places. He spoke of the black people as his brothers and sisters.

The Tree was then picked up and taken on the second stage of its journey. We went a short distance and stopped again, putting the Tree down where the sage has been spread to make its resting place. This time Jesse faced the north with the Peace Pipe and made prayers to the north and its red color. It was here that I first came to understand what red power meant. In praying to the red power, he mentioned all people, the universe, all living animals, and even the fish down in the ocean. As I stood there listening I suddenly realized that red power was the most important gift from Almighty God to all living creatures, for the red power was blood. He also prayed for the red people, called them his brothers and sisters. He concluded by saying, "I dedicate my life to the red power that God has put inside us."

He was right. Red blood is red power, and its power is absolute. If anyone doubts this, all he needs to do is take a razor blade and cut his wrist, and then sit there until he runs out of red power. Then he is done; all through. So we should show special respect for the red power that is placed within us by Almighty God. Using blood alone I can prove to myself that the black, red, white, and yellow races are my brothers and sisters. If I take the black man and cut him, I find that the blood isn't black, it's red, and it is the same for the other races. Therefore, people should live as brothers and sisters under one God, united in all ways and working together spiritually and physically.

So Jesse White Lance talked about the same four colors that we use in the Sun Dance today: black, red, yellow, and white. As well as their representing other things, he made it clear that the four colors stood also for the black, red, yellow, and white races. So you see that through the Peace Pipe, which is our Jesus Christ, we have learned to accept the other races as our true brothers and sisters. Moreover, this is why the Indian calls so many things "his relatives." He speaks of his four-legged brothers and sisters, of his winged brothers and sisters, and he has relatives deep down in the ocean. Red power is the common investment of Almighty God in all living creatures on this earth and in the universe.

We now lifted the Tree up and took it on its third journey, stopping as before at a sage-covered resting place. This time Jesse faced east with the Peace Pipe, holding its stem up toward the sky and saying that the yellow represented the yellow race, which he accepted as his blood brothers and sisters. He also said that the color yellow was a plea for all families to unite and to work for Almighty God. In this blessed task they were to love one another, to share life, and to put all divisions aside.

The Tree was then picked up again and taken on its fourth journey. At the last stop, prayer was made to the south and its white color. Here Jesse said that the white represented the purification of the people of all races. He mentioned that all those of the White race were his brothers and sisters because of the red power. So here was a great prayer that included all the non-Indians, and the White people especially. As all of this happened in 1956, I cannot remember everything that took place. Many things were going on at the same time, and a huge crowd of people was walking with us and singing. It was an exciting experience!

When the prayer was finished, the Tree was picked up and moved on its last journey. First it was brought to the east entrance of the Mystery Hoop and laid down. Jesse stood with his arms raised and his hands open and made the shrill howl of a coyote four times. This was a plea to the Great Spirit that the dance arena would literally become the Mystery Hoop representing the Sioux nation. It was also an answer to those who feel that our Sacred Hoop is broken now. Physically it is, but spiritually it is not broken. The Sun Dance holds it together still.

In addition, the holler of the coyote also indicated that the sneaky coyote of our folklore was going to enter the Mystery Hoop. When the four cries had been uttered, Jesse moved farther into the east doorway of the Mystery Circle and prayed to Almighty God that the Tree, which had been alive and growing only a few minutes ago and now would die out there in the middle of the Mystery Circle, would serve as a symbol of many things. God had provided it for this very purpose. The people had harvested it, and before their eyes the Tree would expire. It was a lesson. Many things would die in this way, including their loved ones and friends. People should realize this was the will of God and an expression of His love. God is the only one who truly loves us, and we die physically so that he can take us to be at His side forever.

After these prayers were made, the Tree was picked up and carried out to the center of the Mystery Hoop, where the hole for it was being dug. It was placed on the ground with its butt facing the hole. Once again the Tree was blessed with the sacred sweet grass, and while this was done the Pipe was laid on the dirt pile which was on the north side of the hole.

At this time rawhide images of a man and a buffalo were brought and placed by the Tree. People have asked me why at my dances the buffalo and the man are painted red instead of black. It is because of the teachings I received from Jesse White Lance; this tradition was handed down to me from him. He spoke of the red power, and since the red power is in both the man and the buffalo, I paint them both red. They carry the red power. Red is also my clan color.

Before these two images were tied on to the top of the Sacred Tree, a narrow stripe of red clay was sprinkled on the Tree's trunk from the base clear to the top. This represented the narrow red path that Almighty God tells us we are to follow as we walk through life. Then, while the buffalo and the man were being secured to the top of the Tree, four cloth offerings were also prepared and tied there. These were seven-yard-long banners: one red, one black, one white, and one yellow.

The image of the man is put on the tree for several reasons. In ancient days it was a prayer for victory over our enemies. But it was also a prayer for the health and well-being of the many youngsters who had been born during the previous year. They had arrived to begin a journey here, and it was a prayer that they would have happy and productive lives. Besides this, it was a prayer for mothers to produce more human beings and more red power. When we Sioux look at the image of the man that hangs on the tree, all this comes to mind. It gives us much to think about, and especially when we consider the image of the "real man" today. Years ago one of our renowned medicine men predicted, and in fact I predicted also, that the Indian would return to wearing long hair, reservation-style black hats, and Indian-style dress. Yet he would return to this with an empty mind and an empty heart. The non-Indian, the White man and the Indian, have returned as predicted. In ever-increasing numbers the White men of today have long hair and beards, and look like the artists' paintings of Jesus Christ, and so many of their minds seem empty, their hearts appear to be empty, they have no religion, no belief in Almighty God, and they need help.

Halfway down from the top of the Tree we placed the cherry bundle. It is a bundle of branches which is put crossways on the Tree for two reasons: In ancient days the cherry tree provided one of our main sources of food, as did the buffalo; today it also reminds us of the cross of Christ.

Just below the cherry branches the medicine man tied one end of each of the three rawhide ropes we would use to pierce in the Sun Dance. All of the ropes were tied on at the same time before the Tree was raised.

The hole into which the Tree is placed represents the hole we can neither overstep or avoid. We all go down into this hole on the day we depart from the earth. So into this hole Jesse White Lance first put sage and then the Peace Pipe he had prayed with and laid down on the dirt mound. Next we placed some buffalo fat in the hole. We did this because the Tree was going on a journey from which it would never return. It would need food for the trip, just as our dead relatives did when they went down in the hole in years past.

Now we took some dried meat, or jerky, and we put it down in the hole. After that *wasna*, pemmican, which is one of our main foods, made from a mixture of pounded cherries and dried meat, was put down in the hole in memory of our past and of our loved ones who had passed away. Each of these items was a prayer to Almighty God. We pray to only one God, and that is the Great Spirit, Almighty God.

When all of these preparations were finished, ten men set the butt of the Tree in the hole, raised it up, and dirt was packed around the base to keep it straight and in place.

Ater the Tree was up, many people came to it and brought cloth offerings of different colors to tie around its base. If black was brought and hung up by somebody, it was the donor's way of saying that he had prayed for loved ones who had died. If red was hung there, it meant that a person who had been ill during the previous twelve months had vowed that if he got well he would bring a red cloth offering to place on the Tree. If someone else brought a yellow cloth offering and tied it on the Tree, it meant that there had been troubles in the family but that everything was better now. Since their prayers had been answered, the cloth offerings were being brought to make public thanksgiving to Almighty God for His help. Other people brought white cloths and hung them up. This revealed that the donors had prayed for purification, health, and wealth, and that some or all of the prayers were being answered. Offerings of these four colors were brought and hung up around the base of the Tree.

On occasion one might see a grain of wheat or grass tied on the

Sacred Tree. This indicated that a person who had been ill had prayed throughout the entire winter that Almighty God would make him well and once more put his feet on the green grass which would come up in the spring that followed. All these things are our traditional way of praying to Almighty God.

Now the Tree was completely prepared, and everything was ready for the first day of the Sun Dance in 1956. On the night of that last day before the Sun Dance we had what we call the ground initiation. Not everyone was present for this. In the old days the only ones allowed were the men who had gone on war parties or horse raids. But in 1956 and now, too, we use our American Indian soldiers, in particular those who have been prisoners of war or wounded. These are the ones that have earned the right to initiate the Mystery Hoop ground.

The medicine man Jesse White Lance passed away some years ago at the age of seventy-one. I can't recall the date. He was an enrolled member of the Rosebud Sioux Tribe, an honest and solid person, who believed deeply in his Sioux culture and practiced his Indian religion right up to the day he died.

Left to right: Jim Wentzy, Dallas Chief Eagle and Arthur Mahoney, standing outside the tribal headquarters building in the town of Rosebud.

VII
Preparations For The Sun Dance Of 1974

EAGLE FEATHER

On July 6, 1974, Jerry Dragg, S.H., and I went to the Rosebud Fairground and removed the sign for the last year's Sun Dance. Then we took it to Melvin Spotted Elk's house. Melvin is an artist, and he was going to print the new dates on these signs and hang them up. This year the Sun Dance would be held on July 11, 12, 13, and 14 at the Rosebud Fairground, which is about a mile north of the town of Rosebud, South Dakota.

On the afternoon of July 7, a group of us drove out to the fairground to build the sweatlodge for the dance. Those who went were: Hazel and I, S.H., L.H., Linda and Melvin Spotted Elk and their kids, C.Q., and Georgaline Little Elk and her daughter. Some White people were there, too: Tom Albright and his son Fran, and Jim Brady and his son.

Therefore, when we built the sweatlodge we didn't just get Sioux Indians, we had different nationalities helping us. Tom Albright and some others went after willow branches and brought them back. Then all of the men who were to participate in the Sun Dance helped build the sweatlodge and its outside fireplace, which we call Old Man Four Generations. The door of the Sun Dance sweatlodge always faces west.

C.Q. and L.H. went after a load of rocks for the sweatlodge fireplace. When they returned, C.Q. and I chopped down the grass where the sweatlodge would be placed. If we didn't do this it would be very hard to sit down in there; so we made the ground as smooth as possible and got it ready. Then all of the men joined in to get the butts of the willows in the ground. Then they bent the branches over at the top to make a dome-shaped structure. We use the bark of the willow branches to make strips to tie the willow framework together. When we are constructing the sweatlodge we never use wires or nails or any other manufactured item. We bend the willows over and tie them with their own bark.

As we did these things, four-generation prayers and ceremonials were performed. There were ceremonies for the blessing of the ground, the blessing of the space after it was finished, the blessing of the rocks, and the sage that would be put inside the sweatlodge was blessed. Many things were being prepared at this time for the sweatlodge by the different people who took part in the Sun Dance; for example, they had to get the coverings and the pail ready, and also the pitchfork.

The custodian for the four main days of the 1974 dance was Floyd Comes a Flying, and he is usually selected for this job because he is a firm believer in the Indian religion and culture, and because he has been healed by our Indian religion and medicines. A while back they said he was going to lose his feet. Gangrene had already set in, and the doctor said it would only be a week before they would need to amputate both of his feet. But he came over to us and we had ceremonies with him and doctored him, and today he is walking around and is in excellent shape.

On the evening of July 8, 1974, Hazel and I, C.Q., Georgaline Little Elk, her daughter, S.H., L.H., B.B.W., J.P., and Sonny all went to the fairground to dig the hole for the Holy Tree. We measured the ground all around the circle until we located the center of the arena. To find the exact center is very important. And we prayed with the Peace Pipe about the dirt we were going to dig up, about the diameter of the hole we were going to dig, and about how deep we should dig it. Usually it is about four feet deep, but prayer helps us to do it just right for each Tree.

It was here that we began to run into some trouble. Hazel, J.D., Sonny, and S.H. drove down to my daughter Ramona's house to borrow a posthole digger. But the car stalled on the way down there, and they had to pay people a dollar to push them. Finally they made it back to the fairground and using the borrowed posthole digger, J.D., C.Q., S.H., L.H., and B.B.W. worked on the hole for the Holy Tree. Later that evening Tom Albright and his son Billy came out to help us, and we finally got the hole ready and were prepared to bring the Tree in and set it up.

One of the other problems we encountered here was finances for the dance. A minister from the House of Friendship in St. Francis had promised to get us money for the Sun Dance, but none of it had appeared yet. In addition, L.C.D. had said he would get us three thousand dollars for the Sun Dance, but he hadn't come through with any of it yet, and he never did.

We were in real trouble, and Hazel and Linda Spotted Elk went out to ask for donations. They came back with a little better than ninety-eight dollars for food and the other things we needed to get ready for the dance. Then on July 9, my son-in-law, Melvin Spotted Elk, typed some letters for me to the effect that there were no funds, no money whatever for the Sun Dance. In the letters, I stated that Mrs. Melvin Spotted Elk was authorized in the name of the Sun Dance Association to collect funds for the Sun Dance.

These are some of the problems we had. The people who promised they would help us couldn't do it, and here we were, only two days before the Sun Dance, with virtually no money. We didn't even have an extra dime.

Yet this only served to prove again that when you believe in Almighty God your needs will be answered. Later on, the tribal chairman of the Rosebud Sioux, Robert Burnette, gave us five hundred dollars. Then on the third day of the dance, Dallas Chief Eagle brought over Thomas Mails and introduced him to me. He said, "I want you to meet Reverend Thomas Mails. He would like to take some pictures of the Sun Dance, and he will pay you substantially for the privilege."

So I talked to the other fellows and they said, "Sure, we've got to have money for food and things, but is this man going to commercialize these pictures and make big money?" We had a discussion there among ourselves until I explained that it would be for education purposes only, and then they agreed. This was a great help from Almighty God. With the money we bought food for the people to eat, and we all felt better. So these were the good things that came out of our troubles.

On the evening of July 9, Melvin Spotted Elk began passing the rocks into the sweatlodge. Altogether, about twenty heated rocks were used that time. This was the very first time a ceremony had been held in a sweatlodge at the fairground. After the first group of rocks had been put in and water was poured on them, the door flap was opened two times. Then Melvin filled the water pail again and passed more rocks in. Twice more, to make four times in all, the door was opened. Finally the Peace Pipe was sent in, prayed with, taken out, and the purified people came out. So that was the first sweatlodge of the 1974 Sun Dance, and at that time we were very aware that even greater history was to be made with the first piercing at the Rosebud Fairground. For although a Sun Dance had been held close by there in 1928, it was without piercing.

On the morning of July 10, Hazel, Titus, S.H., and L.H. went after the cherry tree boughs we needed to construct the pipe rack for the Sun Dance Altar.

On the afternoon of July 10, at our home in St. Francis, L.H., Titus, Hazel, and I tied the eagle feather plumes to the ends of the Sun Dance whistles—only the first wing bone of the golden eagle is used to make a whistle. Later, Jerry Dragg, C.Q., S.H., and I worked on separating the eagle claws we would use for piercing.

At this time another helpful donation came in. Lorraine Metcalf brought over four loaves of bread, five pounds of sugar, some coffee, and eight dollars' worth of meat. She said she'd try to bring more food the next day, and if she could, she'd provide a cow or whatever. She was a great help, and I'm sorry to say that she is dead now. We certainly scraped along to make it through the dance. With the help of Thomas Mails and Mr. Burnette, the food donations, and the free-will offerings taken at the ceremony, we just barely made it over the hump. One of the hopes we have is that we can give a little traveling money to the men and women who are taking part in the dance. Some come a long way and lose work time and we try to help them as we can.

So here we are on July 10, which incidentally is my birthday: Happy Birthday to me! Happy Birthday to me! You know.

Some of the group went down to Spring Creek after Orrie Farrell, but he wasn't there. Hazel and I packed the dishes and food we would need and got things ready. Marcella Little Elk, our neighbor here, made the hamburger meat and corn balls for us. She also fixed C.Q.'s Sun Dance blanket.

About three o'clock, we all went to the fairground to unload and set up the tents we would live in. Even as we drove up there, Hazel was trying to sew Titus' leggings. When we arrived, I was told that there was a White girl looking for me. She wanted to know if she could make tape recordings of the Sun Dance. I said, "No, we don't allow tapings of Sun Dance music and songs, they are too sacred for that."

Now everyone who would take part in the Sun Dance was present. John Fire Lame Deer gave a talk to all the men who were going to dance and pierce. I explained some things about the Sun Dance to the men. I talked about the leader's prayers, the Mystery Circle, the flesh offerings, the blessings, and so forth. Then all of the dancers were touched on the forehead with blood—with red power. All of the pipes were brought into the Preparations Tipi and filled by a holy man. Then each dancer brought his own pipe out into the sun and sang a prayer for a vision.

To receive a vision, the dancer must look directly at the sun for a few minutes without worrying about losing his eyesight. He must have faith in Almighty God in order to do this.

We look right at the sun, and we get visions from it. But the visions you receive are entirely yours, your property, and you make your own decisions as to what you will say and do about them.

THE PROBLEMS OF PUTTING ON A SUN DANCE—
Thomas E. Mails

To fully understand Eagle Feather's statement that the group was in trouble because of a shortage of funds, it would help to know something about the cost of putting on a Sun Dance today.

The earliest expenses incurred are for the preliminary meetings held to plan the dance. It is customary to assist committee members with transportation costs, and while they are present, housing and food is provided. So cash shortages often make the selection of local people expedient. The committee may well consist of relatives and close friends, and criticism for this is inevitable. So too, while the Sioux Sun Dance, Incorporated, is an association of medicine men and women who live on different reservations, not all of them can attend meetings, and Eagle Feather works out many details for himself.

The next outlay is for posters to advertise the event, for stationery, and for telephone calls.

After that, the Intercessor must travel by automobile to make arrangements for purchasing a number of beef or buffalo needed to feed the estimated number of participants and spectators. All who come will expect at least the main course of the noon meal. This reflects the traditional Sioux giveaway custom, and it must be done. The remarkable thing is that although people do not advise the Intercessor in advance as to whether they will be present, the expectation is that sufficient food be on hand and cooked—this latter operation requiring enormous effort in itself. The killing, transporting, carving, and roasting of a cow can be an awesome task on a hot summer day. Joe Staub worked hours on end each day in 1975, and a lesser man would have wilted under the effort required.

A guessed-at amount of coffee, Kool-Aid, bread, and sugar must also be provided to supplement the beef or buffalo.

I should insert here that because of its historic connection with the Sioux life-way on the Plains, buffalo meat is greatly preferred. To be able to offer this is a coup on the part of the Intercessor. But in 1975, the cheapest buffalo were priced at $750 each, while a large cow or steer could be had for $250 each. Therefore, since a cow carries almost as much meat as a buffalo, arrangements were made for three cows.

Individual families supplement the foodstuffs already mentioned with items like canned foods, extra bread, and canned soft drinks. No refrigeration facilities are available, so ice cubes are purchased and kept in small commercial coolers. Beer and liquor are not welcome at Sun Dances, and those who violate this rule are dealt with quickly and summarily.

The few who can afford it camp out in style, using many of the modern-day luxuries available for such purposes. There are always mobile campers and a few bright new tents. Other families live in worn-out tents, stay in their automobiles, or sleep in the open air. Even some pledgers do the latter.

Other expenses include payment for the singers and the rental of a loudspeaker system; it is also customary to give each pledger who travels some distance or who loses work time a small share of the overall income as compensation.

I don't know whether a rental is charged for the use of the fairground itself. Since it was not mentioned, I'm inclined to doubt it.

Adding all of these things up, it can be seen that the cost of putting on a Sun Dance will vary according to the number of participants and spectators, and that it will range from a low of $1,000 to a high of $3,000. When five hundred guests come, it will cost about

$1,500 for a bare-bones ceremony. Moreover, if a powwow is held in conjunction with the Sun Dance, costs for singers and prizes will cause the total price to rise sharply.

Even so, when we compare the outlay for a Sun Dance to what the outside world pours daily into its extravaganzas, the price seems like nothing—until one realizes that the reservation people begin the arrangements for every Sun Dance with little more than empty pockets and a few vague promises of help from friends. It is only their faith in God that sustains them; in their minds the annual performance of the dance is so vital to the well-being of the Sioux, and indeed to the well-being of the universe, that failure is out of the question. One way or another, it will get done. The Great Spirit, Almighty God, will see them through.

Faith notwithstanding, the Intercessor's immediate problem is that in addition to taking on the responsibility for conducting the dance properly, he must also solve its financial demands. If he does this often enough, he learns that God's answers can often come more slowly than he would like them to. Thus he perspires and agonizes a lot, and is commonly heard to say, "This is my last Sun Dance, I'll never do it again." But he does, and he will, and I will have more to say about that further on.

Even though Eagle Feather's financial obstacles were largely overcome before the dance began in 1975, he was disappointed with the way things went as it got underway, and he announced to the small crowd present that it was his "most pitiful Sun Dance ever." The first-day turnout had been disappointing, some of the pledgers hadn't shown up, and there was a considerable amount of bickering among his relatives about money and the way it was being handled. I spent a great deal of time in his camp over a nine-day period, and things were always calm when I was there, but I later learned that much of this was an outward display of serenity for my benefit. At other times there was more than a little friction.

My point in mentioning this is to encourage compassion for the Intercessor. Being human and along with others a captive of the reservation ills, he sometimes makes mistakes. But he also cares deeply, works very hard, and he merits understanding, pity and assistance.

The role of Intercessor is a most demanding one, and it requires a strong man to fulfill it, one who can make everything ready and then expedite the dance once it gets underway.

It should be noted that the Intercessor does receive assistance, for which he is always grateful. Eagle Feather declares that his wife, Hazel, has always been a great help to him. So, too, have his relatives and friends. There are people he can always count on and some perform heroically. Titus works like a full-grown man. Delbert Smith cut and carried wood, dug plants, and labored elsewhere in 1975. Joe and Evelyn Staub are dependable as rocks for whatever is needed. So are Jerry and Mary Dragg. And once the dance gets underway, other medicine men lend constant assistance. Therefore, while one man carries the major burden, the Sun Dance performance is by no means a one-man affair.

80

VIII
Preparations For The Sun Dance Of 1975

THOMAS E. MAILS

So far, Eagle Feather has described many of the things which were done to get ready for the 1974 Sun Dance at Rosebud. But more than a little data was omitted, which I will try to supply here in my description of the 1975 Sun Dance at Rosebud, held on July 3-6.

My plan was to arrive early enough to be present when all of the preparations were made. That way I would see everything for myself. It was not to be. When I reached the fairground on June 27, the vision quests had been completed, and it remained for Eagle Feather to provide me with more information about these. He did, and even supplied photographs.

The sweatlodge framework was already up, and the two fire pits had been dug—the Rock Cradle for the lodge, and Old Man Four Generations, in which the rocks would be heated for the purification ceremony.

Still, I was more than excited about what was yet to come, and as I looked at the fresh white willow framework of the yet-to-be covered sweatlodge, stripped of its bark and standing out crisply against the green grass, my memory took me quickly back to what I had seen the year before, and my imagination on to thoughts of the fascinating things I would watch and learn in the days ahead.

I telephoned Eagle Feather from Mission that night, and he asked me to meet him about 10 o'clock the next morning at the grove of trees below the dirt side road north of the Rosebud dam and lake. I knew the place well, and I was there on time. It was another beautiful summer day, and the crew was already at work cutting wood among the thick growth of cottonwood trees which borders the west side of the road and takes it nourishment from the Rosebud Creek.

I suppose that wood gathering is not thought to be a particularly glamorous part of the Sun Dance. Yet it is essential, and it is the point at which the final preparations really get underway.

Even more important to me was the fact that the Sun Dance Sacred Tree itself was right there, where they were cutting, and I would see it for the first time. Eagle Feather took me to it. I'll admit to a little disappointment at first, for nestled as it was in a thick stand of mostly larger trees, it didn't seem impressive. I misjudged it, though. By the time it was chopped down and set up it was taller than I had thought, and certainly more attractive. Older authorities say that the Tree should be straight. But none I've seen in these modern days are. They all have a bend or two, yet they function perfectly well.

I discovered that cutting and hauling pieces of cottonwood is extremely hard work, even though it didn't take many hours to fill a pickup truck. The men used a long-handled axe and a manual saw

Fools Crow at Bear Butte, South Dakota, wearing his ceremonial costume and holding his sacred pipe.

Evelyn Staub

to do the job, carrying at times astonishingly large chunks of wood to the truck.

Eagle Feather was there, tall and overweight, and dressed in his usual attire: well-worn and rumpled khaki trousers, a soiled white T-shirt, and his red-visored sportsman's cap. It was good to see him again. He was only supervising the job this year, and admitting by that fact that it was work for younger and healthier men.

Young Titus Smith was there. Last year I'd watched him with utmost admiration as he—just a boy of eleven—was pierced. Now he seemed close to being a man, he had grown so much. At twelve he was almost as tall as his father, Delbert, who was back on the reservation after a ten-year absence.

It was Delbert who did most of the work that morning and throughout the preparations stage. Brown, beautifully muscled, and with long black hair, he made a wonderful figure against the dense green forest growth. He would later be the source of several of my oil paintings.

Joe and Evelyn Staub came along shortly, and they, too, would become close friends before I left the Rosebud Reservation. Joe is a superb mechanic, the kind who can teach himself how to fix anything, and Evelyn has turned their house in the town of Mission into a foster home because one is so badly needed. In 1975 the Sioux Nation Sun Dance Association voted her Mother of the Year. She would comfort the pledgers at the Tree when they were pierced.

Joe is an astounding worker, the kind who doesn't know when to say no or how to quit. Evelyn is gentle and a keen observer. They are marvelous people. That morning Joe had already gone to a place where a load of used lumber was available and filled his truck with it. Yet upon arrival he plunged immediately into the forest and began cutting and hauling cottonwood along with the others.

Eagle Feather told me that the mill-cut wood could be used to cook the beef, but only the cottonwood would be used in the sweatlodge fireplace, for it was living wood, while the milled wood was thought of as dead.

Jerry and Mary Dragg arrived, and Jerry joined in the cutting and hauling. He is in training with Eagle Feather and will soon be a medicine man. Mary is White, but wholly immersed in the traditional Sioux religion. She had become pregnant since I met her in 1974, and would have a son, He Brings a Good Day, in September, 1975.

As time passed, a few onlookers joined the group. When the trucks were at last piled high with wood, we went in a truck and auto caravan to the fairground and unloaded the cottonwood by the side of the Old Man Four Generations fireplace. Once that was done, Eagle Feather and the others spent the rest of the day putting up their tents and getting their things arranged.

I watched, and visited, and walked around. It was then that I noticed an important tradition quietly being fulfilled. Short sections of last year's Sun Dance Tree were piled alongside the sweatlodge, ready to be burned in the first fire. Several fragments of the ropes employed by the pledgers were still tied to the pieces, and also a single tobacco offering, wrapped in black cloth rotting and grayed now from exposure to the weather. I found myself wondering who had tied the offering there, and what had come to pass because of it.

On July 1, 1975, Eagle Feather, Delbert, young Melvin Spotted Elk, Jr., and I went on an herb-gathering expedition. The herbs would be used in the healing ceremonies which are held during the Sun Dance. It turned out to be a happy trip, for Eagle Feather was warming to the feel of the dance and in an excellent mood.

We went in his blue, somewhat battered, 1965 Chevrolet. As is the case with most Sioux at Rosebud and Pine Ridge, he had bought it used; few reservation Indians are ever able to afford new cars.

Our first stop was at the bottom of Holy Lodge Hill, where the first plant root was obtained. Eagle Feather told me its name, but since it is a plant he has been shown in a vision, and used often, I suggested that he might like me to keep the name secret. He said he would appreciate that, and so the name must remain unknown.

The plant is hardly noticeable in its weed-bed habitat, and very little of it shows above the ground. Yet the length and size of the root is absolutely astounding. Delbert dug around it with a shovel, and found the going fairly easy in the sandy soil. Yet to get to the bottom of the root he was in the hole headfirst till only his legs were showing.

The root must be taken out intact, so the soil was moved away from it carefully and gently. When at last it was free, Eagle Feather lifted it up for me to see. It was nearly as long as he is tall, close to six feet in length, brown in color and with a bulb at the bottom twice the size of a football. Its principal use is for arthritis. I was even more surprised when he called it a young plant, adding that old ones had roots twice the height of a man!

I asked Eagle Feather how he had learned about the herbs. His answer was: "In dreams, not in vision quests."

While we were standing there waiting for Delbert to finish refilling the hole, Eagle Feather stooped and pulled up a milkweed, rubbing the milk over a sizable burn on the back of his hand. He claimed that this was an excellent treatment for burns.

Following custom, Eagle Feather replanted the top of the plant, smoothed the earth, and we returned to the car and put the root in the trunk. On our way out of the cow pasture which surrounds Holy Lodge Hill, we stopped at a barbed-wire gate. Delbert jumped out and opened it, but as he returned to the car the engine died.

What happened then amused me no end, for obviously it had all happened before. Without saying a word, Delbert turned and flipped up the hood. Then, while Eagle Feather pressed on the accelerator, Delbert tapped roughly on the carburetor with his large pocketknife. In an instant the engine roared to life, and we were on our way again.

It is a reservation custom to carry a small cassette tape player on the front seat, and Eagle Feather had his well-used one along. He snapped it on, and as we bumped down the road it was to the ringing accompaniment of Sun Dance music. Eagle Feather sang along with it in the kind of strong voice any Intercessor must have. I asked what he was singing. "The flesh offering song," he replied.

> Grandfather, have mercy upon me
> that my people will not starve.
> Grandfather, have mercy upon me,
> I'm offering my body to you,
> This is all I have to offer.
> Grandfather, have mercy upon me,
> I have made an offering,
> I have offered my flesh, blood, and tears.
> Grant me my prayers.
> From here on it is up to you.
> This is all I can do.

"We repeat that eight times," he said.

He smiled, clearly enjoying the day and the music. And when the haunting parts which mentioned the old days came, he lowered his voice and sang softly.

We arrived at another gate and again went through the stalled-engine routine.

At this point I said to Eagle Feather: "I feel bad, and am wondering whether you are ashamed of me." "After all," I added, "a White merchant in Mission just told me that all the Indians had plenty of money and new cars. Why, then, are you taking me out in this one?" "Oh well," I went on, "your Chevrolet is probably still under warranty, and it does take awhile to work the bugs out."

Eagle Feather surveyed the interior with a glint in his eye and a wry smile. The dashboard was battered. The upholstery was ripped in half a dozen places, and the stuffing was coming out. My interior door handle hung limp, like a flag on a windless day. In all, it was a sad affair that matched perfectly the banged-up fenders and bent radiator on the outside. In all, it was a typical reservation automobile, the rule and not the exception. How that merchant came to believe in the wealth of the Indians I'll never know. One thing is for sure: He did not venture out of the town of Mission to see how most of the Sioux really lived.

Delbert tapped, Eagle Feather pumped, and in a moment we were on our way again. At this point we were driving across a potholed pasture toward the Little White River, which bisects the Rosebud Reservation.

When we stopped again, Eagle Feather got out and walked straight across the flat meadow to the place where he knew that the second root could be found. The name of this one was not secret. It was called slim root, which turned out to be a fairly descriptive name.

Once again the part of the plant visible aboveground was small—just a few little leaves on spindly stalks. The root itself was not so long or impressive as that of the first plant, but it was still sizable compared to the part of the plant above the surface.

Delbert was instructed to dig four slim roots, which would be given to people who had stomach troubles and ulcers. "The common type," Eagle Feather said. "I have another root for major stomach infections."

We put them in the trunk and drove on down to the Little White River, where some berry bushes grew. Eagle Feather broke off a branch and had me smell the berries. They had a mildy pungent odor. He said that he used them to cure heavy drinkers in the sweatlodge. While they were in the darkness, he tossed a few of the berries on the fire. "The smell," he said, "is awesome." In no time at all the patient would be "throwing up like crazy, and usually didn't want another drink for a long time." I wondered if we might not commercialize that discovery.

On the way back to the gate we halted by a stand of cherry trees and Eagle Feather got his shears from the trunk to clip a few branches. These would be used to make the pipe rack. He shaped them expertly, leaving forks at the end of two branches, and cutting one other piece for the horizontal member.

With two more carburetor tappings we made it back to the fairground, tape recorder going all the way. And by midafternoon, Eagle Feather was seated in front of his tent, cutting the roots into small pieces in readiness for the Sun Dance healings.

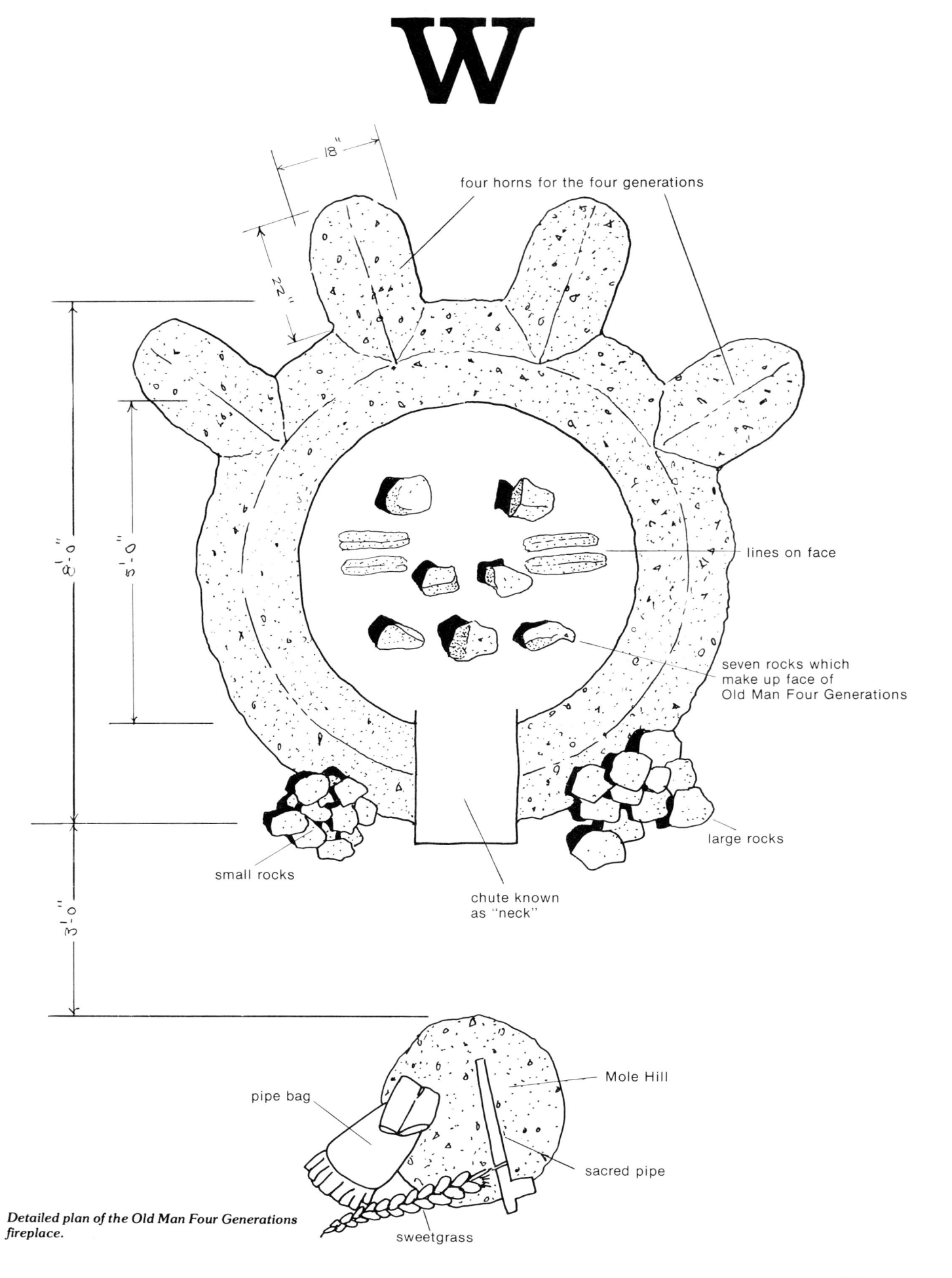

W

Labels on main diagram:
- 18"
- 22"
- 8'-0"
- 5'-0"
- 3'-0"
- four horns for the four generations
- lines on face
- seven rocks which make up face of Old Man Four Generations
- large rocks
- small rocks
- chute known as "neck"

Labels on lower diagram:
- pipe bag
- Mole Hill
- sacred pipe
- sweetgrass

Detailed plan of the Old Man Four Generations fireplace.

86

IX
The Sweatlodge And The Sacred Rite Of Purification

EAGLE FEATHER

We come now to the morning of July 11, 1974, the first day of the Sun Dance. It is before sunrise, only 4 A.M., and somewhat cloudy and cold. The dancers begin the ceremony by going into the sweatlodge, and everyone should understand what the *Inipi* or rite of purification means to the Sioux.

The little shallow, round pit which we dig in the center of the sweatlodge is called the Rock Cradle, and it is considered to be the central Altar.

To make this pit, where later the heated stones will be placed, we first drive a long stick into the earth to mark the center of the lodge, and then around this point we draw a two-foot-diameter circle with a cord of rawhide. When this is done, a larger circle, nine or ten feet in diameter, is drawn for the outside wall of the lodge. Then the pit is dug and the lodge is built of willows, with its doorway to the west. The rocks used in the Rock Cradle are heated outside, within fifteen feet of the sweatlodge, in the larger fireplace called Old Man Four Generations. This outside fireplace is located west of the sweatlodge. It is a round hole less than three feet deep, and the excavated dirt is piled around it so as to make the shape of a man's head with four horns and a neck.

The four horns are on the top of the man's head, and they represent the four generations of a family. When a man and a woman marry, that makes generation number one; generation number two is their children; the third generation is the grandchildren; the fourth generation is the great-grandchildren.

When we consider this fireplace, we also must think of its four prayer colors: black, red, yellow, and white. In this instance, black is associated with the remembrance of our dead relatives. Red represents people who are sick and are asking *Wakan-Tanka*, the Great Spirit, for healing. Yellow is for individuals and families that are in trouble and in need of help; some of their problems might be drinking, or situations where the family is about to break up and separate. So this color is really a prayer for a family whose home is not what it should be, and we are asking the Great Spirit to unite these people. White is for purification, and it represents our thanks to Almighty God for helping us to unite in seeking a closer relationship with Him.

And this is how the four-generations colors are used. When the rocks have been heated and the fire burns down, the pit is cleaned out by the sweatlodge custodian. He cleans the lodge off outside, sweeps it inside, brings the rocks, and prepares and lights the fireplace. He also has a very important pipe of his own that he places on top of the sweatlodge when a ceremony is being held.

As we light the first fire in Old Man Four Generations, always doing this on the side facing west, we pray, "O *Wakan-Tanka*, this is the eternal fire you have given us. It is your will that we have built this humble place in the sacred manner. The eternal fire always enlightens our minds and hearts. So if possible, renew us by making us pure, and by helping us to live according to your power and will."

Bear in mind as I continue that the rocks, the sweatlodge, and the outside fireplace are extremely important to all mankind, regardless of what race or nationality an individual may belong to. This is true even though they represent our Indian way of worshipping Almighty God and uniting and working together. All that we do there brings blessings to the whole of mankind.

So while the dancers are being purified in the sweatlodge, the custodian sweeps out the fireplace hole, the face of four generations. As he sweeps this out he will find ashes of different colors — gray or black or red or yellow or white.

Remember that the fireplace is round and has horns and a neck. So when he starts to sweep he takes the gray ashes he finds and, with a shovel, sprinkles them on the outer edge of the face, moving around the entire face and head and down toward the neck. This is done to acknowledge that the hair of Old Man Four Generations is gray. Then he sweeps up more ashes, and let's suppose he finds a lot of yellow and red. So he spreads the yellow all over the face; he makes the face yellow.

As I said, yellow is for families that are breaking up. So the custodian has discovered in his sweeping that someone in the sweatlodge is praying for the restoration of a family or families that were breaking up, and his prayers have been answered because the yellow dirt showed up in the fireplace. Then he sweeps some more and finds red ashes in there. So below, where the eyes of the face will soon be marked with rocks, and on the cheekbones, he makes four straight and vertical lines in the ground, two on each side and leaving a space for the nose in between. Then he sprinkles the red ashes in the four marks.

So here also the custodian has found out that prayers have been made in the sweatlodge for people who are sick, and they are being answered by God.

When he has finished sweeping and found the colors that are there, the custodian takes seven rocks from the sweatlodge Rock Cradle and puts them on the face of four generations, using two for his eyes, two for his nose holes, and three for his mouth. These seven rocks represent the seven rites we are commanded to do. Our non-Indian brothers have ten commandments, but the Sioux people have only seven. Number one is the use of the Sacred Pipe; number two is the keeping of the soul; number three is the sweatlodge rite of purification; number four is the crying for a vision; number five is the Sun Dance; number six is the making of relatives; and number seven is preparing a girl for womanhood.

The Peace Pipe, or Sacred Pipe, is a very important part of the ritual and is used because the Traditional Sioux of modern times sincerely believe that it is our Jesus Christ, or our Savior, and that He is still here on earth in the person of the Pipe. The non-Indians have killed and crucified their Savior. This is why traditional people do not celebrate Easter at all.

I can explain more about the Pipe by telling you something of what a *Yuwipi* is. We have the different clans, like the Ghost Clan, the Spider Clan, and the Rock Clan, which is mine. The *Yuwipi* and the Rock Clan are associated with one another.

In the Sioux mind there are many similarities between the Christians' Jesus Christ and the Sioux Sacred Pipe. For example, when

W

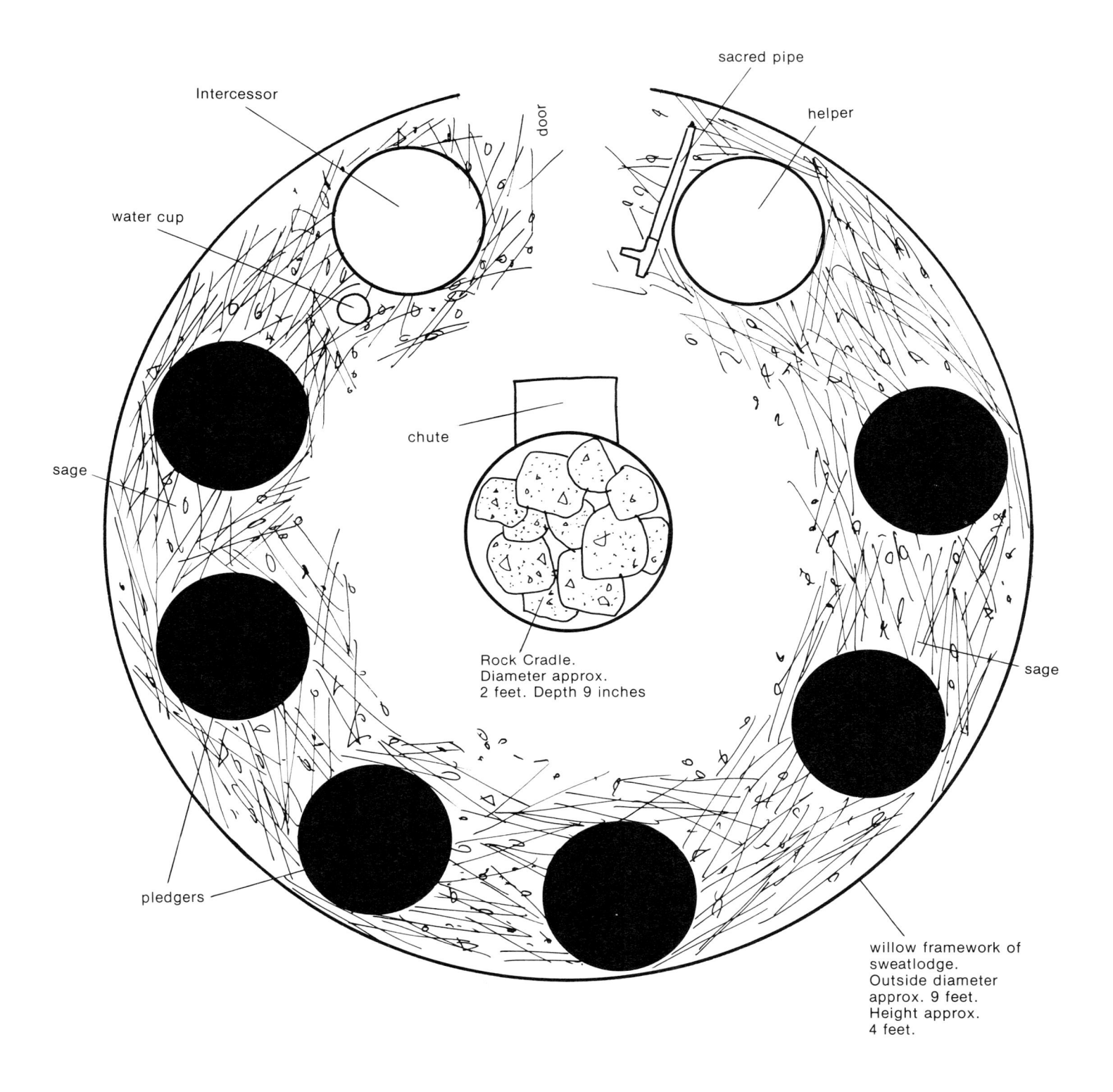

- Intercessor
- door
- sacred pipe
- helper
- water cup
- sage
- chute
- Rock Cradle. Diameter approx. 2 feet. Depth 9 inches
- sage
- pledgers
- willow framework of sweatlodge. Outside diameter approx. 9 feet. Height approx. 4 feet.

Detailed plan of the Sweatlodge when it is being used for a purification ceremony.

Calf Pipe Woman brought the Pipe to the Sioux people it was like Christ being brought into the world by a woman at Christmastime. Christ was wrapped in a bundle, and the Pipe is wrapped in a bundle also. We adhere to this same belief in our *Yuwipi* ceremony, where I am tied up in a bundle so securely that I can't breathe and then laid down while different songs are sung. And the spirit unties me, I never untie myself. No one knows how I am being untied. And when I am freed it is like the opening up of Christ's swaddling clothes so that the world could see Him. And just as when His bundle is being opened the Christian people shout "Joy to the World," and "Merry Christmas," so too we are happy because our lives will be restored, and we rejoice in Almighty God at this time when we are reunited and enjoying the great things which He brings to us.

Now a bed of sage is spread around the perimeter of the lodge for the people to sit on, and in front of the sweatlodge a little mound of dirt is made. This is thought of as a molehill. A mole is an animal that lives under the ground and close to Mother Earth, and this dirt is piled there for the Sacred Pipe to rest on during that part of the ceremony when it is not being used inside the lodge. Sage is used a great deal in the Sun Dance, and it plays a vital part in the sweatlodge ceremony itself. As I mentioned, we sit on it. We also wipe our bodies with it when we begin to perspire, and sometimes we use a handful to breathe through so the steam won't burn our throats. The rocks are red-hot when they are brought into the lodge, and when the water is poured on them the temperature can rise as high as 140 degrees. Bits of sage are dropped into the Rock Cradle itself before the rocks are placed there.

When the lodge is finished, the leader enters it and offers pinches of tobacco to the winged powers of the earth, and to the place where the sun goes down and from which the living water comes that we will use in our ceremony. These powers are invoked and asked to assist us in the rites. After this, *kinnikinnik*, the sacred tobacco, is placed in the Pipe bowl, and a pinch of tobacco is offered to the power of the north, from which comes strength and purification; then to the east, which sends peace and light for the eyes and the mind; then to the south, which is the source of life and growth; and finally to the west, which gives rain and nourishment.

Now the Pipe is filled and everything has been made *wakan*, holy. The leader leaves the lodge, and he places the pipe on the small earth mound, with the bowl on the west side and the stem pointed toward the east. Depending on its capacity, as many as possible of those who are to be pierced now enter the lodge. Eight is about all it can hold.

The leader returns to the sweatlodge and goes in first, and as each man bows low or gets down on his knees to enter the small doorway he prays: "All my relatives thank you. In bowing low while entering the lodge I am acknowledging that I am nothing compared with you, *Tunkashila Wakan-Tanka*, O Grandfather, Almighty God. You are everything. It is you who have placed us upon this great American island. We human beings are the last to be created by you. You who are first and eternal, help us to become pure. I send my voice to ask you to help us in all we are about to do." To further emphasize their humility before God, the participants either strip down to a G-string, as men did in the old days, or else to their shorts. The medicine man who will lead the ceremony sits on the south side of the door. On its north side sits another helper, who may be a medicine man, too.

As the rest of the men enter the lodge, they move around it sunwise, or clockwise, and then seat themselves on the bed of Sacred Sage. All remain silent a little while in remembrance of the goodness of the creator, *Wakan-Tanka*, and how it once was and is now.

Then the Sacred Peace Pipe is handed in by the custodian, who, incidentally, could even be a woman, and who remains immediately outside during the rite. Then he passes in a braid of sweet grass and some hot ashes to put into the Rock Cradle. The sweet grass is lighted from these ashes and burns. There is a very good smell to it, and it purifies everything in the lodge.

The stem of the Pipe is placed so that it faces west inside the sweatlodge. Now the leader takes a pinch of *kinnikinnik* tobacco and holds it toward the west, the black, praying to the place where four generations have journeyed on to the happy hunting ground. Then he prays and mourns for all the dead. After this he asks Almighty God to send from that direction the power needed to purify everyone in the sweatlodge.

Now he takes another pinch of tobacco and holds it toward the north. He prays to the north, the red, for the people that are sick, asking God to heal them and to guide them in every way needed. He also prays to the Buffalo Clan, which is in the north.

Then he takes a pinch of tobacco and holds it toward the east, praying to Almighty God and saying, "From the east comes the sun, and from the east comes the moon, and from the east comes the morning star. We know that many good things come from the east; the dawn comes from the east, and the daylight and the evening and the night." The color of the east is yellow. So here prayers are said for people whose families are breaking up because of disputes. So here the people in the lodge are being taught to share with one another and to live in harmony with all creation.

Then the medicine man holds a pinch of tobacco to the south, to the white. And he says, "Almighty God I want to thank you for all you have provided for me and my brothers throughout the universe. Guide us and watch over us. We want to thank you for everything you have given us. Oh, Grandfather, Almighty God, we need you every day."

Finally, he takes another pinch of tobacco and he holds it up toward the sky, saying, "Grandfather, Great Spirit, today we have humbled ourselves before you and entered the sweatlodge. We are going to tell you of our troubles and our needs. We ask you as we begin the Sun Dance to help us. You have sent the great eagle from above to help the earth. We ask the great eagle for guidance and help. We want you to bless the fire, the water, and the stones that are in here. Help my brothers and sisters that are present to talk to you of the sorrows and the happiness of our Sioux nation and, if you will, guide us in our thoughts as we dance. Give us strength, endurance, and understanding, the kind that we need to be true brothers and sisters in our hopes and accomplishments."

These are the types of prayers that are made inside the sweatlodge before the Sun Dance.

When the opening prayers are finished, the helper who sits on the north side of the doorway takes the Pipe and places it in front of him with the stem pointed toward the west. Using either a forked stick or a pitchfork, the cutodian now picks up one of the heated rocks from Old Man Four Generations, which is also referred to as *Peta-owihankeshi*, The Everlasting Fire With No End. He walks along the sacred path connecting the fire pit and the sweatlodge, and passes the rock inside the lodge, where it is taken by the leader and placed in the center of the Rock Cradle, or Altar. The first rock is always an offering to *Wakan-Tanka*, who, as Black Elk says, is at the center of everything.

The man who has the Pipe touches its stem to the rock as it comes in, and each time a rock is handed in to be placed in the altar he touches the Pipe to it as it passes by him. When he does this all of the men cry, "Thank you."

The next rock passed into the lodge is placed on the west side of the Altar pit, the next on the north, one is set in the east, one in the south, and one is placed in the pit for Mother Earth. After this the pit is filled with another fourteen or so rocks, and the entire pit stands for everything in the universe.

The helper now offers the Pipe to the six directions. Then he lights it, takes a few deep puffs, and blows the smoke out so that he can rub it all over his body. Then he hands the Pipe to the man at his left saying, "*Ho ate*" or "*Ho tunkashila,*" depending on his relationship to the person.

The man who receives the Pipe responds by saying, "*How ate*" or "*How tunkashila.*" "*How ate*" means "my father," and "*How tunkashila*" is "my grandfather." The Pipe is sent sunwise, which is clockwise, around the circle until it comes back to the leader. He generally purifies it with burning sweet grass in case some impure person has touched it, carefully empties the ashes, and deposits them at the edge of the Rock Cradle. Then he passes the Pipe outside the lodge to the custodian, who places it on the little mound where it was originally.

Now the custodian pulls down the canvas or blanket door of the sweatlodge and pushes down all of the bottom edges of the wall coverings to make it airtight and pitch-black inside. You can't see anything and you feel completely shut off. This darkness represents the sinfulness of the soul and our ignorance, from which we must now purify ourselves before we Sun Dance. Then the living water is passed in the pail, and the leader pours it on the rocks. The effect is instant, and the temperature soars! During the course of the ceremony the door will be opened briefly four times and the wall edge will be raised, letting in the air and light. This reminds us of the four generations, and how through the mercy of *Wakan-Tanka* we have in the past and are today receiving forgiveness and enlightenment.

The leader now prays to *Wakan-Tanka,* saying "*Ha-hey,*" four times. This is what we say when we are in trouble; when we are in darkness and in need of enlightenment. We send Him our voice four times because we want Him to hear us four times, which is the sacred number He has taught us to observe.

The leader goes on:

> *Wakan-Tanka,* Grandfather, you are first and always have been. You have brought us to this land, and here our people wish to live in a sacred manner. Teach us to understand and to recognize all the powers of the universe, which is really one power. We pray that our people will always send their voice up to you as they walk the sacred path of life.
>
> *Tunkashila,* you are here with us at this moment. You made the earth, and we pray that our generations will be able to walk in the days ahead without falling. O rocks, you have neither eyes nor mouth nor arms nor legs. You do not move about as we do. But by receiving your sacred breath, the hot steam here in the sweatlodge, we and our people will have the breath and strength to walk the difficult path of a holy life.
>
> We know there is a winged power in the west where the sun goes down who controls the water all life relies on, so help us to please him by using these waters in a sacred manner. To every earthly thing, *Wakan-Tanka,* you have given a power, and because the fire is your most powerful creation

we have placed it here at the center of the sweatlodge. Help us in the purification we are about to undergo.

After the leader has prayed in this manner, the rest of the men pray in turn, with the prayer chain going in a clockwise circle. When they are finished, the leader usually chants a number of prayers in that spine-tingling, high-pitched voice which so often startles those standing outside the sweatlodge and hearing it for the first time. These chants are the equivalent of the hymns sung in a Christian church. When he is done he generally addresses the others, telling them about visions he has seen or the understandings he has come to during the purification ceremony. Some of these may include personal messages for the men having to do with their conduct or future. He may read to them the scriptures he has seen written on the rocks in the Altar, or he may pass on information he has gained from analyzing the shapes of the rocks themselves. He tells about his visions at this time only because they are directly related to the men and to the Sun Dance. Visions he receives at other times are too personal to share.

The ceremony closes abruptly and without fanfare. The Pipe may or may not be taken in and used to pray with again. The leader decides whether or not it is needed again. In either case the leader indicates that the rite is over by calling for the custodian to open the door, and the men exit in a clockwise rotation with the leader going out first.

So the sweatlodge is our purification ceremony which makes us fit to Sun Dance for the nation, and inside the sweatlodge it is very, very warm.

I always pray, "O Grandfather, *Wakan-Tanka*, you are and always were, I have done your will on this earth as you have taught us by placing the sacred rocks at the four quarters of the altar. We understand that it is really you who is at the center of the sweatlodge where the rocks are being placed. O sacred rocks, you are helping us to do the will of *Wakan-Tanka*, Almighty God."

Moses went to the top of the mountain to receive the Ten Commandments, written on the tablets of stone. And on these stones we use in the sweatlodge there are scriptures, too. Anyone who wishes to can pick up a small stone—creek stones are good—and if they hold it in their hand for a period of time they will see valuable messages, visions of hands and faces, and many other things. This being the case, it is sad that the lessons contained in the stones are so often overlooked. People do not learn from the stones as the Great Spirit wants them to in order to live wisely.

The actual shape of a stone has to do with guardian angels and tells us some amazing and helpful things.

Some non-Indians have told me that they believe they have been here before in another life, and that they recognize a person they see now as someone from that other life. They have seen his face before, and they know the man; they recognize him. The face looks familiar and they have the feeling that they should go up and talk to him.

What they are actually seeing is their guardian angel. Let me explain what I mean. Before me at this moment I have two stones. They are glassy stones and quite small. One is an oblong shape, about two inches long and an inch wide. Another is almost an inch and a half long, and it is about an inch wide. The Great Spirit has put these stones on earth for you and me to read on them the scriptures which will help us understand His work here and throughout the great universe.

I will tell you about a stone with the scriptures on it, like this stone I'm holding in my hand now. In my language the stone is *tokahe,* which means "It is first here," and "It will be old here." In comparison, we must bear in mind that we are just passers-by on earth. We are only here so long, and then we die and go on our last journey. While I am here on earth, I must consider the stones in my traditional Indian way and use them to find my guardian, or guiding, angel.

When a Sioux holy man gives a man a rock he says, "You are going to be with someone." He doesn't say whether it will be a man or a woman, but it will be a human being. So when you are given one in the sweatlodge or however it may be, you are to take it and carry it with you wherever you go. In time this rock itself will show how its revelations are the work of Almighty God, and not of any human being.

So on this rock I have in my hand I am going to look for the face or an image of a person. The face that I now see is either a short, fat woman or a heavyset man. The face is round and the person has a double chin. These features are important to me, since when I go out among people I can find my guardian angel among them. Then I know who to go to to get help if I am in desparate need of it. This double-chinned person is my guardian angel of the moment, and is the person I should seek out for whatever help or support I need. This person is the angel that God has given me.

So this is what you have to do to find your guardian angel on the street. You first have to find your guardian angel on a stone. It may be a slim-faced person or it may be a square-faced person. The stones will tell you. Try it and see.

This stone, just as those in the sweatlodge, will do even more. It will help you predict a great many things. I'm sure that such extraordinary claims will cause some non-Indians to say we are ridiculous, or to accuse us of witchcraft and call us shamans. But I simply ask for understanding and for people to realize one day that there is great value in what the Great Spirit, Almighty God, can teach us through these little stones. Each of us should carry a small stone. And we should be able to read them upside down, sideways, or in any direction.

At this very moment, I have another little stone here in my left hand, and I see in it the shape of a woman holding a wrapped bundle under her left arm. And as I turn it and look into her face I see that she is beautiful and has long braids. This stone is going to bring me something. Today this stone is going to bring me happiness. It is a prediction that a bundle of joy will come to my family and myself. The woman is white-headed, and she has a beautiful shawl around her shoulders.

These are the kinds of things we should be teaching each other as we live together as brothers and sisters. It is the way God wants us to dwell on this earth and to appreciate each other. We traditional Indians believe in living in harmony. This is what we should do, and we should help one another in any way that is needed.

The stones also tell us what to do in other ways. Let us say that you want to make a donation to some cause. Sit down with your stone, look at it, and ask it whether this donation will be beneficial or not. The stone will give you the answer. Many people have sent donations to Indians reservations without doing this, and the gifts never get to the average people. They often stop at the tribal-council or the tribal-chairman level, and these people generally use the money as they see best.

So your stone should be used when you want to make a donation. Sit down with it and pray with it to Almighty God. Say, "What I am about to do, will it be good or bad? Where and to whom should I send it?" You can learn the answer—providing you have the right belief and hope in Almighty God, and we say, "It is first here" and "It will be old here." So I hope that everyone will find little stones, carry them, and use them to locate their guardian angels. It's a miracle and a mystery how God works, but it is a truly wonderful thing.

We have a number of White doctors here on this reservation. I have given them many stones, prayed with them about this, and blessed the stones. Not long ago one of the doctors came to see me. He said, "Bill, here is that stone you gave me."

I said, "Oh, I forgot about it."

He said, "Today, if I am going to operate on a person I pick up the stone and talk to it. I look at each of its sides and I try to understand my stone. I find out whether I'm going to have success with a patient or not. I find this out through the stone, and I experience in its fullness the miracle work of Almighty God."

So it has been proven to us many times and in unusual ways that stones can mean a lot to us in our daily life.

STONES—Thomas E. Mails

Fools Crow has seven small stones in his body which spark when he touches pledgers during a Sun Dance on places where they need healing.

Stones, *Ivan Wasico*, also play a vital part in his sweatlodge healing ceremonies. The heated stones speak to him at certain times to gain information from him about his patients. And the good spirits in the stones afterward go to the patient and determine his exact illness. Then they return to the stones and speak to Fools Crow, telling him what illness must be cured and what medicine is to be used.

THE NUMBER OF SWEATLODGES—Thomas E. Mails

The number of sweatlodges is determined by the number of participants. In the usual instance there are no more than twenty pledgers, and one lodge is enough. But the Sun Dance held at Crow Dog's the last two years included as many as ninety men and twenty-four women, and therefore seven or eight sweatlodges were erected to handle the crowd.

THE YUWIPI—Thomas E. Mails

Yuwipi means "They tie him up" or "They wrap him up." It is an ancient nighttime ritual held in a house, in which a special altar is built and the holy or medicine man is sometimes, though not always, tied up with ropes and then wrapped securely in a blanket, which is tied again. Then the lights are extinguished, and while mysterious things occur, such as strange noises or sparks flying, the holy man is quickly "set free by the spirits." When the lights are turned on, he is loose from his bonds, and his blanket and thongs are folded in front of him.

Yuwipi is extremely popular today, and meetings are held on an irregular basis to offer prayers for the sick, to seek visions for guidance, to determine the future, and to find hidden, lost, or stolen articles.

When the formal ceremony ends, feasting begins. The meat is always dog; one which has been strangled and boiled with the skin on. Bread, potatoes, pastry, and coffee are also served.

The practice of *Yuwipi* has many variations and those who attend the meetings on a regular basis say that each one is different in some way from the others.

*Lame Deer adding prayer offering cloths to the
Sacred Tree in 1975.*

X
The Mystery Circle and The Sacred Pipe

THOMAS E. MAILS

In times past, and even now when Sioux Sun Dances are held in remote places where no camping or commercial facilities are available, the dancing arena was formed by erecting a shade arbor around the circumference of a circle left open to the sun.

The size of the open circle varied from 50 to 150 feet, and was determined by the number of participants and spectators involved in the Sun Dance. The exact center of the open circle was marked by the Sacred Tree, or sun pole, and the surrounding shade area was a 10-15-foot-wide arbor. This consisted of a double row of tree trunks set upright in the ground, whose forked tops were connected by horizontal logs lashed together to form a trellis. Over this, fresh pine boughs, and sometimes blankets and robes, were spread to shut off the sun, so the spectators sitting there could watch in relative comfort while the dancers sweltered in the midsummer heat.

Today, the local tribal fairground, with its permanent facility, is often used for the dance. The Rosebud Fairground arena is available for many other purposes, too. Shows of various kinds are held there, including rodeos and the *wacipis,* or social dances, popularly known as powwows. But it is an especially desirable place for the Sun Dance, providing a large and unobstructed arena, adequate camping sites for visitors, running water, and, although they are outdoor ones, latrine facilities. Electricity is available for night lights and the sound system.

The arena is a level, 150-foot-diameter circle, surrounded by a colorful trellised shade area of bleacher seats, with major openings at the east and west, and smaller entrances at regular intervals to facilitate spectator movement. The trellis is covered with pine boughs for the Sun Dance. A small and portable announcer's booth usually sits at the west end, adorned with painted Indian symbols. The booth was used by the Sun Dance leaders in 1974, and the singers sat on a low platform in front of it. For some unexplained reason it was not used for announcements in July, 1975. These were made from the south side, where the singers sat.

Burning sweet grass in the hands of devout holy men, fervent prayers, copious tears, the shining Sacred Tree, and brightly colored flags for the four directions transform the arena into the Mystery Hoop or Circle. The terms are interchangeable, and they are synonymous with the Hoop of the Nation.

On the morning of the first day of the dance proper, as the Intercessor and the pledgers are approaching the east entrance silently and in single file, a medicine man plants four sets of colored flags in the ground at the four directions, about ten feet in from the bleachers and thus about forty feet out from the Sacred Tree. There are

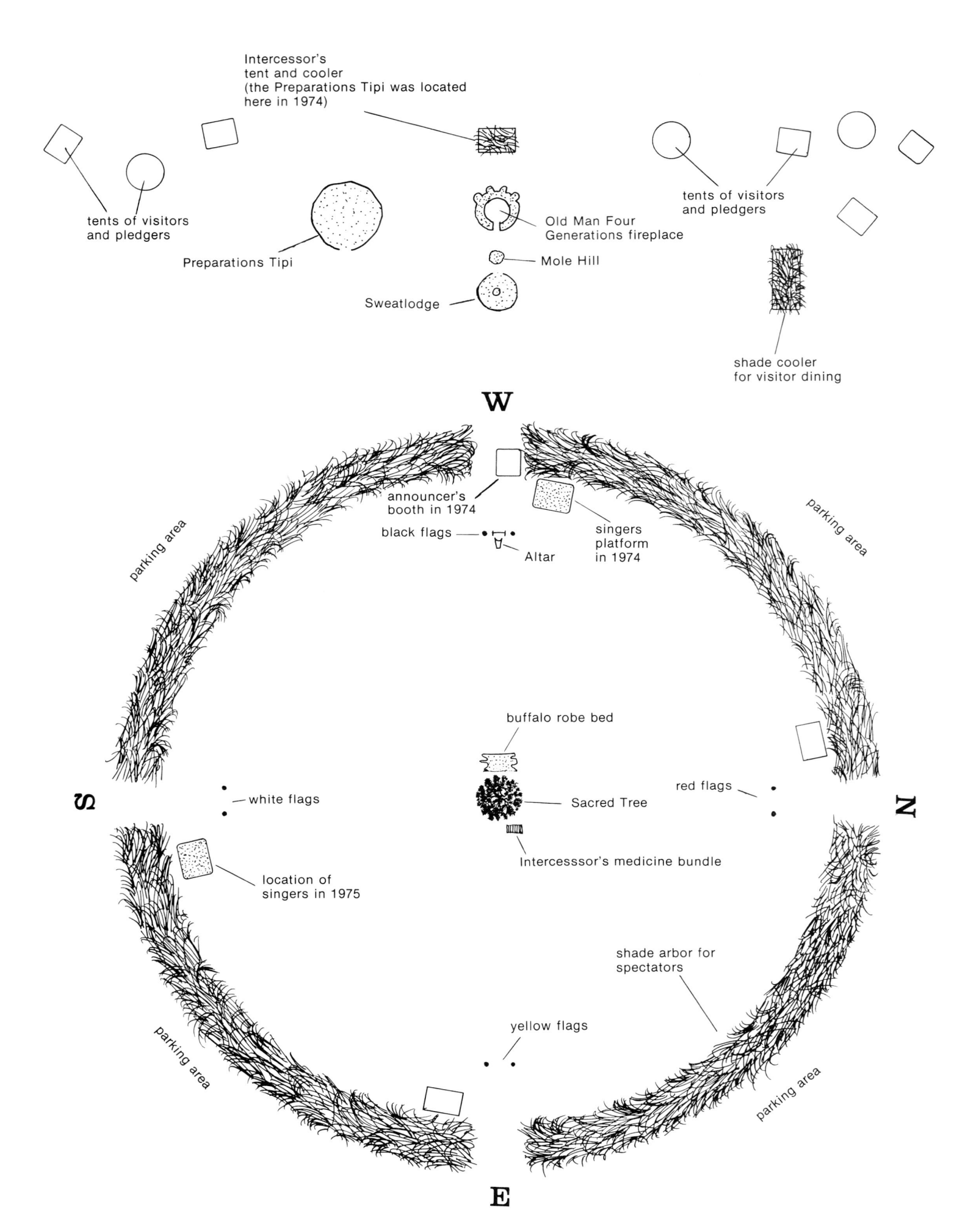

Plot plan of the Rosebud Sun Dance Grounds in 1975.

two flags in each set, placed about six feet apart: red for the north, yellow for the east, white for the south, and black for the west. Eagle Feather has already explained the symbolic meaning of each color.

The flags mark off an eighty-yard-diameter circle within the larger circumference which is restricted to the Sun Dance participants alone from the moment they enter it each day until the dance ends at noon. The rule is that spectators are not to cross in front of the flags when a ritual is in progress. Exceptions to this rule are made for people called to the Tree for special healing, or for a child who has a particular role to play; a rare dispensation can even be granted to a nonparticipant who is, however, required to enter the Hoop area barefooted.

Aside from the full-time participants, people must enter and exit the Mystery Circle through a set of flags, which is regarded as a doorway. Anyone violating this rule through ignorance is summarily sent out of the Hoop and told to come in again the proper way.

At the end of each day's performance, a medicine man, usually the Keeper of the Pipes, picks up the flags, the Sacred Pipe, the pipe rack, and the buffalo skull, and after dancing in concert with the pledgers across the circle in four moves made from the west to the east, takes them to the Preparations Tipi. The next morning he brings them to the circle again.

The flags are slim branches about five feet in length, with long pieces of colored cloth attached to their tops. The branches, unpainted in 1974, were painted by one of the pledgers in 1975, and each set was the same color as its cloth appendages. New branches are cut each year. I was not told what kind of wood is used, but it is safe to assume it is either willow, which is employed for the sweatlodge framework, or cherry, which is used for the pipe-rack framework.

The reverence of the Sioux for the Mystery Circle becomes understandable once one learns how significant a role the circle plays in their life-way.

Above all, it signifies that which is universal and eternal, and it encompasses all creation in its relationship with the Great Spirit, or Mystery. Thus the Sun Dance Circle or Hoop is a sphere of energy or power without limit or end. To be within it during a ceremony is to be exposed to divine power, and when a person responds in awareness and accepts the powers offered by God through the sun, the directions, and the Tree, he becomes energized and powerful. He can then live with a special awareness and in harmony with all creation. He becomes one with all things, and especially with the entire Sioux nation. In performing the traditional Sun Dance ceremony he fuses in prayer and sacrifice with his own kind. The effect of what happens there lasts as long as the power—which fills the participant and then spreads out from him like the ripple effect when a stone is tossed into a pool—and is joyfully received by all those it encounters.

We can see, then, why my prayers are made in the sweatlodge and in the Hoop for all creation, and specifically for living things. We can understand why such powerful things as the sun, other celestial bodies, the Tree, the eagle, and the directions are invoked, and why unity is sought for with such fervency. The Hoop can do its best work only when all of these are working in harmony with man. Every created thing has a role to play in the functioning of the universe as God intends the universe to be. The Sun Dance focuses minds and hearts on this, and it seeks to give every created thing an opportunity to be, in the fullest sense, what God created it to be.

It becomes obvious that the Sun Dancer is transformed, for the four days of dancing, into a special channel or tube through which God bestows His grace upon all creation. As the pledgers dance and sacrifice, power flows from God through the Sun, the Tree, and the directions into the pledgers, and then out from them in the form of visions, healing, and well-being to the nation and to the world.[1]

Therefore, the thrust and purpose of the Sun Dance is as it has always been, two-fold. First, it is a ritual of thanksgiving to the "Great Mystery"—a title readily translated as "God" by the present-day holy men—for past favors granted. Second, it is a ceremony which draws down divine power and puts it to practical use. When the holy men describe the dancing as "bringing down the sun power," this is what they mean.

The sincere Sun Dance pledger dances for the entire nation. It is by no means a selfish act, and it never was. It is also an awesome responsibility, and that is why the purification in the sweatlodge precedes the Sun Dance as the Intercessor and others get ready, and why it is carried out before the holding of each day's performance. All of the participants are being cleansed from sin and ignorance in order to become pure tubes through which God will be willing to work to dispense his power, which will nourish and enlighten all things.[2] They know that nothing of God's relationship with all created things can be taken for granted or is bestowed in perpetuity. This is a circumstance ordained for man's own good, since he is by nature his own worst enemy. Therefore, the Sun Dance must be repeated as an annual event, and since the Sioux are spread out over a large geographic area today, its blessings increase according to the number of times it is held in the divinely appointed season. At least five Sun Dances were done on the Rosebud Reservation in July and August, 1975.

According to present-day Sioux holy men, the origin of the Sun Dance lies in fairly recent history. Around 1685, they say, when the Sioux were beginning to migrate onto the Great Plains, a maiden serving God brought the sacred Buffalo Calf Leg Pipe to the people. At the same time she gave them seven sacred ceremonies to follow in which the Pipe would be used. Those who did this faithfully would find knowledge and the truth, so with the advent of the Pipe and the rites a new and deeper understanding of all things was available to mankind.

Most non-Indian scholars agree that the Plains Sun Dance ceremony is of fairly recent origin, coming into being only after the larger nations moved onto the Plains. It then spread from one tribe to another as newcomers encountered it. This may be so, yet considering the reluctance of the Traditional Sioux to alter their religious patterns, I think it might be wise to hold open the possibility that the Sioux and others already had an ancient and regularly held sun ceremony to which were added certain ingredients common to the Plains area. After all, the reverence of all Indians for the sun seems to date as far back as legends and investigations have gone.

Stories told by the Sioux holy men about the coming of the Sacred Pipe, *Prehincala Hu Cannunpa Kin*, have varied in detail, but they are consistent as to meaning. They all agree that while the details of its first coming will probably never be known, through the Pipe men will get to know God better and this will lead to good fortune for all connected with it.

The first Pipe was entrusted to a man who received the title "Keeper of the Pipe," and it has been handed down in the same family from one generation to the next. The original is said to be kept at Green Grass, South Dakota. Some of those who have seen it question whether the present one is really the original, since it does not appear to be old enough, but this fact does not concern the holy men, since any pipe used in the same way as the original one was meant to be used "is just as sacred and effective." To the understanding person, they become one and the same pipe; *cannunpa kin.*

It is obvious, then, that the Pipe plays a central role in the Sun Dance. At Rosebud the Intercessor, every pledger, the assisting medicine men, and the sweatlodge custodian carries one of his own and prays with it to those things which God has invested with power.

Thus the holy men say that the Pipe itself has power to transport power, and it is sacred, for it came from God. Its ultimate purpose is to center the mind, heart, and soul on God in His relationship with creation, and it follows logically that those who ignore this power or handle it foolishly will do untold damage to themselves. On the other hand, those who use the Pipe with reverence to seek enlightenment regarding sacred things will receive special help. For when the Pipe is understood, smoked, and pointed to the other sources of power as one prays, it becomes the very channel through which their power flows from them to the petitioner.

The holy man knows that the Pipe consists of four parts, each of which represents something important. The stone bowl stands for the earth. The stem symbolizes everything that grows upon the earth. Animal or insect appendages to the stem, or carvings on the stem, represent the four-legged creatures. Attached eagle feathers and the smoke from the Pipe represent everything that flies and which lives above.

When the Pipe is smoked, all these things join with the one who smokes and add their voices and hearts to the prayer, "So how can God do other than respond?" It follows, then, that the one who prays with the Pipe will speak of his relationship with all created things, and will express his concern and love for them.

The way in which the cardinal directions are marked and prayed to in the Sun Dance ceremony has already been emphasized. But something more should be said about the powers of those directions as the Sioux holy men have explained it to me. In their view, God gave each direction a sacred power, named "Grandfather," which is its own to use as it sees fit. They are holy and mysterious beings. God remains above them in power, and they themselves are not separated from Him even though they are distinct and identifiable. The powers do the will of God, yet they have an intellect and a will of their own. They hear and answer prayers, yet their powers and ways remain mysterious. "With them and through them we send our voice to God."

This is why the circular area in which the Sun Dance is held is called the Mystery Circle or Mystery Hoop. Great and wondrous things happen in it, yet because these are supernatural achievements the natural man can never know exactly how they are done. It is a mystery. The proof lies in the happening: in the deliverance from ignorance, in the visions seen, in the healings, and in the sense of well-being when it is over.

The directions, as they are called upon in the Sun Dance, begin with the west. The Altar is made there, and that is where the dance itself begins. It is the source of rain and of the water which is used to purify in the sweatlodge. Joy and growth always follow the rain, and release from ignorance. West is also the home of the powerful Thunder-being who flies in the midst of the thunderstorms in the form of a huge bird. His wings produce the thunder, and the lightning flashes from his eyes. It is this being who stands against evil and who makes certain that the Pipe is used correctly. Each direction is associated with a sacred stone of a specific color; that of the

source of the purifying water
home of the Thunder Being
sacred stone is black
home of the horse power
messenger is the black eagle

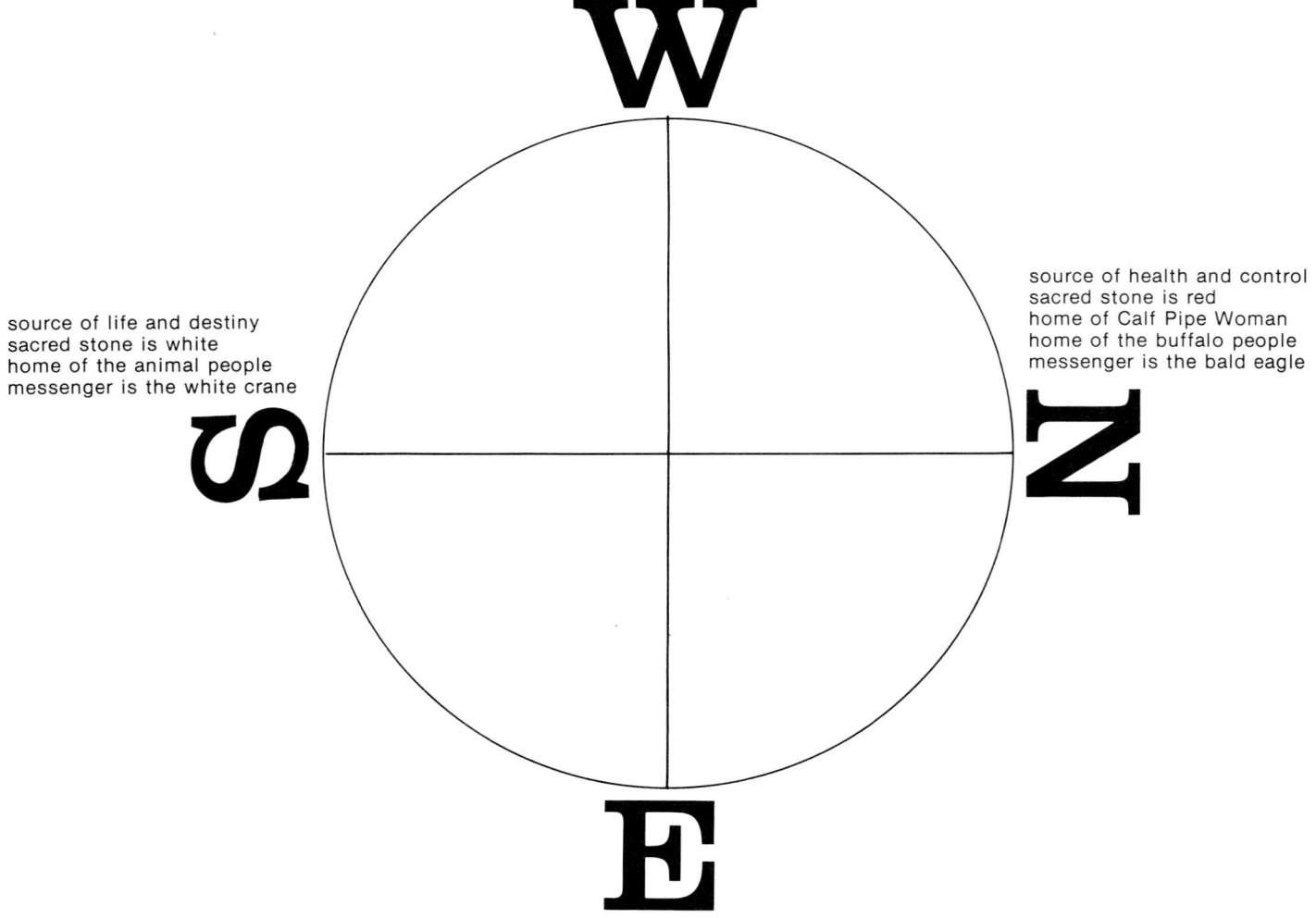

W

source of life and destiny
sacred stone is white
home of the animal people
messenger is the white crane

S

source of health and control
sacred stone is red
home of Calf Pipe Woman
home of the buffalo people
messenger is the bald eagle

N

E

source of wisdom and understanding
sacred stone is yellow
home of the Elk People
messenger is the brown eagle

The powers of the four directions.

west is black. Each of the directions has a messenger; that of the west is the black eagle. The horse family also lives there.

Winter's home is in the north. Its power promotes good health and growth. Those who misbehave look to it for correction and for the wisdom needed to walk the straight path again. It is a challenging power, and it promotes endurance. The rock there is red, so it has a special meaning for the red people and red power. The north is the home of Calf Pipe Woman and the buffalo people. Its messenger is the bald-headed eagle.

The power of the east is closely associated with the sun. It is there that he rises to bring light and enlightenment to all of creation. The path of the sun is from east to west. It is thought of as a clockwise direction, and all good things are to conform to that pattern. Counterclockwise movements are considered bad, so the sweatlodge is round and is entered in a clockwise direction, and the Sun Dancers always walk around the Mystery Circle in a clockwise direction. The Morning Star, which is the star of wisdom and new beginnings, hence a source of inner peace, is in the east and is closely related to the sun. The Elk people live there. The rock of the east is yellow, and its messenger is the brown eagle.

The sacred power of the south is connected with life after death and thus directs men as they walk toward that awesome place. Life begins in the south, and nourishment of every kind comes from there. Warmth and happiness are associated with the power of the south. The Animal People live there. The rock of the south is white, and its messenger is the white crane.

It is believed that the powers of the directions and the Pipe work only toward good, although they may find it necessary to accomplish this good in an indirect way. They may take the time to discipline those whom they love in order to bring the chastized to their senses and to a more receptive and responsible manner of mind and life.

The Lakota think of the heavens as the dwelling place of God. Therefore they pray to Him with the Pipe by holding its stem up in His direction after they have prayed to the four horizontal directions. He is called Grandfather rather than Father, and Great Spirit because he is a spirit. He is the creator of the universe, He is eternal, and everything belongs to Him. Thus He is above all other spirits and powers, and He placed them in their positions and empowered them. His knowledge and goodness are perfect, and He is the author of truth. The red path walked by mankind leads to Him. Since He oversees all things, His help is requested in and through all things.

Mother Earth was made by God, and He watches over her. Men pray to her with the Pipe because their bodies come from her, are rooted in her, and she nourishes all things. Within her all created things are related, and by praying to her unity is achieved.

So there are really six directions which are addressed in the Sun Dance and from which the powers necessary to the well-being of all creation come. Once again, the proof is in the results achieved, and Sun Dances are being celebrated with increasing fervor because this is so. Therefore, any adversity only promotes, rather than diminishes, the frequency and passion of the Sun Dances. The worse things are, the greater the need and the more the Sioux call upon the powers to get the people back to where they ought to be.

BUILDING THE DANCING LODGE—James O. Dorsey and George Bushotter

Next follows the building of the dancing lodge. Forked posts are set in the ground in two concentric circles. Those posts forming the circle nearer the sun pole are a few feet higher than the posts in the outer circle, thus making a slant sufficient for a roof. From the inner circle of posts to the sun pole there is no roof, as the dancers who stand near the pole must see the sun and moon. From each forked post to the next one in the same circle is laid a tent pole; and on the two series of these horizontal tent poles are placed the saplings or poles forming the roof. In constructing the wall of the dancing lodge they use the leaf shields, and probably some poles or branches of trees, the shields and leaves stuck in the wall here and there, in no regular order, leaving interstices through which the spectators can peep at the dancers. A very wide entrance is made, through which can be taken a horse, as well as the numerous offerings brought to be given away to the poor. Then they smoke the pipe, as in that manner they think that they can induce their Great Mysterious One to smoke.

All having been made ready, the aged men and the chief men of the camp kick off their leggings and moccasins, and as many as have pistols take them to the dancing lodge, around the interior of which they perform a dance. As they pass around the sun pole, all shoot at once at the objects suspended from the pole, knocking them aside suddenly. Leaving the dancing lodge, they dance around the interior of the camping circle till they reach their respective tents.

This is followed by the *uúcita*. Each man ties up the tail of his horse and dresses himself in his best attire. When they are ready, they proceed two abreast around the interior of the camping circle, shooting into the ground as they pass along, and filling the entire area with smoke. There are so many of them that they extend almost around the entire circle. If any of the riders are thrown from their horses as they dash along, the others pay no attention to them, but step over them, regarding nothing but the center of the camping circle.

By this time it is nearly sunset. The young men and young women mount horses and proceed in pairs, a young man beside a young woman, singing as they pass slowly around the circle. The young men sing first, and the young women respond, acting as a chorus. That night the tent of preparation is again erected. The candidates dance there. The people gaze towards that tent, for it is rumored that the candidates will march forth from it. [3]

THE SHELTER—Frances Densmore

After the sacred pole was erected and the "sacred place" prepared, a shelter, or "shade-house," was built entirely around the Sun Dance Circle, any who wished to share in this work being permitted to do so. Posts about 6 feet high were erected, and upon these were placed a light framework of poles. This framework was covered with buffalo hides and decorated with freshly cut boughs. Beneath this shade sat the old people, the relatives of the dancers, and any who attended the ceremony merely as spectators.

Orrie Farrell. Oil painting by author.

The piercing. Oil painting by author.

106

George Eagle Elk and Titus. Oil painting by author.

The healing ceremony. Oil painting by author.

On the morning of the Sun Dance those who were to take part in the ceremony were allowed to eat a full meal, after which they entered the vapor lodge while the following song was sung:

SONG OF FINAL VISIT TO THE VAPOR LODGE

> A voice
> I will send.
> Hear me
> The land
> All over.
> A voice
> I am sending.
> Hear me.
> I will live.

After their vapor bath, the dancers were painted by the men whom they had selected for that purpose.[4]

Chief Eagle Feather, serving as Intercessor and praying with the sacred pipe at the Rosebud Fairground in 1974.

110

XI
The Mystery Circle Altar

THOMAS E. MAILS

The legend of the coming of the White Buffalo Calf Maiden mentions instructions she gave as to how to build an Altar. There was to be a framework made of two upright sticks, each forked at the top to receive a horizontal stick. This was the pipe rack, and it was to be painted blue. In front of this, on a bed of sage, was to be placed a buffalo skull.

Eagle Feather says about the making of the Altar only that it consists of the pipe rack, made of cherry wood, and the buffalo skull. Neither of the skulls used in his 1974 and 1975 dances at Rosebud was complete, and both were unpainted. The 1974 skull consisted of about three-quarters of a complete skull, and in 1975 it constituted no more than half a skull. Both were old pieces and this may explain why they were partial skulls, since whole buffalo skulls are somewhat costly, if not that hard to obtain nowadays.

The Altar is made up rather quickly for Eagle Feather's dances. As the line of pledgers enters the Mystery Circle to begin the day, two or three assisting medicine men, including the Keeper of the Pipes, go to the black flags at the west and set the Altar up. If they draw a square in the ground as once was done, the act is neither visible to the audience nor can any evidence of such lines be seen upon close observation. The pipe rack is set up on a north-south line, between and just ahead of the black flags. It is about fourteen inches high and twenty-four inches wide. It is not painted. In 1974, two rosary-like strings of flesh offerings in white packets were tied to the rack in an "X" design. No strings of offerings were attached to the rack in 1975.

All of the pipes of the male pledgers are taken from them when they arrive at the Altar and are set against the rack, with the bowls resting on the ground and the stems leaning against the horizontal member of the rack. There is no sage bed under the pipe bowls.

The buffalo skull, bleached white by exposure to the weather, is laid flat on a bed of sage just in front of the pipe rack, its nose pointing east. The three pipes of the medicine men are leaned against the skull with their bowls resting on the sage on the ground, one of the stems against the nose bridge and the other two resting against the intersecting point of the skull and the horns on each side. There were loose bunches of sage stuffed in the eyes and nose.

At the end of the dancing for each day, the skull and pipe rack are picked up by the Keeper of the Pipes and carried to the Preparations Tipi.

Frank Fools Crow pays closer attention to the traditional Altar customs when he prepares for his Sun Dance. The skull is painted: red on the left side including the left horn, representing fire; and green on the right side including the right horn, because the earth is covered with green and the color is associated with growth. "Green

Floyd Comes A Flying, Keeper of the Pipes, bringing in the sacred buffalo skull on the fourth morning of the Sun Dance at Rosebud in 1974. Floyd had diabetes. He went blind in 1976, and died on Friday, September 17, 1976.

Top: the traditional, bead-wrapped, eagle wing-bone Sun Dance whistle used by the pledgers. Bottom: the buffalo skull as prepared by Fools Crow–red on the left side, and green on the right. Sweetgrass balls are stuffed in the eye and nose holes.

is good for the earth and for growing children." There is no dividing line between the colors.

Balls of sage or sweetgrass are inserted in the eye and mouth holes of the skull, and the entire skull is placed on a bed of sage, facing east and positioned just behind the altar square.

His Altar Square, called The Mellowed Earth, is thought of as a sacred place. To make it he draws lines in the ground about two feet long, and then other intersecting lines in the middle to make a cross —like the divisions of a window pane. Into these grooves he sprinkles tobacco, vermilion paint, and mica dust, in that order. The mica dust is sometimes omitted. If any pledger wishes to, he can place an eagle-down feather at one of the points where the Altar lines intersect. The pipe rack is set up on the east side of, or in front of, the Altar Square, so that the mouthpiece of the leaning pipe stems will be just above the easternmost line of the Altar Square.

George Bushotter says that in his time the leader carried a buffalo skull painted red.[1] He may have meant painted with red stripes, since Frances Densmore was told that the skull was painted with stripes of red extending from the nostrils to the horns,[2] and that "The Leader of the Dancers must provide the buffalo skull for the ceremony," a skull without defect selected by him from the many that strewed the prairie.[3]

THE ALTAR—Frances Densmore

The dance enclosure was about 50 feet in diameter, with a wide entrance at the east. The sacred pole stood in the center of this circle, and about 15 feet west of the pole a square of

The Sun Dance Altar as prepared by Eagle Feather at Rosebud. The buffalo skull has sage in the eyes and nose, and rests on a bed of sage. The pipe rack sits almost between the black flags of the west.

113

The Sun Dance Altar as prepared by Fools Crow at Pine Ridge. The buffalo skull has either sage or sweetgrass in the eyes and nose, and rests on a bed of sage. All of this sits on a two-foot square of overturned earth. The pipe rack is placed in front of the skull.

earth was exposed, all vegetation being carefully removed and the ground finely pulverized. This square of earth was called owaṅ, ka wankaṅ, "sacred place," and no one was allowed to pass between it and the pole. Two intersecting lines were traced within the square of earth, forming a cross, these lines being parallel to the sides of the square but not touching them. After tracing these lines in the soil, the Intercessor filled the incisions with tobacco which had been offered to the sky, the earth, and the cardinal points. He then covered the tobacco with vermilion paint-powder, over which he spread shining white "mica dust." At the intersection and ends of the lines he placed bunches of downy white eagle feathers. Very beautiful was the contrast of green turf, soft brown earth, shining white lines, and downy eagle feathers. West of this was placed a bed of fresh sage, on which the buffalo skull would be laid during the ceremony.

The Intercessor sang a song as he prepared the square of earth. When this and similar songs were sung by the Intercessor, there was absolute silence in the great gathering of people.

XII
The Preparations Tipi

THOMAS E. MAILS

The Preparations Tipi is a special lodge provided for the pledgers as a place to assemble, to rest, and to dress and undress before and after each day's ceremony. It is also the place where the buffalo skull, the flags, the pipe rack, and the Sacred Pipe are kept on a bed of sage between one day's ceremony and the next.

Authorities sometimes refer to it as the "Tent of Preparation."[1] I prefer to use the word "tipi," since "tent" has a non-Indian connotation. To do so would violate the consistent use of the Circle for holy purposes.

Those Preparations Tipis I have seen are canvas-covered pole structures about fifteen feet in diameter. They are set up the day or evening before the first day of the Sun Dance. At Rosebud in 1974, the Preparations Tipi was furnished and erected by American Indian Movement members, who brought it on the last evening before the dance and set it up then. One pole extending higher than the others above the Tipi was topped with a skunk-fur pendant. Perhaps that was a commentary on something, but no one explained what it was and when I mentioned it to Eagle Feather, he just smiled. There were no painted symbols on the outer surface of the Tipi, and it had no dew cloth.

At Rosebud in 1975, the Preparations Tipi was rented by Eagle Feather from a friend at Standing Rock. He attempted to erect it on the afternoon before the first day of the dance, but his unfamiliarity with that particular Tipi frustrated him no end. The poles were put in place in the traditional way, but when the cover was raised into place and wrapped around, it just wouldn't come together properly. Since the wind was blowing, it whipped the loose cover about and caused it to balloon out like a huge white sail on a running ship. It was a grand sight.

Others pitched in and tried to solve the problem, but they were amateurs in the art and failed also. When darkness came the entire assemblage was lying in a heap on the ground, just as it had been when construction attempts first began. I wondered, as I returned to my motel at Mission, whether there would even be a Preparations Tipi when the dance got underway in the morning.

I needn't have worried. When I arrived at 6 A.M., there it was, a ghostly gray pyramid against the violet-hued hills of the early South Dakota morning. An unknown professional had come during the night and put it up. There is always someone who knows the ancient ways of doing things.

In the old days, new sticks were used to pin the Tipi front, and thre were quilled or beaded decorations especially made to adorn it.[2] No one worries about such attention to detail anymore. Plain rented pins were employed in 1975, and the exterior of the canvas cover was left plain. No skunk-skin pendant hung from the poles either.

In 1974 at Rosebud, the Preparations Tipi was located about twenty feet west of the Old Man Four Generations fireplace. In 1975, this site was occupied by Eagle Feather's tent and cooler, and the Preparations Tipi was situated about twenty feet to the south of the Old Man Four Generations fireplace.

TENT OF PREPARATION—James O. Dorsey and George Bushotter

After this there is set up within the camping circle a good tent known as the tent of preparation.[3] When the managers wish to set up the tent of preparation, they borrow tent skins here and there. Part of these tent skins they use for covering the smoke hole, and part were used as curtains, for when they decorate the candidates they use the curtains for shutting them in from the gaze of the people and when they finish painting them they throw down the curtains.

In the back part of this tent of preparation are placed the buffalo skulls, one for each candidate. A new knife, which has never been used, is exposed to smoke. A new ax, too, is reddened and smoked.

Wild sage is used in various ways prior to and during the Sun Dance. Some of it they spread on the ground to serve as couches, and with some they wipe the tears from their faces. They fumigate with the plant known as "ćan śilśilya," or else they use sweet-smelling leaves. Day after day they fumigate themselves with "wácanga," a sweet-smelling grass. They hold every object which they use over the smoke of one of these grasses. They wear a kind of medicine on their necks, and that keeps them from being hungry or thirsty for occasionally they chew a small quantity of it. Or if they tie some of this medicine to their feet they do not get weary so soon.[4]

When the tent of preparation is erected, there are provided for it new tent pins, new sticks for fastening the tent skins together above the entrance, and new poles for pushing out the flaps beside the smoke hole. These objects and all others which have to be used are brought into the tent of preparation and fumigated over a fire into which the medicine has been dropped. By this time another day has been spent. Now all the candidates assemble in the tent of preparation, each one wearing a buffalo robe with the hair outside. One who acts as leader sits in the place of honor at the back part of the tent, and the others sit on either side of him around the fireplace. They smoke their pipes. When night comes they select one of the songs of the Sun Dance, in order to rehearse it. Certain men have been chosen as singers of the dancing songs, and when one set of them rests, there are others to take their places. The drummers beat the drum rapidly, but softly (as the Teton call it, kpankpanwela, the act of several drummers hitting in quick succession).

Three times do they beat the drum in that manner, and then they beat it rapidly, as at the beginning of the Sun Dance. At this juncture, as many as have flutes—made of the bones of eagles' wings, ornamented with porcupine quills, and hung around their necks, with cords similarly ornamented, some with eagle down at the tip ends of the flutes—blow them often and forcibly as they dance. While the drum is beaten three times in succession all the candidates cry aloud, but when it is beaten the fourth time they cry or wail no longer, but dance and blow their flutes or whistles.

When the candidates take their seats in the tent of preparation, they select a man to fill the pipe with tobacco. When they wish to smoke, this man passes along the line of candidates. He holds the pipe with the mouthpiece toward each man, who smokes without grasping the pipe stem.

When the candidates are allowed to eat, the attendant feeds them. No one can be loquacious within the tent of preparation. If a dog or person approaches the tent, the offender is chased away before he can reach it. No spectators are allowed to enter the tent. And this regulation is enforced by blows whenever anyone attempts to violate it.[5]

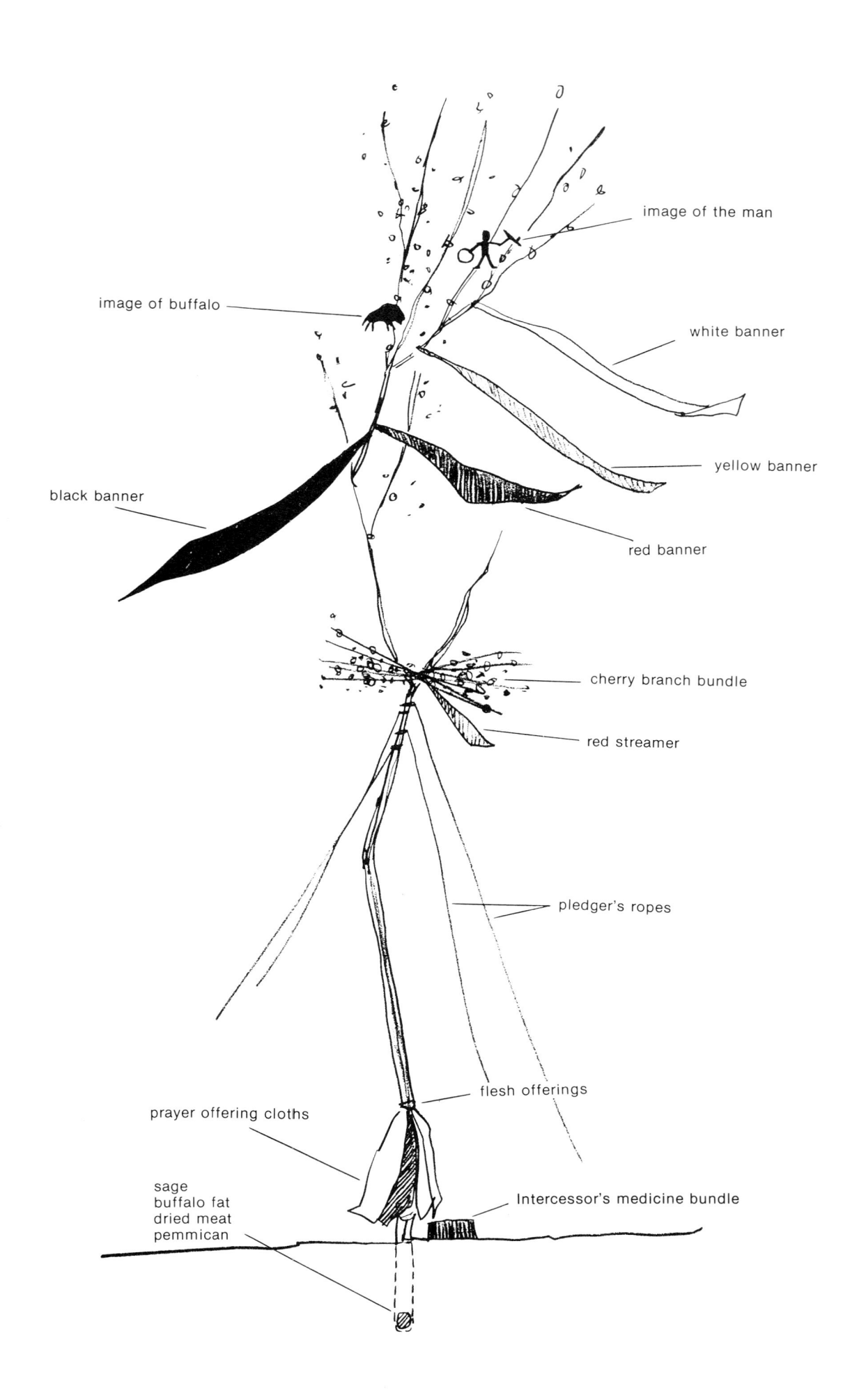

XIII
The Sacred Tree Of 1974

EAGLE FEATHER

The Sun Dance Sacred Tree, also called the Sacred Pole, is a cottonwood tree that is chosen by the Intercessor twelve months in advance of its use. Then, at intervals during the twelve months prior to the dance, flesh offerings are cut from the arms of the holy men, medicine men, and others, and are taken and placed as offerings at the base of the Tree. During this time other sacrifice offerings, such as tobacco and cloth, also are tied to the Tree while prayers are made. Each of these is directed toward the success of the forthcoming dance. This manner of selecting the Tree differs from that of ancient times, but I feel it is a better way for today's circumstances.

When the time comes to cut the Tree, four virgin and unmarried girls are chosen to hit the Tree with an axe from each of the four directions before it is chopped down. Helen Marshall, age ten, was one of the girls who did this in 1974. A regular axe is used for the cutting.

In 1974, the Tree was transported by truck to within one-quarter mile of the fairground. It was carried in from there by twelve men, six on each side of the Tree, and holding cross poles to make a litter on which the Sacred Tree was placed.

No feints or passes were made at the hole before the Tree was put in it. Offerings of sage, tallow, jerky, and pemmican were placed in the hole, and the Tree was set directly into the hole on top of the offerings. Pemmican was also one of the foods given to the guests during the ceremony.

The women who furnish the pemmican and tallow which are placed in the hole, as well as the pemmican used for food, do so because they have made a vow to do this in return for God's help with their problems. Since the Tree is considered dead once it is cut, it is thought to be going on a journey from which it will never return. Therefore, the food placed in the hole is a lunch whose spiritual counterpart will go with the Tree and nourish it as it travels.

When the Sun Dance has ended, the Tree is taken down and laid aside in a carefully selected place. Then, on or before the first day of the Sun Dance of the following year, it is cut up and used for firewood to heat the rocks used in the sweatlodge.

The different colors of the cloth offerings which are tied to the top and to the base of the Sun Pole indicate what each of the donors is praying to Almighty God for. After the Tree is taken down, these cloth panels are burned in the sweatlodge fire pit, Old Man Four Generations, although women sometimes take small pieces of cloth as souvenirs of the dance and keep them for many years. In such instances they also serve as visual aids to be used in instructing their children about the dance.

The meaning of the black, white, red, and yellow colors used on the Tree is the same as it is for the four sets of flags marking the

Diagram of the completely decorated Sacred Tree.

north, east, south, and west directions in the Mystery Hoop, and for those colors associated with the sweatlodge.

I fashioned the rawhide man and buffalo figures which were tied to the Sacred Tree in 1974. A small piece of buffalo hide with the hair left on was used to make both, and it is my plan to use the same figures for the Rosebud Fairground dance of 1975. The color of the paint used on the effigy of the man depends in part upon the clan the medicine man belongs to. I use red paint because of my clan, and because I have been taught what red power is. Black is associated with the Thunder Clan, which may account for its use as recorded in some early accounts by historians. The buffalo effigy was left its natural color on one side, and some splotches of black paint were daubed on its other side.

The cross bundle on the Sacred Pole was made entirely of cherry branches.

The four cloth pendants tied to the branches at the top of the Tree had tobacco-offering bundles secured to each corner of each pendant.

On the evening of July 10, a group of those of us who were going to participate in the dance went to get the Tree I had picked out a year ago. We got it from a place along a creek east of Rosebud. When we went to get it we took four virgin girls to hit the Tree on the four directions with an axe. Then it was cut down, and we put it on a truck and trucked it back up near the fairground. From there we took the Tree in four moves to the center of the Mystery Circle and laid it down. One man went after the cherry bush branches, brought them back, and tied them onto the Tree. The cloth offerings attached to the top of the Tree always consisted of a five-to-seven-yard-long strip of each color: black, red, yellow, and white. In 1974, these were given by the Rosebud Police Department as prayers for peace, quietness, and no trouble from radicals at the dance. They also prayed that the people of the Rosebud Brule Sioux Tribe and Pine Ridge Oglala Sioux Tribe would live in peace. This hasn't come to pass yet, but now we are beginning to feel the effects of some of the prayers.

My wife, Hazel, obtained some buffalo meat and made a jerky, a dried meat. She also acquired some tallow taken from the same buffalo. Besides these she had saved some pounded cherries from the year before, and she made *wasna*, pemmican, with it.

So on the bottom of the hole for the Tree we first put a small amount of sage, and then we put down the tallow. On top of the tallow we put the jerky and on top of that we put the *wasna*. As we set these in, prayers were made with burning sweet grass and the Peace Pipe was filled. All who were going to participate prayed with it. And then the Tree itself was made ready.

To prepare the trunk of the Tree we took *wasaya*, which is a traditional color we put on our face, and we made a narrow and straight red line from the bottom of the Tree to its very top. When this was done we tied the images of the man and the buffalo on top of the Tree along with the cloth offerings.

Now the Tree was ready to be raised and put into the hole. The 1974 Tree was about sixteen inches in diameter and close to sixty feet long. And I'm telling you, to set a tall green cottonwood tree upright in a hole is a great job, so a great many men joined in here to help us raise the Tree. And then when the Tree was set in and straight up, of course, the ropes were tied on there for the men who were going to do the piercing.

So the Tree was set, tamped, and readied the day before the Sun Dance. When it was set, prayers were said there again, offerings were tied to its base, and everything was ready for the Sun Dance.

Rawhide images of the man and the buffalo used during an ancient Sun Dance. A breath feather is attached to the man's head. Both images are black. Museum of Natural History, New York City.

Rawhide images of the man and the buffalo used during an ancient Sun Dance. A breath feather is attached to the man's head. Both images were black, and were designed to symbolize the Sun Dance prayer for growth, fertility and new life in mankind and all creatures.
Height of man, 13". Peabody Museum, Harvard University, Cambridge, Mass.

The images of the cardboard man and the rawhide buffalo which were tied to the Sacred Tree at Rosebud in 1975. Height of man, 14". . . . Color: scarlet red. Length of buffalo 15". . . . hair left on, not painted.

Some of the male Pledgers in 1975.

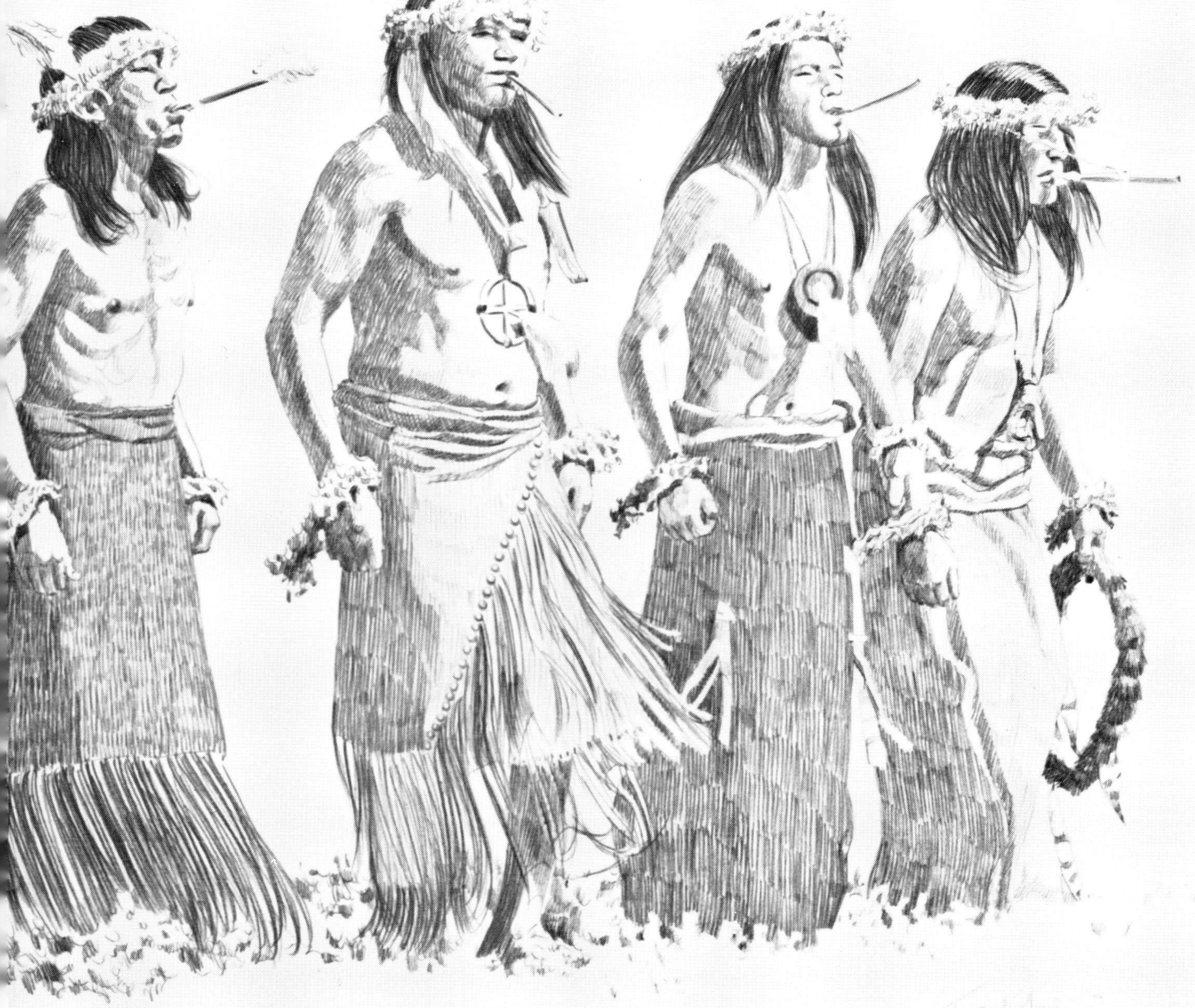

At this time we took the first flesh offerings. Many small pieces of skin were taken off of our shoulders and arms. I have made over a thousand. These flesh offerings were mixed with some herb medicine, wrapped in cloth to make little bundles, and then tied on a long string which takes the form of a rosary, either in a single color or in different colors.

Why do we do this? Because the Indian religion is designed to be more painful than any other religion in North America. And when the flesh offering is made, no antiseptic or anesthetic is used. The Peace Pipe is handed to the person making the flesh offering, and while he or she holds it, the flesh is taken off with a needle or razor blade. As many pieces are taken as the person has promised the Great Spirit, Almighty God, in return for His blessings.

Lots of people are horrified when they see the flesh offerings and do not understand why they are made, so they have criticized the Sioux people for doing such things in public. But the meaning of the sacrifice goes deeper than what is seen.

It is a very painful experience to give flesh offerings, and as the flesh offerings are being cut, the person says:

> Almighty God, Great Spirit, have mercy upon me. I humbled myself today in the sweatlodge and here. I make these flesh offerings as prayers on behalf of my people. These pieces of flesh that I offer came from you in the first place. I have shed tears as I stand here and talk to you. I have shed blood as I talk with you. So I have offered you my body and my heart O Great Spirit, Almighty God. This is all I can do for you. I have humbled myself. This is as far as I can go on my own. From here on it is up to you. Help me, and give me strength and faith and hope.
>
> Please watch over the next generation that is to come, giving them strength and faith and hope and knowledge, so that they, too, may be strong and faithful toward you. Also bless the ones that are sick in the hospital, and the shut-ins.
>
> O Great Spirit, help me to understand the nature of our human race, and lead us all in such a way that we can live closer together regardless of our nationality. Help our churches to think of one another as brothers and sisters, for you have given us the red power to make this possible.
>
> Bless our four-leggeds and our winged brothers. Also bless even the little ants that are upon the earth. Remember in particular the little animals, such as the squirrels, chipmunks, prairie dogs, and all the other tiny animals you have put on this earth.
>
> Grandfather, Great Spirit, help me to be careful and reverent as I travel about from day to day. Make me a responsible person, and help me to remember the sacredness of the ground that I walk upon. If I should cross a river or creek, I will make a little offering in remembrance that I am a trespasser. The fish live under the water, as do the turtles, frogs, and many water people. And if I make a mistake in so doing, help me correct it. Help me as I travel in my daily life, for I wish to preserve your world for my brothers and sisters who are yet to live on this earth.

Flesh-offering prayers are always of this nature, and the piercing to come is a flesh offering, too. I have been pierced twenty-five times. Sometimes I have been pierced twice in a year. It is very painful, for I say again that we do not use any antiseptic or anesthetic. When we are being pierced and the stick or eagle claw is being pulled through our flesh, which is tied by the rope to the center

Sacred Pole, we pull back to the pounding rhythm of the drum and we sing:

> Have mercy upon me
> O Great Spirit.
> Wakan Tanka,
> Great Spirit,
> have mercy on me
> that all my relatives shall live.

When the Tree was set and the flesh offerings were done, we had the ground initiation, just as it was done with Jesse White Lance way back in 1956. Prayers were made as the Sacred Pipe was passed, and a song was sung in honor of our own boys who went overseas and were prisoners of war, or wounded.

After the ground initiation we brought the mourners in, those who had loved ones that had passed away in the fall of 1973 or the spring of 1974. We brought them in and we gave them a feed. As the feed was going on, encouragement was offered to them by different medicine men, and if any minister or preacher is ever there at the time, we usually ask them to make a speech of encouragement.

THE SACRED TREE OF 1975—Thomas E. Mails

On July 2, 1975, we went in a sizable group to get the Sacred Cottonwood Tree. The Sun Dance principals were somewhat dressed up for the ritual, indicating its importance. Eagle Feather had on a clean yellow short-sleeved shirt. Four young girls, whose ages ranged from something like eight to eleven, were brought along to assist with the ceremony. They wore no costumes, just their regular school clothing—brightly colored shirts and jeans—and their hair was done up in braids or pony tails.

The girls were lined up on the west side of the Tree, and a medicine man held a twist of burning sweet grass over their heads for purification while he prayed for them. Then Eagle Feather painted a round red spot on the palm of each girl's hands and a round red spot in the middle of their foreheads, using his index finger as a brush. As the paint was applied he prayed that each one would be acceptable to God for the task.

When this was done he held the mouthpiece of his pipe against the Tree, with his left hand placed above the pipe and also touching the Tree. As he prayed again, he looked up at the sun.

Using a long-handled axe, each of the girls in turn hit the Tree once in the four cardinal directions, moving from east to south to west to north. Eagle Feather showed each girl where to hit the Tree. The last one was so small she could hardly lift the huge axe.

After this was done, Delbert chopped the Tree down. It fell heavily and no attempt was made to keep it from striking the ground, as was supposedly done in ancient times. I wondered if anyone could have done so, since it was really heavy and at least forty feet tall.

Joe Staub trimmed off the lower branches with the axe. The bark was not removed. Eight men then dragged the Tree a short distance to a waiting flatbed truck. There it was hoisted aboard, with its trunk projecting forward over the cab, trucked to within half a city block or so of the Mystery Circle, and removed from the truck. This time the men were careful not to let it touch the ground.

Ten men carried it trunk-first into the Mystery Circle, with a medicine man who carried an eagle-wing fan leading the way. No pause for prayer was made at the east entrance to the Circle. The Tree was taken straight to the hole and laid on the ground before it.

Now a few more branches were removed, and Joyce Crane, the

oldest of the four girls who had chopped the Tree, brought four colored banners which were to be tied to the top of the Tree. She waited there patiently while a medicine man painted a single red stripe from the butt of the Tree to the first fork of its lower branches. This represented the red path which the people walk upon.

A bundle of cherry branches, with a red banner wrapped around it, was tied crossways at approximately the midpoint of the Tree. Then Eagle Feather tied the four cloth banners onto the top branches, with the white highest, then the yellow, the red, and the black. Next came the images of the man and the buffalo, with the man secured higher on the Tree than the buffalo.[1] Finally, the ropes of the pledgers were tied on just below the bundle of cherry branches.

Now the hole was smoked with burning sweet grass by a medicine man and the necessary items were placed inside: first sage, then buffalo fat, then dried meat, and last pemmican. In depositing each item, Eagle Feather first held it toward the six directions and prayed. Then as it entered the hole it was smoked with sweet grass by the medicine man who was assisting him.

After this, Eagle Feather stood at the butt of the Tree and drove a long steel spike into the ground to keep the Tree from moving forward when the men began to lift it. Eight men walked the Tree up, and when they had it up as high as they could reach, six men got on three ropes and pulled it the rest of the way like tug-of-war crews. As Eagle Feather said earlier, it was a real job to hoist it. No feints were made as some authorities claim was the ancient custom. Once the trunk was in the hole and straight up, the dirt was packed around it. Until this was finished, the men really had to wrestle to keep it there.

None of the women had approached the Tree until now, but at this point two of the female pledgers brought cloth offerings for the trunk of the Tree. The men tied them on—two red ones first, followed by the other colors.

The Tree was splendid to behold! Its leaves glistened in the sun and as the wind picked up, the banners streamed out like brightly colored arms reaching for tomorrow, the first day of the dance. By this time it was late afternoon. The participants seated themselves cross-legged in a large circle and passed the Pipe, each person smoking it and praying with it. The ground was being initiated. It was becoming holy, the nation's Hoop. The moment was very personal, and while we observers could have joined them, we left them to themselves.

A concluding item of some mystery to me, and for which I have received no satisfactory explanation, is why in the old days the Sacred Tree was considered "an enemy" by the men who went to cut it down. (The accounts of Dorsey and Densmore that follow both make references to this.) I have received no such inference from the oldest living holy men. In fact, the Tree to them would seem to represent more of "a friend." Nor is the Tree considered dead at the moment it is chopped down. It only begins to die "for the people," and the dying continues during the four-day ceremony. "It is going on the long journey we will all go on some day," says Eagle Feather.

Fools Crow tells of a remarkable moment at Crow Dog's 1974 Sun Dance when the seventy-four male pledgers went forward to touch the cottonwood Tree and as one, they all believed it felt like human flesh. "It wasn't a tree, it was flesh to all of the pledgers: They all felt the same thing at the same time." After that the twenty-four women pledgers touched it and reacted the same way: "Then they all said, 'That's a man there.'"

THE SACRED TREE—James O. Dorsey and George Bushotter

> At length orders are given for all the people to pitch their tents in the form of a tribal circle, with an opening to the north. It takes several days to accomplish this, and then all the men and youths are required to take spades and go carefully over the whole area within the circle and fill up all the holes and uneven places which might cause the horses to stumble and fall.

Miss Fletcher says, "The people came in a circle, with a large opening at the east. In 1882 over 9,000 Indians were so camped, the diameter of the circle being over three-quarters of a mile wide."

Though Bushotter has written that this work requires several days, it is probable, judging from what follows in his manuscript, that only two days are required for such work. For he continues thus:

> On the third day some men are selected to go in search of the *Can-wakan* or Mystery Tree, out of which they are to form the sun pole. These men must be selected from those who are known to be brave, men acquainted with the war path, men who have overcome difficulties, men who have been wounded in battle, men of considerable experience.

Miss Fletcher's account names the fourth day as that on which they sought for the sun pole.

> The men selected to fell the Mystery Tree ride very swift horses, and they decorate their horses and attire themselves just as if they were going to battle. They put on their feather war bonnets. They race their horses to a hill and then back again. In former days it was customary on such occasions for any women who had lost children during some previous attack on the camp to often wail as they ran towards the mounted men, and to sing at intervals as they went. But that is not the custom at the present day. Three times do the mounted men tell of their brave deeds in imitation of the warriors of the olden times, and then they undertake to represent their own deeds in pantomime.

> On the fourth day, the selected men go to search for the Mystery Tree. They return to camp together, and if they have found a suitable tree, they cut out pieces of the soil within the camping circle, going down to virgin earth. This exposed earth extends over a considerable area. On it they place a species of sweet-smelling grass (a trailing variety) and wild sage, on which they lay the buffalo skull.

> The next morning, which is that of the fifth day, they prepare to go after the tree that is to serve as the sun pole. The married and single men, the boys, and even the women, are all ordered to go on horseback. Whoever is able to move rapidly accompanies the party. When the chosen persons go to fell the Mystery Tree they rush on it as they would upon a real enemy, just as tradition relates that the Omaha and Ponka rushed on their sacred tree. Then they turn quickly and run from it until they arrive at the other side of the hill (nearest to the Mystery Tree), after which they return to the tree. They tie leaves together very tightly, making a mark of the bundle, assaulting it in turn as a foe.

> The Tree is reached by noon. The persons chosen to fell it whisper to one another as they assemble around it. They approach someone who has a child, and take hold of him.

The Blackfoot Sun Dance buffalo skull.

Then they bring robes and other goods which they spread on the ground, and on the pile they seat the child, who is sometimes a small girl, or even a large one.

Each of the chosen men takes his turn in striking the Tree. Everyone must first tell his exploits, then he brandishes the ax three times without striking a blow, after which he strikes the Tree once, and only once, making a gash. He leaves the ax sticking in the Tree, whence it is removed by the next man. He who leaves the ax in the Tree is by this act considered to make a present of a horse to someone. As soon as he gives the blow, his father (or some near kinsman) approaches and hands him a stick, whereupon the young man returns it, asking him to give it to such a one, calling him by name. For instance, let us suppose that a young man, Grizzly Bear With an Iron Side, requests that his stick be given to Leaping High. The old man who is employed as the crier goes to the camp and sings thus: [in Dakota] "The last word is a sign of a brave deed on the part of the donor, and it is so understood by everyone." On reaching the tent of the other man, the crier says, "O Leaping High, a horse is brought to you! A horse is brought to you because Grizzly Bear With an Iron Side has given a blow to the Mystery Tree!" On hearing this, Leaping High says "Thanks!" as he extends his hands with the palms toward the crier; and he brings them down toward the ground and takes the stick representing the horse. Then the crier passes along around the circle, singing the praises of the donor, and naming the man who has received the present.

After all the chosen men have told of their deeds, and have performed their parts, the women select a man to speak of what generous things they have done, and when he has spoken, the larger women who are able to fell trees rise to their feet, and take their turns in giving one blow apiece to the Tree. By the time that all the women have struck the Tree it falls, and all present shout and sing. Many presents are made, and some of the people wail, making the entire forest echo their voices. Then those men who are selected for that purpose cut off all the limbs of the Tree except the highest one, and do not disturb the treetop. Wherever a branch is cut off they rub paint on the wound.

They make a bundle of some wood in imitation of that for which they have prayed, and hang it crosswise from the fork of the Tree. Above the bundle they suspend a scarlet blanket, a buffalo robe or a weasel skin, and under the bundle they fasten two pieces of dried buffalo hide, one being cut in the shape of a buffalo, and the other in that of a man.

Though Bushotter did not state the circumstance, it is remarkable that both the figures have *membrum virile rigid*. The author learned about this from two trustworthy persons, who obtained all the paraphernalia of the Sun Dance, and one of them, Capt. John G. Bourke, U.S. Army, showed him the figures of the man and buffalo used at the Sun Dance at Red Cloud Agency, in 1882. In the former figure, the lingam is of abnormal size. The connection between the phallic cut and the sun is obvious to the student.

No one of the company dares touch the sun pole as they take it to the camp. Before wagons were available, they made a horse carry most of the weight of the pole, part of it being on one side of him and part on the other, while the wakan men chosen for the purpose walked on both sides of the horse in order to support the ends of the pole. At present day, a wagon is used for transporting the sun pole to the camp. While they are on the way no person dares to go in advance of the pole, for whoever violates the law is in danger of being thrown from his horse and having his neck broken.

Miss Fletcher states that the sun pole is carried to the camp on a litter of sticks, and must not be handled or stepped over.

> The married men carry leaf shields on their backs, and some of the riders make their horses race as far as they are able. Any member of the party can appropriate the small branches which have been cut from the Mystery Tree.
>
> When they reach the camp circle, all of the party who carry branches and leaves drop them in the places where they intend erecting their respective tents.

Judging from Mr. Bushotter's first text, the tents are not pitched when the people return with the sun pole. But as soon as they lay the pole in place where it is to be erected, the tents are pitched. Then all the objects that are to be attached to the sun pole are tied to it, and some of the men take leather straps, such as the women use when they carry wood and other burdens, and fasten them to the sun pole in order to raise it into position.

> This raising of the sun pole seems to be symbolic of the four winds, or "four quarters of the heavens," as Dr. Riggs translates the Dakota term. Those who assist in raising the sun pole must be men who have distinguished themselves. They raise the pole a short distance from the ground, and then shout, making an indistinct sound; they rest awhile and pull it a little higher, shouting again; resting a second time, they renew their efforts, pulling it higher still. They shout a third time, rest again, and at the fourth pull the pole is perpendicular. Then the men around the camping circle fire guns, making the horses flee. Those who raised the pole have a new spade, and they use it one after another in throwing a sufficient quantity of earth around the base of the pole, pressing the earth down firmly in order to steady the pole. [2]

THE SACRED TREE—Frances Densmore

The tree to be used for the sacred pole was selected and cut, and the sacred pole was decorated and raised on the morning of the day preceding the Sun Dance. All the tribe were present when the four young men set out from camp to select the tree. For some time before their departure the drummers and singers sang the songs of war, for the tree was regarded as something to be conquered. The following song might be sung as the people assembled. This song was composed by the singer, a man who is known in the tribe as a composer of war songs:

WITH DAUNTLESS COURAGE

> On the warpath
> I give place to none.
> With dauntless courage I live.

The following song was frequently used in this connection, and was used also before the departure of a party going on the warpath or in search of buffalo:

THE MANY LANDS YOU FEAR

Friends,
The many lands
You fear
In them without fear I have walked.
The black face-paint
I seek.

Four young men left the camp for the woods to select the tree which should form the sacred pole. Any who wished to accompany the young men were permitted to do so, but they had no part in choosing the tree. On arriving at the woods the young men searched for a straight, slender tree. It was stated that cottonwood was preferred for the sacred pole and for all the articles of wood used in the Sun Dance, because the white down of the cottonwood seed resembles the downy eagle feathers used in the ceremony. If a cottonwood could not be obtained, elm was selected, because the elm is the first tree to blossom in the spring. The tree for the Sun Dance pole must be a standing tree and particularly fine with respect to straightness, branching, and fullness of leaf. It was required that the first tree selected should be cut, no change or choice being allowed. It is interesting to note that all articles devoted to a ceremonial use must be the best obtainable. A high standard of excellence prevailed among the Sioux, and this is especially shown in their ceremonies which expressed their highest ideals.

Cottonwood was used also for the post in the spirit lodge, also in offerings placed on the Sun Dance pole.

When the young men had decided on a tree they returned to make their report to the Intercessor. Their return had been anxiously awaited, and in response to their signal a number of friends went on horseback to meet them, riding around them in wide circles and escorting them to the camp. There they found their friends dancing around the drum and singing a song used to welcome a returning war party or men who had gone in search of buffalo. After the singing and dancing a feast was provided by the friends of the young men. There was abundance of food, and all were invited to partake.

The announcement of a choice was followed by preparation for cutting the tree and bringing it to the camp. The cutting of the tree for the Sun Dance pole was an important part of the ceremony, and many went to witness it. Some went from curiosity, and others wished to make offerings when the tree was cut. Even the children went to see the cutting of the pole. The young people, riding their fleet ponies, circled around the party. The leading members of the company were the Intercessor (or, in his absence, one of the old medicine men), the four young men who selected the tree, the four young women who were to cut the tree, and the pole-bearers, who were to carry it to the camp. It was the duty of the Leader of the Dancers to provide the ax with which the tree was felled, but he did not accompany the party who went to cut it. In the old days a primitive implement was used; in later times this was replaced by an ax purchased from the trader, but it was required that the ax be a new one, never used before.

Great interest centered in the selection of the tree, and when it was indicated by the young men the Intercessor raised his pipe, holding the stem toward the top of the tree and lowering it slowly to the earth, repeating a prayer in a low tone. When he held the pipe toward the top of the tree, he spoke of the kingbird; lowering it about one-third of the distance to the ground, he spoke of the eagle; lowering it half the remaining distance, he spoke of the yellowhammer, and holding it toward the ground, he spoke of the spider. The tree was regarded as an enemy, and in explanation of the reference to these animals it was said that "The kingbird, though small, is feared by all its enemies; the eagle is the boldest of the birds; the yellowhammer cannot overcome its enemies in open fight but is expert in dodging them, darting from one side of the tree-trunk to another, while the spider defeats its enemies by craftiness and cunning."

One of the four virgins was selected to cut the tree, but she did not fell it at once. It was considered that she had been given the honor of conquering an enemy, and before she wielded the ax a kinsman was permitted to relate one of his valiant deeds on the warpath. The maiden then lifted the ax and made a feint of striking the tree. Each of the four virgins did likewise, the action of each being preceded by the telling of a victory tale by one of her kinsmen. The ax was then returned to the first virgin, who swung it with effect, cutting the tree in such a manner that it fell toward the south. While the tree was being felled, no one was allowed near it except those who wielded the ax, the Intercessor, those who wished to make offerings, and those who were to carry the pole. At this time the following song was sung:

SONG OF CUTTING THE SACRED POLE

(first rendition)
The black face-paint
I seek.
Therefore I have done this.

(second rendition)
Horses
I seek.
Therefore I have done this.

Throughout this part of the ceremony the tree was regarded as an enemy, and a shout of victory arose as it swayed and fell. Care was taken that it should not touch the ground. The medicine men, some of whom usually accompanied the party, burned sweet grass, and offerings were presented. The branches of the tree were cut off close to the trunk except one branch about one-fourth of the distance from the top, which was left a few inches long in order that the crossbar of the pole might be fastened to it. In some cases a small branch with leaves on it was also left at the top of the pole. From this time the pole was regarded as sacred and no one was allowed to step over it. Jealousy frequently arose among the women in regard to the privilege of cutting the tree, and it is said that on one occasion a woman was so angry because she was not chosen for the purpose that she stepped over the pole. Half an hour later she was thrown from her horse, dragged some distance, and killed. The horse was known to be a gentle animal, and the event was considered a punishment justly visited on the woman.

Between 20 and 40 men were required to carry the sacred pole to the camp. These walked two abreast, each pair carrying between them a stick about 2 feet long on which the pole rested as on a litter. The pole was carried with the top in advance, and the Intercessor or his representative walked behind the bearers. No one was allowed to walk before the sacred pole.

The songs of carrying home the pole were songs of victory. The following song could be used at any time after the pole had been cut and was frequently sung as it was carried to the camp:

SONG OF VICTORY OVER THE SACRED POLE

(words addressed to the sacred pole)

> "I am only a man"
> You falsely implied.
> Now you cry.

Around the pole-bearers circled the young men and women of the tribe on their ponies. It was the custom of the young people to decorate their ponies with trailing vines and to wreathe the vines around their own bodies. They made hoops of slender branches, with crossbars like the framework of a shield, and on this they draped vines and leaves, thus forming a striking contrast to the dignified procession of pole-bearers.

Four times on the way to the camp the pole-bearers were allowed to rest. The signal for each halt—a throbbing call beginning on a high tone and descending like a wail—was given by the Intercessor. At this signal, the pole was lowered for a few moments upon crotched sticks provided for the purpose.

The sacred pole was brought into the Sun Dance circle as it had been carried, with the top in advance. As the pole-bearers walked across the circle the medicine men cried, "Now is the time to make a wish or bring an offering." The people crowded forward, shouting and offering gifts of various kinds. So great excitement prevailed that no one knew who brought a gift, and a man could scarcely hear his own voice.

The Intercessor then prepared the sacred pole, first removing the rough outer bark, fragments of which were eagerly seized and carried away by the people. After the pole had been made sufficiently smooth, it was painted by the Intercessor; native red paint or vermilion was used. The pole was painted in perpendicular stripes, beginning at the branch where the crossbar would be fastened and extending to the base.

As the Intercessor painted the sacred pole, he sang the following song, which, like the other songs pertaining to his ceremonial office, was sung alone and without the drum, the people listening attentively:

SONG OF PAINTING THE SACRED POLE

> Father,
> All these he has made me own:
> The trees and the forests
> Standing
> In their places.

The Sun Dance pole was usually about 35 feet in length and 6 to 8 inches in diameter. A crossbar "the length of a man" was tied on the pole, being securely fastened to the short branch left for the purpose. At the intersection of the pole and the crossbar there was tied with rawhide thongs a bag, which constituted one of the offerings made by the Leader of the Dancers. This bag was about 2 feet square, made of rawhide decorated with beads, tassels, and fringe, and was wrapped in cherry branches 4 or 5 feet long which completely concealed it. Inside the bag was a smaller bag of tanned buffalo hide containing the offering, which consisted of a large piece of buffalo hump, on a sharpened stick painted red. The stick was cottonwood and, according to Chased-by-Bears, symbolized the arrow with which the buffalo had been killed and also the picket stake to which a horse stolen from an enemy was fastened when it was being brought to the camp. The additional offerings fastened to the crossbar were two effigies cut from rawhide, one in the form of an Indian and the other in the form of a buffalo, indicating that the enemy and also the buffalo had been conquered by supernatural help. To the crossbar were fastened also the thongs, or cords, by which the men would be suspended. One cord was made ready for each man, the middle of it being fastened to the crossbar and the two ends hanging, to be fastened to the sticks passed through the flesh of the man's chest. At the top of the pole was hung a tanned robe of buffalo calfskin. In the later ceremonies a banner of red list cloth was used instead of the buffalo robe.

After painting the sacred pole, the Intercessor examined the hole which had been prepared for its erection, in which he placed an abundance of buffalo fat. It was said that, while doing this, he "prayed and talked in a low voice."

The command to raise the pole was followed by absolute silence on the part of the assembled people. Thus they watched the pole as it was raised slowly and carefully by the men who had brought it to the camp. The moment it was in place all gave way to cheers and rejoicing, and the three following songs were sung. These three songs were recorded by a man said to be the only Teton Sioux living (1911) who had filled the office of Intercessor. These songs comprise part of the instructions he received from the man who preceded him in that office. The singer was about 80 years of age when the songs were recorded.

SONG SUNG AFTER RAISING THE SACRED POLE

> (the pole speaks)
> Sacred
> I stand
> Behold me,
> Was said to me.

SONG SUNG AFTER RAISING THE SACRED POLE

> At the center of the earth
> Stand looking at you.
> Recognizing the tribe,
> Stand looking around you.

SONG SUNG AFTER RAISING THE SACRED POLE

> At the places of the four winds
> May you be reverenced.
> You made me wear something sacred.
> The tribe sitting in reverence,
> They wish to live.

The sacred pole was placed in such a manner that the crossbar extended north and south, and the earth was packed solidly around the base.[3]

134

XIV
The Sun Dance Costume and Body Paint

THOMAS E. MAILS

As a rule, the male Sun Dancer wears no clothing on the upper part of his body. On the lower part, with some exceptions, the pledger wears a traditional-style wrap-around or fitted cloth skirt which reaches from his waist to his ankles. Some add long, narrow panels like breechclouts, front and back. Often, ribbons of different complementary colors are attached horizontally or vertically for decoration. The color most commonly used for the skirt is red—in various hues ranging from red with a blue cast to red-orange. A few dancers wear blue skirts and, more rarely, purple cloth may be selected. A belt secures the wrapped skirt and holds it up.

In 1975, one pledger wore a cloth shirt and legging outfit which was dyed, cut, and fringed to look like the old-time buckskin garments. A few people remarked about it, but perhaps it was worn to prevent sunburn. In any event, the shirt came off at piercing time and the pledger stood up to the sacrifice very well. It is not the costume that makes the man.

The female pledgers wear their finest full-length dresses of the traditional Indian style. Some of those worn today are light-weight white buckskin, and others are cloth, of which many colors—ranging from red to blue to purple—are used. Long fringes are common and sometimes a shawl is wrapped around the skirt. The dresses are belted with as expensive a silver concho belt as the owner can afford.

Every pledger wears a head wreath, wristbands, and anklebands made of plaited sage.

In 1975, I went in a small auto caravan with Eagle Feather, a few children, including the four girls who had struck the Sacred Tree before it was cut, and some of the Sun Dance participants to gather the sage. Most of it was collected along the eastern slopes of Holy Lodge Hill, where Eagle Feather vision quested. A special variety of sage is selected for the Sun Dance. It grows on a single stalk and has larger leaves than other varieties. It is soft as silk, gray-green in color, and has a shallow root, so it is easily pulled from the sandy soil.

Nearly a trunkful was collected, and it was a warm experience to see how seriously the children, in their colorful outfits, went about the collecting. As each bunch was gathered, the roots were cut off with shears.

In a half hour or less we had enough and returned to the camp area. Shortly thereafter I watched as Eagle Feather sat in the shade area before his tent and deftly plaited the first head wreaths, after which he encouraged several other Sioux sitting there to do the same.

Some boasted that they could do it easily, but none managed to

Body painting for the Sun Dance at Rosebud. Top left: paint for the fourth day. Bottom left: paint for the third day.

do so without first receiving guidance from Eagle Feather. As it turned out, he was the only one of that group who really knew how to do it right. Since the sage items used in the dance must all be circular in form, making them correctly consists of taking a handful of sage by the root end and then feeding the next handful into it at a slight angle, while someone assists by wrapping it with a white string to hold it in place. Inexperienced people neglect the slight angle and make a straight intersection instead; they then have a very difficult time bending the long length into a circle and holding it there, since it tends to twist and spring back.

Some dancers add handsome windings of red cloth to their head wreaths, and some wrap groups of ribbons of different colors around the side, allowing the ribbon ends to hang long and free along the sides of the head and over the chest. As an option, they can also hang golden eagle feathers or eagle-down feathers from the back of the wreath. It is permissible to have a golden eagle tail feather secured to the wreath in an upright position at each side of the head, and I was told that the women who do this are those who have vowed to give flesh offerings during the dance. Some pledgers have a single stalk of sage placed upright at each side of the head wreath.

I'm certain that some of this is done in remembrance of the old days when men belonging to dream cults wore either fur-wrapped animal horns or cut and curved eagle feathers on their heads, which were attached either to the wreaths or to a rawhide strap. The few old photographs and pictographs available show such headdresses on pledgers who were animal or bird dreamers. Women in the old pictures appear to be wearing only a single eagle-down feather above the wreath and placed at the back of the head.

The sage wristbands are made in the shape of a horseshoe with extended legs, and the legs are tied together with string when the band is on. The legs of the Lead Dancer's wristbands are left quite long so that the Intercessor can grasp these extensions when he leads him around the Mystery Hoop. Eagle Feather said that once a man has put on his sage pieces he is holy and alone before God. No one is to touch him until the dance is over. Nevertheless, dancers are touched when they are pierced, led around, comforted, and congratulated.

In ancient times the wristbands and anklebands were usually made of buffalo fur.[1] When the buffalo became extinct in the eighteen eighties, they switched to rabbit fur, and Densmore quotes Red Weasel as saying that when he was Intercessor, he wore otter skin around his wrists and ankles.[2] According to Fools Crow, sometime between 1928 and the present, rabbits were in short supply, too, and the switch was made to sage, which was also used in some of the old dances.

It is traditional to let the hair, when it is not cut short, hang long, free, and straight. More and more young men are letting their hair grow long today, and it adds significantly to their overall appearance when they dance. Unbraided hair has always been the ceremonial style among the Sioux, for the hair is believed to be an extension of the soul.[3]

Except for the women, who usually wear moccasins, nearly all of the pledgers dance barefooted. This allows Mother Earth to send her sustaining power into them as they dance. Men whose feet are not conditioned to take the punishment are allowed to wear moccasins. Now and then a pair of tennis shoes—even beaded ones—will be seen. I was told that sage anklebands ward off evil powers that inhabit the ground.

Each male pledger wears a buckskin cord around his neck, to

which is attached a whistle, made either of wood or from the wing bone of an eagle. When a white plume feather from a golden eagle can be obtained, the whistle is tipped with it, since its long quill can be bound to the whistle so as to extend the feather straight out in front of it. If the quill isn't long enough, a piece of straight wire is used as a bridge between it and the bone. In lieu of the plume, a white down feather is used. In the old days the Sun Dance whistles were decorated with porcupine quills or beads, and the mouthpieces were wrapped with sage.[4] But few whistles have these additions today. Most are left quite plain. The wooden whistles are larger than the eagle-bone whistles and are straight, while the bone whistle is slightly curved. Some of the innovative and experienced young men attach their whistle to a double cord, one length of which is shorter than the other. The shorter end is tied to the front end of the bone and looped over the ears, thus holding the whistle up and in place, and also easing the burden of its use as the long hours of dancing go by.

Pledgers wear an assortment of items around their necks for medicinal purposes. Some wear small medicine bags containing items seen in visions. Most wear a cord to which is attached a round beaded or painted disk. The symbols placed on these all relate to powers associated with the dance: the sun, the four directions, the Pipe, or a sacred color.

Some of the necklaces represent the sunflower, which has traditionally been connected with the dance and grows in abundance in the Dakotas. Standing Bear tells how the sunflower was used by the Sioux in this dance: "They cut out a piece of rawhide the shape of a sunflower, which they wore on a piece of braided bucksin suspended around the neck, with the flower resting on the breast. It is the only flower that follows the sun as it moves on its orbit, always facing it."[5]

Contemporary pledgers who intend to be pierced with eagle claws wear the claws suspended on a cord around the neck—one for a single piercing, and two if they wish to be pierced on both sides at once.

The Intercessor may dress as he pleases, but most wear traditional garments such as buckskin leggings, breechclouts, and moccasins. Fools Crow sometimes wears a bone breastplate over his store-bought shirt and at other times wears his full ceremonial attire. He does what he feels is right for the moment but usually whatever he is wearing is topped off by his high-crowned, Navajo-style cowboy hat. Eagle Feather wears the leggings, a long red breechclout, beaded moccasins, and a necklace. His upper torso is bare. In 1974, he wore his double-tailed headdress for the first three days, and then tied a piece of red cloth around his head as a band for the last day. In 1975, he wore a braided headband all four days. It was fashioned from lengths of yellow and red cotton cloth, and I'm pleased to report that when the dance ended he gave it to me as a memento of the ceremony.

The Keeper of the Pipes and the Sweatlodge Custodian wear regular street clothes. There is nothing about their costume which would distinguish them from any of the male spectators. They do not wear paint.

When the male pledgers emerge from the sweatlodge their perspiration is so heavy that it is as if they had been doused with a garden hose. They dry themselves off with a towel and then go into the Tipi of Preparation. Here they put on their shirts and sage, fill their pipes, and then come outside where, on the third and fourth days, the Intercessor paints the men. The women are not painted at all, and at Rosebud, paint was applied to the men on the third and fourth days of the dance only.

Red is the nation's color, and in 1974 and 1975 at Rosebud the paint was put on with a red felt marking pen. This punctured my romantic ideas slightly, and I remembered having had the same feeling of disappointment when I watched the Apache at Fort Apache, Arizona, paint their Sunrise Ceremony tipi trees with a similar commercial instrument. I wish they still used the natural earth colors.

The pledgers stand erect to be painted, with the Intercessor simply moving around them as he carries out the task freehand. It is completed in a matter of minutes.

The paint for the pledgers' backs on the third day consists of a circle eight inches in diameter, with four short, straight lines like sun rays at the top. Seven dots are placed within the circle in such a way as to make the eyes, nose, and mouth of a face. Taken as a whole, the design is similar to the layout of the Old Man Four Generations fireplace, and it probably has the same meaning.

The paint placed on the pledgers' backs on the morning of the fourth day consists of a circle eight inches in diameter with a single dot in its center. This time the circle represents the Mystery Hoop of the nation, which is synonymous with the Sun Dance Mystery Circle. The dot stands for the Sacred Tree, which is the living center of the Hoop.

When the circles are done, the Intercessor begins at the shoulder and draws a carelessly applied zizzag line down each arm to the wrist. There is no forked line at the wrist, such as is usual when designs like this are intended to be lightning lines. Perhaps this is because tradition restricts use of the lightning line to thunder dreamers.

When the Intercessor is finished with their backs and arms, the men may or may not apply paint designs to their own chests. Among those symbols used by some in 1974 and 1975 were small red circles representing the sun, and a quarter moon done in blue and yellow.

BODY PAINT—Fools Crow

In describing the body painting done at Pine Ridge, Fools Crow said it was usually more extensive than that which I witnessed at Rosebud. He told me that for his modern-day Sun Dances the medicine men paint each man according to his vision. If, for example, a message came to a man through a buffalo, the upper portion of the man's body from the ribs up would be painted black and, below that, red. If the vision brought a message through thunder beings, lightning lines were painted on his arms, legs, chest, forehead, and the sides of his face. Other visions might call for spots to be painted all over the body.

In addition, Fools Crow has his assistants draw small red circles on the pledgers' chests to indicate where they will be pierced. For this, they use red earth paint Fools Crow received from an uncle in 1908; one circle is drawn on one side to indicate a single side piercing, and two circles if the man wishes to be pierced on both sides.

I was interested to note that while Eagle Feather did not follow the practice of using the red piercing circles in 1974, he did employ it in 1975.

Densmore's informants told her that men of known artistic ability were hired as body painters by the pledgers during the days before the ceremony, and that there was a prescribed ritual for this involving the use of a pipe.[6]

DECORATION OF CANDIDATES—James O. Dorsey and George Bushotter

The candidates spend the night in decorating themselves. Each one wears a fine scarlet blanket arranged as a skirt and with a good belt fastened around his waist. From the waist up he is nude, and on his chest he paints some design. Sometimes the design is a sunflower. A man can paint the designs referring to the brave deeds of his father, his mother's brother, or of some other kinsman, if he himself has done nothing worthy of commemoration. If a man has killed an animal, he can paint the sign of the animal on his chest, and some hold between their lips the tails of animals, signifying that they have scalped their enemies. Others show by their designs that they have stolen horses from enemies.

Each one allows his hair to hang loosely down his back. Some wear head-dresses consisting of the skins of buffalo heads with the horns attached. Others wear eagle war-bonnets. Each candidate wears a buffalo robe with the thick hair outside. He fills his pipe, which is a new one ornamented with porcupine quillwork, and he holds it with the stem pointing in front of him. Thus do all the candidates appear as they come out of the tent of preparation. As they march to the dancing lodge the leader goes first, the others march abreast after him. He who acts as leader carries a buffalo skull painted red.[7]

COSTUME AND BODY PAINT—Frances Densmore

On the morning of the Sun Dance those who were to take part in the ceremony were allowed to eat a full meal, after which they entered the vapor lodge while the following song was sung:

SONG OF FINAL VISIT TO THE VAPOR LODGE

> A voice
> I will send.
> Hear me
> The land
> All over.
> A voice
> I am sending.
> Hear me.
> I will live.

After their vapor bath, the dancers were painted by the men whom they had selected for that purpose. A few of the writer's informants stated that the bodies of the dancers were painted white on the first day of the ceremony, the colors being added on the morning of the second day, but others, including Red Weasel, stated positively that the painting in colors was done before the opening of the dance. Red Bird stated that each man who was accustomed to paint the dancers had a special color, which was "associated with his dream," and that he used this color first in the painting. The colors employed were red (the "tribal color"), blue, yellow, white and black, each color being a symbolism connected with the sky. Thus, it was said that red corresponds to the red clouds of sunset, which indicate fair weather; blue represents the cloudless sky; yellow, the forked lightning; white corresponds to the light; and black was used for everything associated with night, even the moon being painted black because it belonged to the hours of darkness.

Teal Duck stated that when he took part in the Sun Dance his face and body were painted yellow, with dark-blue lines extending down the arms and branching at the wrist to lines which terminated at the base of the thumb and the little finger. Similar lines extended down the legs, branching at the ankles. There was also a dark-blue line across his forehead and down each cheek. A black deer's head was painted over his mouth, the man who painted him saying that this decoration was used because the deer could endure thirst for a long time without losing its strength. On his chest was painted a red disk representing the sun, and outlining this disk he wore a hoop of wood wound with otter fur and decorated with four white eagle feathers tipped with black. On his back was painted a dark crescent representing the moon. Bands of rabbit fur were worn around the wrists and ankles.

Those who took part in the Sun Dance wore their hair loose on the shoulders after the manner of men who had recently killed an enemy. A lock of hair was tied at the back of the head and to this was fastened upright a white downy eagle feather. Small sticks about 8 inches long were also fastened in the hair, four being the usual number. These sticks were decorated with porcupine quills, beads, and tassels. A dancer was not allowed to touch his body during the ceremony, the decorated sticks being taken from his hair and used for this purpose.

No moccasins were worn by the dancers. Each man wore a white deerskin apron (*nité iyapehe*), which was fastened at the waist and extended below the knees both front and back; he had also a robe of buffalo skin in which he was wrapped while going to the Sun Dance circle and returning to his lodge. A whistle was hung around his neck by a cord. This whistle was made of the wingbone of an eagle, wound with braiding of porcupine quills and tipped with a downy white eagle feather fastened above the opening so that the breath of the dancer moved the snowy filaments. The mouthpiece was surrounded with fresh sage. The man blew this whistle as he danced. The instrument was decorated by the woman who decorated the Sun Dance pipe.

After being painted and arrayed, the men who were to take part in the ceremony assembled in the dancers' lodges of their respective bands and awaited the summons of the Crier.

The Leader of the Dancers was with the Intercessor in the council tent. His costume was not necessarily different from that of the dancers. Chased-By-Bears stated that when acting as Leader of the Dancers he was painted white with black streaks across his forehead and down his cheeks. The deerskin *nité iyapehe* which he wore was elaborately wrought with porcupine quills by the women among his relatives who wished to do the work, although such decoration was not required.

The costume worn by an Intercessor was somewhat similar to that of the dancers, but on his wrists and ankles he frequently wore bands of buffalo skin on which the hair was loosening, and his robe was the skin of a buffalo killed at the

The Cheyenne Sun Dance buffalo skull.

time when it was shedding its hair. Bits of hair shed by the buffalo were tied to his own hair, and he wore buffalo horns on his head, or he might wear a strip of buffalo skin fastened to his hair and hanging down his back. In contrast to the dancers his hair was braided, but like them he wore one white downy eagle feather. His face and hands were painted red. The costume of an Intercessor varied slightly with the individual. Red Weasel stated that he wore otter skin around his wrists and ankles, that the braids of his hair were wound with otter skin, and that he wore a shirt of buffalo hide trimmed with human hair, which was supposed to represent the hair of an enemy.

On the morning of the day appointed for the Sun Dance the Crier went around the camp circle, announcing the opening of the ceremony in the following words: "Now all come. Now it is finished. Hasten!"

In the procession which approached the Sun Dance circle the Intercessor was the most prominent figure, the others acting as his escort. The Intercessor held before him with uplifted stem his Sun Dance pipe, which would be smoked during the ceremony. The Leader of the Dancers walked beside him, carrying the ceremonial buffalo skull, which had been painted with stripes of red extending from the nostrils to the horns. Near him walked some close relative or friend, who carried the Leader's sealed pipe, which would be placed with the buffalo skull beside the square of exposed earth. Those who were to fulfill their vows walked on either side of the Intercessor and the Leader of the Dancers, and around them were the war societies and other organizations of the tribe. On reaching the entrance of the Sun Dance circle the procession paused. The Intercessor directed the attention of the people to the east, and it was understood that each man offered a silent prayer; this action was repeated toward the south, the west, and the north, after which they entered the enclosure. Amid impressive silence the procession passed along the southern "side" of the circle to the western "side," where the Leader of the Dancers, pausing, laid the buffalo skull on the bed of sage, with its face toward the east. He then placed his sealed pipe in its ceremonial position, the bowl resting on the buffalo skull and the stem supported by a slight frame of sticks painted blue, the mouthpiece of the pipe being extended toward the Sun Dance pole. When the Intercessor rose to sing or pray, he held this pipe in his hand, afterward replacing it in its ceremonial position; it was also extended toward the sky, the earth, and the cardinal points, but the seal on it was not broken until after the ceremony.

The pipe which was smoked at the ceremony was that of the Intercessor. He first burned sweet grass, the ascending smoke of which was said to symbolize prayer. Then he lit the pipe, and extended the stem toward the sky, the earth, and the cardinal points. The following explanation of this action was given by Charging Thunder: "When we hold the pipe toward the sky, we are offering it to *Wakan-tanka*. We offer it to the earth because that is our home and we are thankful to be here; we offer it to the east, south, west, and north because those are the homes of the four winds; a storm may come from any direction; therefore we wish to make peace with the winds that bring the storms." After this action, the Intercessor, having first smoked the pipe himself, offered it to the Leader and all the dancers. The procedure was repeated at infrequent intervals during the period of dancing.

Beside the Sun Dance pole the men who were to fulfill their vows stood facing the sun, with hands upraised. The Intercessor cried, "Repent, repent!", whereupon a cry of lamentation rose from the entire assembly.

The opening song of the ceremony was sung three times with a tremolo drumbeat, after which the drum changed to a definite, even stroke, and the men began to dance with faces still turned toward the sun and with hands upraised.

During the excitement of the opening dance many gifts were given to the poor or exchanged among the people and many paid their respects to the parents of young men who were taking part in the dance for the first time.

The drum used in the Sun Dance was placed south of the pole. It was a large dance drum of the usual type and elaborately decorated, the sides being hung with beadwork and fur, and the supports wound with beads and fur. In addition to the drum a stiff rawhide was beaten. This gave to the accompaniment of the songs a peculiar quality of tone, which marked a difference between that of the ordinary dances and that of a religious ceremony. The men who had carried the sacred pole were seated at the drum and the rawhide, together with special singers, both men and women, the latter sitting behind the men and forming an outer circle. The voices of the women singers were an octave higher than the voices of the men.

The Intercessor was seated west of the "sacred place" during the entire ceremony. The Leader of the Dancers was with the others who were fulfilling their vows, but during the brief periods of rest which were allowed the dancers he lay on the ground at the west of the "sacred place" face downward, with his head pressed against the top of the buffalo skull.

The man who had spoken the vow for a war party assumed some responsibility in the proper fulfillment of their vows, and the dancers were attended by the men who had painted them. All who took part in the dance were required to abstain from food and water during the entire period of dancing.[8]

XV
Sun Gazing and Dancing

EAGLE FEATHER

Now it was the morning of July 11, 1974, the first day of the Sun Dance. To begin each of the four days, the pledgers go into the sweatlodge. This ceremony may take an hour and a half. When they come out they get dressed and are painted. Then they start in single file for the arena, with the Intercessor going first, the men next, and the women last. On the way they stop four times, making their final stop at the east entrance.

Since we follow virtually the same procedure on each of the four days, I will describe a typical day. The dancers enter the Mystery Circle walking in a clockwise direction, and as they go in, the singers assemble and the Altar is being made up by one or more of the medicine men. It consists of a pipe rack and a buffalo skull. The pipe rack is made with two vertical branches called crutches which have a fork at the top and a horizontal branch across. The rack frame is made of cherry wood, and the numerous tiny white packets tied on the strings tied to the rack are flesh offerings wrapped in white cloth. The buffalo skull is put on the Altar because we remember it as one of the greatest things God provided for the Sioux. It was food for us, and the skin was used for our clothing. Many things came to us from the buffalo. This is why we remember it and try to take spiritual care of the buffalo even today.

The entering line of dancers stops in front of the Altar. There they are placed in a single line facing west toward the Altar, with the women at the north end of the line. Here the Intercessor leads them in a prayer to Almighty God about four special things. He says:

> Grandfather, the first and greatest thing you have put on this earth for us to care for, in the way you have instructed us, is the Peace (or Sacred) Pipe. You have put the Pipe on this earth for us to use in praying to you, and the Pipe is like our Jesus Christ; our Savior. Second, we remember the relationships that we have established with the other Indians and with the non-Indians, and also our need to uphold these relationships as you have asked us to do. Third, Grandfather, bless the earth, the herbs and the trees you have provided for us, and also the water we drink and use for purification. Give us the strength we need to care for this beautiful earth. Fourth, we remember the food that you have provided. Help us to not waste it foolishly, but to use it only as necessary to nourish our bodies and make them strong.

These are the four things it is our custom to pray about before we go through the Sun Dance.

Then the pipes are taken from each participant and leaned against the pipe rack. As the pipes are being put down, the singers start singing the first song. It is called the Entering Song or the

Starting Song. Then as they stand there other songs are chanted. The songs are mostly chanting. Meanwhile the dancers face west and blow on their whistles and try to see a vision in the clouds. Many great visions or spiritual helpers have been seen there, such as buffalo, horses, and men praying that are in need of help. And here eight songs are sung. Then we generally move the dancers to the north side of the Hoop. But just before we move them, because the two black flags are there at the west, we pray for the black people, and also for our loved ones that have passed away and gone on to the Happy Hunting Ground. Prayers are also made for all who have passed away, Indians and non-Indians alike. Then we are through there.

Now the dancers are moved in a clockwise circle to the north. Here two red flags are stuck in the ground to make the north a doorway. At this stop the dancers face north, away from the Tree, and look up and blow on their whistles while eight songs are sung by the singers. Visions are sought and prayers are made to the red color, which represents the red power. We are again reminded that red power is an investment by Almighty God in the entire human race, so prayers are made for the red race and the red power. We ask God and the power of the north to strengthen the red power and so on.

When the eight songs are finished, we move the pledgers to the east. Here they face east and look up into the sun.

The flags here are yellow. Since among other things the yellow represents the yellow race, it is also involved with red power. So we ask Almighty God to care for the yellow race as our brothers and sisters. While we are at the yellow color, one of the mystic things about the Sun Dance takes place. The Sun Dancers, you will notice, will be looking directly at the sun. As they do this they pray and cry many times, for they see visions in the sun. But don't get me wrong and believe that the sun is our God. We believe only in the same God the Christian worships and honors as Almighty God.

As to exactly what we think about the sun, it is very hard for us to explain. All I can say is that as we look into the sun, we see visions, many visions, and we do not all see the same visions. But as we stare into the sun and dance and pray, the glare and the reflection build until something, the power, hits you like a fire bolt. If you watch carefully you will see that all of the dancers seem to be hypnotized! At this moment they are all alone, and they pray passionately to Almighty God. Then as they look away from the sun and into the crowd, they do not see people there. Instead they see a black spot or a blue spot or some other color. Then when we rest we tell each other of these color spots we saw, and we look at the spectators to see who is sitting where the spots were. We know they need healing, and the color tells us what kind. And when a healing ceremony begins, these are always the people who come forth to be healed.

Let me insert something more here about the healing ceremony. I'm sure that the churches do something of this same nature. Our healing ceremony has to do with health, of the soul and the flesh. People who want to be healed go to yellow flags at the east side of the arena and form a single line facing the Tree. The dancers are moved to the east side of the arena and face east. Then each male and female dancer, led by the Intercessor, passes along the line of people, placing his or her hand on the head of each person. The Intercessor comes next to last, giving them a medicine herb to eat, and another medicine man finishes by blessing them with an eagle-feather fan. Then the people return to their seats and the dancers go back to the center of the arena, where each one dances and blows on his whistle.

During the first healing ceremony in 1974, there seemed to be a lot of clouds over the sun, and I wondered if it was important. On the third day of the dance, Titus and I were pierced at this time—right after the healing. I laid down the buffalo hide and the dancers faced me, blowing their whistles and dancing while I prayed with the Peace Pipe. As a representative of the young, Titus was pierced also—Titus and I will both pierce as long as we are alive and the Indian language and culture is alive. I used the sound system to announce to the spectators why he was going to pierce. Albert Stand pierced us with a knife. When Titus was cut, I helped him up and then put a stick through his skin to hold the rope. Titus danced and pulled on the rope until the stick broke loose. It didn't take him long. I pulled for quite a while before I broke mine too, and the flesh offering was finished for that day.

Besides the healing colors we see, after we look directly at the sun we are able to predict many things that will happen in the coming year. Eight songs are sung by the singers while we dance at the east, and then I move the line over to the south, facing south, away from the Tree. Two white flags mark the south, and the white color represents purification, wealth, and health. It also represents the White race, whom we are to accept as brothers and sisters, and we are reminded again at this time that they are also involved in the red power. So here prayers are made to the powers of the south for purification, for living together, and for our uniting under one God.

As the sixteenth song is being sung here, the leader generally takes the lead dancer's Peace Pipe from the Altar and goes to the four directions and prays. Then he brings it back and presents it to the first dancer in the line and says, "Here, cousin (or brother, whichever the case may be), are you ready to receive this Pipe that you should sincerely believe in, as Almighty God has taught you?" He nods his head in agreement, I give him the Pipe, and he carries it in both hands to the two white flags, where the medicine man who acts as the receiver of the pipes awaits him. In offering the Pipe he pretends he is going to give it three times, and each time the receiver pretends he will take it, but does not. In doing this the pledger asks, without actually speaking the words, "Are you sincere about receiving this Pipe? Let us move backwards before I present you with the Pipe."

The three make-believe gestures mean the following: the first time the question is, "Would you lie with this Pipe that I fake to you?" "I won't." The second time the question is, "Are you sincere in your belief that this Pipe is holy?" "I am." The third time the question is, "Do you believe our teachings as to why Almighty God put this Pipe here on earth?" "I do." The fourth time the Pipe is presented the dancer releases it to indicate that he now presents the Pipe to the receiver to be smoked.

After the Pipe is presented, the dancers retire to the shade area to rest and to talk over what has happened so far. This is why they rest. They sit down and they share their visions in a joking way, to make the trial of the dance a little easier. In a manner of speaking, this is like the congregation after the minister gives his sermon on Sunday morning. These are religious experiences they have had and visions they have seen. Then they start putting their visions together to make all they can out of their first session in the Mystery Hoop.

While the pledgers talk, the Pipe is being smoked by the medicine men and the singers, and the first of the pledgers is presented to the audience. This was not done years ago, but needs have changed. Today, when I am conducting a Sun Dance, I like to take the man that has just presented the Peace Pipe to the Receiver of the Pipes and have him get on the microphone and say what he believes about the value of the Sun Dance, what he can predict from his dreams and visions, and what his hopes and promises are for the future. Then the people can know what he has in mind, what his intentions are, and they can follow through and see how they turn out.

So while this is something that was not done many years ago, it is what I enjoy doing with the dancers during the four days of the dance. It gives them an opportunity to share their viewpoints concerning the Indian religion and culture. They can tell the audience what their visions and predictions are, what they have seen, and what they think. All this is brought to the attention of the people and I think this is great. It is my idea of the right way to run a modern Sun Dance. Some men do a good job with their presentation and some don't, but it is all worthwhile.

When the first man has finished his talk, the Peace Pipe is returned to the pipe rack and the dancers return to the west side of the Mystery Hoop. This time they are placed so that they are facing the Tree in the center of the circle. Sixteen songs are sung to begin this second session, and during this time they gaze at the Sacred Tree while they dance. They fix their eyes on the four colored banners that are hanging up there, and in time they begin to see visions in the Tree. Many visions are seen by the different dancers. While they do this I generally go to the microphone and remind the spectators why these long pieces of colored cloth are tied up there, and also talk about the meaning of the cloth offerings which are hung at the base of the Tree. Once more, prayers are made from that direction, the west. Here each dancer receives a message from the west and the Tree, and he communicates with the Tree about it from that direction.

When the sixteen songs are finished I move the dancers to the north side of the Tree and place them in a line facing it again. Now each man and woman communicates with the Tree about what he had visioned from the north during the first session, and also about the visions he is now receiving from the Tree as he faces it from that direction. Here, too, sixteen songs are sung.

Then we move the line of pledgers to the yellow flags at the east, and place them so they are facing the Tree from that direction. Now they talk with the Tree about the visions they received from the sun when they faced it while at the east, during the first trip around the Hoop. While they do this eight songs are sung.

Then we move the line to the south and do likewise, with the pledgers talking about the colors they have visioned and communicating with the Sacred Tree. So the line of dancers is always moved around the Hoop clockwise, everything goes clockwise. Finally, I rotate them back to the west direction where they began, and I position them facing south, toward the Tree and the sun. While they are standing there eight songs are sung, and at this time I generally take the Pipe and go to the colored flags at the four directions, praying with it to the powers of each of the directions. Then I take the second pledger's pipe from the rack and present it to him. He takes it, goes to the south, and after using the three fakes, presents it to the medicine man who receives the pipes. In turn, the pipe holder takes the pipe and gives it to the singers. This ends the second session.

The dancers go to the shade area to rest. They sit down, and once more share their visions and the things they have heard. They talk about this and they put it all together again—I guess I could say they try to "get it in line" and "in focus"—so they can make sense of it all and put it to use.

When they are through talking, the second pledger retrieves his pipe from the singers and brings it back. Then we put it on the pipe rack. After this we enter the Hoop again and move a little closer to the Sacred Tree. I generally split the pledgers up into groups of four, or groups of whatever size they may be when the full number of pledgers is divided by four. Then I place each group at a different direction, facing the Tree. A song is now sung while they meditate about the first visions they saw from the west and about the visions they saw in the Tree, and they communicate with the Tree about these things. Then the dancers are sent forward to the center of the Mystery Circle and up to the Tree itself.

Heartfelt prayers are said here as they go and physically touch the sacred source of the visions they have seen. They back up and return to place their hands on the Tree until they have touched it a total of four times. Eight songs are sung here by the singers, in one set, and then four more songs, and by the time this is done all of the pledgers will have touched their vision and communications center. In other words, you might say they have shaken hands with the Sacred Tree.

When they have backed away from the Tree four times, I line them back up again and take them clockwise to the west. Here I set them in the order they are to be given their pipe.

Now, while they dance, I take number three man's pipe and I go and pray with it to the four directions. Then I present it to him. Then once more we exit and return to the shade to sit and rest again. And here we talk about the communications we have had, the feeling of facing the Sacred Tree, and about what the visions mean.

So this is the way the Sun Dance is done each day. And when the Pipe has been smoked and returned we go back to the west position, facing west, and we begin again.

Now if my mind slips and I start to give the pipe to the wrong man, he generally refuses it, so I have to be very careful. We do now as we did before. The first time we go to the west, then we move to the north. However, as soon as we begin praying to the west, the man at the microphone announces that those in the audience who are sick and would like to be physically and spiritually healed are asked to come out to the yellow flags at the east side of the Mystery Circle.

From the north we go to the east, and when the songs stop, each dancer goes to the sick people, and if we have decided to give them herbs or roots, I generally give them the medicines. As the pledgers move along the line laying their hands on the people, prayer is made for each one for healing, because with these hands the dancers have touched the Sacred Tree, the Holy Tree, and their hands are holy and full of power. They put their hands on the head and the shoulders while they pray, and when each pledger has gone along the entire group, he gets back in line with the other dancers. When all of them have touched and prayed for every person, the healing ceremony is over.

Now we return to the dancing, and I continue moving them around the circle and exchanging the pipe and so on. This is the way the first day goes and, in a general way, each day that follows.

When number four pipe has been taken back we make flesh offerings. The old-timers generally pierce on the first day, and both they and the others make flesh offerings. Many of us have scars on our arms from these sacrifices. I generally make a vow to give two hundred flesh offerings every year. So now the flesh is removed and tied up in small bundles, and the prayer we make at this time goes like this: "Almighty God, I have shed tears. I have even walked in my tears, and I have shed blood. Today I offer you the flesh of my own

Bringing forward the pipe.

body. Almighty God, this is really all I have to offer that is of importance to you. My body is yours, my flesh is yours, my blood is yours, my tears are yours. You have helped me survive this long, and if you will, grant me more years to come. I ask you to answer my prayers, and I leave it in your hands. I shall patiently wait for the answer." These are the kinds of things which are said when the flesh offering is made.

As we continue with the sacrifices, the Sacred Pipe is sent around the assembled pledgers—I'm sure you understand by now that it is always moved clockwise. And here again, when we have the flesh offering, I frequently do something, as a result of a vision, that was not done years ago: I ask all the mothers at the Sun Dance to join with us in a special way. I ask them to come out in the center of the Hoop and to stand there. Then I have them raise their hands while I ask God to bless these hands that have done such thankless but needed works as making meals, mending our clothes, washing our clothes, and so forth. This is an hour in which we praise and honor all the mothers in the universe, including our four-legged and winged brothers and sisters, and the other creatures. This hour in which we pray for Sioux mothers, and in fact for all mothers, is something I didn't make up. I was instructed to do it during a vision quest. And I have tried to put it into a form which causes the Indians and non-Indians present to think about how important a mother is. The Sun Dance touches on everything that matters. If our younger generation could only see how important a mother is, and understand why she says, "Don't do that, or that isn't good," this would be a far better world for us to live in.

I always urge the mothers to raise their hands as high as they can, and while they pray I ask Almighty God to, in the same zeal they are reaching up, help and guide them as mothers, and to give them special strength for their task. The mothers themselves pray touching prayers. I remember one who said, "I used to be a drunkard and a bad mother. But I know now that the greatest honor and pleasure I have had is that of being a mother to my children. And I didn't know how important the word 'mother' was until I found you. So continue to guide me, and help me to be a real good mother to my children." That is just an example of the things the mothers pray about out there.

When this is over and the circle of pledgers has been made with the Peace Pipe, we go to the microphone and tell the people about the old-timers who are going to pierce. We also call upon the Mother of the Year to say something. Each year we try to select a Mother of the Year. This is another thing that I have been told to do in my vision, and I have tried to put it to good use. When the piercing is taking place I have the Mother of the Year sit there with us and comfort the suffering men. She does this by putting her hand on their forehead, holding their hand, and wiping off blood with sage and rags. In my vision I saw that when Christ was taken down from the Cross, his mother was there to comfort Him. Then, after the men break loose from the Tree, I try to get their own mothers to go to them with a cloth to wipe the tears from their eyes and also the blood off their chest. They also comfort them with words.

In the piercing the flesh is cut pretty deep, and it is cut with a knife. Then a pin or an eagle claw is inserted and the rawhide is tied to it. The white substance in the paper cup which we keep at the base of the Tree is lard. We use it to grease the stick that is inserted into the dancer's skin so it can slide through easier. The wooden skewer sticks used for piercing are made of ash and cedar; cherry wood has been tried, but has a sticky surface which makes it more difficult to insert. Then we tie the rawhide rope onto the stick, and we also tie a knot between the skin and the stick. Some call it skin and some say flesh—it all depends on how deep you've been gotten. I was pierced pretty deep there in 1974, and I had an awful time pulling it loose. If it was just under my skin I'd have pulled loose right away. So a rawhide is tied between the skin of the man and the pin, which draws it up very tightly, and then the man is stood up on his feet. I didn't use a wooden pin in 1974, I used an eagle claw. The eagle claws used in piercing are a recent innovation. They are employed by some dancers today because the Sioux believe that the eagle was the first messenger to be sent by God to the people.

I repeat that we do not use antiseptic or anesthetic to cleanse the wound or to dull the pain. And it is very painful, believe me, it is very painful! I have gone through twenty-five piercings, and I know.

After the Sun Dance is over it is our custom to go into the sweatlodge, where the medicine men put herbs on the pledgers' wounds, using the heat also to draw out the pus. I cannot tell people exactly how we draw the pus out, because that's another sacred thing to us, and I shouldn't be revealing such things. However, I will say that a certain herb is used inside the sweatlodge to take the swelling down and to take the pain away. The manner of treatment depends upon the reaction the pledger has had to his piercing. Some have the smoke from burning sweet grass blown on their wounds, but most have a small herb rubbed on the torn places and then have dirt rubbed on them. Doctors once claimed that because of my diabetes I was certain to get gangrene in my wounds, but that has not happened.

Some men are pierced deeply and some not so deeply. You ought to hear some of the fellows plead when they are lying down there to be pierced! Some cry, "Don't pierce me too deeply, just pierce me a little bit." There is a way you can tell how deeply a person is being pierced. When he pulls back on the thing he is fastened to, you will notice that it sometimes snaps clear back to the tree and even beyond that. When you see that happen, the man was pierced pretty deeply. On the other hand, when you see that the minute he pulls on the rope it just tears off and falls where he's standing, then you can know that he hasn't been pierced very deeply. These are things not many spectators know. Standing on the sidelines, they can't see how deep the pledgers are pierced.

However, this pleading is understandable. A fellow has got to look at it like this: In any church there are some who come to the services just to put on good clothes and make an impression. So, too, now and then we have a few pledgers in the Sun Dance who are there just to put on a show. Misguided people exist in the church or out of the church, and also take part in the Sun Dance.

I have been asked whether there is any conversation during the piercing. You bet your life the men talk to us when they are being pierced. They pray ardently, they groan, some beg. And they get excited. All the men are excited when they are lying down and have the sage or something else in their mouth so they can have something to bite on to ease the pain. Unless you know how to do it, the hardest thing imaginable is to pierce a person when he is tense. It's very hard to pierce then because you have to pull the flesh up to put the pin through. But I've grown wiser over the years. The more they tighten up, the better it is for me. I just take a small knife, make two little parallel cuts on each side, and then put the pins or claw through.

It hurts plenty when the stick or claw is pushed through. So before the insertion, either two small vertical gashes are made with a commercial knife or, if the skin can be pulled up, the knife is pushed through to make a hole. The modern knife is less painful than the bone knife used in ancient days and thus has replaced it.

There's a lot of talking and a lot of praying that goes on out there at the Tree, and there is plenty of commotion that the spectators don't hear. How the men hang on to you when they are pierced! Sometimes they will grab your leg or your arm and just about break it off. This is where the great showdown is!

We do a lot of praying there for them, and we give them all the encouragement we can, yet each man should have had that encouragement built up in him before he started the Sun Dance.

The dancers do not gather together to talk or to do anything else at night during the four days of the dance. They gather at meals and may discuss problems that come up, but otherwise they meditate or pray.

I have been asked about fasting. The old-timers did fast, but as I said, times are changing. Today we are just like a bunch of cattle in a stockyard getting ready for market, being fed cattle food. And our bodies do not have the nourishment our older people once had. They were able to continue from sunup to sundown. We're not able to make it from four o'clock in the morning until noon. The 1974 dancers did not abstain entirely from food and water. They fasted from midnight until twelve o'clock noon. Then they ate lunch and dinner, and did other things until midnight, when they quit eating and drinking water again. They followed that plan from day to day.

We generally dance each day till noon and at twelve o'clock food is served. On the second day we follow about the same procedure, except that on this day we invite the people with especially serious problems to come out in the center and to pray with us with the Peace Pipe.

Everything went as we planned it in 1974, and it came out well. I don't think we ran into any serious trouble at all. We were told that the American Indian Movement people planned to come over and boycott us and all that. Instead they came and gave us a mighty big helping hand. Perhaps that was an answer to the prayers of our cloth offerings that were tied to the Tree.

I was very happy about the ceremony when it was over. Of course, what one thinks about it is conditioned by his understanding. For some, and particularly for non-Indians, a Sun Dance is as puzzling as your church service would be for my great-grandmother. She would hear the organ, and the choir singing, and she would have a difficult time understanding what was going on. I'm sure the non-Indian feels the same way when he comes without understanding to the Sun Dance, hears the songs and beating of the drum, the whistles being blown, and sees the flesh offerings.

To even begin to appreciate what the ceremony means, people would have to understand—I mean sincerely understand—what the Sun Dance is and why it is called the Sun Dance. Actually, its Indian name, *Wiwanyag Wachipi*, translates as "Sun gazing and dancing." It brought great blessings to most of those who shared in it in 1974; you can feel the spiritual power surging within you when you are there.

A few of the participants did have some troubles after the dance. Here again, we are not alone in this. Some church people will come and vow, with good intentions, "Reverend, I'm not going to drink any more and I'm never going to do this or that. I'll never lie and or steal again." Well, we have them here too. Many of them have made their Sun Dance vow saying, "Bill, I'm never going to steal again and I'm never going to drink anymore." And boy, the next time I see them on the street they are drunker than a hoot owl. But these are the things that happen, and we have to learn to live with it just as ministers, and unchurched peoples also, must do. We do this from one day to the next in the best way we can, rather than to tear one another down. Things are hard enough without that. We do what we can as brothers and sisters; we keep on trying to unite under one God. This is the way that I look at the situation.

One pledger or another might have trouble after the Sun Dance because he didn't do the dance with a good heart. Once again, it is probably this way in other churches, too. Some prayers are being answered and some are not; some people are happy when they come out of church, and some are not. It's the same way with our Sun Dance. Some come away from the dance with great feelings in their heart, and some leave it with a broken heart. You know how it is. You pray for different ones, and the first thing you know something goes wrong or someone dies. Then some will say, "Well, the reverend didn't pray right so the person died." We have that situation here too. Now and then word comes to me that someone has said, "Eagle Feather didn't pray like he should out there at the Sun Dance; this is why my uncle and my brother died." But no matter, we all have to keep our faith and hope in Almighty God. I sincerely believe that.

I have read what others have said about the Sun Dance, and I have talked to a great many people about it. I have lectured in colleges, schools, and among my own people. I have taught a lot of young people and old people, including non-Indians. There are many I have taught and worked with. And I feel good about it.

I don't make the decisions to have the Sun Dance ceremony. Somebody comes in and says, "I have vowed to Almighty God to do the Sun Dance and the vision quest." This is how these things begin.

I learned nearly everything I know about the Sun Dance from Frank Fools Crow, an Oglala, who is the Ceremonial Chief of the Teton Sioux. Fools Crow was eighty-two years old in 1974, and lives near Kyle, on the Pine Ridge Reservation, South Dakota.

Now I'll answer some of the questions that you have asked at different times. Thomas Mails has asked me about what happened to the young girl he saw me praying for out there with the Peace Pipe, and how it affected her. The doctor had said she was dying, and she is doing very well and seems to be in good health today. In fact, she will be participating out there in the 1975 Sun Dance. However we have lost two others. Mrs. Picket Pin, the lady that went out there in a wheel chair to be healed, is now no longer with us. She passed away in January. And another lady that made a Sun Dance vow, a little short woman, Mrs. Vera Eagle Roach, is no longer with us. She passed away here at St. Francis in March.

So two people who were involved in the 1974 dance healing ceremonies have passed away. Another one, Mrs. Lorene Metcalf, gave food and didn't come out there to be doctored, and she has passed away with cancer. Two of these ladies passed away with cancer, and Mrs. Eagle Roach died from a heart attack. These three have passed away, but I haven't heard of any of the others passing away that we have had the healing ceremony with. The lady that had prayed with the Peace Pipe out there in the center of the circle is doing very well. Her name is Mrs. Matilda Brayes.

We still have the problem of C.Q., the gentleman that quit on us. He had vowed to pierce every year, and I still have his Peace Pipe hanging here in my house, his whistle, and his costume. But he said that the Indian religion was only good for him for three weeks, and the White man's religion was no good at all, so I don't know how you would describe his condition. I think the demons had hold of him for a while. However, he has licked his alcohol problem,

Straining to break free from the Sun Dance rope.

even though he said, "No more of this Indian religion or the White man's religion for me." I cornered him the other day here and told him, "Well, C.Q., you know what I'm going to have to do. I'm an old man of sixty-one, and here you are a very strong young man who has vowed to Almighty God to pierce every year, so I guess I'm going to have to pierce for you this year. Maybe I'll have to do it for you."

So these are some of the results of the 1974 Sun Dance. In fact, many of the things we prayed for and visioned out there have already happened. The Police Department, as I said before, put up the cloth offering banners as prayers for peace, and visions were seen in the Tree regarding them that are coming to pass. You might have heard that an American Indian Movement leader is said to have committed murder, and that another AIM leader is being held in jail. In fact, many of the American Indian Movement leaders who cause continual trouble are beginning to fall by the wayside. And while the AIM movement does some good things, we are hoping that this will continue to happen to some of its leaders, so that we can unite and not fight one another. Then we can work together as brothers and sisters as the four colors tell us we should, teaching us what the real red power is. It has been seven months since the policemen made their prayers and statements, and it's going to have to come out as their prayers said it should.

We also had Sun Dance visions which told us that President Richard Nixon was going to resign from office, and we learned that he was going to pass away before long. We also knew that Onassis was going to go. These predictions were made at the 1974 dance. Another prediction made there at the Sun Dance was that the meningitis disease would soon spread throughout the country. At the same time here, an herb was shown to us in a vision to use for treating this meningitis. My wife, Hazel, has the disease now; she was in the BIA hospital with it and came out without being helped, but she is starting to feel better because of this herb she is taking.

These are some of the predictions that were made as a result of our visions, some of which are beginning to surface and beginning to go the way we were told they would at the Sun Dance. So I think I have brought out fairly well how the Sun Dance is done today, and your understanding and my understanding of it should be about the same. As I have said in the beginning, I studied to be a lay reader in the Episcopal Church, and I was baptized and married there. And I sincerely believe in Almighty God in both the non-Indian and Indian ways, because we pray to one and the same God. For this reason I wish other ministers and myself and some of the others could sit down and thrash out what red power really means. Then we could have better understanding and better communication, and look each other in the eye and say in a meaningful way, "Brother."

Now I've been asked to comment about the great Oglala Sioux medicine man, Black Elk, and changes which have taken place in the Sun Dance. Black Elk has told us a few things about how the Sun Dance was done in his time. However, in both the churches and the Indian religion there has been tremendous change. The world and man's needs are constantly changing, too, so some of the customs that Black Elk talks about are not being done as they once were. However, we do try to follow the old ways as much as we can.

Part of this came about because back in the late eighteen hundreds the government stopped the Sioux from practicing their culture and their religion. So, you see that many of the changes were forced upon us, and others have happened because things aren't as they once were anymore. Some of the changes that are being made today are the result of our work with other churches, and our coming to realize that we both believe in the same person, Almighty God. But progress is slow. Friction between the Roman Catholic clergy and the Indians about our 1975 dance caused us to move from our preferred location at St. Francis to the Rosebud fairground. A few of the things we do differently now have resulted from the mixture of the non-Indian culture and the Indian culture. You must remember that at the time period described in the book, *Black Elk Speaks,* the Sioux were still quite isolated and there was very little mixture of Sioux and non-Indian ideas.

But the non-Indian is the dominant factor in religion now and must be dealt with accordingly. There are many denominations and different religious organizations, and we are continually seeking to understand more of the non-Indian culture, and at the same time attempting to discover how we can all unite in common purpose under one God. In fact, some of this striving toward unity was predicted by Black Elk and is coming to pass now. So I've always described these changes as "the echoes of *Black Elk Speaks.*"

The Sioux are beginning to comprehend these ancient prophecies of Black Elk and other holy men. However, we recognize the need to vision quest more about them as well as the need to vision quest together. Then it will be necessary to discuss the visions we have received, just as this is being done in the modern Sun Dance.

As to the effectiveness of the Sun Dance today, and its future, in my time I have been in twenty-five Sun Dances and I've conducted quite a few of them. In addition, I have had the honor of being made a chief of the Sioux Nation Sun Dance, Incorporated. As all the medicine men do, I have also trained many people. However, just as is the case with the non-Indian religions, many of the youngsters we have trained in religion are wandering off to worldly things; smoking marijuana, drinking, and having a good time. So it's very hard for us to avoid giving people the impression that we are not saying enough and we're not doing enough in the Sun Dance. And we do admit in the sweatlodge and our conversations that we are not all working together as we should under one God. However, we do criticize each other and we do attempt to evaluate our work from time to time. Some of this takes place when we pray to the Sacred Tree and to the different directions for guidance and instruction. But spiritual education as a whole is not what it ought to be today. All we need to do is compare it with the education of years and years ago and consider how things have changed.

Yes, many things have changed in both the non-Indian and the Indian religions. So all I can give you today is my vision and my view of the world we now live in. Even more dramatic changes are ahead of us. I have seen the following in a Sun Dance vision and therefore predict that it will come to pass. Millions of people are starving today in Asia and the Orient, and within the next few decades this same thing is going to happen here in our own beloved United States. Things will get to a point where the government will control everything, and one result will be that in desperation we are going to starve each other out. In ever-increasing measure the poor people will not get the proper nourishment. In fact you already find it happening in our big cities; in the slum areas and on skid row.

And I'll tell you something else, I believe the psychiatrists of today, through their books and teachings, are going to ruin this beautiful world of ours if we do not get rid of them. We can live without them. Your White grandparents, my Indian grandparents, and our great-grandparents lived without psychiatrists, and look how beautiful their world was by comparison. Psychiatrists are tearing this beautiful country apart.

Another vision I have had is of men throwing a huge bomb up at the moon one day. It will blow a hole through the crust and there will be water up there. When human beings have completely ruined this world they will move up to the moon and stay there for a number of years until they finally spoil it. Then they will be forced to come back to this dirty world they ruined. This is my vision, and even though I hate to tell it, I just can't help it, for this is the way it will be for our world.

Perhaps, though, we deserve such a fate. We want to know too much and we constantly try to advance ourselves at the expense of others in every way. But whatever we think we are, without God we're nothing. We must have Almighty God in us at all times, and perhaps we ought to remember this when we cut ourselves and the red power starts coming out. For it is only then that we pray desperately, "God help me, help me, I need help!" But you know and I know that we cannot get God's help the moment we need it unless we are prepared. I must prepare myself. I must get myself ready. We must all be prepared by remaining close to Him.

THE SUN DANCE STEP AND MUSIC—Thomas E. Mails

In dancing, the male pledgers assume a standing position and dance in place. Their bodies are straight, chests thrust slightly forward, and their arms are held close at their sides. Their heads are at a slight angle toward the sky with the chin protruding, and while they dance they blow sharp, high-pitched blasts on their eagle-bone whistles.

The dance step for most consists of a simple rising on the balls of the feet and then dropping down again in time to the music. Now and then a passionate young pledger will hop energetically back and forth from one foot to the other, much like a boy might do who stepped barefoot on hot concrete. At intervals, in response to the Intercessor's command, the dancers raise both hands to the sky in supplication, and then lower them to their sides again.

The women perform in a more demure fashion, using the same rising and falling movement but in a less energetic manner. They do not bounce around. Their eyes are usually downcast, but their heads are not bent downward. They also raise their hands to the sky at intervals.

On the whole, the dance as done today is not as exhausting an experience as it was when the dancing was more continuous and lasted all day long. There are frequent intermissions and interruptions which allow the dancers to rest, and each day's performance, beginning at about 8 A.M., terminates no later than noon.

A Sioux elder who stopped by a Mission, South Dakota, restaurant one day during the 1975 dance expressed his utter disgust over the fact that the dancers rested so frequently, and in the shade. "It's not," he said, "like the old days when men really suffered!" But he did not say whether he had ever danced or pierced.

Perhaps the modern Sun Dance is not so challenging as the older form. Yet it is no picnic either. The pledgers perform diligently when they are dancing, and the overall effect upon them is somewhat conditioned by how hot it is. July and August days in South Dakota can be miserable even without dancing under the blazing sun for four straight hours. The dancers are usually barefooted, too, and the sticky burrs on the ground can cut their feet badly.

One day I asked Orrie Farrell how the burrs felt, and he replied with a grin that they only made him step higher. Yet I saw the evidence of plenty of sore and cut feet as some of the men winced while walking gingerly around in the afternoons.

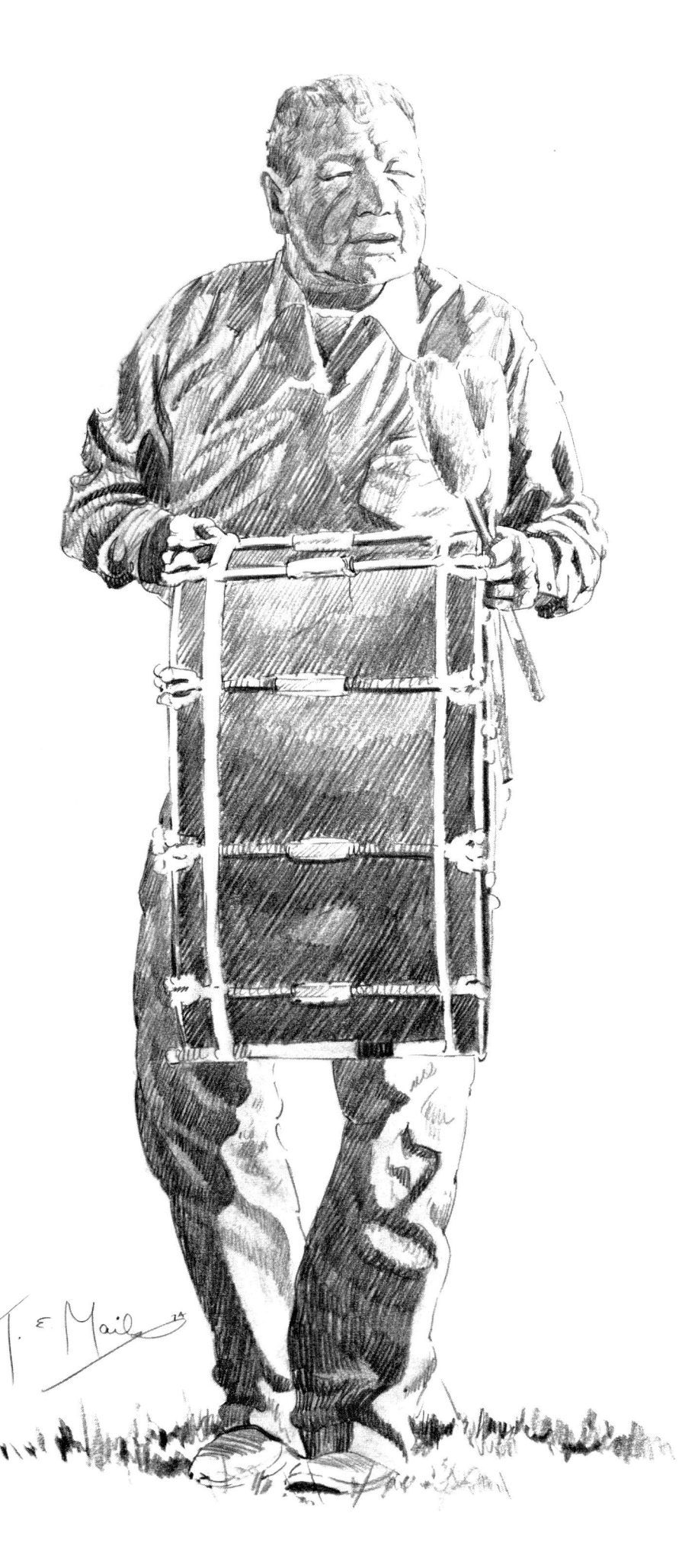

The lead singer bringing in the drum on the first morning of the Sun Dance in 1974.

The music for the Sun Dance is provided by singers and a single drum. In the old days, the drum was a large dried and flat piece of rawhide. Today a regular commercial drum, like that employed by dance bands, is used. Black Elk says: "The voice of the drum is an offering to the spirit of the world. Its sound arouses the mind and makes men feel the mystery and power of things."[1]

Singing groups range in number from three to eight. A basic group is arranged for by the Intercessor, and anyone else who is qualified may join in as he wishes. The group's payment consists of a share in the food and the income of the dance. It is not uncommon for the Intercessor himself, along with other medicine men, to sit in for a while to spell the regular singers or to pick up the tempo.

All of the singers sing, while from two to four of them beat the drum with padded sticks at the same time. The singers wear their regular dress clothing, which often consists of a brightly colored shirt, Levi's, and a cowboy hat with an ornate headband.

Sun Dance songs are considered sacred and taping by the public is frowned upon. The dance leaders usually specify that no one is to bring tape recorders to the Sun Dance, although the medicine men and some pledgers have in the past taped parts of the music, and such tapes are in existence.

By and large, the tempo of the music is not as quick as one hears for the fancy dancing at powwows. It is a measured rhythm, one to which the pledgers can keep time in their vertical movements. Now and then the tempo will increase slightly, and at such times the Intercessor will usually issue a command to the pledgers to stretch their arms and hands up toward the sun in prayer.

A detailed analysis of Sioux music, and particularly that of the Sun Dance, is beyond the scope of my qualifications. For this purpose I recommend what I believe to be a fine book in all respects, *Songs of the Teton Sioux* by Harry W. Paige. *Teton Sioux Music*, by Frances Densmore, is also of value for such investigations.

CAPT. BOURKE ON THE SUN DANCE—James O. Dorsey

After the reading of the paper, Capt. John G. Bourke, U.S. Army, remarked that he had seen the Sun Dance of the Dakota several times, and once had enjoyed excellent opportunities of taking notes of all that occurred under the superintendence of Red Cloud and other medicine men of prominence. Capt. Bourke kindly furnished the author with the following abstract of his remarks on this subject:

In June, 1881, at the Red Cloud Agency, Dakota, there were some twenty-eight who went through the ordeal, one of the number being Pretty Enemy, a young woman who had escaped with her husband from the band of Sitting Bull in British North America, and who was going through the dance as a sign of grateful acknowledgment to the spirits.

The description of the dance given in the account of Bushotter tallies closely with that which took place at the Red Cloud Agency, with a few immaterial exceptions due no doubt to local causes.

At Red Cloud, for example, there was not a separate buffalo head for each Indian; there were not more than two, and with them, being placed erect and leaning against a frame-work made for the purpose, several elaborately decorated pipes, beautiful in all that porcupine quills, beads, and horsehair could supply. Buffaloes had at that time disappeared from the face of the country within reach of that

Page 157:
The piercing of Robert Blackfeather. Oil painting by author.

Page 158:
Pulling back on the rope. Oil painting by author.

Page 159:
Gilbert Yellow Hawk. Oil painting by author.

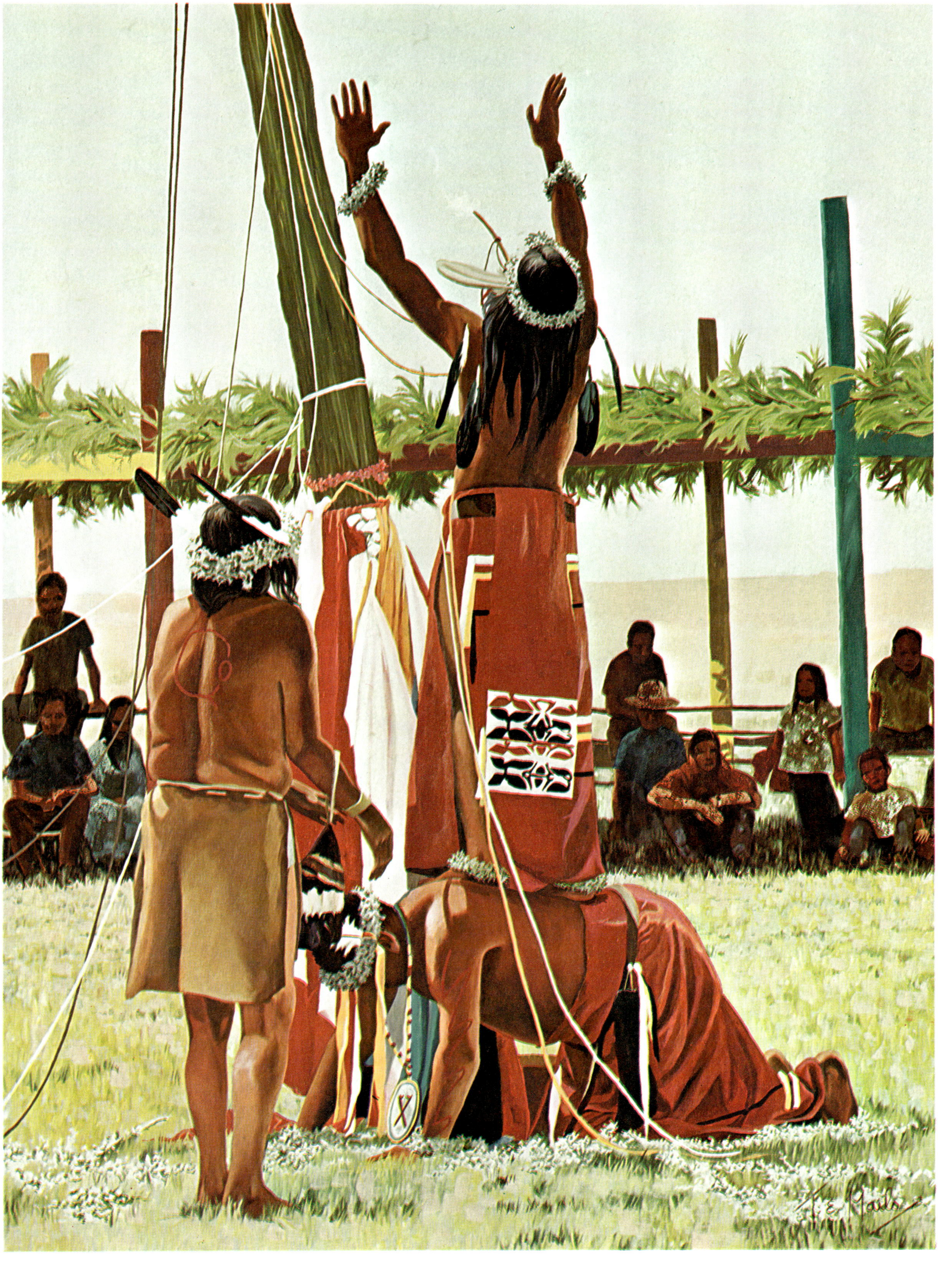

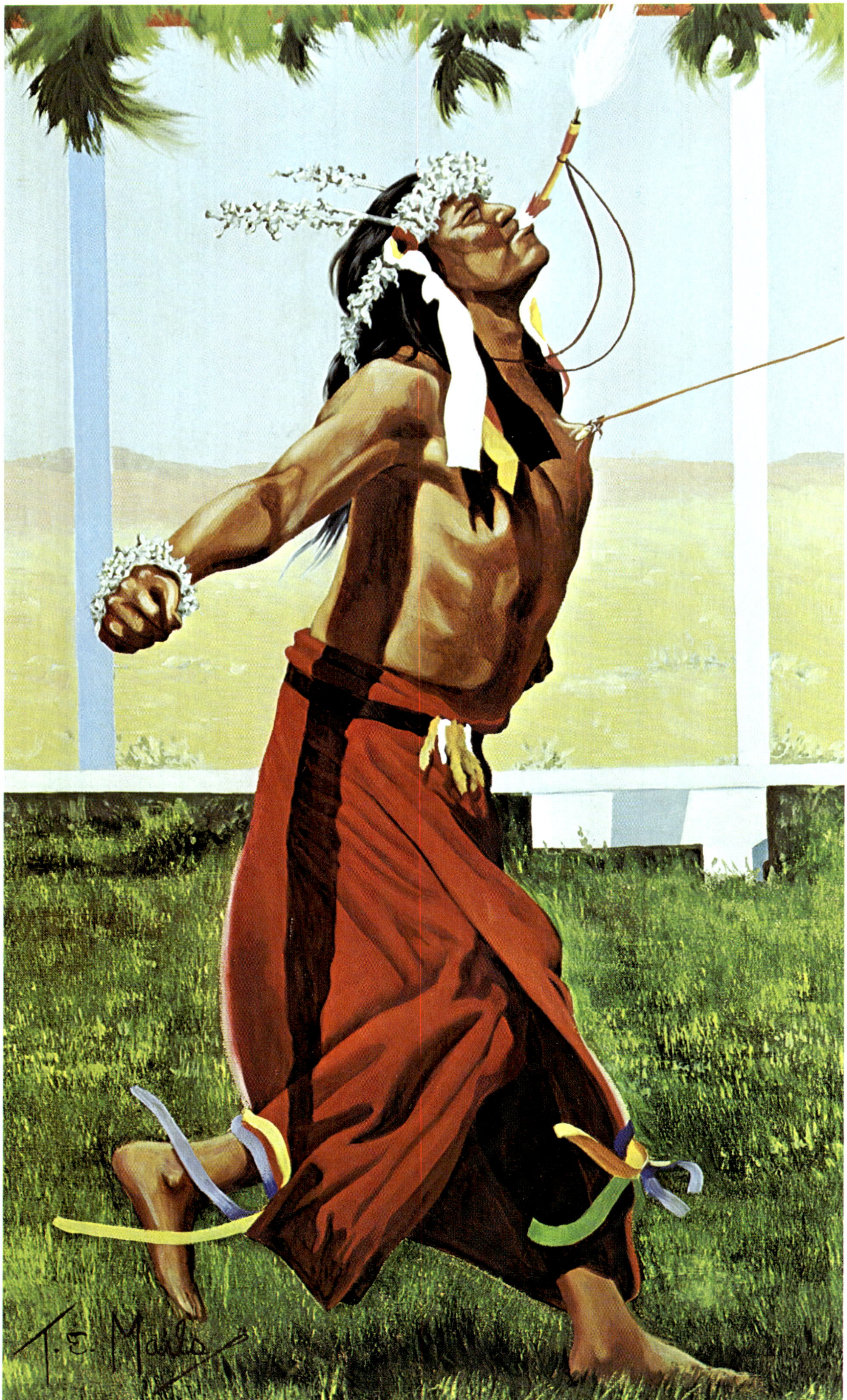
T. E. Mails

159

*Going forward to touch the Sun Pole.
Oil painting by author.*

agency, and there was also an increasing difficulty in the matter of procuring the pipestone from the old quarries over on the Missouri River.

First, in regard to securing the Sacred Tree, after the same had been designated by the advance party sent out to look for it. The medicine men proclaimed to the young warriors that all they were now to do was just the same as if they were going out to war. When the signal was given, the whole party dashed off at full speed on their ponies, and as soon as we arrived at the Tree, there was no small amount of singing, as well as of presents given to the poor.

Next, a band of young men stepped to the front, and each in succession told the story of his prowess, each reference to the killing or wounding of an enemy, or to striking coup, being corroborated by thumping on the skin which served the medicine men as a drum.

The first young man approached the Sacred Tree, swung his brand-new ax, and cut one gash on the east side; the second following precisely the same program on the south side; the third, on the west side, and the fourth, on the north side, each cutting one gash and no more.

They were succeeded by a young maiden, against whose personal character, it was asserted, not a breath of insinuation could be brought, and she was decked in all the finery of a long robe of white antelope skin almost completely covered with elks' teeth, as well as with beads. She seized the ax, and, with a few well-directed blows, brought the Tree to the ground.

In carrying the Tree to the camp it was placed upon skids, no one being allowed to place a hand upon the Tree itself. Upon reaching the summit of the knoll nearest the camp the Tree was left in charge of its immediate attendants while the rest of the assemblage charged at full speed upon the camp itself.

When the Tree had been erected in place, it was noticed that each of those who were to endure the torture had been provided with an esquire, while there was also a force of men, armed with guns to preserve order, criers to make proclamations, and heralds and water-carriers armed with long staves tipped with bead-work and horse-hair. These water-carriers did not carry water for the men attached to the Tree, they were not allowed to drink, but if they happened to faint away the medicine men would take a mouthful of water apiece and spray it upon the body of the patient, producing coldness by the evaporation of the water.

All the Indians on that occasion were attached to the Tree itself by long ropes of hair or by thongs fastened to skewers run horizontally under the flesh.

The young woman, Pretty Enemy, was not tied up to the Tree, but she danced with the others, and had her arms scarified from the shoulders to the elbows. All this scarification was done by a medicine man, who also slit the ear of the babies born since the last Sun Dance.

The young men were scarified in the following manner: Their attendants, whom I have called esquires, seized and laid them on a bed of some sagebrush at the foot of the Sacred Tree. A short address was made by one of the medicine men; then another, taking up as much of the skin of the breast under the nipple of each dancer as could be held between his thumb and forefinger, cut a slit the length of the thumb, and inserted a skewer to which a rope was fastened, the other end of the rope being tied to the Tree.

The young men placed eagle pipes, as they were called, in their mouths. These pipes were flutes which were made from one of the bones in the eaglet's wing. They had to be sounded all the time the young man was dancing. This dancing was done in the manner of a buck jump, the body and legs being stiff and all movement being upon the tips of the toes. The dancers kept looking at the sun, and either dropped the hands to the sides in the military position of "attention" with the palms to the front, or else held them upward and outward at an angle of 45 degrees, with the fingers spread apart, and inclined towards the sun.

When laid on the couch of sagebrush before spoken of, each young man covered his face with his hands and wailed. I was careful to examine each one, and saw that this wailing was a strictly ceremonial affair unaccompanied by tears.

Before approaching the Tree the victims were naked, with the exception of blue cloth petticoats and buffalo robes worn with the fur outside, giving them the appearance of monks of the olden time. The buffalo robes were, of course, thrown off when the young men were laid on the sagebrush preparatory to the scarification. One young man was unable to tear himself loose, and he remained tied up to the Tree for an hour and seven minutes by my watch. He fainted four times. The medicine man put into his mouth some of the small red, bitter, salty seeds of the Dulcamara, while the women threw costly robes, blankets, articles of bead-work and quill-work, and others of the skin of the elk and antelope upon the rope attaching him to the Tree, in the hope of breaking him loose. The articles thus attached to the rope were taken away by the poor for whom they were given. There was any amount of this giving of presents at all stages of the dance, but especially at this time, and the criers were calling without ceasing. "So and so has done well. He is not afraid to look the poor women and children in the face! Come up some more of you people! Do not be ashamed to give! Let all the people see how generous you are!" or words to that effect. (I had to rely upon my interpreter, who was reputed to be the best and most trustworthy at the agency.)

One of the prime movers in the organization of this particular dance, Rocky Bear, at the last moment, for some particular reason, decided not to go through the terrible ordeal. He explained his reasons to the tribe, and was excused. He gave presents with a lavish hand, and it was understood that on some subsequent occasion he would finish the dance. There was no sign of dissatisfaction with his course, and everyone seemed to be on the best of terms with him. All through the ceremony there was much singing by the women and drumming by the medicine men, and a feast of stewed dog, which tastes very much like young mutton, was served with boiled wild turnips.

By a comparison of the accounts of Miss Fletcher, Capt. Bourke, and Bushotter it will be noticed that while there are several points of disagreement which, as Capt. Bourke remarks, are "due no doubt to local causes" the accounts are in substantial agreement. Miss Fletcher says that the opening of the camp circle was toward the east; but Bushotter gives it as toward the north. She states that the tent of preparation was erected on the first day after sunset but Bushotter says it was set up on the fourth day. She represents the selection of the men who go to seek the Tree, the departure to fetch the Tree, the felling of the Tree, the bringing it and setting it up within the camp circle, as all taking place on the fourth day. Bushotter states that the men were selected on the third day; they went to seek the Tree on the fourth day; they went to fell the Tree on the fifth day, and on the same day they brought it to the camp and set it in place. Capt. Bourke saw four men and one girl employed in felling the Tree. Miss Fletcher mentions that five men and three girls did this in 1882; but Bushotter recorded that several men and women took part in this performance. The ears of the children were pierced on the fourth day after the raising of the sun pole, according to Miss Fletcher; but Bushotter says that this did not occur till after the devotees had been scarified and fastened to the pole and posts, on the sixth day. Bushotter agrees with Miss Fletcher in saying that on the sixth day the earth was "mellowed," the devotees scarified, and they danced with the thongs fastened to the pole, etc., attached to the skewers running under their flesh.[2]

FORMS OF TORTURE AND EAR PIERCING—
Frances Densmore

Women sometimes took part in the Sun Dance by fasting and standing beside some relative who was dancing, or by assuming part of the obligation of a vow made by some relative and permitting their arms to be cut. The gifts distributed by relatives of the dancers and the feasts given in their honor were also the work of the women.

Even the simplest form of the Sun Dance was a severe test of a man's endurance. He was required to abstain from food and water, to dance with face upraised to the sun from morning until night, and to continue dancing during the night and on the following day until he fell exhausted.

If he had vowed to have his arms cut, he left the line of dancers and seated himself beside the pole for the operation, after which he resumed his dancing. The number of cuts varied from 10 to 100 or even 200, according to the man's vows, though if the vow required the larger numbers named part of the number was usually assumed by his relatives. The cutting was done by a man of experience, to whom the dancer gave one or more horses. The man had an assistant, who lifted a small portion of flesh on the point of an awl, whereupon the man then severed it with a quick stroke of a knife, lifting the first portion which he cut toward the sky, saying, "This man promised to give you his flesh; he now fulfills his vow." The cuts were usually placed close together. The writer has seen the scars of a man whose arms were cut 100 times—small dots on the upper arm, about half an inch apart, in regular order.

Another manner of cutting the arms was by gashing, which left broad white scars. As already stated, the relatives of a man might assume part of the obligation of his vow by allowing their arms to be cut. Thus Lone Man said that he vowed 200 gashes, but his relatives divided half the number among themselves.

If a man vowed that he would be suspended from the pole the operation of fastening the thongs to his chest was as fol-

Seeking visions from the sun.

lows: The dancer lay on the ground, and the man who performed the operation, bending over him, lifted the flesh of the chest between his thumb and finger; then thrusting an awl through the flesh, he followed this with the insertion of the pointed stick. This stick was painted blue, and the man moistened it with his lips before inserting it in the flesh. He then lifted the man to his feet and tied the thongs hanging from the crossbar of the pole to the sticks in the man's flesh. Medicine was applied if the bleeding was excessive. In old days the awl used in this operation was of bone. Chased-By-Bears, who performed this office many times in the Sun Dance, stated that he used a knife, the blade being ground to a point, and the handle and part of the blade being wrapped with rawhide.

The thongs by which a man was suspended were usually of a length permitting only his toes to touch the ground, though the height of the suspension depended somewhat upon the man's physical strength. When first suspended each man was given a stick by means of which he might raise his body slightly to ease the strain upon the flesh of his chest. After discarding this support, any effort at rest or any cessation of the motion of dancing only increased the suffering.

The men were suspended soon after 9 o'clock in the morning on the north side of the pole in such a position that their upraised faces were in the full glare of the sun. It was expected that they would make an effort to free themselves as soon as possible. Sometimes this was accomplished in half an hour, and according to John Grass and other informants a man seldom remained in that position more than an hour. If he was unable to tear the flesh in that time by means of the motion of dancing, he might give horses for his release, or his relatives might give them in his behalf. In that event the man who had done the cutting was allowed to cut through the flesh either partially or entirely. If a considerable time elapsed and the man could not free himself, and neither he nor his relatives could give the requisite horses, he was jerked downward until the flesh gave way. While suspended, each man held his eagle-bone whistle in his mouth, blowing it from time to time.

If a man vowed to take part in the Sun Dance by carrying buffalo skulls, the number varied from two to eight. If two were used they were fastened to the flesh of the upper part of the back, near the spine. The flesh having been lifted on an awl, a small stick was inserted. A thong of buffalo hide was fastened to this stick, the other end of the thong being passed through the nostril-openings of the buffalo skull, suspending it at some distance from the ground. The man then danced until the tearing of the flesh released the skull. If four skulls were used, the additional pair was fastened to the back, halfway between the spine and the point of the shoulder. With six skulls, the third pair was fastened to the upper arm. If more than six were used, the additional skulls were fastened anywhere on the upper part of the back, it being permitted also to fasten more than one skull to a thong. When several skulls were employed, their weight made it impossible for a man to stand erect, hence the man had to lean forward upon a stick, dancing in a bowed position. The scales indicated 25 pounds weight for a buffalo skull which was obtained by the writer. The skull was shown to Chased-By-Bears who, after lifting it, said that although the specimen was a large one it was not unusual for men to carry such in the Sun Dance. Buffalo Boy stated that he carried six buffalo skulls for four or five hours, at the expiration of which he was set free by the cutting of the flesh from which they were suspended, the proper number of horses being given for his release.

A more severe form of torture was the hanging of the body clear of the ground by means of thongs passed through the flesh on each side of the lower part of the back. Seizes-the-Gun-Away-From-Them told of an instance in which a man rode to the Sacred Pole, and was suspended by his back, after which the horse was led away. The most severe form of torture was the suspension of the body between four poles, by means of thongs passing through the flesh of both chest and back, the body hanging so that only the toes touched the ground. Under these conditions the flesh tore less readily. John Grass stated that a man had been known to remain in that position from one morning until the evening of the next day, when gifts were given for his release.

While the men were dancing, they "prayed for all in the tribe, especially the sick and the old." Red Bird said: "The warriors went on the warpath for the protection of the tribe and its hunting grounds. All the people shared in his benefit, so when the warrior fulfilled his vow he wanted all the tribe to share in its benefits. He believed that *Wakań Tanka* is more ready to grant the requests of those who make vows and fulfill them than of those who are careless of all their obligations; also that an act performed publicly is more effective than the same thing done privately. So when a man was fulfilling his vow, he prayed for all the members of the tribe and for all the branches of the tribe, wherever they might be."

As soon as a man enduring torture was set free by the breaking of the flesh, it was customary to apply to the wound a medicine in the form of a powder. It was said that the wounds healed readily, blood poisoning and even swelling being unknown. The writer saw a large number of Sun Dance scars, which appeared slight considering the severity of the ordeal.

After the medicine was applied, the man returned to his place with the dancers, continuing his fast and dancing until exhausted. During the period of dancing the men who painted the dancer occasionally offered a pipe, holding the bowl as the man puffed; also putting the dancer's whistle into his mouth, as participants were not allowed to touch any objects while dancing.

Each man remained in one place as he danced, merely turning so that he continually faced the sun, toward which he raised his face. In dancing he raised himself on the ball of his foot with rhythmic regularity. At intervals of a few hours the men at the drum were allowed to rest, and the dancers might stand in their places or even sit down and smoke for a short time, but if they showed any hesitation in resuming the dance they were forced to their feet by the men who did the cutting of the arms and superintended the fulfillment of the vows.

Women whose relatives were fulfilling vows frequently danced beside them during part of the time. White Robe, singer of the following song, stated that she composed it while taking part in a Sun Dance in which her brother was fulfilling a vow. As the result of a successful raid against the Crows, he brought home many horses, which were divided among his relatives, she receiving part of the number. He had vowed that if he were successful he would be suspended from the pole and would also have 200 cuts made on his arms. She and her sister assumed one-half of this number, each having her arms cut 50 times. She and his other female relatives danced while he was dancing, and without preparation she sang this song which was readily learned and sung by all the women:

WAKAN TANKA, PITY ME

Climbing Eagle [man's name]
Said this:
"Wakan tanka,
Pity me.
From henceforth
For a long time I will live."
He is saying this, and
Stands there, enduring.

The aged members of the tribe were seated comfortably in the "shade house" on the outer edge of the dancing circle. There they listened attentively to all that took place; indeed, the utmost reverence and respect for the ceremony were shown by all who attended. The spectators realized that when prayer was offered by the Intercessor "it was their duty to join in his prayer with their hearts."

Meantime many incidents were taking place in the great tribal gathering. Those who rejoiced were asking others to rejoice with them, while still others joined their friends in lamenting chiefs who had died during the year, or warriors who had been slain by the enemy. The relatives of those who took part in the Sun Dance provided feasts, and little groups were seen feasting here and there in the camp while at the same time songs of lamentation could be heard. The following song was used at a Sun Dance in commemoration of Sitting Crow, a Sioux warrior who was killed in a fight with the Crows. The words of this song are a warrior's best memorial:

SONG OF LAMENTATION

Sitting Crow [man's name],
That is the way he wished to lie.
He is lying as he desired.

Even the children had a part in the Sun Dance, which consisted in the piercing of their ears. Frequently this was done in fulfillment of a vow made by their parents; for instance, in the event of a child's illness the parents might vow that if the child should live until the next Sun Dance its ears would be pierced. This was considered an honor, and the gifts which were required made it impossible for poorer members of the tribe. The piercing of the ears was done publicly by any experienced person, in some instances by the Intercessor, assisted by those who cut the arms of persons fulfilling vows at the ceremony. The parents of the child gave gifts to those who pierced its ears, the gifts varying according to their means. Some gave 1 horse, some 10 horses, and wealthy persons added large and valuable presents of goods to show their affection for the child. A wealthy family provided also rich furs on which the child was laid during the operation—soft robes of otter, beaver, or buffalo, elaborately wrought on the inner side with beads or porcupine quills—and brought a pillow filled with the soft hair scraped from the deer's hide, or the down of the cat-tail reeds that grow in the marshes. All these articles were left in their places after being used and were appropriated by the poor of the tribe.

The piercing of the ear was originally done with a bone awl, this instrument being replaced later by one of metal. After the puncture, a piece of copper was inserted so that the wound would heal rapidly. One or both ears might be pierced, and if desired more than one hole was made in each ear.

The children whose ears were thus pierced were considered somewhat related in status to the men whose flesh was lacerated in the Sun Dance and feasts were given by their relatives in honor of the event.

About noon of either the first or second day of the dancing the Intercessor sang the following song, the drum being silent and the entire assembly listening as he sang:

NOON SONG

(first rendition)
Where
Holy
You behold
In the place where the sun rises
Holy
May you behold.

(second rendition)
Where
Holy
You behold
In the place where the sun
    passes us on his course
Holy
You behold.[3]

PUBERTY CEREMONY AT THE SUN DANCE—
James O. Dorsey

Among the Oglala Dakota, according to Miss Fletcher, the rites incident to the puberty of girls take place on the fourth day of the Sun Dance festival. In a note on page 260 of the Peabody Museum Report, vol. III, the same authority says:

"Through the kindness of Rev. A. L. Riggs I learn that among the bands of Eastern Sioux living near Fort Sully, Dak., a feast, called the reappearance of the White Buffalo Skin, is held for the consecration of a girl on her arriving at puberty. The feast is sacred and costly, and not everyone can afford it. Those who have once made the feast become the privileged guests at every such feast, occupy the feast tent, and are served first. A prominent feature in the feast is the feeding of these privileged persons, and the girl in whose honor the feast is given, with choke cherries, as the choicest rarity to be had in the winter. The feast can be held at anytime. Bull berries, or as the Dakotas call them, 'rabbits' noses,' may be substituted, or finely pounded meat fixed with fat, in case no berries are to be had. In the ceremony, a few of the cherries are taken in a spoon and held over the sacred smoke, then fed to the girl. The spoon is filled anew, incensed as each person is fed. As each one is given the cherries, he is addressed thus: 'You will eat this chief's food.' The eaters are not chiefs; they only partake of chief's food."[4]

THE CONCLUSION OF THE SUN DANCE—Frances Densmore

Those who had taken part in the Sun Dance returned to their respective lodges at the close of the dancing. Before partaking of food or water they spent some time in the vapor lodge. Their first sip of water was taken in the following manner: A large bowl was filled with water, and beside it was placed a bunch of sweet grass. Having dipped this into the water, the dancer placed it to his lips. He was then given a small piece of cooked buffalo meat, and later sat down to a meal which was spread in his own lodge.

When the entire ceremony was finished the Intercessor took from its ceremonial position the pipe given by the Leader of the Dancers, and carried it to his own lodge. There he broke the seal of buffalo fat, and having lighted the pipe, offered it to such of his friends as felt themselves worthy to smoke it. No one who knew himself to be unworthy ever dared to touch the Sun Dance pipe.

Among the Indians here dealt with, camp had to be broken before the evening of the second day. The Sacred Pole and its offerings, the red-painted buffalo skull, and the bits of white eagle down remained on the prairie. As the last man left the camping ground, he looked back and saw them in their places. Then he left them with *Wakan tanka* and the silent prairie.

After the people reached their homes the boys of the tribe began a childish enactment of the Sun Dance, which continued at intervals during the entire summer. Boys whose fathers or grandfathers had taken part in the ceremony were given preference in the assigning of parts. Mr. Robert P. Higheagle, the interpreter, stated that he well remembered the gravity with which the grandson of the Intercessor imitated the actions of that official. A fine was exacted from any boy who failed to do his part in the proper manner, or showed disrespect toward the performance. Whistles in imitation of Sun Dance whistles were made of reeds, the plumy blossoms representing the eagle down, and long red and green grasses being wound around the reed in imitation of the porcupine-quill decoration.

Through the summer woods the boys sought for wild grapes and berries with which to color their bodies and their decorations. Removing the outer bark from trees, they took long, thin layers of the inner bark for streamers, coloring these with the juice of grapes and berries. The tree for their Sacred Pole was carefully selected, and was brought home with much pomp and ceremony. Boys with good voices were assigned the parts of singers and seated themselves around an old pan. A hoop was sometimes covered with a bright handkerchief or cloth; this more nearly resembled the Sun Dance drum in appearance; but the pan was considered more satisfying. The torture was imitated by thrusting a stiff cactus-spine through a boy's skin; this was fastened to the Pole by means of a very frail thread. When his movements in dancing broke this thread the boy was considered released.

Thus the boys of the tribe were trained in their play to become the men of the future.[5]

XVI
The Rosebud Sun Dance
Of July 3-6, 1975

THOMAS E. MAILS

Using the procedure for a typical day, Eagle Feather has given a summary account of how the Sun Dance goes: what the participants say, what they think, and what they do. The impression we are left with is that each day is about the same. But there are absorbing variations of considerable importance which he did not cover and which make it worthwhile to render an account of an entire ceremony from beginning to end.

Since I attended and made notes on the entire Sun Dance of July 3-6, 1975, I can reconstruct the sequence of events as they happened. Also, variants from the dance of 1974 will be included to indicate the kinds of differences which may occur from year to year.

I can account for the variations only by assuming that features are included or left out as need or circumstance arises. For example, a young woman who had been given a special healing ceremony in 1974, died shortly before the 1975 dance was held. Since she had vowed that if she was alive in July of 1975 she would be in the dance, a Spirit Keeping Ceremony was held to accomplish her presence and thus to keep her vow. This was a variant; there was no Spirit Keeping rite in 1974.

The Spirit Keeping Ceremony was one of the seven rituals given to the Sioux by the White Buffalo Maiden. It is performed for a deceased loved one, usually a child or youth,[1] and it serves a double purpose. The first is to keep at earth level the spirit of a person for a specified period of time, sometimes as long as a full year, after which the spirit is ceremonially released. The second is that the performance is thought to promote good thoughts, love, and unity among the living.

Spirit Keeping is a demanding role for the one who agrees to accept it. The Keeper must be of good repute and is expected to separate from worldly concerns and involvements in order to concentrate intently upon the purpose of the ceremony, which is to prolong the usual mourning period and to keep the loved one close, all of this making the sudden parting caused by death more bearable.

After the traditional purification rites have been conducted, a lock of hair and some other article belonging to the deceased are rolled into a spirit bundle and kept in a place of honor in the Keeper's home. In the old days a Spirit Post was carved from cottonwood, painted to resemble the deceased, and placed in front of the Keeper's tipi for the duration of the rite.

Missionaries considered the ritual "heathen" and attempted to suppress it. But it continues to be done both as a part of the Sun Dance and privately. I can testify personally to having seen it in 1975, and to discussions with a person whose family did it at a Sun Dance in 1974.

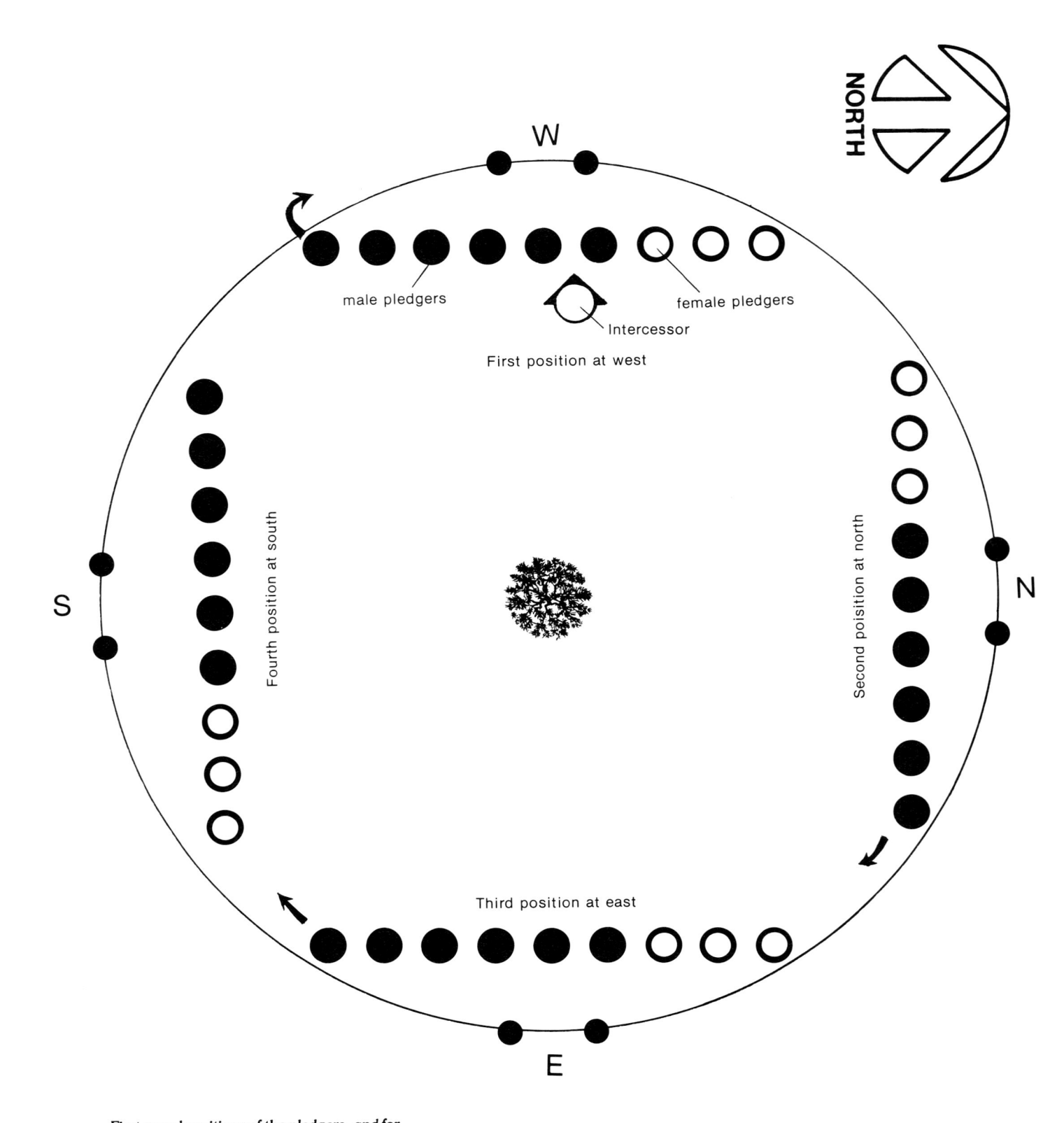

W

NORTH

male pledgers female pledgers
Intercessor
First position at west

S Fourth position at south Second position at north N

Third position at east

E

First round positions of the pledgers, and for each circuit where they face away from the tree.

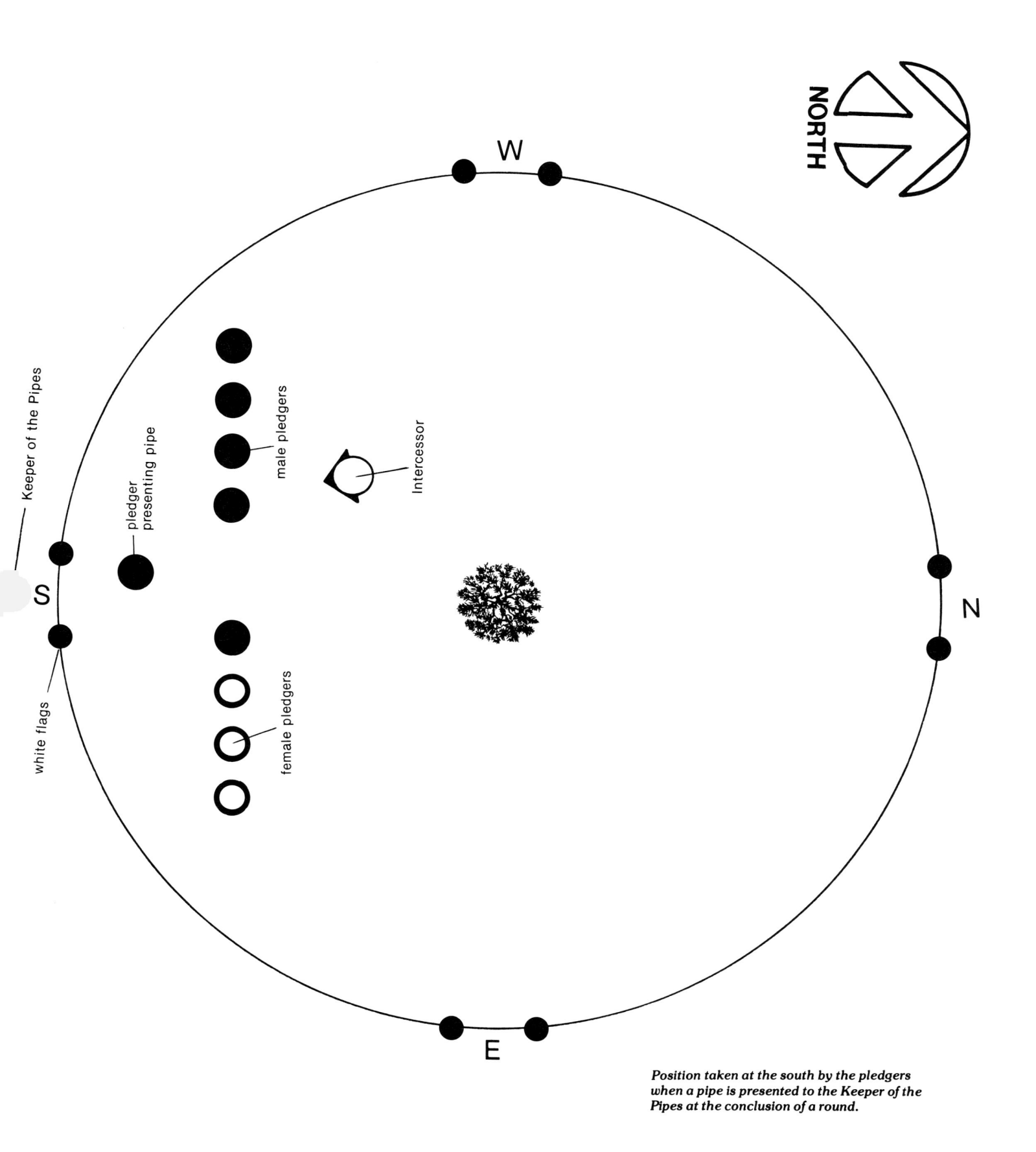

Position taken at the south by the pledgers when a pipe is presented to the Keeper of the Pipes at the conclusion of a round.

Other acts may be deleted or added according to the whims of the Intercessor, and perhaps because of persuasion by the Intercessor's assistants.

JULY 3, 1975: THE FIRST DAY OF THE SUN DANCE

The first group of pledgers was awakened at 4:00 A.M., and the second of two sweatlodge purification ceremonies ended at 7:15. By 7:35 the pledgers were dressed and ready to proceed to the Mystery Circle. They moved in a single line, with the Intercessor going first and carrying the buffalo skull on a bed of sage; the assisting medicine man, George Eagle Elk, coming next; followed by the Lead Dancer, the male pledgers, and the women pledgers last. The participants made four stops along the way, around the outside of the shade and directly to the east entrance of the Mystery Circle. At each stop the Intercessor prayed with his pipe. This same procedure would be followed every morning.

After a prayer by Eagle Feather, the line moved clockwise into the Circle, turning left and circling around until they stood facing the Altar at the west. Eagle Feather put the buffalo skull down, and then the pledgers' pipes, one at a time.

When the singing started and the drum began to boom, the line was moved to the north, then to the east, then to the south. For this circuit the pledgers faced away from the Tree. Please remember that whenever the line stops at a cardinal direction, the pledgers dance continuously and blow their eagle-bone whistles until the line moves on to the next direction.

At the south, the first man's pipe was presented to the Keeper of the Pipes and Eagle Feather went to the microphone to address an audience of only twelve people. While he had expected a total of nineteen pledgers to be present, some who had vowed did not come. He was plainly disappointed. Later I would learn that he also didn't like something that had been said in the sweatlodge. "This is," he lamented, "the most pitiful Sun Dance I have ever conducted." It was a sad moment. No matter, though, things would get better soon, and his personal vow to me that this would be his last dance was broken at least twice before the summer was over. He did not, however, pierce at this dance, ending a string of twenty-five piercings at consecutive dances.

The pledgers rested for ten minutes and, as is the custom, to begin the next round the pledger retrieved his pipe from the keeper in four gestures.

A second circuit of the Mystery Circle was made, beginning as always at the west and then moving clockwise to the other three directions. This time the pledgers faced the Sacred Tree. As a rule, four complete circuits of the Mystery Circle are made each day, with four stops at each cardinal direction during each circuit. James Hanson reports this pattern as having been followed at Pine Ridge in 1965, thus indicating that it has been the custom for at least the last ten years, and thus the ancient custom as well.[2]

At the south the second pipe was presented to the Keeper of the Pipes, and the pledgers rested.

After the rest period, the pledgers were divided into four groups, each of which was placed midway between two cardinal directions. While in this position, the pledgers danced and then Eagle Feather made announcements and introductions.

The third pipe was presented, and the pledgers rested.

The dancing resumed at the west, and another circuit of the circle was made. This time the pledgers faced away from the

Sacred Tree. Since the singers were few in number, Eagle Feather assisted them for a while. During this time the Lead Dancer moved the pledgers from point to point. By now the spectators numbered thirty-five.

At 10:45 on this first day, Eagle Feather gave two hundred flesh offerings, one hundred from each arm, "for the health and welfare of the people." To precede this, as a form of announcement, the fourth man presented his pipe by coming forward to the Keeper on his knees. The pipe was refused. Then when the offerings were finished, he came forward again on his knees to the Keeper, and this time the pipe was accepted. I learned later that this form of presentation is customary whenever a sacrifice or healing ceremony is about to take place.

When the flesh offerings were finished, the wounds were rubbed with saliva and sage by the women and then a coat of plain dirt was applied. The ritual ended at 11:15, and the participants left the Mystery Circle, exiting through the east flags and going directly to the Preparations Tipi.

JULY 4: THE SECOND DAY OF THE SUN DANCE

The sweatlodges were again completed by 7:15 A.M., and the participants formed the customary line to proceed in four moves to the Mystery Circle.

Once in, the line proceeded to the west, and the singing and dancing commenced at 7:30. The first circuit of the directions was made with the pledgers facing away from the Sacred Tree.

The fifth pipe was presented, and the pledgers rested.

When the dancing resumed, the pledgers were divided into four groups and faced the Sacred Tree, from which positions they were sent forward four times to lay their hands upon the Tree. There were now nine men and two women dancing, plus the Intercessor. By 8:15, the audience numbered seventy. A third woman, holding a red scarf wrapped around sage, was sitting at the base of the Sacred Tree. I was elated. She was the Keeper of the Spirit, and there had to be a lock of hair in the bundle too.

The sixth pipe was presented, and the pledgers rested.

When the dancing resumed, the pledgers faced away from the Sacred Tree and, continuing to face in this direction, made the circuit. I should add that each time the pledgers reach the flags at the east they look up into the sun and pray for a vision from it or in it, whichever the proper terminology should be.

The seventh pipe was presented, with the pledger bringing it on his knees to the Keeper, and the pledgers rested while Eagle Feather spent a great deal of time walking around the Mystery Circle and meditating.

The next circuit was done with the pledgers facing the Sacred Tree. As they began their move from the west to the north, Eagle Feather invited people who felt they needed help to come forward for healing. A line of twenty-seven people assembled, and from 9:55 until 10:05 a healing ceremony took place. The Keeper of the Spirit joined with the pledgers and the Intercessor for this, laying her Spirit Bundle alongside the heads of the people as she prayed for them. In doing the healing, each pledger in turn lays his hands on the shoulder and head of the person to be healed and says a fervent prayer for them. The Intercessor comes along next and may or may not administer a piece of herb or root as he prays for the person. The last man in line is a medicine man, who touches the patients with an eagle-wing fan in a fluttering motion. When your eyes are

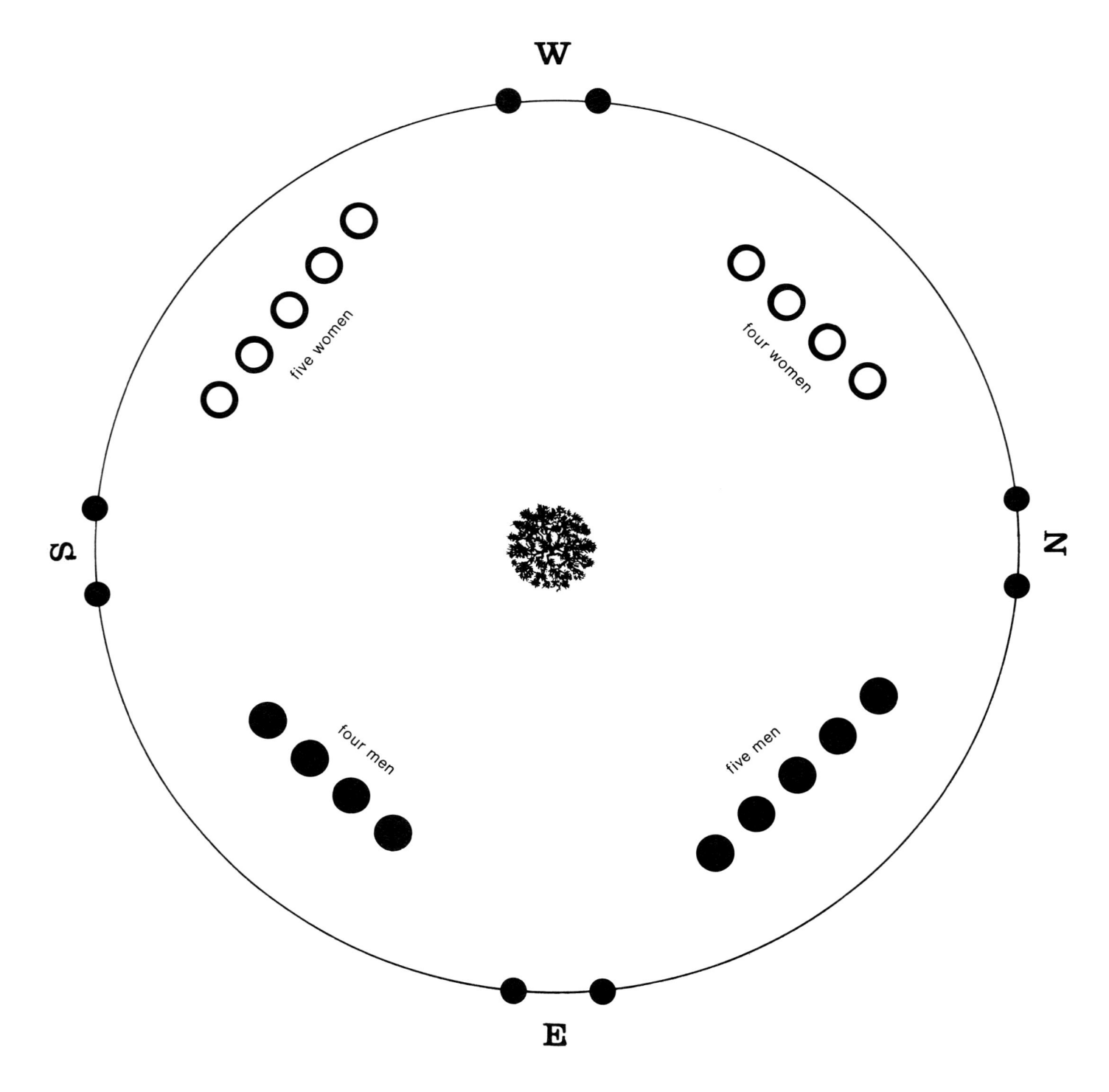

*Positions taken by pledgers when subdivided
into four groups in 1974.*

W

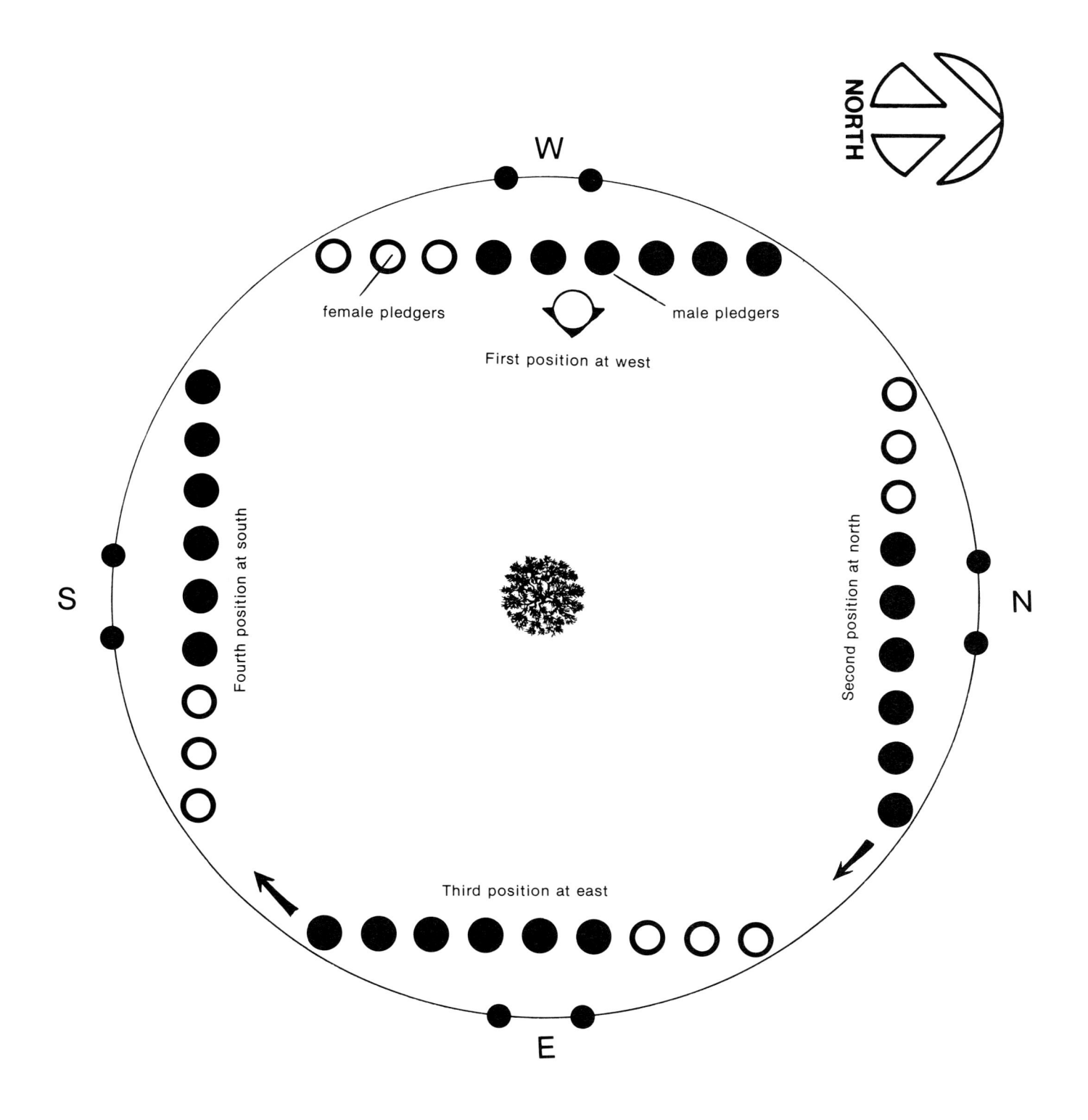

female pledgers — male pledgers

First position at west

Fourth position at south

Second position at north

S N

NORTH

Third position at east

E

Second round positions of the pledgers, and for each circuit where they face the tree.

closed as this is done, you would swear that a real eagle was hovering around you and gently caressing you with its soft wings. It is an uncanny experience to be blessed in such a way.

At 10:10 the first piercing took place as Reuben Fire Thunder was pierced on both sides of the chest and tied to the Sacred Tree. When he had pulled loose, dirt was rubbed on his wounds, he was comforted, and the ordeal was over. He was then taken by Eagle Feather to the flags at the east, where a line of spectators formed to congratulate him on his sacrifice.

The entire group of participants then assembled at the Altar, facing east, and with the Keeper of the Pipes carrying the Altar and the flags, moved in four equally spaced moves across the Mystery Circle to the east, where they stood in line while the spectators came forward to congratulate them.

The ceremony for the second day was completed at 11:00.

JULY 5: THE THIRD DAY OF THE SUN DANCE

Sweatlodge ceremonies were held as usual, and the pledgers processed in four moves to the Mystery Circle, entering it at 7:15 A.M.

As always, the first circuit began at the west, and with the pledgers facing away from the Sacred Tree, moved clockwise from there to the other directions. Now there were nine male pledgers and seven women, for a total of sixteen (including George Eagle Elk) plus Eagle Feather.

At 7:30, the first pipe was presented to the Keeper of the Pipes, and the pledgers rested.

For the next circuit, the pledgers faced the Tree and moved in sequence to the four directions, seeking visions and power from each place.

At 7:50 the next pipe was presented to the Keeper, and the pledgers rested while announcements were made about three of the pledgers: Titus Smith, Reuben Fire Thunder, and George Eagle Elk.

At 8:00 the pledger whose pipe had been taken retrieved it, using the four gestures, and at 8:30, with the pledgers facing the Tree at the west, the next circle began. Now the pledgers were divided into four groups: three women at the northwest, four women at the northeast, four men at the southeast, and four men at the southwest. At the Intercessor's ringing command of *Hoka He,* the pledgers were sent forward four times to lay their hands on the Tree, walking backwards each time to their original positions. Then the pledgers were assembled in a single line at the south, while Eagle Feather took the pipe of the third pledger to each of the four directions and prayed aloud with it. Then the third pledger presented his pipe to the Keeper, and at 8:20 the pledgers rested.

At 8:30 the pipe was retrieved and the next circle began at the west. Eagle Feather announced that if the Keeper of the Pipes refused to accept the next pipe, they would have a healing ceremony. The pledgers faced away from the Sacred Tree and were moved to the north.

While the pledgers were dancing at the north, George Eagle Elk escorted the Keeper of the Spirit to the yellow flags at the east cardinal point. Eagle Feather announced that the girl who had vowed to dance had died. But since she had promised to be here, the Keeper of the Spirit had placed a braid of her hair in the Spirit Bundle. Now the girl's parents, Mr. and Mrs. Floyd Comes A Flying, who had been given the Spirit Bundle to keep overnight when the ceremony for the second day ended, brought the Bundle forward and presented it to the medicine man, George Eagle Elk. He

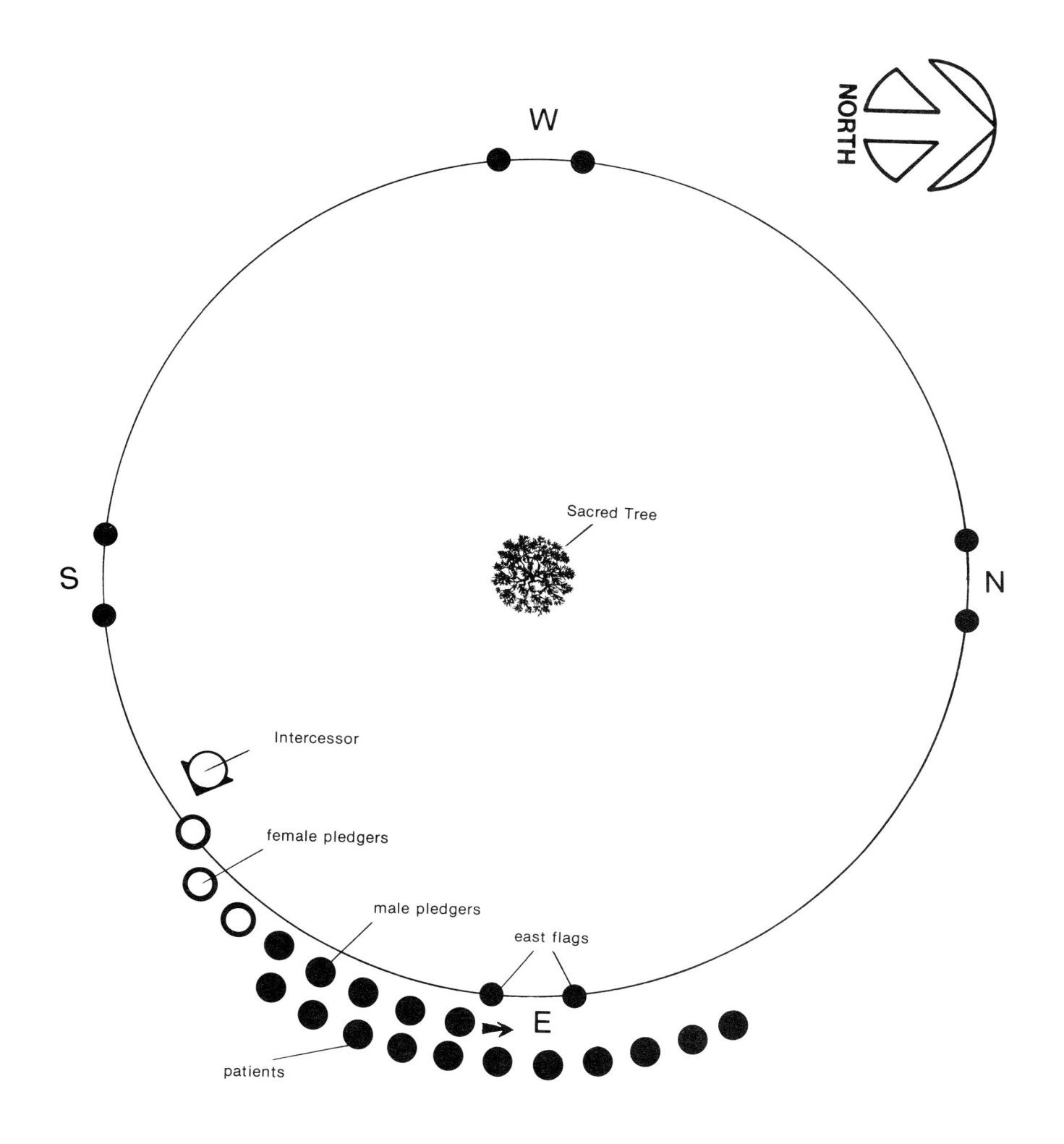

Positions taken at the east flags for the healing ceremonies.

handed it to the Keeper of the Spirit and then purified it by passing a braid of burning sweet grass around it. At 8:37 the Keeper of the Spirit took the Bundle to the Sacred Tree.

Eagle Feather took the fourth pipe from the Altar, prayed with it at the west, and blessed the Keeper of the Spirit with it before presenting it to its owner to give to the Keeper of the Pipes. The pipe owner went forward to the Keeper on his knees. It was refused, meaning that there would be a healing ceremony.

The pledgers rested.

When the fourth pledger returned to the Keeper to get his pipe back, on the fourth gesture the Keeper gave him the pipe but also held on to its stem, moving with the owner as he walked backwards to rejoin the line of pledgers. At that point the Keeper released the pipe and returned to the white flags at the south. This is another variant; it was not done in 1974.

As the pledgers danced at the west, a healing line of thirty-eight people assembled at the yellow flags of the south. The dancers were moved clockwise to the north and then to the east, at which time the healing began. This time Eagle Feather gave bits of root to each person, and again Eagle Elk blessed the people with the eagle-wing fan. As Eagle Feather ended his Sioux prayer for each person, he said in English, "Thank you and God bless you." At 9:08 the healing ceremony was finished.

The pledgers were reassembled at the east and then moved to the south, where at 9:15 the next pipe was presented to the Keeper, the pledger again going forward on his knees.

The pledgers rested, and Eagle Feather announced that those who had made a vow to give flesh offerings were to come, with their shoes off, to the Sacred Tree. Three female pledgers, five male pledgers, and George Eagle Elk came forward. As the offerings were taken from their arms, Lame Deer sang a single mournful flesh-offering song. Then a great stillness settled over the Mystery Circle as the bits of flesh were cut off, prayed over, wrapped in tiny red cloth packets, and then tied on a string to the Sacred Tree. As each flesh bit was removed, the medicine man held it up to the six directions, or powers, and prayed to them before it was wrapped. The offering ceremony was finished at 9:45.

At 9:47 Eagle Feather, the Intercessor, returned the pipe to its owner, who took it to the Altar and placed it on the buffalo skull. Now the next circuit of the Mystery Circle began, with the pledgers facing the Sacred Tree.

At 10:08 the next pipe was presented to the Keeper at the south, and while the pledgers rested the Intercessor brought a fine-looking little boy to the microphone to introduce him to the audience, which now numbered about one hundred and fifty. The boy was Delbert Lone Walker, son of the young woman for whom the Spirit Keeping Ceremony was being held. Now he was without both father and mother, and Eagle Feather urged everyone to make every effort to assist him and his grandparents, who would now care for him.

The pipe was retrieved and the next circuit began at the west. The pledgers were then divided into four groups and placed as they had been earlier in the morning. Once again they were sent forward four times to touch and pray at the Tree.

After this, the pledgers formed a single line at the south and the Intercessor touched the Tree four times with the stem of the pipe. Then George Eagle Elk blessed the line of Pledgers with his fan and the sixth man presented his pipe to the Keeper.

At 10:25 the pledgers rested.

At 10:38 the pipe was retrieved and the next circuit of the Mystery Circle was made, with the pledgers facing away from the Tree.

Eagle Feather at the entrance to the Mystery Circle on the fourth day of the Sun Dance in 1974.

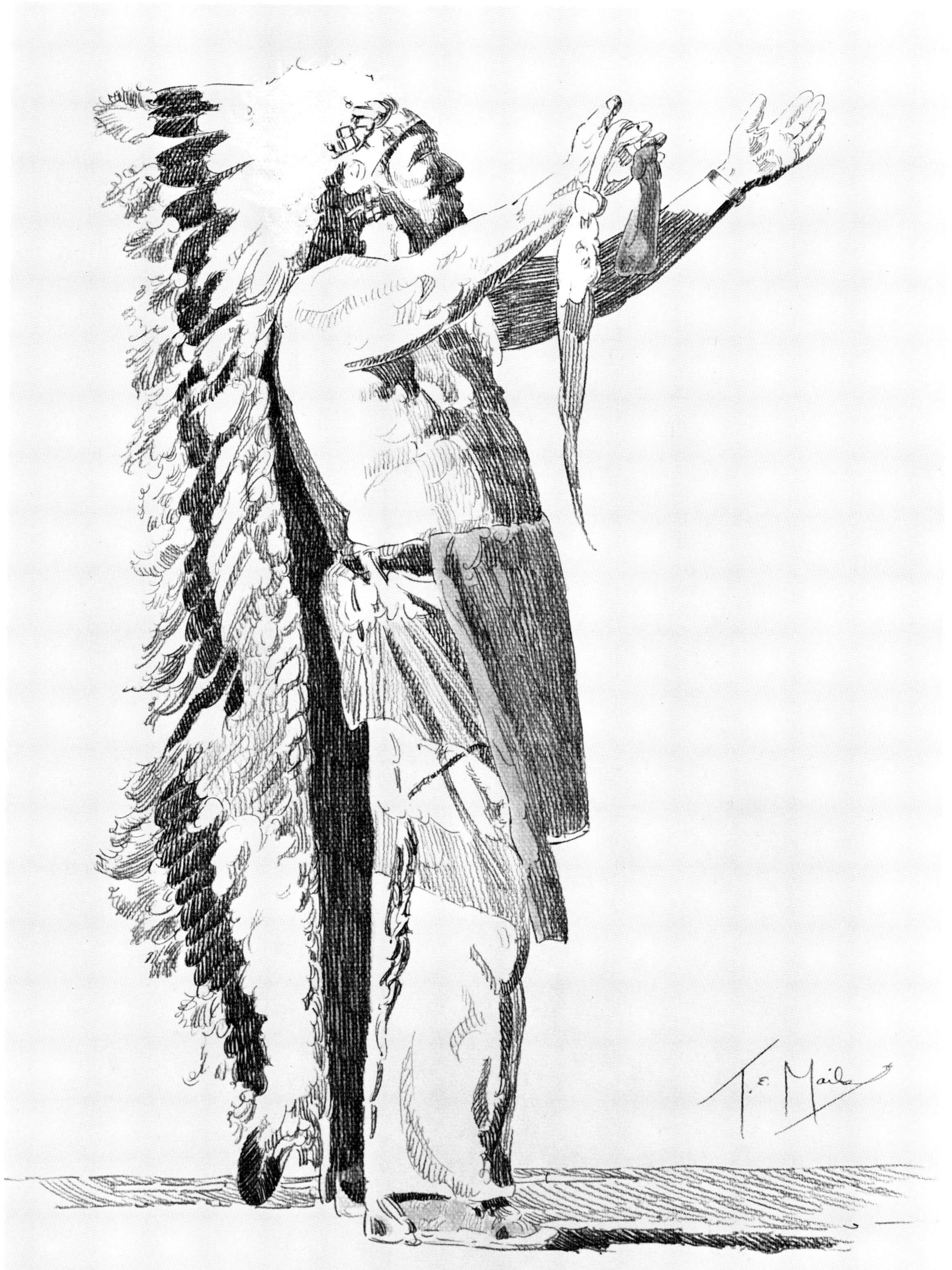
T. E. Mails

At 10:50 the next pipe was presented to the Keeper and the pledgers rested.

At 11:00 the pipe was retrieved by its owner from the Keeper and the participants assembled at the west, facing the Tree. The ceremony for the day ended with the group moving in four equally spaced moves across the Mystery Circle to the yellow flags at the east. Here they remained for a time while people from the audience came forward to congratulate them.

The participants exited the Mystery Circle through the east entrance, turning right to go around the outside of the shade arbor in a clockwise direction as they returned to the Preparations Tipi.

JULY 6: THE FOURTH DAY OF THE SUN DANCE

It was another beautiful day, not too warm and not a cloud in the sky at 7:00 A.M. By 7:30 the sweatlodges and preparations were finished, and the participants processed in the four moves to the Mystery Circle. After they reached the Altar at the west, the medicine man and the Keeper of the Spirit went to the south flags to meet the parents of the deceased girl and received the Spirit Bundle in the same manner as on previous days.

The first act of the day began at 7:40 with the pledgers at the west facing away from the Tree. From here the pledgers were sent in turn with their pipes to pray at each cardinal direction. The Dance Leader, Gilbert Yellow Hawk, went first, followed by Reuben Fire Thunder and then the rest. This was not done in 1974.

When the last pledger returned to the Altar at the west, the entire group turned in the direction of the Altar, away from the Tree, while Eagle Feather went to the microphone and talked about the significance of the last day of the dance.

The line of pledgers formed at the Altar and was blessed by George Eagle Elk with the fan. Now there were eleven male pledgers, five female pledgers (including the Keeper of the Spirit), George Eagle Elk, and Eagle Feather, for a total of eighteen participants. The audience was already very large and by midmorning would swell to more than five hundred. Eagle Feather's disappointment of the first day had faded noticeably. It was not his most pitiful dance anymore. The drum boomed, the singers' voices swept across the arena, and the pledgers made their first circle to the four directions, facing away from the Tree.

The pledgers formed a line at the Altar at the west, facing it, and when the singers began, danced in place while the Intercessor passed behind them down the line and blessed them with his eagle-wing fan. When he finished he took the sage wristband of the Lead Dancer and led the circle to the four directions. The pledgers faced away from the Tree. When the line reached the white flags of the south, Eagle Feather took the first man's pipe to the four directions and prayed with it. After this he gave it to the lead man, who danced forward in a splendid gliding style and, using four gestures, presented the pipe to the Keeper.

The pledgers rested. During this time announcements were made and several pledgers were introduced to the audience.

While the Intercessor sang "A Song to the Four Winds," the first man retrieved his pipe and placed it on the buffalo skull. Now the next circle began, with the line of pledgers facing the Sacred Tree. When the line reached the south, the Intercessor prayed to the four cardinal directions with the second pipe, then gave it to the second man, who presented it in four gestures to the Keeper.

At 9:00, while the other pledgers rested, the Intercessor brought two of them to the microphone to address the audience. What they said is typical: The first man told where he was from, what his problems and hopes were, and added that he had vowed to pierce four times in the Sun Dance. The next man ended his talk by saying that he was happy to see everyone there, especially his estranged wife with their children. He was in tears; it was an emotional and impressive moment. An announcement was made explaining that Sun Dances had been held at the Rosebud Fairground in 1908, 1928, 1974, and now, in 1975, although the first two were not in this precise location. (I learned later that the 1928 Sun Dance, a huge affair drawing more than five thousand Indians, was held half a mile northwest of the present arena.) He also said that the 1974 piercing was the first to be done in that area.

In 1974, at this point in the dance, a special healing ceremony had been held for an exceedingly frail and very young girl. Only in 1975 would I learn that she was the mother of Delbert Lone Walker. She came to the yellow flags at the east and was treated there by a medicine man, who ended his ritual by giving her a pipe. She accepted it, to express her trust, and remained there holding it horizontally at waist level until the next circle got underway. She lived much longer than the White doctors had expected, but she was gone now, so at this point in the 1975 ceremony Eagle Feather introduced her child, little Delbert, to the spectators again and for a second time urged everyone to care for him and watch over him.

The pledgers assembled at the Altar and, as the music began, faced the Tree. The Intercessor quickly divided them into four groups: three women at the northwest, five men at the southwest, four men at the southeast, and five women at the northeast. From this position the Intercessor sent them forward four times to touch the Tree.

Next, the pledgers formed a single line at the south and danced in place as the tempo of the music increased noticeably. Eagle Feather took the next pipe from the Altar and gave it to its owner, who presented it to the Keeper. Then the pledgers rested.

At this juncture in the 1974 dance, while the pledgers rested a medicine man added six cloth prayer offerings to those already on the base of the Sun Pole. Cloth offerings may be added at any time during the ceremony, although most are secured there on the morning of the first day.

As the next circle began, the pledgers faced the Tree and danced in place while an announcement was made inviting all who wished to assemble at the yellow flags at the east for a healing ceremony. Approximately seventy-five people joined in the line, and while they did this the announcer began to offer prayers for them in the Sioux language. The healing ceremony was underway at 9:50. In 1974, a woman whose health problem was especially severe was brought out to the Sacred Tree and given a pipe to hold. She remained there for some time with it. She did live longer than doctors had told her she would, but died in the spring of 1975. The music continued all during the long healing ceremony. When each pledger finished his trip down the line of patients, he rejoined the other pledgers and all danced in place while they waited for the rest, facing the east and the sun.

When the healing was done, several men began to stretch and prepare the ropes for piercing. Each rope is pulled out to its fullest length and tied to a wooden stake driven in the ground to mark the place where each pledger will go to begin pulling back on his rope.

When all the stakes were in, the pledgers formed a line at the Altar and prayers were said by a medicine man over the microphone. Then a medicine man went to the Sacred Tree and offered a prayer to the directions, to God, and to Mother Earth. After this, while the pledgers stood reverently in place, a long address was made by the Intercessor about the significance and tradition of the Sun Dance.

At this point in 1974, the Sacred Pipe was passed down the line of pledgers and smoked by each. As it moved from one to the next, the announcer said: "This is the sacred pipe of the Sioux nation. When they have all received the pipe, the piercing will begin."

The pipe was not passed in 1975. Instead, Eagle Feather brought a metal bucket of water and a dipper. He passed down the line with this, pausing in front of each pledger to extract a dipper full of water from the pail. He raised this up before the pledger's face and then deliberately poured it back into the pail. In this manner he offered each pledger some water and each refused it in turn. The pledgers' stalwart refusal after hours of dancing in the hot sun, showed their determination to make the full sacrifice in the dance.

I was also told that refusal has something to do with rain during a Sun Dance. Tradition has it that it never rains during a properly conducted dance, but if the water is offered and refused, it will rain before the last day is over. I smiled at that and looked up. The sky was absolutely clear in all directions, and a gorgeous cobalt blue. At 4 P.M., when the last tent had come down and Eagle Feather was on his way back to St. Francis, it was windy but still clear. At 5:15 the sky was coal-black with clouds, the wind was blowing so furiously and the rain coming down in such torrents that at Mission we were all anxiously watching for a tornado. At 7:15 the sky was clear again.

There are many beliefs about rain and the Sun Dance, an interesting sidelight of which would develop at two dances before the summer of 1975 was over. Those who believe that the "traditional" dance at St. Francis was not carried out properly find part of their proof in the fact that it rained hard during the dance on the first two days.

It also rained on the fourth day during the Sun Dance at Crow Dog's Paradise. I was told that a troubled Lame Deer persuaded Leonard Crow Dog to put a turtle design on the dirt mound where the pipe was kept (in front of the sweatlodge) to stop the rain. Eagle Feather argued that when God makes rain nothing should be done to spoil it. But the design was drawn and the rain stopped.

Eagle Feather believed that this interference caused a serious injury to the young man who had served as custodian for the sweatlodge. After the dance he went swimming, at which time he dived off a bridge into shallow water and broke his neck. But another person had heard that it was because the custodian had handled the stones from the Old Man Four Generations firepit carelessly, dropping some, that the accident occurred.

Eagle Feather's own 1976 Sun Dance at Rosebud was plagued by rain for the first two days. More than once it rained so hard that the dance was discontinued.

Ater the refusal of water at the 1975 ceremony, the announcer said, "Pain and sincerity go together. Piercing proves a man's sincerity."

The Intercessor took the next pipe from the Altar, prayed with it at the Sacred Tree, and at the south, and then gave it to its owner to present to the Keeper of the Pipes. Now the pledgers recessed out and rested.

The announcer gave the names of the old-timers in the dance who would be pierced first. Usually these are holy or medicine men. In 1974, they were George Eagle Elk, Albert Stands, and Gilbert Yellow Hawk. When they pulled free, they would do the piercing for the other pledgers.

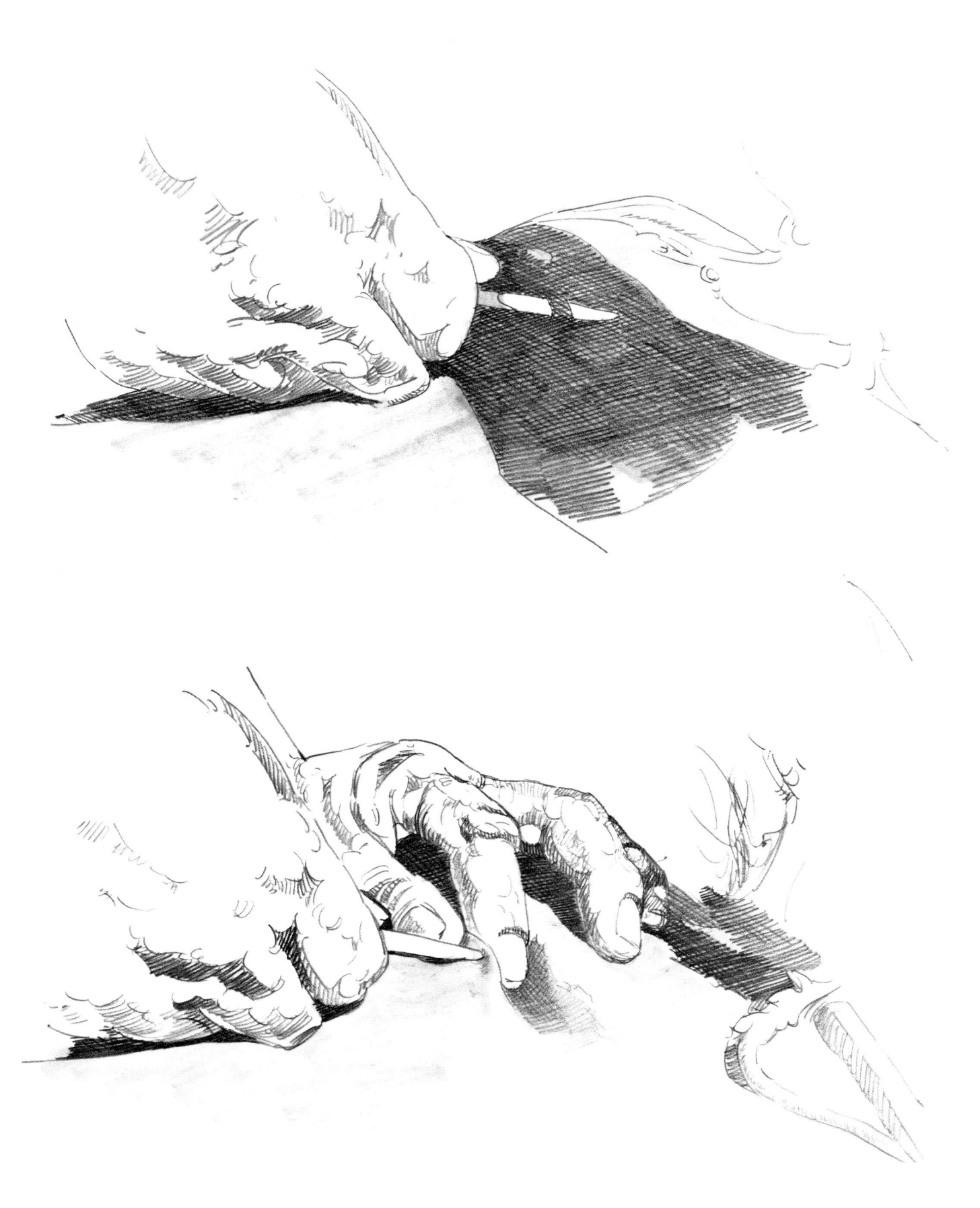

Piercing details using the skewer stick. Bottom: after two parallel cuts are made in the skin, the skin is pinched and pulled up, and the wooden skewer stick is inserted through the cuts. Top: the stick after it is inserted. Note that it is at an angle on the chest, not straight across.

Piercing details using the eagle claw. Top: first step is to cut the skin, and then to hold it up with a sharp instrument while the claw is inserted. Second step is to push the claw through until it is securely hooked in the skin.

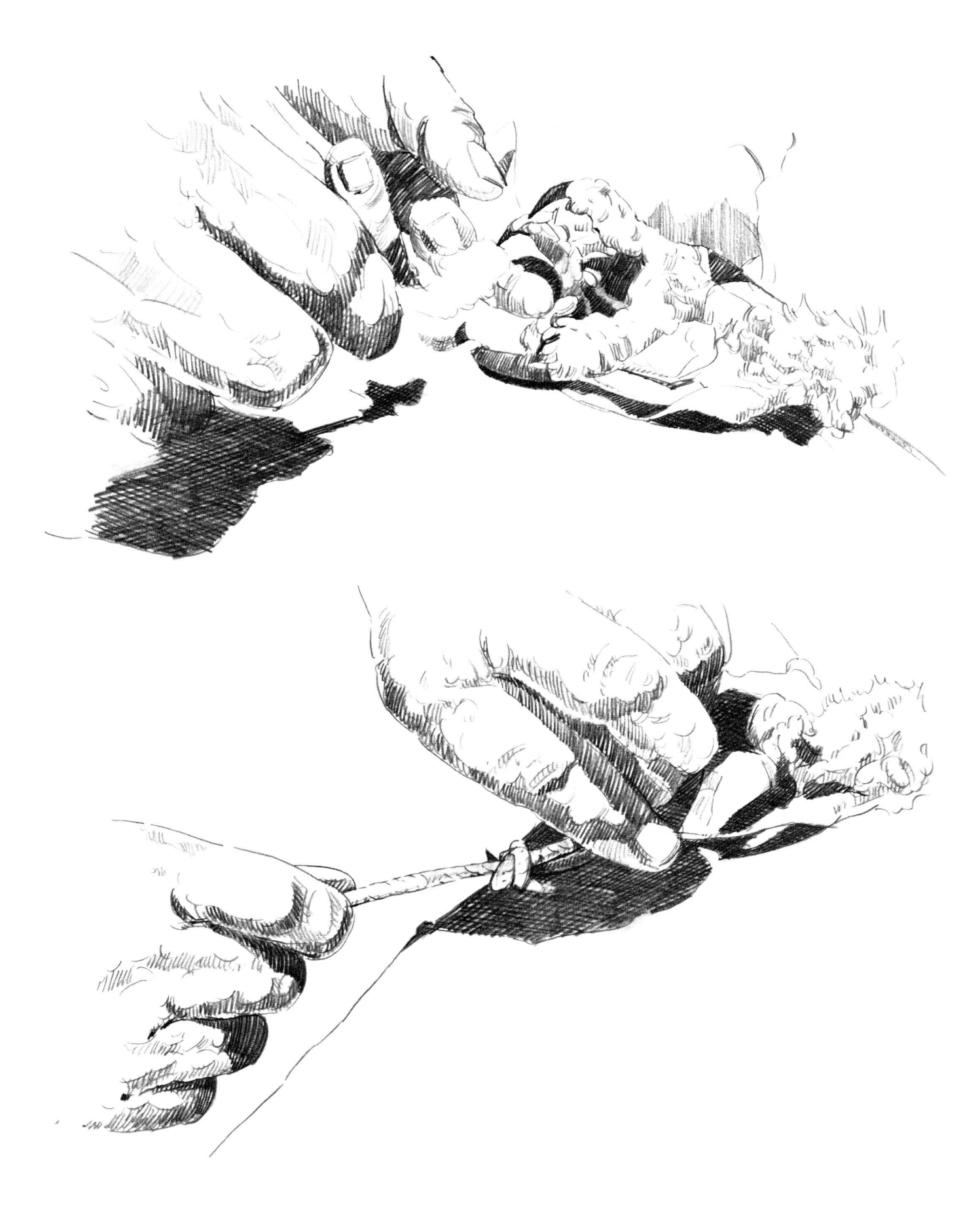

Top: *third step is to use a small piece of rope about 1/8" in diameter to secure the claw in place.* Bottom: *the knot is tied around the skin and the claw, and pulled very tight.*

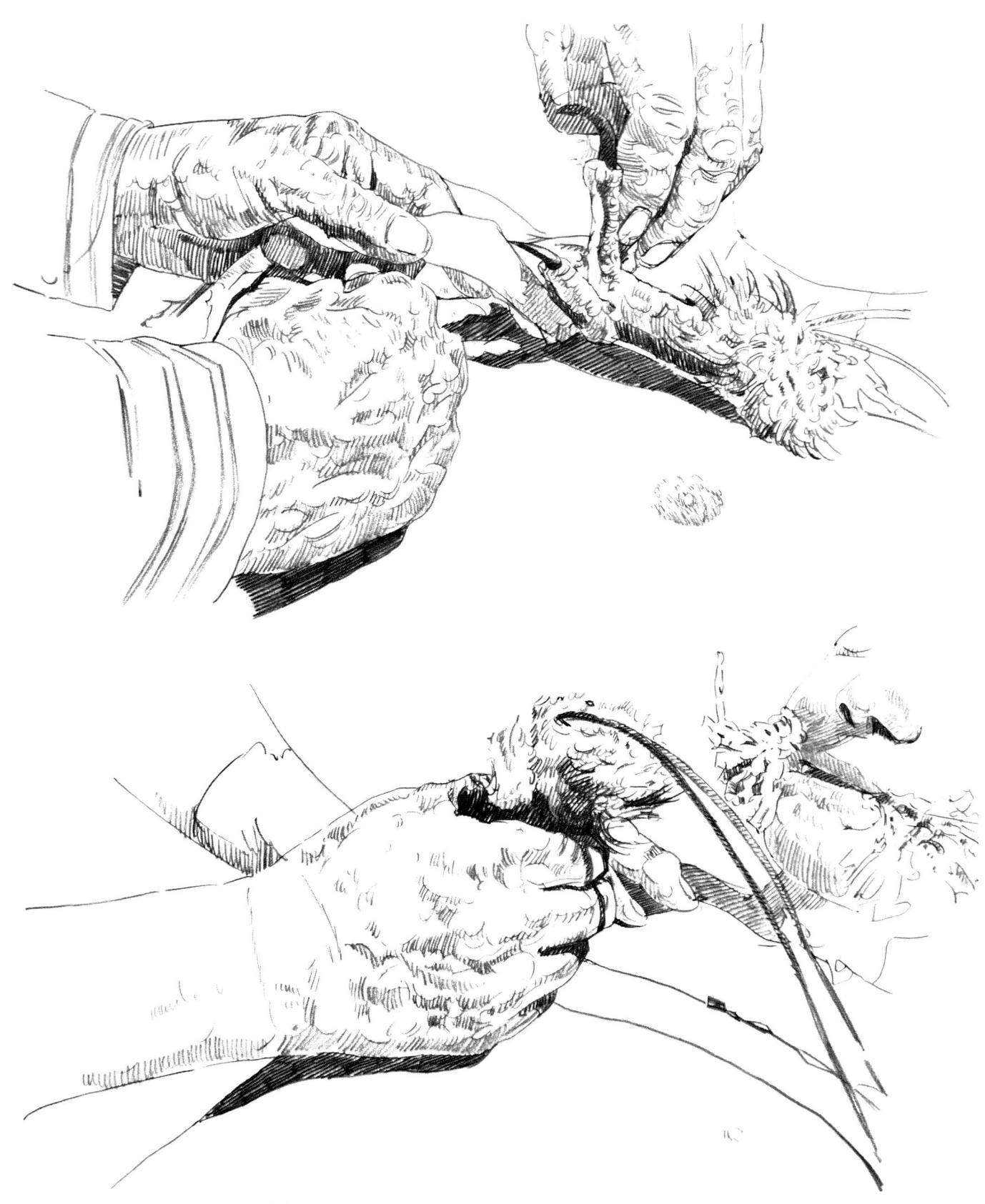

Top: *fourth step is to wrap a strip of cloth around the knot and the claw to secure it further. Fifth step is to test the claw to make certain it will hold when the pledger pulls back. Finally the loose end of the small rope is tied to the heavier rope which is attached to the Sacred Tree.*

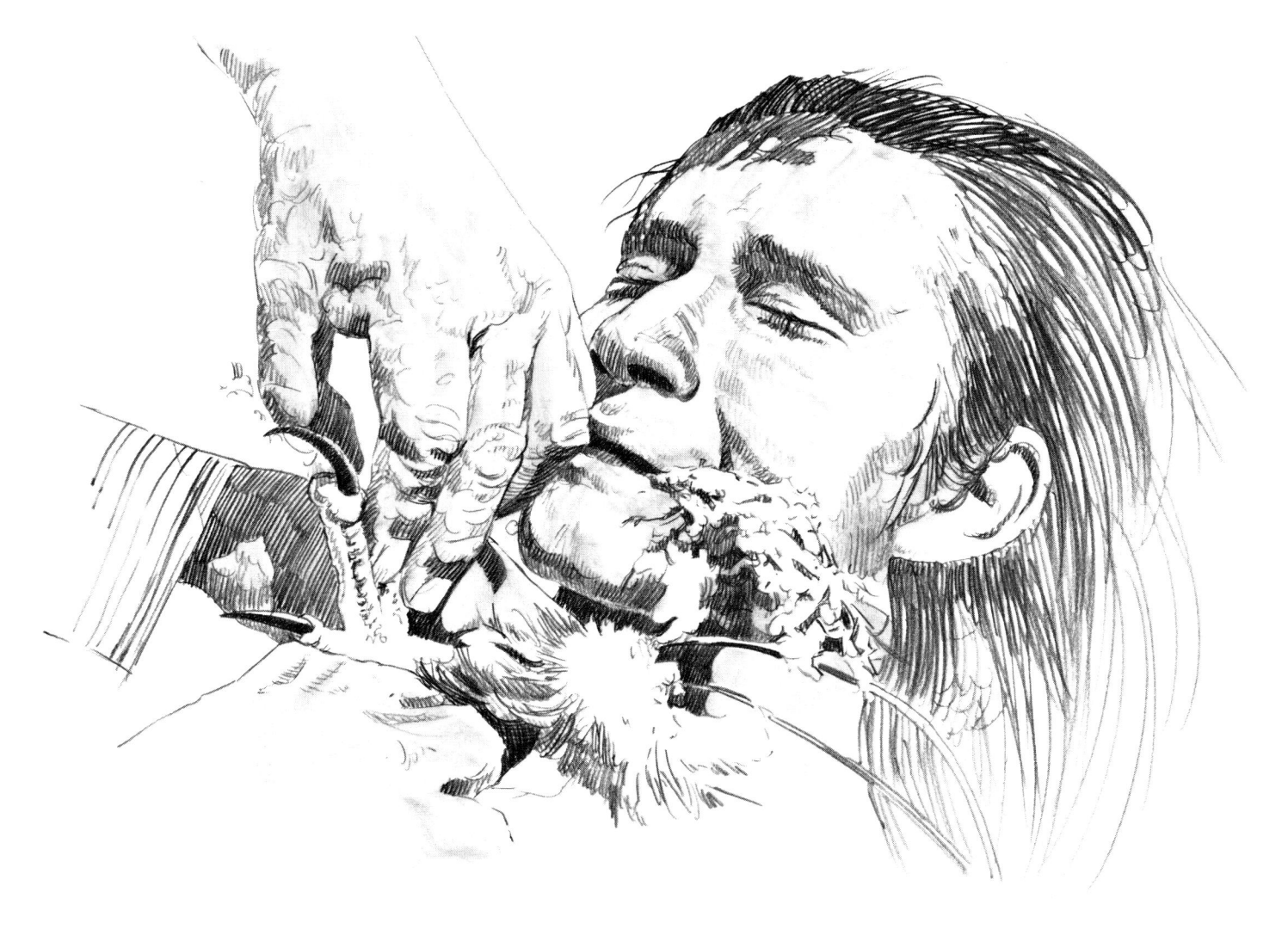

To withstand the pain, as the stick or claw is inserted and secured, some pledgers bite down hard on a bunch of loose sage.

The piercing takes place at the base of the Sacred Tree, where a mat is prepared on the west side for the pledger to lie on. The mat consists of an old buffalo robe covered with sage. The pledger lies down with his head to the north and his feet to the south. He usually removes his sage headband. All those being pierced bite on something to gird themselves against the pain. One man bites down on his pipe stem, another on a handful of loose sage. Most have their eyes tightly closed. Their fists are clenched, and a leg may twitch or raise up to show how much it hurts. The piercing is done deftly. If the skin is loose, the medicine man simply rubs the spot hard with his fingers, pulls up the skin, pushes a knife or an awl through it and, still holding it up, puts a skewer stick or an eagle claw through the holes. If the skin is tight, he cuts two parallel and vertical slits, and pushes the stick or claw through them. Then a thong is tied to the stick or claw, sometimes being inserted along with the stick or claw through the openings in the skin. The other end of the thong is then tied to the free end of the rope, whose other end is in turn secured to the Sacred Tree. There is no music while the piercing is done. Silence reigns, and the spectators are particularly attentive.

When each piercing is completed, the man is helped to his feet by the Intercessor and an assistant and led out to where his stake is. Here he remains until all who are being pierced in a particular group are at their places and ready to pull. When the music begins, now in a resounding way, the pierced pledgers are sent forward four times to touch the Tree.

When they have touched it for the fourth time they may, if shallowly pierced, run backwards and attempt by that to tear the stick or claw loose. But if they are deeply pierced they usually walk backwards until the rope is stretched out as far as it will go, and then begin leaning back and pulling steadily as they blow on their whistles.

It is an extraordinary exhibit of courage, and the perspiration pours out as they struggle. Some break free in an instant, so quickly you can't catch it. Others may take from fifteen to twenty minutes. The old men, whose skin is loose, take the longest, for the skin can stretch an incredible amount before breaking.

Sometimes a stick breaks or slips out, and the rope drops to the ground. Then the pledger is tied up again and starts over. Remarkably little blood is seen, although some does trickle down the front of a few pledgers. When the piercing is deep, it can leave a gaping wound. Otherwise the skin is hardly marred. Eagle Feather rubs dirt on the wounds, that is all; no medicine is applied while the pledgers are still in the Mystery Circle. Fools Crow does apply medicine before and after piercing.

In 1974, Eagle Feather was pierced on one side on the second day of the dance, and on the other side on the third day. On the third day his rawhide rope broke three times, and it took him forty minutes in all to break loose, with Titus helping by holding his grandfather's arm and pulling. Titus was pierced on one side on the third day. He ran backwards once and broke loose so suddenly that he fell backwards and made a complete somersault. Most ropes are cotton or nylon clothesline, sometimes painted red. Only three of those used in 1974 were rawhide.

This pledger bites down hard on his sage head wreath as he is pierced, and the Mother of the Year wipes his brow to comfort him. Some pledgers bite down on their pipe stems, and even a stick.

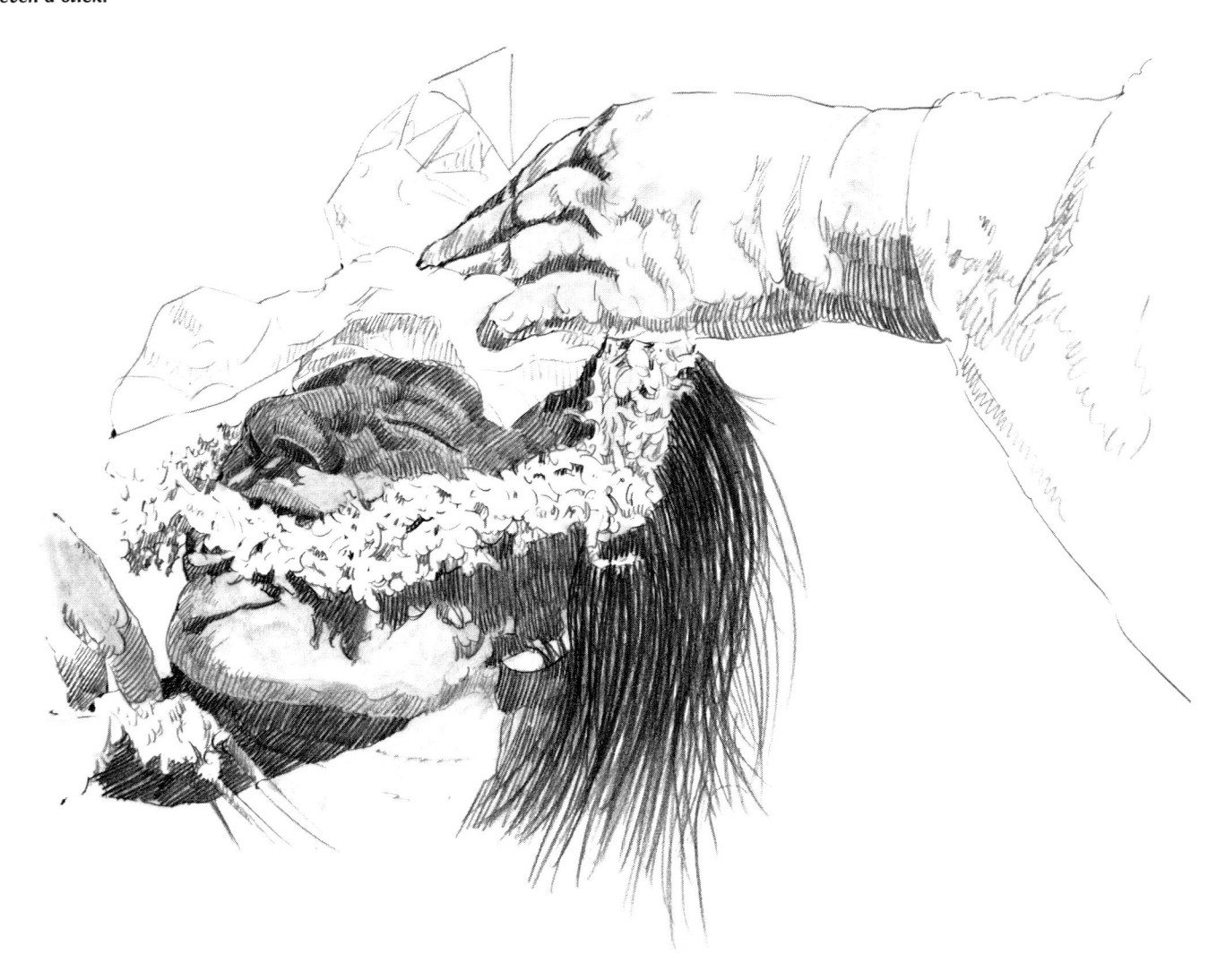

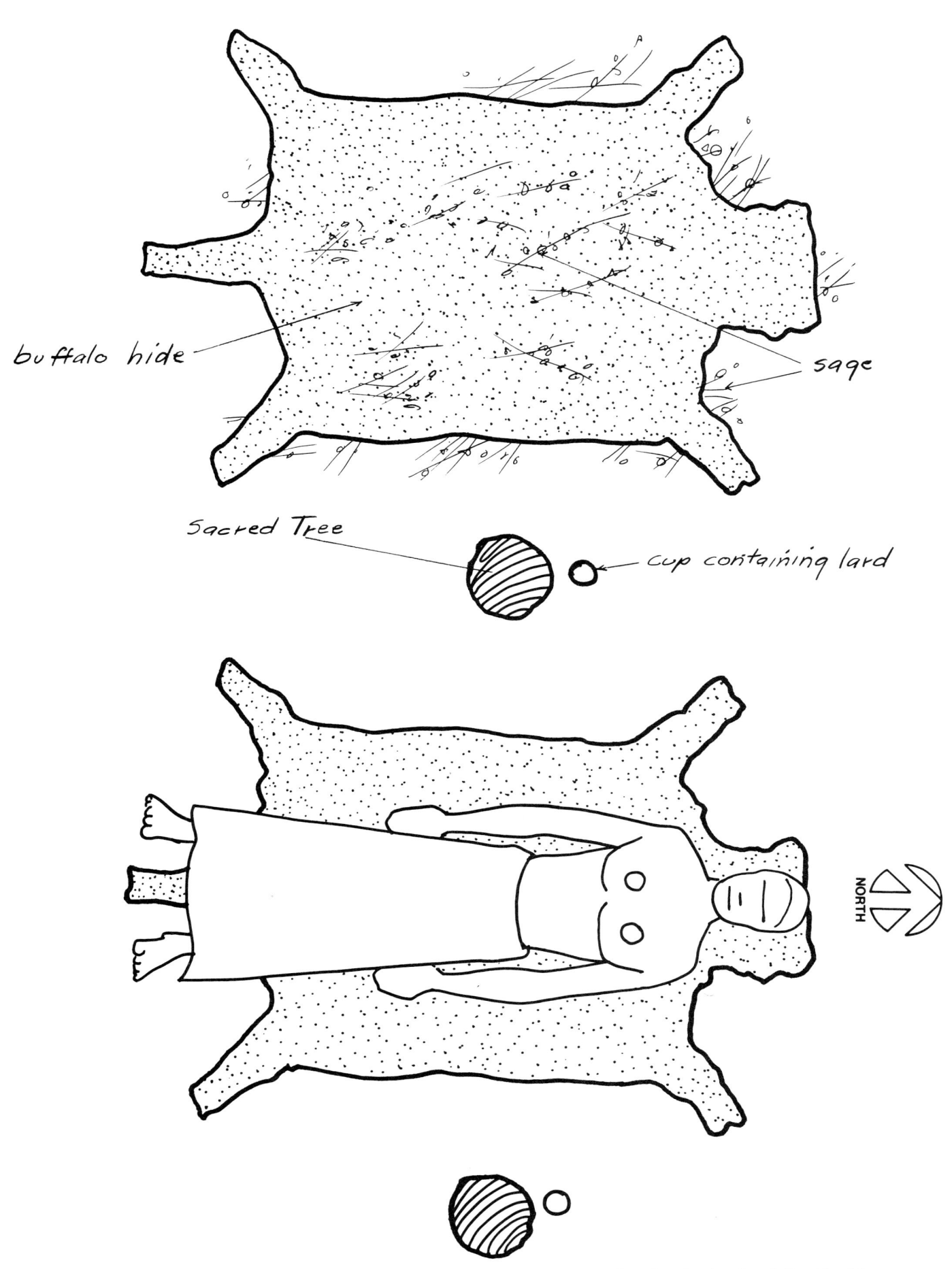

*Top: plan showing the relationship of the buffalo hide and sage bed to the Sacred Tree.
Bottom: the position taken by the pledger as he lies on the hide to be pierced.*

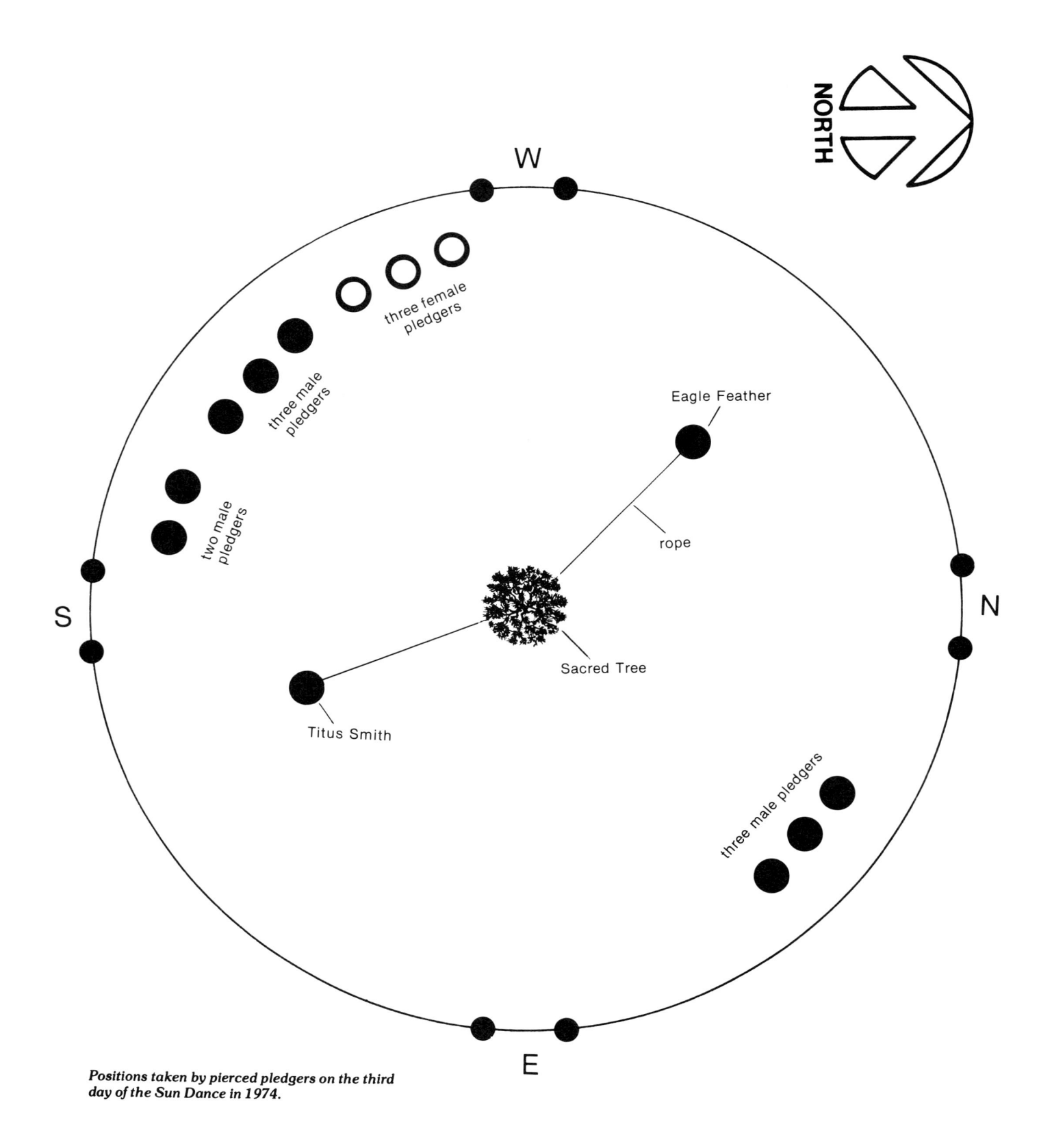

Positions taken by pierced pledgers on the third day of the Sun Dance in 1974.

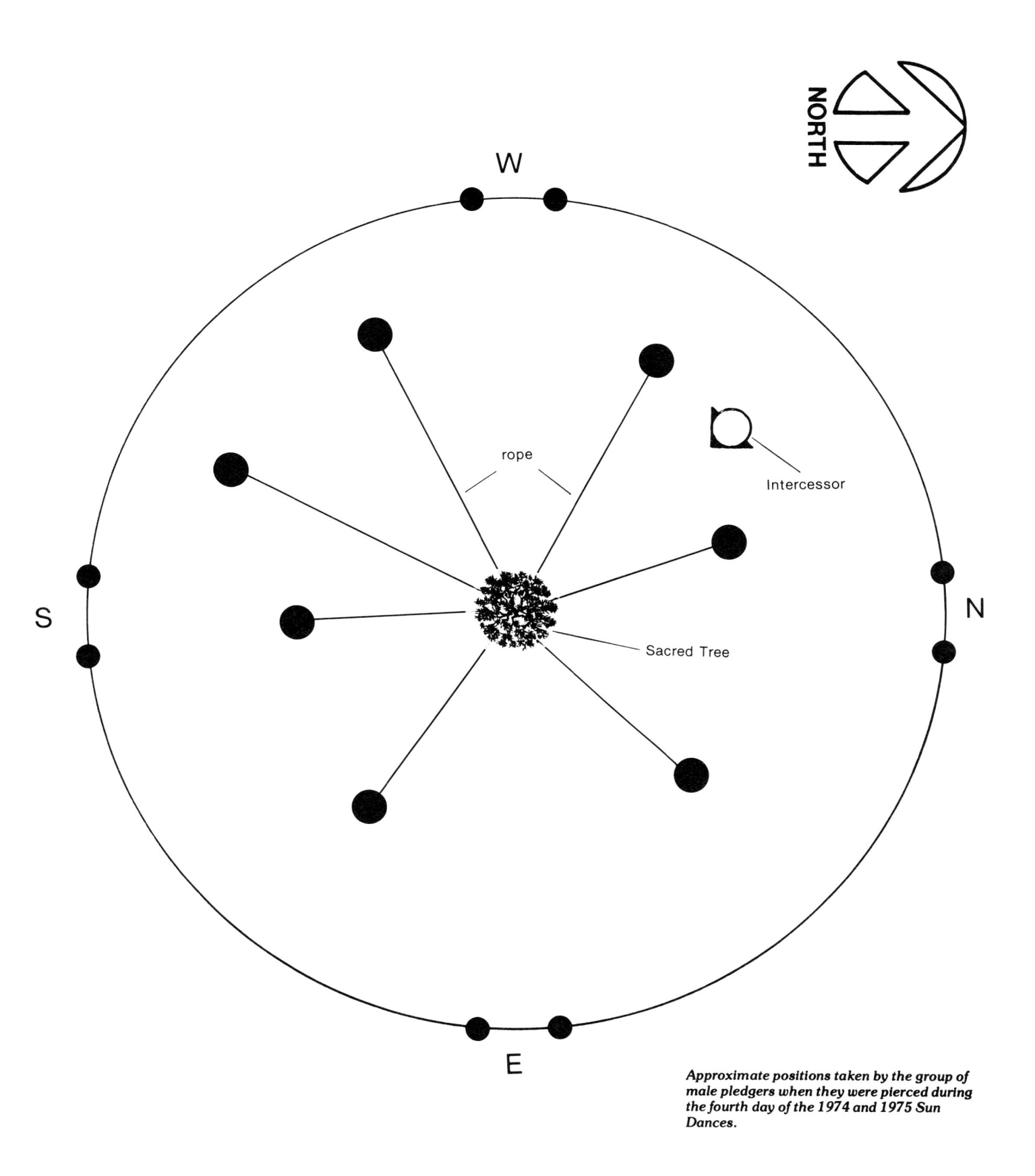

Approximate positions taken by the group of male pledgers when they were pierced during the fourth day of the 1974 and 1975 Sun Dances.

191

In 1975, the family and friends of the pledgers were invited to stand just behind them after they were pierced to give them encouragement, and the Mother of the Year was with them at the base of the Tree to wipe their wounds with sage and cloths when they were skewered. Neither of these things was done in 1974.

The medicine men pierce and pull free first; then the other pledgers pierce, go four times to the Tree, and pull free. As each man succeeds, Eagle Feather puts his arm around his shoulders, congratulating and comforting him. In 1974, it took only five minutes for the entire second group to break loose.

"Don't call this a ceremony," said the announcer. "This is our religion."

In 1975, one of the piercings was of such a nature as to make even the most experienced spectators gasp. Robert Blackfeather waited until all of the other pledgers had pierced and pulled free. Then he was brought to the microphone, where he said a few words about the Sun Dance and followed that with the graphic details of a vision in which he foresaw a great calamity coming upon the world in the form of famine, earthquakes, pestilence, violence, and war. Because of this, he would be pierced in a special way as a prayer for the deliverance of mankind.

Two long ropes were attached at one end to the Tree and then pulled apart and stretched back to the black flags at the north to make a corridor for Blackfeather's relatives and friends to walk along as they went from the shade to the Tree, where they stood to give him encouragement and support. Robert's two ropes were shortened to one-fourth the usual length. Then Gilbert Yellow Hawk got down on his hands and knees at the foot of the Sacred Tree. Robert stood on Gilbert's back and was pierced on both sides of the chest while standing there. He raised his arms and blew his whistle. Then Gilbert moved swiftly from underneath him, and Robert dropped like a shot, bringing audible cries from the flabbergasted spectators. For a few moments he swung back and forth freely like a pendulum. Then medicine men added their weight to his, but the skewers still held. Finally they had to cut him free. Most of us wondered whether he could stand up. But in a few minutes he did, to the obvious relief and admiration of the crowd. It was a stunning performance. No such piercing took place in 1974.

The wounds in Robert's chest were large and deep. Later, he said this was his last piercing, but others have said the same and changed their minds surprisingly soon.

Orrie Farrell and Jerry Dragg both pierced in 1974 and did so again in 1975. But on this second occasion they were pierced more deeply and took some time to pull free. The holes torn in Jerry's chest were the size of a quarter, ragged and ugly. I could see exposed muscle, it must have hurt terribly. Besides these two men, Reuben Fire Thunder was pierced a second time on both sides on the fourth day—a truly amazing feat of courage.

Such extreme piercings are becoming more common each year. During the Sun Dances held at the AIM headquarters at Crow Dog's, on the Rosebud Reservation, as many as eighty-nine male pledgers and twenty-four female pledgers have joined in a single dance. Of the men, forty-seven were pierced in the usual way, and eighteen dragged buffalo skulls behind them which were held by ropes skewered to their backs. I was told by some who witnessed the event that the piercing in some instances was done badly, and the result was such a bloody mess that it made a number of spectators ill.

Besides the common type of piercing, some men do what is called "feather piercing." To do this, the quill of an eagle feather is cut and then tucked in to form a loop. A needle and thread is run through the loop and under the pledger's skin to attach the feathers to him on his back, arms, and shoulders. Depending upon the instructions received in his vision, a man might carry as many as twelve such feathers for one or more days of the dance.

As a further comment about piercing, I am forced to wonder, whenever I read that in the old days men were pierced under the muscles, whether that is true. Having seen how pledgers are forced to pull to break a deep skin piercing, I am inclined to doubt that a skewer under or through a muscle would ever pull free without first breaking the stick. The skin itself can be exceedingly tough. The outer layer, or *epidermis*, is itself many-layered. The underlying dermis, called the *corium*, or "true skin," is a dense, elastic layer of fibrous tissue that contains and supports many important structures of the skin. This is the part of animal skins that makes leather when tanned. Then comes an indefinite layer of subcutaneous tissue. All this must be penetrated before muscle is reached. When the Intercessor speaks of the *"flesh,"* he is referring to a piercing which penetrates the dermis, not a muscle.

The most common form of piercing nowadays is that of being tied to the Sun Pole. But the recent intensification of the dance has caused the more fervent pledgers to resort to more painful and dramtic forms.

I have mentioned the pendulumlike hanging of Robert Blackfeather, the deeper piercings of Orrie Farrell and Jerry Dragg, the

Jerry Dragg is caught up in pain and ecstasy as he struggles to break free of the rope that ties him to the Sacred Tree in 1975.

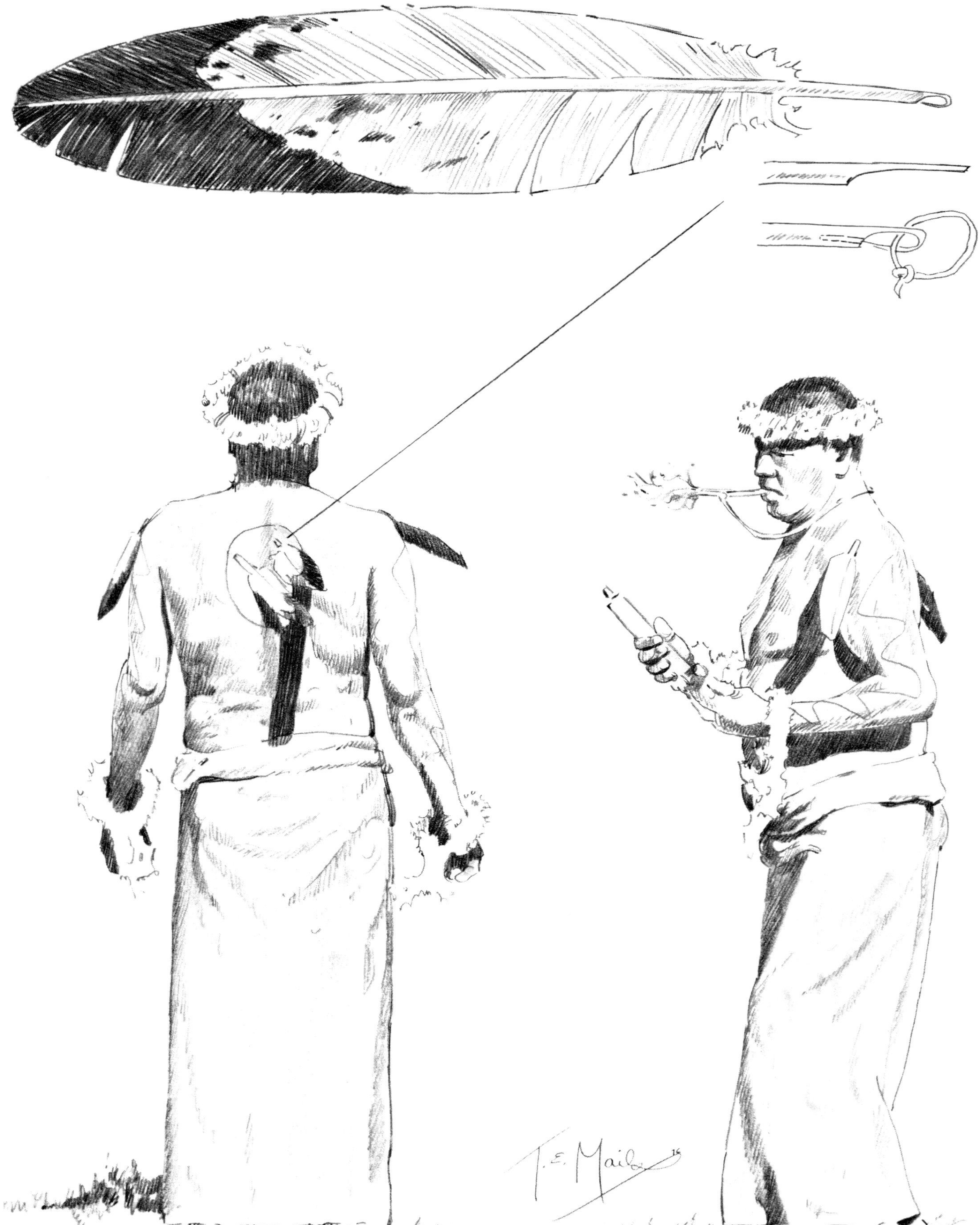

double piercing of Reuben Fire Thunder in a single dance, and the dragging of the buffalo skulls at Crow Dog's Paradise.

In ancient times four methods of piercing were observed, and judging from what has already happened, I am certain that all four methods will be seen again in forthcoming Sun Dances.

One method consisted of being hung in midair from the pole by ropes tied to skewers inserted in the chest or back.

Another consisted of being tied to the pole in the commonest way, with the pledger then pulling back on the thongs.

A third way of piercing was to have buffalo skulls, each weighing as much as twenty-five pounds, either hung from the chest and/or back, or else tied to ropes so that the pledger could drag the skulls behind him. Fools Crow saw this done several times in the old days, and in each instance the pledger dragged a single skull which was turned upside down so that the horns dug into the soil.

The fourth way was the most severe. For this sacrifice the pledger was secured by skewers and thongs from the chest and back to four corner posts. The pledger stood on his toes in the middle of the square formed by the posts, and attempted to pull himself free.

Fools Crow also saw this done once. "The pledger," he said, "was amazingly brave. He pulled all day, all night, and part of the next day before he tore loose." In discussing it with him, I got the impression that Fools Crow was more stirred by this piercing than any other he had seen over the years.

At 11:45 A.M., the sacrificing of the 1975 Sun Dance was finished.

The pledgers formed a single line and were led in a circle from the west, to the north, to the east, and to the south. Eagle Feather brought a pipe from the Altar and gave it to a woman pledger, who then presented it to the Keeper in the customary way. At this point the pledgers proceeded to the shade area, while the Intercessor made a concluding speech to the audience about the dance. I noted that the pledgers were shaking hands and congratulating one another.

When he finished his talk, Eagle Feather had the pledgers assemble in front of the Altar and face the Tree. Then he asked those who would participate in the dance on the following year to step forward. All but two men did. Then the audience, including the non-Indians, was invited to join the pledgers for their final four moves across the Mystery Circle. In both 1974 and 1975 a great number of people did join in. When the east flags were reached, the Sun Dance was over.

In 1974 the pledgers proceeded directly to the Preparations Tipi, and by 1:00 the Tipi cover had been removed and the poles taken down. Then the sweatlodge was dismantled.

In 1975 a social gathering followed the dance and continued for an hour or more, with speeches being made and women spreading out beautiful star quilts and other items for sale.

Eagle Feather's 1976 Sun Dance, held at the Rosebud Fairground July 1-4, followed in a general way the pattern of his 1975 dance. There were no significant variations, and a parallel account is not needed. Plans were announced for the inclusion of a Grey Owl Ceremony, whose nature I do not know, but it was not performed.

Feather piercing. Top: *method of looping quill to receive thread loop that passes also through the pledger's skin.* Lower left: *back piercing.* Lower right: *shoulder piercing.*

position 1

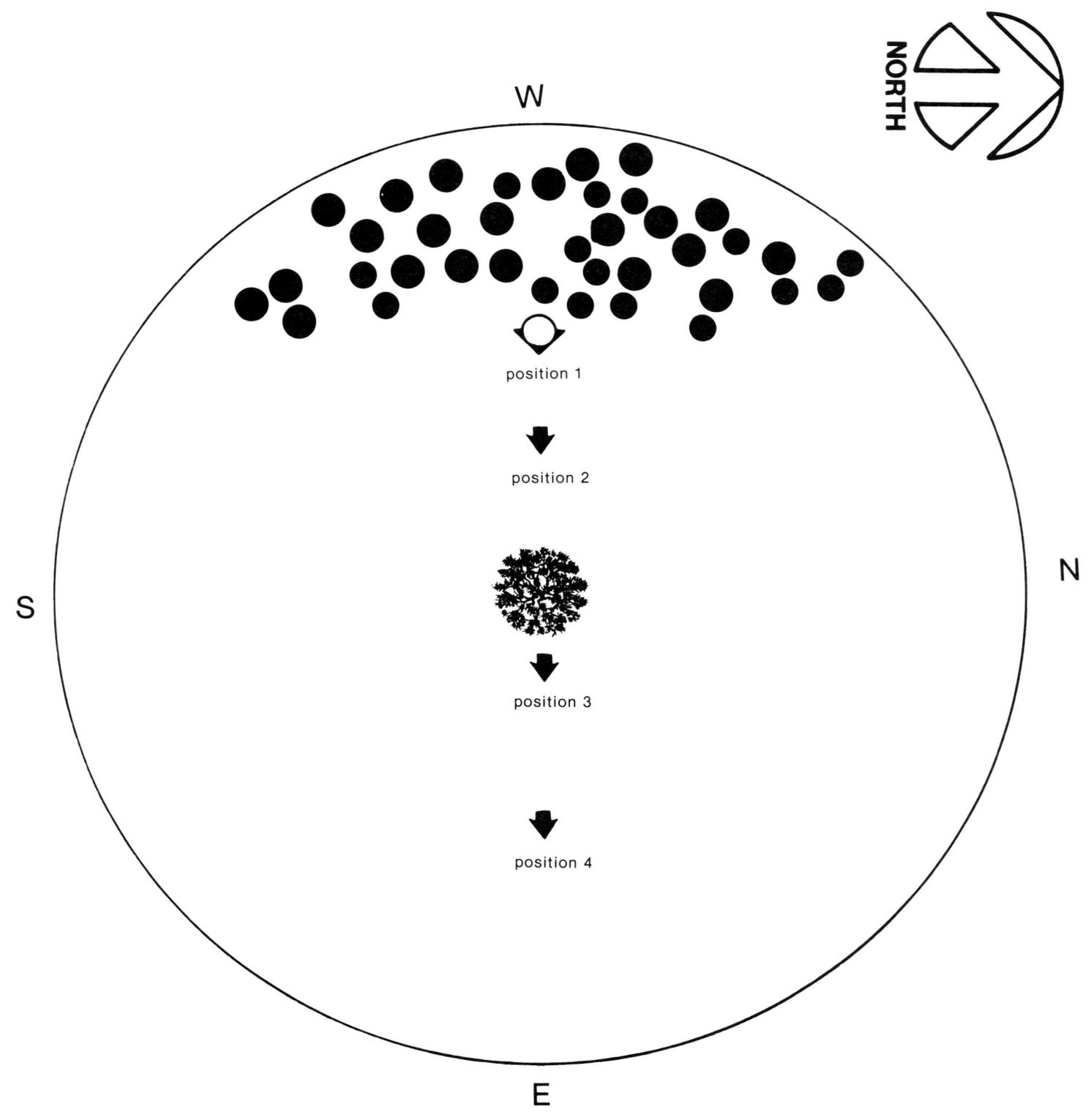

position 2

position 3

position 4

W / N / S / E

NORTH

Positions taken by pledgers and spectators as entire group makes four moves across the Mystery Circle at the conclusion of the Sun Dance on the fourth day.

196

XVII
The Pine Ridge Sun Dance

FOOLS CROW

Over a period of several years, it has been my great privilege to discuss with Fools Crow the way in which he conducts a Sun Dance on the Pine Ridge Reservation. This chapter is a summary of those discussions, which were translated by Dallas Chief Eagle.

To begin with, he told me it is commonly believed that when the government agents told the Sioux in 1881 to stop doing the Sun Dance, they obeyed and held no further dances until two large public dances were held with government permission in 1928 at Rosebud and in 1929 at Pine Ridge. But this is not so. Fools Crow states that the Sun Dance was celebrated at Pine Ridge almost every year, and with piercing. It was always held in a remote area, where the crowd would be small, and precautions could be taken to avoid discovery. It had to be so. The Sun Dance is their religion, their highest way of paying honor to God; therefore they celebrated it in secret nearly every year, and the favored time was the last part of July. Fools Crow attended many of the ceremonies.

Other Sun Dances were held at intervals without piercing, because these were not flatly outlawed so long as they did them quietly. For private purposes the Sioux could go ahead with everything but the torture aspects: there could be no flesh-piercing or flesh-offerings. White spectators, friends of the Sioux, were present at some of the Sun Dances where there was piercing. But they knew what was being done was against the law, and did not report it. Sometimes White men even joined in the dances with the Indians, although they did not pierce at any Fools Crow attended.

"As I said, the Sun Dances with piercing were done in secret and with the ominous threat of arrest hanging over us. We were even afraid of the Indian police, so we started dancing each day when the sun came up and would quit and scatter when the sun went down. We did this every day for four days, going home at night and coming back the next morning. The piercing always took place on the fourth day, about 10:00 A.M.

"Most of the piercing was the commonly known type, where the man was attached to the Sun Pole by long thongs tied to sticks which pierced his chest. Occasionally, a man would be pierced in the back and drag around a single buffalo skull, with the skull turned upside down and the horns digging into the ground. I saw several men do this, but I never in those days saw anyone pull more than one skull at a time. They are very heavy, weighing as much as twenty-five pounds, and with the horns digging in, one is plenty to handle.

"When I was only five or six years old, I was taken to a secret Sun Dance at a place south of Whiteclay. There were quite a few Indians there, and one young man was pierced and tied to four poles, two in the front and two in the back. He was held up, pierced and tied, and when they let him go, only his toes touched the ground. He hung there between the poles for two days, with the skin of his chest and back continuing to stretch and stretch. He was in terrible pain, and struggling all the time. Even at my age I could see what an ordeal it was for him. Finally, he tore loose from all four of the ropes. Even then, he continued on for another two days and nights without food and water. I don't know his name, but he was about the bravest man I ever saw."

I told Fools Crow that at the Sun Dances I attended at Rosebud, I had heard the announcers say repeatedly, "This is our religion, this is our religion." Did his announcers say the same thing? If so, why and what kind of spiritual power does the dance really have for the people?

He said in reply that the Sioux are raised with the Sun Dance, and it is the highest expression of their religion. All share in the fasting, in the prayer, and in the benefits. Some in the audience pray along silently with the dancers. Near relatives will often fast for the full four days, and these will come to the Sun Pole and stand close to the pledgers as they are pierced on the fourth day. Their presence in the Mystery Circle at that time indicates that they have been praying and fasting. They do not just come to stand with them as a token gesture of sympathy and comfort. Everyone is profoundly involved, and in consequence both the Sioux nation and the world are blessed by *Wakan-Tanka*.

As previously indicated, Fools Crow's earliest training as an Intercessor, the one who leads the Sun Dance, came from a medicine man named Stirrup. He then observed many of the secret dances done with piercing, and so added in this manner to his knowledge. However, his first direct involvement came in 1929, when the now famous public dance was held at government request at the town of Pine Ridge. Spotted Crow, who was the Intercessor, asked Fools Crow to assist him, "because from then on Fools Crow's role would be that of Intercessor." He did not at once accept the invitation. But Fools Crow's father, Eagle Bear, said, "Look, Spotted Crow is an old man now, and he has asked you to help him. He is in a pitiful condition, you must go and assist him."

So Fools Crow did as his father asked, and each year since then when the Sioux have wished to have a Sun Dance, Fools Crow has served as the Intercessor. He is notified several weeks before a dance is to be held, and it takes place over the last two days in July and the first two days of August. He also leads Sun Dances on other reservations, and has probably conducted a total of seventy-five or more.

Despite his previous experience with Stirrup and the secret dances, his actual training of import took place during the 1929 ceremony. Spotted Crow used the occasion to instruct him in every facet of the ritual, teaching him how and why each thing was done —except piercing. He had to teach himself to do that.

Over the years after 1929, the Sioux pleaded with the agency superintendents to let them pierce. Finally, in 1952, Fools Crow was called to the agency office and informed that he could pierce the male pledgers, with a certain condition. "They asked me whether I had my medicine to pierce. When I said yes, they told me that if there was any infection or other ill effect, the responsibility would be mine—not that of the agency or the local doctors. So I said I would take it, because I had the proper medicine."

A letter of permission was issued in 1952, and Fools Crow pierced eight men that year. Since then, he has pierced pledgers yearly as a regular part of the Sun Dance. Fools Crow once had a copy of the letter, but it was lost in a fire which burned his home. He thinks that another copy is on file at tribal headquarters.

Since either a four or five-inch long wooden stick or an eagle claw is usually employed for the piercing, I wanted to know whether Fools Crow allowed the use of the eagle claw which is so common at Rosebud today. He answered that neither the people, the pledgers, or he wanted to use it in the early days. Eagles handled dirt, snakes, and small animals, and they felt the claws might transmit germs. Did he permit the use of claws in his dances today. "No," he said, "I have pledgers who would like to, but I won't permit it at Pine Ridge. When I'm elsewhere and they want to do it, I let someone else insert the eagle claw."

"Is there more than one Sun Dance on the Pine Ridge Reservation each year?"

He answered, "Just one."

"At Rosebud," I said, "there are several, as many as four or five."

"We only have one, which is the way it was done in the old days."

"What then," I wanted to know, "is the role of the cottonwood tree in the Sun Dance? Do you select it?"

"Others go out first to find a selection of trees that might do. Then they take me to the area on the day before the dance and I make the final choice. Once we have selected it, we form a circle around the tree. We pray, and then I wipe the tree trunk with a braid of sweetgrass. After this I light my sacred pipe, and smoke it, and offer it to the seven powers. Then I touch the tree with the mouthpiece of the pipe at the four cardinal directions. I light the sweetgrass and smoke the tree on all sides to purify it. Then a young girl, a virgin, takes an axe and chops the tree once at each of the directions. Following this, several men cut the tree down with saws and axes."

"Could you use a power saw if you had one?"

"Yes, it wouldn't matter or do anything to the sacredness of the ritual."

"Does it matter whether the tree touches the ground when it falls? I have read that it does."

"It is all right if it touches the ground. We do use wooden crosssticks, branches, to make a litter to carry it to the truck which transports the tree to the dance ground, and when it is unloaded from there into the Mystery Circle."

"Is there any difference between the tree used nowadays and the tree used for the old secret dances?"

"To avoid attracting attention, we made a small clearing for a Mystery Circle in the middle of a grove of trees. The Sun Pole was always a short one compared to the fifty-foot trees used today. We cut it short so that it would not stick up and be seen. But the bundle of cherry branches and the rawhide effigies of the man and buffalo remained on the tree for the four days. We did not take them down at night. Anyone who found it would have known what it was."

"I have read that the Sioux consider the tree to be an enemy. In the old days they rode up to it and attacked it with this idea in mind. Do you think of the tree that way, and if so, why? Quite frankly, I fail to understand why this should be so."

"Yes, the warriors did that years ago. They made attacks upon the tree, and when it was chopped down they killed it."

"But why is the tree, being so sacred a part of the dance, an enemy?"

"What they killed was not, in spiritual thought, the tree, but its growth."

"How does that fit into the pattern of thought regarding the dance?"

"It is to destroy an enemy to the people, it symbolizes destroying an enemy."

"I still don't understand. During the Sun Dance, visions are sought from the tree. You touch it with your hands to draw power from it and you pray to it. How do you reconcile this with the idea of an enemy?"

"We kill the tree to stop its growth, so that it will remain exactly as it was at the moment of cutting while we pray to it."

The light dawned, and another marvelous insight was revealed. The Sun Dance is, among other things, a ceremony of renewal and restoration. So the Tree, like Christ on the cross and in the tomb in the Christian concept, represents the lull between the casting off of the old—of the past, ignorance, sin, hopelessness, and, at the end of the four days of ritual, the bursting forth of the new growth—of future, knowledge, forgiveness, and hope. It is an enemy in the sense that at a given point all negative things must cease while the course and attitude of life is altered and redirected through ritual.

"Frank, the Tree is brought to the Sun Dance ground, removed from the truck, and carried on cross sticks to the east entrance of the Mystery Circle. Do you, as is the custom, stop four times on the way, and do you lead the procession?"

"I walk beside the Tree and we do stop four times to pray."

"What kinds of prayers?"

"I pray to the two higher powers and to Grandmother Earth, saying that this Tree has come from her. We have taken it from her to use for a special purpose. In our humble way we will help her make it holy. Then I pray for all of the people in the world, that beginning today and for the four days following we will ask the powers to give us their special attention. We want them to hear our prayers and to grant our requests, because we are all people who need divine pity. I say this: From the earth, from you, Grandmother, we have been given this Tree. And you have given us many things from yourself, and I name some, including minerals. These come from you. Make our hearts feel good, give them rest, make us happy and contented wihout ill feelings. We have taken things from you, but only because we feel you have given them to us for this special occasion. May it be that from this point on all the people, including the children, will walk the one good road together."

"Do you pray approximately the same prayer each time you stop?"

"The same."

"In the old days, as the Intercessor walked with the Tree he sometimes made the noise of a wailing coyote. Do you do that?"

"They did do this, they made the sound of a coyote or a wolf—the two are thought of in the same way—and even today some Intercessors make it. But I don't. I feel that people do not want me to, because as the Tree is brought in they are lost in meditation, and the shout would surprise and disturb them."

"At Rosebud, it is the custom to place *wasna*, buffalo fat, pemmican, and sage in the hole before the Tree is placed in it and raised. What do you place in the hole?"

"The day before the Sun Dance begins, I give flesh offerings as a prayer to *Wakan-Tanka* for good weather during the dance. As I was told to do in a vision, I take these from my forehead, the palms of my hands, and the soles of my feet. First I put herb medicine on the places where I intend to cut. Then I lift the flesh with a needle and cut the pieces off with a razor blade. I then wrap the flesh bits in pieces of cloth and put them in the hole where the sacred Tree goes.

"I do this same thing when I make offerings to the powers at Bear Butte. God gave me the healing medicine I apply before and after I cut the pieces. He did not tell me to share it, so I don't. If He wanted me to do that He would have said so plainly. When I use the medicine I feel no pain, and the cuts heal quickly. Also, you will notice I have no scars, while others who give flesh offerings have scars and even black spots. This does not happen to me. I have good medicine.

"The only other items I place in the hole are sage and a little saucer of *wasna*, which is a mixture of all the things you mentioned are used at Rosebud. What I put down there is taken by the good spirits. When the Tree is removed after the Sun Dance everything is gone, including the saucer. It just disappears, and is never there when we look for it."

"What do you attach to the Sun Pole Tree before it is erected?"

"I make a large bundle of cherry branches, and in the middle of it I place a special medicine bag containing a cherry tree root, fat or tallow, and dried meat and sage. The bag is not visible from the ground when the Tree is up, but this does not matter since it is an offering to God in thanksgiving for what he has done and will do for us. The *wasna* under the Tree is an offering too, but is given in honor of the people of all nationalities who have died and left needy dependents. It is a prayer that God will watch over them, and feed the dead and their widows and children."

"Do you hold the *wasna* and sage out to the directions and up to the highest powers before placing it in the hole?"

"No, because it is going down into Grandmother Earth."

"Before you put these things in the hole, do you smoke the hole with sweetgrass to purify it?"

"Yes."

"What comes next?"

"We tie the ropes which the pledgers will pull on to the tree, just below the place where it forks."

"I assume that you also tie to the upper branches an image of a man and a buffalo?"

"I do."

"What is the man like?"

"Both are rawhide and cut from a piece of buffalo hide, which has the hair removed. The man holds the hoop of the Sioux nation in one hand, and its sacred pipe in the other. The man is painted red on both sides, while the buffalo is painted red on one side and green on the other—the same as the buffalo skull for the altar—and the colors mean the same thing. The red is for fire and the Lakota people, and the green is for growth."

"In ancient times, some of the images had an erect reproductive organ. Do yours include that?"

"No, the green color is used now as a prayer for reproduction and healthy growth."

"Do you tie the four customary cloth banners to the Tree?"

"The highest one I put on the Tree is white, the next lower one is yellow, then red, and the lowest banner is black. Their purpose is to help the pledgers and the people, as they pray and seek visions in the Tree, to move up the scale of colors from sin and ignorance, symbolized by the black banner, until they reach the white banner, which stands for purity and enlightenment."

Having completed our discussion about the Sun Pole, I turned our thoughts to the sweatlodge. On the last night before the Sun Dance begins, a purification ceremony is held in it, and then each of the four days begins and ends with all of the participants sharing in a similar ritual.

"Frank, in constructing his outside fire pit when the sweatlodge rocks are heated, Chief Eagle Feather forms at Rosebud four piles of dirt at the top of the pit which spread out like rays of light, and he calls them 'horns.' Do you do this?"

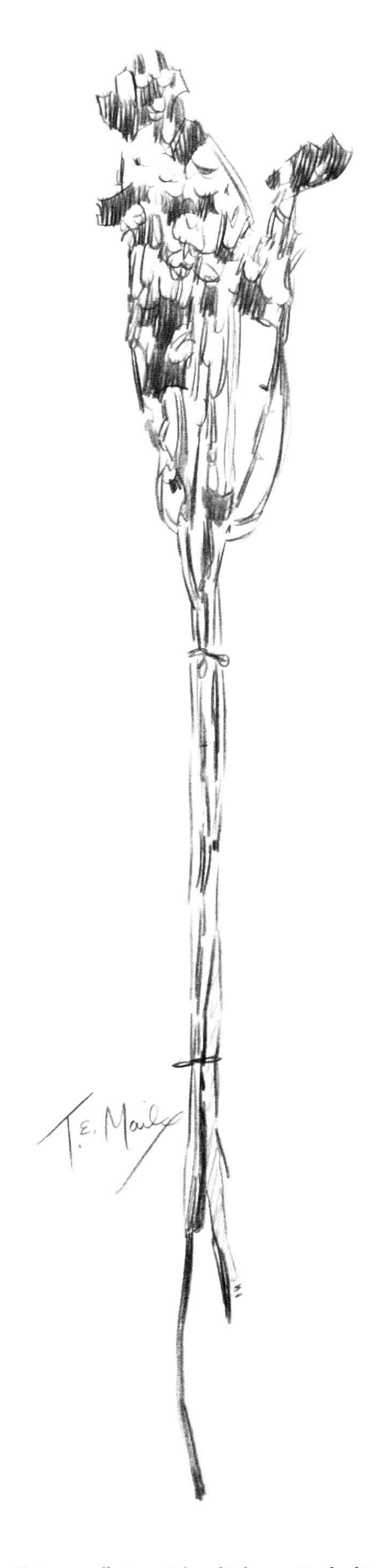

Tobacco offering sticks which are attached to the shade arbor posts and to the Sun Dance Tree.

"No, I just dig a regular pit, and it has no symbolism attached to it."

"Where do you suppose he got the idea?"

"I haven't the slightest notion."

"How many rocks do you use for the Sun Dance sweatlodge fire pit?"

"Twelve. Of these I select the one that will be the seventh passed into the lodge and I paint a red circle on it. This is to show that in the lodge we will be seated in a circle, and our hearts will be one; unified."

"How are the heated rocks placed in the pit which is within the sweatlodge itself?"

"Beginning with the west, four rocks are placed at the four cardinal directions. Then there is silent prayer. After this a rock is placed near the center for Grandmother Earth, then one there for Grandfather, and the seventh with the painted circle is placed at the exact center for *Wakan-Tanka*, the highest power. The remaining five rocks are simply piled on top of the first seven as we all pray quietly."

"How do you enter the sweatlodge, and how are the participants seated?"

"The entrance door always faces west. I enter on my hands and knees and crawl around the outside edge in a clockwise direction. I seat myself on the south side of the entrance. My helper sits on the north side of the entrance. Then the others enter and are seated around the edge of the lodge in the area between us. My helper has either a forked elkhorn or wooden branch which he uses to arrange the hot rocks in the fire pit. He also has a pipe, and as each rock is passed in from the outside by our custodian, he touches it with the mouthpiece of the pipe. This is to bless the rock and to infuse it with *Wakan-Tanka's* power. When all of the rocks are in, we first of all bow down and pray in silence, each person in his own way and with his own thoughts."

"Frank, the chanting in the sweatlodge is absolutely beautiful. How does a typical song go, what do you say?"

"The custodian closes the door flap, and seals out all air and light. Then everyone stops praying and raises up. I have with me a bucket of water and a cup. I fill the cup and pour the water on the rocks, first on the west, then north, then east, and finally south. Then I pour some to each of the higher powers, and finally to Grandmother Earth. The steam rises, and we all stretch and clear our throats, because we will soon be singing. There is a brief pause, and then I pray about the powers that are in the lodge with us. Then I sing to them. I say, 'You are coming, you are coming among us. We have prepared everything for you and we are waiting.' I repeat this three times. Then I sing the same thing three time to *Wankan-Tanka* and Grandfather. Then I do the same for Grandmother Earth. After this I do it all over again, but my song this time is, 'You are all here. You are among us, you are with us, you are in our presence!' Then I make my little 'whoo' sound to the spirits, the one I made for you before. By this time the spirits are answering me with the same sound, and we hear it everywhere, inside around, above, outside. They are there!"

At this point we deviated from the sweatlodge conversation and held a brief discussion about how Fools Crow distinguishes between the high power and the highest power. I wanted to know what the exact difference was between *Tunkashila*, Grandfather, and *Wakan-Tanka*. He answered that *Tunkashila* is only slightly lower than *Wankan-Tanka*.

I asked for a proper translation of *Wakan-Tanka;* was Great Spirit adequate? "No," Dallas Chief Eagle replied, "not Great Spirit, I would say the Holiest One."

"*Wakan*, taken literally, means holy. *Tanka* means big or great. But 'Big Holy' doesn't do it. A better translation would be 'Holiest of All,' or 'Holiest of Everything.' "

Fools Crow agreed at that point. "Perhaps that is the closest we've come, since He is everywhere, even across the sea and sky; the Holiest of Everything." I thought it a beautiful descriptive name, The Holiest of Everything.

I asked him then about the role of the sun in the Sun Dance. Several writers have claimed that the Sioux were and are sun worshippers, and while some ancient informants may have led them to that conclusion I personally doubted it. What was Fools Crow's opinion, I wanted to know?

"Much has been said about the role of the sun in the dance. To us it is like the Sacred Pipe. It knows everything. They are both instruments used by *Wakan-Tanka*, and the greatest instrument of service he has next to the directions is the sun. The sun is not God. It is something He created for the world. We pay homage to it because it watches over the world and sees everything that is going on. It also serves God by bestowing its peculiar gifts upon the world. I want to emphasize again that the sun is not God. There is only one true God, and the Sioux have believed this for as far back in time as we can remember.

"It is also said that we stare continually at the sun while we dance. But we have never done that. Part of the time we have our backs to it and stare at the cloth banners on the top of the Tree. These are the same four colors as we use in the *Yuwipi* ceremony, but their sequence is just the opposite. The pledgers and I do pray to God through the sun. We ask for strength to complete the Sun Dance, and that all our prayers will be heard. As the pledgers continue to do this, they are finally able to see the sun with their eyes completely open. It doesn't blind them, and in it they see visions — which the pledgers usually keep to themselves. No one should be surprised at all this. Many wonderful and mysterious things happen at the Sun Dances to prove that Grandfather's power is active in our midst."

We returned to the sweatlodge. "I assume," I said, "that you follow the custom of opening the sweatlodge door four times during a purification ceremony?"

"We do, and the total length of time the ceremony lasts after I have completed my part is determined by the duration of the individual prayers of the pledgers. Each man offers a prayer which explains why he is participating in the Sun Dance. He concludes by expressing his gratitude to the powers for what they have done and will do for him. Any form of prayer or expression of need is acceptable in such instances. For example, one man might be concerned about personal illness or illness in his family and another about financial problems. Whatever it is, he asks for help, and then ends his prayer by expressing his assurance that the request will be answered."

"What is the last thing you do to complete a purification ceremony? How does the custodian know he is to open the door flap for the fourth and last time?"

"The last thing I do is pray, 'Well, God, I am going to be outside pretty soon. But before I go, make everything well. When I leave here and these people leave here let us do so with a clean heart, soul, and body. Let us be pure and keep us that way. And, show us the good road we must all walk in unity and as close friends—whether we are red, white, black or yellow.' Then I shout 'HO' four times in

Lakota, and the custodian knows we are finished. 'HO' means, we are through now. He opens the door flap. If there is any water left in the bucket I give it to the pledgers. They can drink it or rub themselves with it. If there is still some left over when I have done this, I pour it on the rocks. The water must be entirely consumed. Then we exit the sweatlodge in a clockwise direction."

"When exactly are your purification rituals held?"

"Each man shares in one after the Tree is up on the evening of the day before the Sun Dance begins, then we have one each morning before sunup and one at sundown on each of the four days of the dance. On the final day, when the piercing is finished, we have our last sweatbath. The principal reason for this one is to avoid the crowd and to be alone with our thoughts. Once we are in the lodge people understand that we are in deep prayer and remembrance, and should be left alone."

Before considering the procedure which is followed during the four days of the Sun Dance, I felt it would be valuable to know how Fools Crow makes the Sun Dance Altar, which is located at the west cardinal direction of the Mystery Circle, and also whether and how his pledgers are painted.

"While some Intercessors do not paint the buffalo skull used for the Altar, I paint it in the traditional Oglala way. I make a dividing line down the middle of the skull and paint it red on the left side and green on the right, including the horns. The red symbolizes the Lakota people and fire, and the green stands for fertility and growth. The earth is covered with green, and children are just like the earth's covering. They grow. So green is good for the earth and good for growing children. I also put the balls of sage in the mouth and eye openings for purification, and the skull itself is placed on a bed of sage.

"To make the rest of the Altar, I draw a grooved line in the ground making a two-foot square. Then I cut out the square of dirt and turn it over. After that, I trace two shallow intersecting lines within the square in such a way as to divide it into four equal parts, like a window pane, so there is a cross within the square. Then I fill these shallow grooves with tobacco which has first been offered to *Wakan-Tanka*, Grandfather, Grandmother Earth, and the four cardinal directions. Over this I sprinkle powdered red paint, and then shiny white mica dust. It only takes a minute to do this. If any of the pledgers want to, they can place a downy eagle feather at any of the points where the Altar lines intersect. It is not necessary that this be done; they only do it if they wish to make a special prayer through the eagle. Sage is then spread over the Altar square, and during the dance the buffalo skull is placed in its center, facing the rising sun in the east.

"The pipe rack is made of three cherry-wood sticks, painted green. It is set up to the immediate west of the Altar Square, so that when the pledgers' pipe stems are leaned against it during the dance their bowls will be even with the westernmost line of the square. The pipe stems of the Intercessor, assistants, and the dance leader are leaned against the buffalo skull on its south and north sides. A pipe rack can hold about a dozen pipe stems, so when there are more pledgers than that, the men share the pipes. They do not all carry one."

"What about body paint, do your pledgers use it?"

"When I am the Intercessor for the Sun Dance, the medicine men assist me by painting each of the pledgers according to their vision. If a man has received his message through a buffalo, his body is painted black from the waist up, and red from the waist down. If he has received his message through a thunder being, lightning lines are painted on his arms, legs, chest, forehead, and the sides of his face. Lightning lines are usually forked at the end, and only those who have had thunder-being visions should use this design. The elk and deer vision men are painted from head to foot with white spots. There is no base paint, just the spots.

"In the old days, men who had visions of buffalo wore curved eagle feathers on their heads, and those with elk or deer visions wore the horns of the animals wrapped with fur, such as otter skin. Nowadays we often paint the men in the old way, but they do not wear the curved feathers or the horns on their heads. At Pine Ridge, all of the painting is done on the first day of the dance after the sweatlodge and before the pledgers come into the Mystery Circle.

"In addition to their body paint, the male pledgers have either one or two red circles drawn on their chests to indicate how many times they wish to be pierced. The Intercessor is not told what this will be before the dance. He learns it when he sees later how many red circles there are. If a pledger wants to be pierced on one side, there is one circle there. If it is to be on both sides, there is a circle on each side. I have an old earth-paint which the medicine men use to make the circles. An uncle of mine, named Bear Comes Out, brought it home from Utah in 1908, and gave it to me. The supply is getting low now, but I have a little left; probably all I'll ever need."

"Frank, as the first day of the Sun Dance gets underway, what do you, as the Intercessor, think about? What thoughts are running through your mind?"

"Whatever I do I am thinking at the same time that it must be done right; that I must make no mistakes. I know each of the things we all do during the four days by heart, and I have done them over and over again down through the years. I am ready. Being the Intercessor is part of my role in life, yet for the sake of all concerned I must now fill the role perfectly, even in the way we offer our prayers to God. I also think about those who are sharing in the dance with me. I wonder what they have on their minds, and my hope is that they are agreeing we should together follow the good road with one heart. I pray constantly, and I concentrate fully upon leading the Sun Dance as it ought to be led. As I do so I feel good in knowing that I am there, that I am in good health and able, thanks to *Wakan-Tanka's* power, to help the people fulfill their vows."

"So, how does the great Sun Dance ceremony begin?"

"As I have said, each day of the Sun Dance opens with the sweatlodge purification ceremony. It begins before dawn, and is finished by the time the sun has risen completely. Then the crier calls out several times to the people to come. In the meantime the pledgers and other participants get painted and dressed, and line up in single file. The man, usually a young good-looking one, who carries the buffalo skull, is first in line. Behind him, side by side, is the Keeper of the pipes and the Intercessor. Then come the male pledgers and after them the female pledgers, all carrying their own pipes, already filled with sacred tobacco.

"We start from a place near the sweatlodge, which is located to the west of the Mystery Circle, and circle outside the shade arbor to the west. We stop at this cardinal point when we are directly opposite and west of the Sun Pole, and we pray in silence to the west wind and its powers."

"Do you ask the powers to come?"

"No. We do not call them because we don't want the Sun Dance to be disturbed by their wind forces."

"Do you make four such stops?"

"Yes. We move forward a short distance, stop, and then pray to the north wind and its powers. Then we move again, stop and repeat the same prayer to the east winds and their powers. The last pause for prayer is made at the east entrance to the Mystery Circle, where we pray to the south. We enter the circle and walk clockwise, passing behind the Altar at the west and turning back to a position directly in front of it, facing the sun and the Sun Pole. We quickly make up the Altar square, and while the pledgers remain there the singers sing four songs. The pledgers dance in place and offer their pipes up to the Sun.

"When this is done the buffalo skull is set down on a bed of sage on the Altar. The leader of the dancers places his pipe on the north end of the pipe rack, with the bowl on the ground and the stem leaning at an angle on the rack's horizontal bar. Then the pledgers place their pipes next to his side by side, moving from north to south. They return to their place in line, put their eagle bone whistles in their mouths, and blow sharp, piercing blasts on them while they dance in place and the singers sing three more songs.

"If you remember the story of Calf Pipe Woman, this is exactly what she did. She entered the circular tipi in a clockwise direction and placed the pipe bundle on the ground. She also gave the Sioux seven bags for the seven powers, and there are four colored flags in the lodge. We put our pipes down in memory of this, and the four and three songs, which make a total of seven songs, are done in memory of the seven bags.

"At this point I go to the cardinal directions, and ten feet or so inside the perimeter of the Mystery Circle set up, spaced about four feet apart, four pairs of flags, which are sticks with cloth banners tied to them. Two are set at each direction; two black for the west, two red for the north, two yellow for the east, and two white for the south. After this, no member of the audience can step without permission inside the boundary of the circle marked out by the flags, and if any of the participants wish to leave the Mystery Circle, they must exit through a pair of flags and enter again the same way."

"Any pair?"

"Any pair. Once the flags are set up the circle becomes holy ground. Even the other creatures know this. At the last Sun Dance held before the Wounded Knee incident at Pine Ridge in 1973, we suddenly saw a meadowlark dancing on the north side of the Mystery Circle. No one knew where he came from, he was just there. The shade arbor was packed with people and cars were packed all around outside the shade arbor. But the commotion didn't bother him in the least. As we danced four times up to the Sun Pole and back, he danced along with us. Then he danced out between the north flags and flew off. Everyone there saw it, and later said they were amazed that a bird should join us, and even exit the circle in the traditional way."

"What would happen if someone made a mistake and stepped over the boundary line or walked in or out without passing through a pair of flags?"

"It would be a bad omen for that person. Trouble will follow him, and his life will be plagued by suffering, tragedy, or hard times. It might even be that lightning will strike and kill him."

"But it won't hurt the dance or affect the power which is loosed?"

"The bad things will strike the offender after the Sun Dance is over, but tragedy for that one is assured. The point is, that the power of God and the spirits is so great they must not be disobeyed or offended. This is why, as Intercessor, I rely so heavily on the intercessory pipe. Once those flags are set up and the dance begins, power is within the Mystery Circle in a most special way. It also pervades the audience. A careful observer will notice that we now and then point our pipes toward the audience as we dance. This is to make certain they too receive the full blessings of the ceremony, and that their prayers will be heard by *Wakan-Tanka* and *Tunkashila*."

"Frank, what are the words sung by the singers for the first seven songs?"

"Most of it is melody, but the words they do sing are, 'Tunkashila, Grandfather, have pity on us. We have come here and are doing this so that everything will be right with us.' It is a very sensitive time as we begin the dance, and as the singers sing it is common for some of the pledgers and their relatives in the audience to sob openly. We feel no shame in this, it is a wonderful moment."

"What do you do next?"

"I take hold of the left sage wrist-band of the leader of the dancers and lead him in a circle around the Altar. The pledgers come behind us in a single line. We follow the sun, walking past the north this first time because the sun is fairly high now, and we go directly to the flags at the east. Four more songs are sung here while the pledgers dance in place. Then we move to the south and repeat the performance. When the four songs are finished there, I give the leader of dancers his pipe, and he takes it forward and presents it to one of the singers, who stands between the white flags to receive it. Then the dancers exit the circle and rest. While they do, the singers smoke his pipe. This completes the first circle, and the entire procedure is repeated throughout the day, changing the direction we face, toward or away from the Sun Pole, for each circle, until all of the pledgers' pipes have been presented to the singers and smoked.

"It is three o'clock in the afternoon or later when we are done, and we are all very tired from dancing in the hot sun. Some of the pledgers will be in agony, because they are not supposed to eat or drink water for four days."

"How do you end the dancing for the day?"

"The pledgers go to the west, form a line, and dance in place. While they do this, I go and pick up the flags, and the person who brought in the buffalo skull picks it up. Then I lead the pledgers out of the Mystery Circle and to the Preparations Tipis. On the way we stop four times, twice before we get to the east entrance and twice shortly thereafter. The singers continue to sing until the last pledger is outside the Mystery Circle. Once we reach the camp area the women go to their tipi and the men go to theirs. They change clothing, and go to their individual camps, where, except for the sweatlodge ceremony, they remain for the night. The dance begins again the next morning with a sweatlodge purification ceremony."

"In an average dance you have fourteen pledgers, and fourteen pipes to present. But some Sun Dances have as many as seventy-five pledgers. Would that not take forever if the pipes were presented one at a time?"

"At Green Grass we had seventy-two pledgers, so four men at a time took their pipes forward. Even then we finished each day just as the sun went down about 9:00 P.M. It was an exhausting experience."

I thought to myself, yes, and how do you manage to do it when you are past eighty-five years of age? This led me to wonder out loud, since Fools Crow had not mentioned it, whether he was training anyone to take his place?

His answer was that he is teaching several young men: Philip Brown Eyes to be the lead dancer; Dawson No Horse, John Attacked Him, and a certain "Means" who works at the Pine Ridge hospital, to perform the various details; and Everett Lone Hill and Silva Young Bear to be lead singers. Most of the training takes place during the Sun Dances. Whenever the trainees overlook something, deviate or make a mistake, Fools Crow goes to them at the end of the day and discusses it with them.

"Does the training continue at other times during the year?"

"They either come to my house individually, or sometimes they all come together. Then I talk with them about the Sun Dance."

"Have they learned a great deal already?"

"They have, and these young fellows are very good. So when the Sun Dance is in progress I express my gratitude to *Wakan-Tanka* for that. At night, when everything has gone well, when all is quiet and the camp is at peace, I thank Him that we've had no arguments, no conflicts, no bad winds and no rain to disturb the ceremony."

"I have heard," I said, "that it is not supposed to rain on a Sun Dance. But sometimes it does. Why?"

"The last Sun Dance at Porcupine is a good example. It rained on the second day because someone present was impure. Either we or some in the audience were not cleansed properly, so the Thunder spirits brought rain down to help cleanse us."

"Was there lightning?"

"Yes, but it didn't harm anything."

"Did it strike the Sun Pole?"

"No, and we all remained happy because we understood what the problem was. We finished the dance and went home pleased as we usually are."

"Is the second day of the Sun Dance exactly like the first day?"

"The dancing and basic procedure is the same, but the Sun Pole is different in that we see it differently. It not only looks different to us, sometimes we see eagles flying among the branches, or even an airplane in there."

"Does everyone see these things?"

"We do, and we see different things each day."

I knew better by now than to ask what this meant. Sights and visions are one's own property—but I wondered whether fasting had anything to do with what they saw. Several non-Indians have speculated to this end; that fasting causes delusions. "Do your pledgers really go, as you do, without food and water for the entire four days?"

"They can smoke, but they are not to take water or food. They smoke because the act is associated in the Indian mind with ceremonies, and the spirits have never told me to deny the men commercial cigarettes."

"Did not any of your pledgers ever sneak a little food or water, and were then caught so that you found out about it?"

"Some have been unfaithful and secretly drunk water. Some have even had friends sneak them a hamburger."

"What do you do about that?"

"I neither say nor do anything. It's their problem, and God will handle it. Their offence does not affect the rest of us."

"You said earlier that the procedure on the second day was almost the same as the first. What change is there?"

"On the second day I choose, according to what I know about their goodness, certain of the male and female pledgers to be placed around the Sun Pole in four groups of equal number and at the cardinal directions. These go forward together at my command to place their hands on the Sun Pole. We do this four times, twice in the morning and twice in the afternoon, while those not chosen remain in their places and blow their whistles."

"What do you say when you tell them to go forward?"

"*Ho Ka Hey*, and the first three times they only act like they are going to touch the Pole. On the fourth approach they touch it, and remain there in deep prayer with both hands on the Pole for about a minute. The special thing is that when they do so, the Tree feels exactly like human skin."

The Preparations Tipi and the Sweatlodge at Pine Ridge in 1968.

The Sun Dancers entering the Mystery Circle at Pine Ridge in 1968.

The Sun Dance costume at Pine Ridge.

All photos courtesy of Roy Dale Sanders

The Mystery Circle at Pine Ridge.

Fools Crow leading the dancers.

Presenting the Pipe at Pine Ridge.

All photos courtesy of Roy Dale Sanders

Fools Crow placing the bird sound among the prayer cloths.

Fools Crow blessing the women pledgers.

Dancers praying at the Sun Pole.

All photos courtesy of Roy Dale Sanders

Fools Crow pierces a pledger at Pine Ridge in 1968.

The pledgers ready to be pierced.

The pledger ready to pull back on the rope.

All photos courtesy of Roy Dale Sanders

"Where do they touch the Tree? Is there a special place?"

"Before the dance begins on the second day I paint two red lines around the tree trunk about five feet up and eighteen inches apart. The pledgers place their hands on the area between the lines, and that is where it feels like human flesh. The rest just feels like any cottonwood tree."

"What makes that part different from the rest?"

"While I paint the two lines I pray very hard about it; that this area will be holier and different, and when I finish, it is. Once when I was conducting a Sun Dance at Crow Dog's place at Rosebud in 1974, the seventy-four pledgers said as one that when they went forward to touch the Tree in the designated area, it felt just like warm human flesh. They really had to believe in what they were doing to have that happen. So the Tree, even though its growth was stopped, became a living thing for them. When the men finished, twenty-four women went forward and touched the Tree, and had the same experience. They came away saying it was a human being.

"During that same Sun Dance, a small, oblong black stone fell from above and landed at my feet. I don't know where it came from, but there it was. I picked it up, and on its surface was printed WEJOT 68. I do not know what language it is or what it means, but I'm hoping it is a sign that the Treaty of 1868 will be re-negotiated—and we will either get back our South Dakota land or receive proper compensation for it. A Roman Catholic priest, who was one of the pledgers, was dancing right beside me. He had seen the stone fall, so I offered it to him. But he was afraid and wouldn't take it. So I put it in my shirt pocket, went on with the dance, and when I looked for it later it was gone.

"The even more amazing thing is that when I was leading the Sun Dance at Pine Ridge six years earlier, in 1968, I kicked a rock, and when I picked it up found the same thing, WEJOT 68, printed on it. This rock was reddish in color, flat like a disk, and not much larger than a nickel.

"One more thing about the Sun Dance at Crow Dog's in 1974. The same meadowlark who danced with us at Pine Ridge was back again, lifting its little wings and dancing with us again."

I wanted to know whether Fools Crows used commercial paint or mixed his own earth paint for the lines around the Tree.

"Lipstick," he answered.

"Lipstick?"

"Well, it's pretty hard to mix your own paint and hold on to it. If someone, particularly a medicine man, finds out you have it, he asks for some, and it is impossible to say no."

"So the paint you use has no medicine power then?"

"It becomes a medicine and has power when I pray over it as I put it on the Tree."

"Is any other paint put on the Tree?"

"No. That is the only place."

"Are we ready for the third day?"

"Yes. Early on the morning of the third day, those who wish to be pierced let me know this. I separate them from the rest of the pledgers and place them at the cardinal directions, from which they go forward four times, touching the Tree and praying the fourth time. After they have gone forward, I go to the Tree and push my head in among the colored prayer cloths which are hung on its trunk. There in secret I quietly make several times the hoot of an owl. That places the spirit of the owl in there for a reason I'll soon explain. Then I proceed with the piercing."

"When you pierce the candidates, do they lie on a buffalo hide and carpet of sage?"

The wacipi.

"I place a carpet of sage on the ground on the west side of the Sun Pole. On top of this I put down a buffalo robe, hair side up. The head is to the north and the tail is to the south."

"Is there any paint on the robe?"

"None whatsoever."

"What kind of wood do you use for the skewer sticks that are inserted in the pledger's chest?"

"Cherry. It is a very strong wood."

"Do you grease the sticks with anything like lard to make the insertion go easier?"

"No."

"Will you," I asked, "describe the piercing for us?"

"The pledger lays down on the robe on his back with his head toward the north. I take a special medicine which *Wakan-Tanka* has given me for the purpose, and I rub it on the man's chest where the circles are. I won't say what it is because He has not given me permission to do so, but it crumbles up fine and looks like dirt after it is applied. Then I grab the skin, pull it up, and push the stick, whose ends are sharpened, through. They don't feel a thing."

"You don't cut parallel slits in the chest as is sometimes done at Rosebud?"

"No."

"Several authors, writing on the Sun Dance over the years, have said that in the old days the skewer sticks were inserted under the muscle. Is that true?"

"Never have we put the stick under the muscle, never!"

"I thought not," I replied, "skin itself is plenty strong. If it went under a muscle they could never pull it loose."

"I just grab enough skin to get a firm hold, so that I can stretch it, and then I push the stick through the skin."

"Frank, do you make the skewer sticks?"

"Each pledger makes his own sticks, making his own decision as to their diameter and length. He brings them with him when he comes to the Sun Dance."

"It is hard to tell from my vantage point in the spectator seating area how the rope is tied to the skewer. Do you use a smaller rope whose other end is then tied to the large rope which is already secured to the Sun Pole?"

"In the old days the large and main rope was cut from a buffalo hide, and a smaller deerhide thong was tied to that at its middle, so that its two ends extended out in a V-shape to be tied to the skewers. We don't have buffalo hide for the main ropes anymore, so most pledgers use commercial rope such as clothesline. But I still use a single deerhide thong to tie the rope and skewers together."

"What is done next?"

"Then I help the pierced man to his feet and take him out some distance from the Tree to a place previously marked out for him. I never touch him because he is very holy now, except that when he is in place I once more wipe my medicine on his chest to control the bleeding. Some men do not bleed at all, and if others do bleed a little, it stops before the ceremony is ended that day."

This statement conformed to what I had seen in Sun Dances. The bleeding was minimal. And I was reminded of the recent movie, *Return of A Man Called Horse*, wherein Richard Harris, when pierced with a skewer four times the size of any I'd ever seen, shed more blood than all the fifty or so pledgers I'd watched put together. Readers who saw the movie will also be noting by now that it was a poor and most inadequate portrayal of the Sun Dance.

"The candidates are pierced in turn and then all pull on the ropes at the same time?" I asked.

"Same time."

"And before they start to pull back, do you have them go forward and back four times to the Tree?"

"Four times, and when they touch the Tree on the fourth approach they hear the owl hoot, the spirit I put in there. They will not have known I did it, yet they will always hear it."

"What time of day does the piercing take place?"

"Once about 10:00 A.M. so that we will be done with the first group by noon, and again about 3:00 P.M. for the second group, so that we will finish about 5:00 P.M."

"Do some pledgers ever pierce on one side in the morning and on the other side in the afternoon?"

"No. Each man must finish at the time I select for him to be pierced."

"So that ends the third day, and now I want to ask a pertinent question: Why do the Sioux pierce in the Sun Dance? Many people think it is such a terrible thing to do, and some of the other tribes who still do the Sun Dance never pierced."

"The Sioux received the Sun Dance from *Wakan-Tanka*, and we honor Him by doing it as He told us to. Since the White man has come to us and explained how He sent his own son to be sacrificed, we realize that our sacrifice is similar to, or in memory of Jesus' own. As to how the White man feels, there was a far more terrible thing done by Jesus Christ. He endured more suffering, more pain, was even stabbed here [pointing to his side], and died. And as far as the other tribes are concerned, they must speak for themselves. But I will say that the Sioux feel a special closeness to God in the dance and the piercing. We even duplicate Christ's crown of thorns in the sage head-wreath the pledgers wear. Apparently, some of the other tribes don't know this. In any event, the pledgers seldom lose a particle of their flesh if they are pierced and tied properly—and even if they do, it is considered as a thank offering returned to the God from whom it came."

"Frank, you have told us that you take seven flesh offerings from yourself, for the seven bags, before the Sun Dance begins. Do any of the others give flesh offerings?"

"Yes, and when I bring the pledgers in on the first day, I collect all these bits of flesh in a cloth and take them to the Sun Pole, where I dig a little hole at its base and bury the offerings bundle in it."

"Do you pray with it before covering it up with dirt?"

"To *Wakan-Tanka* and *Tunkashila*."

"Can anyone besides yourself and the pledgers give flesh offerings?"

"They can be given by anyone, even a spectator."

"How do you do this? Do you bring them into the Mystery Circle and to the Tree?"

"They take their shoes and stockings off and come barefooted into the circle between the flags. Once the flesh offerings have been taken, they go around the Tree clockwise and then exit the circle through the same pair of flags."

"On which day might they do this?"

"Any day."

"What do you do with their offerings?"

"We wrap them in cloth and bury them at the base of the Tree with those of the pledgers. I have even heard of one man at Rosebud who gave two hundred and fifty flesh offerings for this purpose."

I remarked that I had seen Bill Schweigman, the Intercessor at

Rosebud, give as many as one hundred flesh offerings from each arm, or a total of two hundred.

"I don't hurt them," Fools Crow muttered, "because of my medicine I put on the cuts."

"How do you take the bits of flesh?"

"With a needle and a razor blade," he answered.

"How does the fourth day of the Sun Dance differ from the third day?"

"The fourth day is identical, except that if pledgers wish to, they can perform their sacrifice by pulling one or more buffalo skulls, suspended from their back. I divide the number who wish to do this equally. If there are eight, four will pull theirs in the morning, and four in the afternoon. The buffalo skulls are turned upside down and one end of each of two ropes is tied to a skewer stick placed in the man's back, while the two loose ends are threaded through the eye holes of the skull and a little hole which is next to the eye hole. The ropes, when they are stretched out, look like two parallel clotheslines. I have had pledgers pull as many as three skulls at one time. The skulls are placed one behind the other about two feet apart, and then tied together."

"When such a pledger is pierced, does he lay face down on the buffalo hide?"

"He kneels down on the hide, and has circles painted on his back similar to those put on the chest. Then he is pierced with wooden sticks in the usual way."

"What about feather piercing, do you do that? And, do you do it by bending the end of the quill back to make a loop, then inserting a thread tie through the loop and the pledger's skin?"

"Yes, and whoever wishes to can have this done."

"How do they decide how many feathers to use?"

"The traditional number is twelve, six running from the right shoulder down the right arm, and six running from the left shoulder down the left arm."

"None on the back or on any other part of the body?"

"Never."

"What," I asked, "have we forgotten? You mentioned healing a boy at a Sun Dance, and I have seen healing ceremonies performed at Rosebud. Do you have these at Pine Ridge where the pledgers pray for people who have problems and need healing?"

"I do, and all such rituals must be done before the dance ends; within the four day period. The people are asked to come forward, and the pledgers and I bless them. We do not give the people medicine. We just lay our hands on them and pray for them, because they could have any kind of illness ranging from headaches to appendix to paralysis or heart trouble. We might give them the wrong thing. Then too, not all of the problems are illnesses, they could be alcoholism or family strife or something similar."

"You never know what's wrong with anyone?"

"Sometimes *Wakan-Tanka* tells me what is wrong with certain people. Some of the pledgers who have real dedication and faith become different as they dance, infused with insight and extra power. They too might know what ails some of the people who appear before them."

"But you still do not give them medicine?"

"No. In the usual instance, if they want healing they must come to me later and bring a pipe. Sometimes I do make exceptions, as in the case of the boy with the bent leg I healed at Greenwood in 1976."

"In dancing, part of the time the pledger's arms are down, and other times held up to the sun or the Tree. What is the difference and what are they doing?"

"Whether they raise one or both hands they are appealing to *Wakan-Tanka* and *Tunkashila*."

"Do they not also appeal to the Tree and the sun?"

"When they do this, some of them even feel a special power in their hands. And they may see the answer to what they are looking for up there in the sun or the Tree—an eagle, a buffalo, a bear; things like that."

"When they see something, do they understand what it means, or do they tell you about it and ask you to help them interpret it?"

"If they do want to talk with me, we discuss it in the Preparations Tipi at night. Some of the pledgers know the meaning, some may have only a question or two about it, others need a great deal of help. If so, I interpret the vision for them in private. No one else hears what we say.

"A final thing I'd like to tell you about visions has to do with the man hanging up there above the buffalo in the Sacred Tree. While we are dancing, even though he has no whistle, we hear the sound of one coming from him. And the buffalo, he's pretty smart up there. He remains silent, but sometimes he sits down, sometimes he lays down, and sometimes he stands up. The pledgers watch for this, and they see it. As for the bundle of cherry branches, on the first day of one Sun Dance we all looked up and saw an airplane land on it. It was puzzling, but quickly explained the next day when Ed Magaw, the pilot, flew in by airplane to do the rest of the Sun Dance with us."

"There are so many things to be seen up there, but the crowd seldom notices them. They might look up there for a moment, but most of the time their eyes are glued on the pledgers."

"So what makes the real difference, might it not be the four days of fasting, would that in itself not cause the pledgers to see unusual things?"

"The pledgers are dancing, praying very hard, concentrating and calling for God's pity. People forget that, but it brings great power."

Fools Crow and I spent a long time discussing the Sun Dance. As far as I could tell we had, by now, covered the important and valuable things—everything except the vision quest as it is associated with the Sun Dance.

"Frank," I asked, "do all of your pledgers go on a vision quest before they do the Sun Dance?"

"A long time ago a vision quest was required of every pledger, but I cannot truthfully say it is an absolute requirement now. Some of the men work and do not have time for it. A few are afraid of ghosts, and hate to be left alone like that. But others do quest, even as far back as a year before their dance is held."

"Do you prepare them for this in any way? Do they come to you and ask how to do it or anything like that?"

"Yes, whoever wishes to make a vision quest as part of the fulfillment of their vow comes and tells me. It might not even be a pledger, but someone else who wants to do this in connection with a forthcoming Sun Dance. If in my judgment they are sincere, I first have a sweatbath with them. Then I take them out to wherever they want to go to vision quest and get them situated there. They choose their own place. After this I return to my sweatlodge, enter it, close the door flap, and I remain there in deep meditation and prayer, giving them support until they are through. It may be one day, two days, three days, or even four days. I know how long it will be because they tell me in advance. Then when the time period is up, I go and get them."

"When you are in the sweatlodge, do you fast as the vision-questor himself must do?"

"One of the main purposes of what I do is to share fully in what he is doing, so I do fast. Then whatever he sees up there in his vision, I see it too."

"At the same time he sees it?"

"Yes."

"When you go to get him you can tell him exactly what he saw?"

"I can. The reason some medicine men are not able to do this is that after they have placed their pledgers they do not join with them in spirit and prayer. They get into their automobiles and drive around. They go somewhere shopping or even get a bottle and have a party, only returning when it is time to get the pledger. I don't do this. The vision quest is too sacred, too holy. I want to share completely with them and give my full support. I want us to be of one mind, and I want to feel and suffer with them."

I thought then that it is not hard to see what makes the difference between what Fools Crow accomplishes and the accomplishments of most other holy men and medicine men. His dedication and spirit are seldom matched, and his work is all the richer for it.

"How," I asked, "do you make the vision questing place? What is it like? Do you set out cherry tree or cottonwood branches to mark the four corners of a square?"

"I set four tall cherry tree branches in the ground to mark, in the usual instance, the corners of a seven or eight-foot-long by six-foot-wide rectangle. It could be a square. The leaves are removed from the branches, and I tie to these the four sacred colored cloths to establish the cardinal directions."

"Is there a pipe rack such as is the case in vision questing at Rosebud?"

"No pipe rack. I cover the rectangle with sage, and if the pledger brings a pipe he places it on the sage. I also place there on the sage a saucer with *wasna* on it. Then if there is time I prepare a single string of 405 tobacco offerings for the good spirits, and I wrap this around the four tree branches, beginning at the west, where the black cloth is, and bringing it back and tying it at the west. The string is not tied to the other branches. When it is done, the questing place enclosure looks like a prize fight ring with only a single rope."

"Can the pledger face in any direction when he is within the enclosure?"

"He faces the direction he is praying to, and he will also look up as he prays to *Tunkashila* and *Wakan-Tanka*, then down to Grandmother Earth. If he stays there several days he will follow the sun as he prays whether he sits or stands. It is permissible also for him to lie down at night and part of the time during the day."

"Suppose the candidate decides in advance he will stay several days, but has his vision on the first day. Does he stop then, or does he complete the full number of days?"

"If the pledger chooses the longer period, he is religiously obligated to complete the number of days he has vowed."

"Do they ever talk to you about what they see in their visions?"

"I already know. Some may have a question or two as to how their vision should be interpreted, and if so I answer that."

"Is there any other way to make a vision questing place?"

"What I have described to you is the only way to do it. When I make any vision questing place at Bear Butte it is identical."

"Then you do a Sun Dance and all its preparations exactly as you saw it done at the secret dances years ago?"

"Yes, I do it the same way, and to do this without error is harder than it sounds. A leader and a medicine man walks a hard road and carries a heavy burden. I could even be praying and crying at my father or mother's grave, and if someone brought me a pipe I would have to leave there and go. But, that is my life."

It was difficult to look at Fools Crow right then, for he had quietly drifted away in thought from us, and it was a very private moment. I knew my endless questions had caused him to reflect on some things he'd not thought about for a long time. I had stirred up a number of things from the bottom of a century-old pond.

THE TRADITIONAL SUN DANCE OF JULY 26-29, 1975—
Thomas E. Mails

It was mentioned earlier that a number of problems plagued the arrangements for the Traditional dance. The last of the preliminary obstacles came only a week before the dance, and it consisted in the withdrawal of permission to use the proposed site, located one-half mile west of St. Francis. At that point the Sun Dance was cancelled.

Although the owners changed their minds, and the dance was soon on again, it was quickly realized that the location could certainly have been better, since it was in the heart of a prairie dog town and there were also a lot of rattlesnakes around.

By this time George Eagle Elk, a medicine man, had been chosen to manage the dance. Although he was not asked to do so at the time, Eagle Feather would lend a hand later on.

Perhaps to emphasize the concern for tradition, a decision was made regarding the Sacred Tree which was later regretted, and certainly questioned. As has already been stated, in ancient days the Tree was cut on the last day before the Sun Dance was to begin, and then brought into the Mystery Circle in four moves. Yet the college representatives and the other dance leaders decided to cut the Tree four full days before the dance, at a place four miles away from the Circle, and to carry it by hand one-fourth of the way each day.

The Tree was cut down early in the morning of July 22. It was struck first by a little boy and a girl, then felled. The Tree was carried one mile and then laid down for the night. When the bearers returned for it at sunup the next morning, they found that deer had eaten some of the leaves. The next night cattle broke off some of the branches. After that, guards stayed with the Tree day and night until it was in the Mystery Circle and up. By this time, though, it was only about ten feet tall and a sad-looking affair. It was a solemn portent of things to come.

On July 22, work was started on a larger cooler to be used for feeding the spectators. By July 23, the cooler was finished, two Preparation Tipis had been put up and two sweatlodges built, seven campers were in place, and a small cooler to serve as a place to feed the pledgers had been erected. Hopes were high.

Little happened on July 24. On July 25, the Sacred Tree was carried on its last mile-long move and set up. By this time some worries were being expressed about having enough experienced leaders to direct the dance. One witness said that no *wasna* (pemmican), buffalo fat, or sweet grass had been placed in the hole before the Tree was put up.

JULY 26: THE FIRST DAY OF THE
TRADITIONAL SUN DANCE

On July 26 the Sun Dance got underway. No purification ceremony was held in the sweatlodge. At 8:00 A.M. seven male pledgers including one White man and a man from Canada, all wearing the conventional Sun Dance costumes, entered the Mystery Circle together with two medicine men, made one circuit, and got ready to pierce. The Flags were set out and the Altar consisting of a pipe rack and a buffalo skull, was put up in the customary way. Only one pipe was used by all of the dancers.

Five of the men were pierced, two of them on one side of the chest only.

There was no Mother of the Year present to comfort them and to wipe their wounds. Eight singers provided the music.

One man who did not pierce quit dancing at 10:00 and did not return.

At 10:45 the torture ceremony was finished and the men were led on their sacred circuit of the Mystery Circle. To avoid needless repetition, let it be understood that whenever a circuit was made the customary stops were observed at the four directions, and when the south was reached, the pipe was presented in the usual way with the four gestures to the Keeper of the Pipes. Then, after the men rested, it was retrieved as the next circuit began, and in the manner described in the previous chapter. The same is true regarding the occasions when the pledgers approached the Tree. Each time they did this, they went forward and touched the Tree four times, backing away after each contact to their starting places. The pledgers rested.

Then it was announced that a White man had donated a buffalo to the Sun Dance.

At 11:20 the pledgers began the next circuit, resting at 11:30.

At 12:00 noon another circuit was made, and the pledgers rested. At 12:15 the Intercessor took his pipe to the Sacred Tree, where he prayed for health and wealth for the Sioux.

By 12:30 the pledgers had left the Mystery Circle and were resting in the Preparations Tipi. The singers ate their lunch, but the pledgers did not eat.

At 1:25 the pledgers emerged from the Tipi, and by 1:30 they were waiting at the western entrance to the Mystery Circle.

At 1:35 the singers commenced singing, the pledgers started their next circuit of the Mystery Hoop facing away from the Tree, finished it, presented the pipe, and rested.

At 2:00 the next circuit was made, with the pledgers facing the Sacred Tree.

At 2:25 the next circuit was undertaken, with the pledgers facing away from the Tree. This routine was standard: One time the pledgers faced the Tree, the next time their backs were to the Tree.

At 3:10 the pledgers began their eighth circuit of the day, dancing as always and blowing on their eagle-bone whistles to the accompaniment of the drum and the singers. The pledgers had been without food and water since sunup, but they still smiled and joked about their situation to make it easier.

At 3:35 another circuit was made.

At 3:55 the next circuit began. It was followed by a very long rest period.

At 4:55 the eleventh circuit was made, and at 5:05 the pledgers rested.

At 5:30 the next circuit was carried out. Even at this late hour the temperature was reported to be 102 degrees. In the middle of this circuit one of the older dancers fainted. Some wondered if it was from hunger. Chief Eagle Feather was not leading the dance, but he was asked to see if he could get the man back on his feet. What he attempted did not work immediately, so Eagle Feather took the man's place and finished the circuit. During the rest period Eagle Feather continued to minister to the suffering man.

At 6:10 the twelfth circuit was made.

At 6:50 another circuit was completed.

At 7:30 the fourteenth circuit of the day was made, during which time another of the pledgers became ill and was taken to the rest area. All of the men rested, one smoking and another drinking water.

At 8:30 the pledgers went around the Circle again. As they finished, the pipe was picked up by the Keeper and the pledgers exited from the Mystery Circle.

When the sun went down at 9:00 the pledgers were fed, after which they participated in a purification ceremony in the sweatlodge.

JULY 27: THE SECOND DAY OF THE TRADITIONAL SUN DANCE

At 7:50 A.M. five pledgers, led by a layman rather than a medicine man, entered the Mystery Circle. The Altar was set up, and again there was only a single pipe which would be used by all of the men. The standard flags were erected at the four directions, and a hind of the donated buffalo meat was placed at the Sacred Tree. The pledger who had fainted the day before was dancing again.

As the first circuit got underway, some interesting announcements were made. One was that two of the men had cut their feet so badly the day before that they would be permitted to wear either shoes or moccasins. Another was an admission that the participants could not do "as well as was done at the Rosebud Fairground." This was a startling acknowledgment from people whose dance was intended to be the really Traditional one.

While the pledgers rested, a medicine man talked for forty-five minutes.

As the next circuit got underway, it was noted with some discomfort that black clouds were moving toward the Mystery Circle. One spectator remarked: "If they really meant it, the clouds would split, and no rain would fall in the Circle." When the line of dancers reached the south they all raised their hands to the sky and prayed that the clouds would separate.

When the pledgers rested this time some smoked cigarettes again and even lay down. By 9:15 it was raining so hard that the twenty or so spectators ran for the protection of their automobiles.

At 9:30 it was still raining hard, but the next circuit was begun anyway. At this point a medicine man told the participants that if they prayed and really meant it, the rain wouldn't spoil their dance.

The pledgers raised their hands and prayed, but the rain did not stop and the wind began to blow hard. Another comment of some import was offered now by one of the spectators, to the effect that the man leading the dancing had never danced the Sun Dance or even gone to a *Yuwipi* meeting. "He sure is misleading them," this observer remarked. At 9:50 the pledgers rested, and shortly thereafter the rain stopped.

When the pipe had been retrieved two men made preparations for their piercing by stretching their ropes and staking them down. As the first man was pierced, his legs really shook. When both men were pierced and ready, they went forward four times to touch the Tree, and the pulling began. By 10:20 both had broken free and rejoined the other pledgers.

Another circuit was made around the Mystery Circle. It was raining again.

At 10:50 the rain slacked off, the audience returned, and the next circuit of the morning was made. When the pipe was presented at the south, the Keeper accepted it on the third gesture. That was unusual.

At 11:00 an appeal was issued to all of the women present to move to the north side of the shade. One of the pledger's skewer sticks had broken inside of his chest, and it was feared that some woman's "monthly sickness" had caused it; it was either that or the two cats which had been brought to the Sun Dance by some White people. The Sioux believe that animals should not be present where a Sun Dance is held. Their presence assures serious problems.

At 11:15 the sixth circuit of the day was undertaken.

At 11:35 another circuit was made.

At 12:00 noon the pledgers made the next circuit, facing away from the Tree. During this circle their hands were raised constantly as they prayed to *Wakan-Tanka* to have pity on them.

At 12:30 Eagle Feather went to the Sacred Tree and prayed, then moved to where the singers were and prayed there. After this he went with a man to the Tree and took thirteen flesh offerings from the man's arms.

When the pledgers made their next circuit they were divided into four groups, went forward and touched the Tree four times, and then finished the circuit at 12:50.

At 1:30 eight pledgers, including Eagle Feather, made the tenth circuit of the day. When the pipe was presented, it was by the pledger going forward on his knees. It was refused and a healing ceremony followed with Eagle Feather giving the spectators herb medicines.

At 2:00 the spectators were fed for the first time during the dance. Among other things, they were given some of the buffalo meat.

At 2:15 six pledgers, including one new man, began to dance again and made their circuit facing the Sacred Tree.

At 3:15 another circuit was made.

At 4:00 circuit number thirteen was carried out. By now the dancers appeared very tired, and a spectator remarked that they looked "pitiful."

At 4:30 the fourteenth circuit was executed, and at 4:40 the dancing ended for the day.

JULY 28: THE THIRD DAY OF THE TRADITIONAL SUN DANCE

No sweatlodge ceremony was held. The pledgers slept late and did not enter the Mystery Circle until 9:15 A.M. Now there were seven pledgers, three singers, and an audience consisting of one adult and four children. It was cool and windy but the forecast was for a temperature of 105 degrees by midafternoon.

There was some discussion this morning about the way in which the donated buffalo meat had been apportioned. Each of the pledgers had received a sizable piece but the singers had received none; one leader's wife was said to have left with the rest of the meat, which turned out to not be true. It was apparent that internal friction was not unique to Eagle Feather's Sun Dances, dissension also focusing on the fact that the pledger line had not paused and prayed the customary four times on its way from the Preparations Tipi to the Mystery Circle.

At 9:20 the first circuit began.

At 10:20 the next circuit was made.

At 11:00 the third circuit got underway, with the pledgers facing away from the Sacred Tree.

By this time the wind was increasing, and while the pledgers rested men were sent to take down one of the tipis.

Now it was announced that five men would be pierced, and preparations were made for this. Two men would be piercing for the third straight day! The announcer said, "These dancers really believe in the Indian religion, because this is the only way to prove to yourself that you do believe."

The men were pierced in succession in the customary fashion at the base of the Sacred Tree. This time their blood relations stood by them to give comfort and encouragement as they pulled free. Two men had to have some skewer slivers dug out after they broke away.

All of the pledgers went forward and touched the Tree four times, then formed a line and moved to the south, after which they rested.

At 12:25 P.M. Eagle Feather introduced two of the oldtimers who were dancing, and stressed how deeply they were involved in the Traditional culture.

At 12:30 the next circuit was made. The pledgers seemed very tired, and someone speculated that resting too long might be doing that to them.

At 1:45 the next circuit was executed, with the pledgers facing the Tree. They seemed to have gathered their second wind and danced very hard while blowing more sharply than ever on their whistles.

Whispered word was going around that there was drinking among a few of the spectators, including one of the medicine men who was involved in the dance. "This is a very bad thing," observers said.

At 2:30 the sixth circuit was made, while the wind roared and the dust flew.

At 3:30 the seventh circuit was undertaken.

At 4:30 the eighth circuit got underway, and by 5:00 the ceremony was over for the day.

JULY 29: THE FOURTH DAY OF THE TRADITIONAL SUN DANCE

No purification ceremony was held in the sweatlodge.

By 9:14 A.M. six dancers had entered the Mystery Circle and the first circuit was underway. At this hour the weather was pleasant. There was little wind and it was cool. The only spectators present were the pledgers' families.

While the dancers rested a medicine man announced that the pledgers were praying with the Peace Pipe because they didn't want trouble. That sounded ominous and, as it turned out, was indeed prophetic. "This dance," he concluded, "is different from all the rest." Indeed it was.

A second medicine man said that he was unhappy because people were criticizing some things about the dance and the pledgers. "The pledgers will be praying for the ones who are saying that," he remarked. He went on to admit, though, that he, too, did not like the fact that the medicine man who was supposed to be running the Sun Dance had gone to Parmalee, come back really drunk, and now was crying around the Holy Tree.

Perhaps I should insert here that I learned later that the same medicine man would be drunk and bring a supply of liquor to Crow Dog's Sun Dance. There, however, they took it away from him, smashed the bottles and cans, and threw him out of the dance area. Then, when he had sobered, they took him over to the refuse dump

Waiting to enter the Mystery Circle.

to make him look at and consider the accusing evidence of what he had done.

At 9:45 the pipe was removed from the Circle and taken back to the Preparations Tipi. It was another bad sign. To make matters worse, there was a dog in the Tipi!

One of the dance sponsors said, "They are not doing this right, so all of the days they have danced have been bad days." It had rained during parts of two days and been really windy the last two days, so windy, in fact, that the flags kept falling down. The "power" was not good, and it was affecting everything in the area. There had been a killing down at Crow Dog's place. A boy named Ervin Stewart had been shot through the head, and when the girl with him ran to escape some boys had chased her and hurt her so badly that she was in the Rapid City hospital. Now a wake for the boy was being held at Crow Dog's for two days and the funeral would take place on the third.

The pipe was brought back to the Mystery Circle and the pledgers made their next circuit. The announcer said that it was time for the flesh offerings, and as the pledgers danced they raised their hands and prayed for those who would make the offerings.

While the pledgers rested the spectators were told that the Sun Dance would end today and the St. Francis powwow would begin tomorrow. The announcer went on to admit that while the pledgers were not supposed to eat or drink water for the four days, they just couldn't follow this rule and so the Intercessor had let them eat and drink; that was really why there was "so much talk."

At this point, one of the few positive notes emerged. Eagle Feather took one of the pledgers to the Sacred Tree and announced that the man's sister, who had not walked for years and had been confined to a wheelchair, was walking today because of her brother's sacrifices on her behalf.

Two men had flesh offerings cut from their arms at this time. A few minutes later another man made flesh offerings, saying that he had promised a year before that he would do so if he lived this long.

At 11:20 the next circuit was made and during it the Intercessor prayed for "peace at the Sun Dance ground today." Almost immediately thereafter someone said something that offended Eagle Feather, so he took his sound-system speaker down. Now the singers and the announcements could hardly be heard, an unhappy situation made even worse by the twenty-five-mile-an-hour wind and the thick dust. It was especially bad for filming.

When the pledgers rested, they smoked and drank water, and also exited for trips to the latrine.

When they returned the fourth circuit was made. This time the men were divided into four groups—one man on the northwest, two on the northeast, two on the southeast, and one on the southwest. From these positions they went forward to the Tree four times.

Now it was announced that whoever wanted to do so would make flesh offerings. Five of the pledgers gave them, including the man whose sister had been healed. He bled considerably this time, indicating that his cuts were large and deep.

At 2:00 P.M. the Intercessor brought the water bucket and dipper out to see if he could tempt any of the men to take the water and refuse to pierce. They had already had water, though, so it seemed a hollow gesture. When the Intercessor finished, another circuit of the Mystery Circle was made.

After this, the ropes were stretched in preparation for the piercing. All six pledgers were pierced and pulled free quickly. Eagle Feather was back and helped with the piercing. When all of the men were loose, he led them one by one to the north, the east, and the south.

The pledgers rested, and the old-timer who had fainted the first day was sick again.

The Altar was picked up by the Keeper and even before the flags were removed the little Sacred Tree was swiftly taken down. Then the flags were picked up and the pledgers exited from the Mystery Circle by crossing it in the customary four moves.

The Traditional Sun Dance was over, but its many problems were cause for considerable and profound reflecting by all who shared in it.

It did not come off well at all, and we should ask why this was so. It would be far too simple to dismiss it as just a bungled attempt to copy a ritual so ancient and superior as to make duplication impossible. As the respected medicine man, Robert Stead, said earlier at Rosebud, "No one knows exactly how it was done in the old days," and it is generally conceded that some important details are lost forever. Nor did it fail, if that is really what it did, because of the presence of the things so often criticized about modern Sun Dances, such as insincerity or commercialism. Neither of these were involved or ever became issues.

We can easily identify some of the visible culprits. Inadequate planning was one, and poor execution by inexperienced leaders was another. It is painfully evident that sincerity will not replace competence. Holy men who were there for some of the time as observers put the blame on Divine reaction (or perhaps better said: lack of Divine reaction), careless handling, and poor attitudes. "The powers do not come down when it is not done right." The cats, the dog, or "those women" might be at fault. The holy men also criticized on a personal basis two men who were involved in leading the dance: one for his drinking, which is especially forbidden for medicine men, and another for prior immoral conduct so grievous it should have disqualified him from carrying the pipe. And surely the failure to have purification ceremonies every morning was a serious breech of custom.

Some further explanation may be derived from re-examining the goals and assumptions of those who proposed the Traditional Sun Dance in the first place. One goal was to make the most of the dramatic possibilities attached to the bringing in and raising of the Sacred Tree; another was to have the pledgers fast for the entire four-day period; a third was to have them dance from sunup to sundown; and finally, the planners assumed a kind of cooperation that seldom occurs on the reservations.

In other words, they made disaster inevitable from the very beginning by establishing standards which could not be met. Here again, this only proves the wisdom of experienced Intercessors such as Fools Crow and Eagle Feather, who readily confess that contemporary life does not provide men with the strengths required to match the performance of the pledgers of olden days. Their diets are inadequate, some have jobs that contribute nothing to physical conditioning, and others suffer from the softness which comes from having no jobs at all. So these Intercessors face reality and do not attempt to exceed the bounds of their pledgers' capabilities. "It is hard enough," says Eagle Feather, "to do what we do." His advance opinion, and that of several of the pledgers at the 1975 Rosebud Fairground Sun Dance, was that the Traditional Dance would not fare well in this regard.

Having said this, credit must still be given where it is due. The men certainly did dance longer each day than is usually the case at Rosebud and Pine Ridge. Moreover, two of the pledgers endured piercings that were simply amazing. Ordinarily a man will be pierced only once during a dance if he is pierced on both sides simultaneously. He might pierce twice if he does only one side at a time. But at this dance the two men were each pierced four times — which means that they had had eight holes torn in their chests by the time they were through. Further, the men did finish the full four days of the dance and no doubt accomplished some divine good for themselves and the people. Although the leadership might be faulted, the pledgers were profoundly sincere, and did well considering the situation.

Was the Traditional Sun Dance of 1975 only a hollow replica of the ancient form? Yes and no. Did it show the futility of the modern Sioux in this respect? By no means. Remember that it was not the only dance held in the summer of 1975, and the others were most impressive by comparison.

Perhaps no further attempts will be made now to put up a really Traditional Sun Dance. Yet the very fact that an effort was made will spur on the Intercessors who conduct annual Sun Dances to make additions and changes which will make their performances more traditional, and thus more truly representative of the religion of the Sioux.

All in all, I feel the attempt at a Traditional Sun Dance was worth it, both for what it did accomplish and for the special insights provided into contemporary life and thought at Pine Ridge, Rosebud, and the other Sioux reservations. I also think that now that they have had a taste of how it goes, the organizers of the Traditional Sun Dance will feel less free to criticize the Intercessors and pledgers who put on their Sun Dances on an annual basis. No doubt a mistake now and then, and a little "commercialism" here and there, will be less offensive than it was before!

XVIII
Postlude To The Sun Dance

THOMAS E. MAILS

From this insider's view of the Rosebud Sioux Sun Dance we can now draw some final conclusions. One is that the Sun Dance consists of a great deal more than piercing, the other parts of the modern rite being much more than mere incidentals in its scheme. For those with "eyes to see and ears to hear," the Sun Dance is a carefully orchestrated symphony of the *entire* Sioux religion, which builds in pulsating cadence from the opening movement around the Mystery Circle to the mesmerizing climax in the group piercing. When it is over, everyone is very quiet because the gamut of emotions has been run. Power has been called in and set in motion for another year.

The individual days of the Sun Dance as Eagle Feather presents them may seem to be quite similar, but we can see that this is not really so. As the days go by the interest of the community picks up, the healing lines grow longer, the tempo of the dancing increases, and the intensity of the pledgers mounts. Everything shapes and points toward the final, crowning moment. When you are there among the people, as I have been, you can feel the electricity spread.

The accumulation of prayers pulls down increasing power from God, Mother Earth, the Sun, the Sacred Tree, and the Directions. The flesh offerings and the individual piercings of the first days whet anticipation for the final hour in which all of the pledgers will unite in offering themselves in thanksgiving to *Wakan-Tanka*.

Careful conditioning, orderly preparation, and group involvement are all there, as are deepest sincerity and reverence. More than once I have seen tears in Eagle Feather's eyes as he prayed and meditated during dances, and I have seen pledgers so caught up in the dance as to be oblivious to all else around them.

For Eagle Feather, the preparations for the following year begin the day after the Sun Dance is over. The dance ends with a community vow aimed at the next one. In a very short time he selects the Tree and begins to address himself to it through prayers and offerings. Several months before the next dance is to be held the actual planning gets underway, at which time other people are brought in and involved. Vows are made known by pledgers and donors. This is followed by a period during which attention is increasingly focused on the coming dance. A full three weeks or more before the dance is to begin the vision quests are undertaken, and during the last week all of the final items are obtained or built: the food, the camping gear, the costumes, the Preparations Tipi, the sweatlodges, the coolers for eating, the singers, the sound equipment, and whatever else remains to be taken care of.

True group involvement is heightened perceptibly when the first day of the dance is immediately at hand. As many people as possible

Feather piercing.

are invited to share in the gathering of the wood and the sage, and in the chopping and setting up of the Sacred Tree. Every age group is called upon. Children play an important role in the cutting of the Tree and are taken along to gather sage and herbs. It is part of their training in the Sun Dance religion. The young and the middle-aged do the more strenuous tasks, but some of the old will even dance, and along with others will contribute valuable advice.

The sharing continues as the Sun Dance gets underway. It is seen in the purification ceremonies, in the dancing, in group healings, and when relatives stand with the pledgers to give them encouragement and comfort. The social dancing which follows the Sun Dance is but one more step in promoting the nation's unity and happiness —insofar as such is possible in reservation circumstances.

Traditional ritual adds its obvious benefits, too. In a time when the Sioux suffer greatly in their struggle to maintain cultural identity, the annual Sun Dance tells them each year who they are and why they are. It gives them roots, it gives them a sense of being needed, and it shores up their belief that they either are or can become valuable contributors to a troubled world. More than that, the antiquity of the ceremony gives them the sense of longevity. Theirs is an old and a proven culture. They need apologize to no one for it.

All of these are commendable attributes for any religion to have, and they are essential to the well-being of the Sioux today. This should be borne in mind by the observer who, looking at living and political conditions on the Rosebud and Pine Ridge reservations, might decide that the Sun Dance produces nothing of consequence; that it is actually an exercise in futility by a self-deluded people. Not all of its benefits are easily seen. When one looks in the right places one finds they are there in abundance.

Seen in its proper light, the Sun Dance of today becomes an exciting religious experience for participants and spectators alike. No one should seek to downgrade it by selling it short or by making comparisons between it and the grand Sun Dances of former days. Actually, more men and women are participating in the Sun Dances now than was the case in prereservation times. It appears from what early informants wrote that relatively small numbers of pledgers took part in the annual Sun Dance of any given year, and when details of past and present are compared it seems also that the old-time dances were not really that much better than the well-done dances of today.

Again, while the men of past times did submit to more stringent forms of torture, the same men did not pierce year after year as some men do now. To my knowledge, there is no ancient record of anyone piercing two years in a row, let alone doing it six times on both sides in one summer, as Reuben Fire Thunder did on the Rosebud Reservation in 1975. If anyone cares to champion the claim that piercings are no longer deep enough to be of consequence, I invite that person to prove how much he believes it by being pierced. As Eagle Feather says, "It hurts plenty." And the same is true for the flesh offerings. Even he flinches now and then when the small bits of flesh are cut off.

Dancing in the hot South Dakota summer is not so easy either. The sun beats down unmercifully in July and August. Even though a complete circuit of the Mystery Circle seldom takes more than fifteen minutes, the pledgers are exposed to at least two and a half hours of sun every morning. So over the four consecutive days their upper torsos and heads receive at least ten hours of blistering heat.

While we are on this subject, it is often said that Sun Dancers "stare continually at the sun" as they dance. This is not so now, and I doubt that it ever was. The only times they face the sun directly are when they are in the west facing east and in the east facing west. The rest of the time either their backs or their sides are to the sun. Photographs, too, will clearly support the fact that even when the men and women seem to be facing the sun, their eyes are, for the most part, nearly closed. Only for a few minutes now and then do they actually stare at the sun and seek visions in it.

The same situation applies when they are pierced. The eight to a dozen men are positioned equidistantly around the Sacred Tree, so only a few of them are actually facing the sun as they pull on the ropes. One writer claims that the pierced dancers circle around the Tree, constantly facing the sun as they attempt to pull free. But anyone who has seen how the ropes are secured to the Tree would know that they would become hopelessly entwined if the pledgers did this. Also, the ropes are not attached to the Tree in such a way that they would slip to allow circling. Fools Crow witnessed and took part in a number of the old dances, yet never mentions seeing a pierced dancer circle the Tree while he pulled against the skewer and the rope.

It is fair to ask how the Sun Dance compares to other traditional forms of worship. In my estimation, it compares very well indeed. All of the proper elements of worship are there: confession, petition, reception, sacrifice, and service. There is no reason whatsoever to consider it inferior, heathen, or even primitive—if anyone should happen to think of that as a negative word, which I do not. The healing ceremonies themselves are most impressive and effective. Therefore, while I can appreciate the reasons for doing so, it remains a serious blunder for the United States Government to have interfered with and suppressed the performance of the Sun Dance. This, unfortunately, is exactly what it did, taking forty-three long years to rectify its error. It was not until 1934 that John Collier, appointed Commissioner of Indian Affairs by President Franklin D. Roosevelt, cancelled the suppression by an order which said: "No interference with Indian religious life or ceremonial expression will hereafter be tolerated. The cultural liberty of Indians is in all respects to be considered equal to that of any non-Indian group."

Sadly, corrective orders of this kind do not lead inevitably to fulfillment. And, while in 1975 the evidences of a strong Sun Dance revival are plain, despite claims to the contrary there are always subtle pressures by both church and state either to prevent the holding of the Sun Dance, or if it is held, to adulterate its impact upon the community.

Perhaps no one will ever be able to solve to everyone's satisfaction the question of whether or not the Sioux of ancient times addressed themselves to a Supreme Being in the Sun Dance and other ceremonies. Yet it is clear that for the entire period of the twentieth century this has been the case. The primary source of power called upon in the Sun Dance is the same God that Christians worship, and it is not without consequence that the men who lead and pledge in the dances often claim to be both Traditionalist and Christian.

Fools Crow, whose memory takes him as far back as 1897, declares that his people have always believed in a Supreme Being who is identical with the God of the Bible. Some say the concept actually has its origin in Christian influences, but then they must explain how it came into being before Christianity was known in the New World and spread so completely to a people mostly at war against those from whom they supposedly were learning it. I fear that people who believe that the Indian idea of a Supreme Being came into being only with colonization may be forgetting three things: first, that while the Sioux life-way did change over the years, it was exceedingly slow to do so, and never changed without good reason; second, that circumstances were against changing spiritually to White ways, the nature and conduct of the people who took their land by force and scorned their culture hardly being conducive to such conversion; third, that records show the Indians were open to accepting the White man's God only because they found that He compared favorably with the One they already worshipped. Christian ideas assuredly did influence Indian religious practices once contact was made, but one need not conclude from this that their concept of a Supreme Mystery came into being only during this time.

To take an opposite tack for a moment, I have heard a few young Indians say that they sincerely believe that the torture aspect of the Sun Dance is a "real" or "true" expression of thanksgiving as compared with that of the Christian religion, which renders lip service to God, but avoids pain and sacrifice. Even some non-Indian authors have found great comfort in this aspect of Indian religion. One writes as follows: "Unlike the Christians who passively revered Christ's example of self-denial through crucifixion, and yet profess a comprehension of that denial, the Indian who would purport to understand the implication must himself experience sacrifice physically, mentally, and spiritually."

Accusations like this about Christians are unwarranted and untenable for two reasons: The first is that, despite their mistakes and shortcomings, thousands upon thousands of devout Christians have submitted throughout the ages to persecutions of every kind, including death. Others have undergone tremendous hardships in order to bring assistance as well as the Gospel to people in need. The assertion that Christianity is painless and thus renders its followers incapable of comprehending the Crucifixion is unwarranted. The percentage of Christians who have deprived themselves and suffered for the sake of others certainly matches any such performances by non-Christians. I have no wish in saying this to demean the bravery of those who Sun Dance, and the very existence of this book on the ceremony makes that clear. However, most Sioux have never pierced in the Sun Dance and never will. It can also be said that pledgers rarely suffer for long, and there are few ill effects from the piercing and flesh offerings. The men know this when they vow to be pierced, and often they will do more than one dance within the space of a few weeks.

The second reason is that it is just not necessary to make such statements in order to give the Sun Dance the status it deserves. It can stand on its own without that, and it is enough to say that it compares favorably with the sacrificial offerings of other religions, which are made as they are demanded. One is seldom able to exalt anything by attempting to tear a comparable thing down.

In each of my previous books on Indians, I have lauded the traditional faith of the nations involved as being wholly acceptable to God and sufficient. I have said that I believe, as do a number of other non-Indians, that we worship the same God, and that there is no need to convert an Indian who is practicing his traditional faith. I have also stressed my conviction that the traditional Indian religions have much to teach the world, if the world will just realize that and listen. I can even empathize with Black Elk when he claims that Indian teachings can be the bridge which will lead the world out of its present darkness and into a brighter tomorrow.[1]

More than a few of the younger contemporary Indians are saying the same thing, but go beyond it to believe they have a religion which is superior to Christianity and all others. Some boast that other faiths will fade away or come to a bad end, while the Indian peoples will triumph and endure. I can appreciate the actual reasons for such views. As these young Indians evaluate what has been done to them, justice demands that the scales should be balanced. Yet wishing, contrary to the old song of that name, will not make it so. When and if we go down, we will all go down together. I am pleased to say that Fools Crow, Eagle Feather, and Dallas Chief Eagle understand this, and make no such boasts of one religion's superiority to the other.

When I praise the traditional Indian faiths, therefore, my intent is not by so doing to shortchange Christianity or to suggest that it is inadequate by comparison. It is simply to recognize that natural religion is also an avenue whereby God has had successful communion with man since the beginning of time. Scripture affirms this position in Romans 1:19-20, when it says, "For what can be known about God is plain to them, because God has shown it to them. Ever since the creation of the world his invisible nature, namely, his eternal power and deity, has been clearly perceived in the things that have been made."

If my position is a reasonable one, what can be of great benefit to religious people is the sharing of the different things we learn from the same God, so that by this we may each increase in knowledge and brotherhood as we glorify His Holy Name. Eagle Feather has already stressed this same point in his account of the Sun Dance, and Fools Crow speaks freely of his love for all races of mankind.

Nor have I ever intended, by what I have said about the Indian religions, that those who are active Christians should abandon their faith in favor of natural religion. And, I do not in any case think that many non-Indians are capable of practicing the traditional kind of Indian faith. In most instances one must grow up into it and over the years reach its understandings through the unique Indian environment and manner of mind.

So I say again that what we can have is rapport and mutual profit. We each have valuable understandings to contribute to the other. The Indian, on the one hand, can help the Christian understand the supernatural powers which are available through harmony with creation. The Christian, on the other hand, can give the Indian specific answers to some questions with which he must otherwise deal in the abstract.

Finally, as we compare the different accounts of the Teton Sioux Sun Dances, we discover that significant changes in attitude and conduct have taken place over the years. My informants do not attempt to debate or to justify the differences. Eagle Feather simply points out that everything, including the Christian Church, changes as the times change. "We are not," he says, "alone in this."

No one would contest that, or would argue that the contemporary Sun Dance should do other than serve the present needs of the people. It is with good reason that the modern ritual is different in some ways from the one performed one hundred years ago, and there is little question but that the dance of 1881 was different in some ways from that enacted one hundred years before, when the associations of the Sioux with the Plains horse and buffalo culture were just beginning.

It appears that changes in the Sun Dance are related to new resources encountered by the people themselves and to influences by outsiders. When the emphasis was placed upon the buffalo, horse raids, war, and societies, the dance meant one thing. When all of these were taken away, the pattern altered again. Now the Sun Dance includes that which fulfills the religious requirements of the modern Sioux.

However the changes have come about, the present-day ceremonialism indicates that traditional ritual practices are not so fixed in nature among the Sioux as they are among some other Plains peoples, and especially as compared with the rituals of the Pueblos of Arizona and New Mexico.

The latter believe that unless an entire ceremony is performed with absolute faithfulness to ancient times in terms of songs, words, and gestures, it will fail to achieve its purpose and might even bring disaster. The Sioux do think in these terms, and several instances have been mentioned in previous chapters wherein it was believed that failure to do a task or to conduct some part of a ceremony properly resulted in tragedy or Divine retribution. But my studies indicate that Sioux ceremonialism offers some latitude in performance, with each individual allowed the privilege of developing his personal approaches around a central core of fixed requirements. In other words, a given number of things in any ceremony must be done exactly as they have been for as long as can be remembered, while the rest can vary according to needs or individual views.

If this is an accurate assessment, it can be asked whether or not the Sioux position is called into question by its license. Can an ancient ceremony in a traditional society be reshaped and still accomplish its purpose?

My answer, and that of the medicine men, is a firm Yes, so long as the practices still draw upon the same Primary Source. And I am sure that the Sioux holy men would go on to say that their viewpoint actually offers greater hope of effectiveness, because it combines the ancient commands, hope, and basis with an acute awareness of modern needs and circumstances.

If by now you would like to attend a Sun Dance there are some sobering facts you ought to bear in mind alongside the exciting ones. One is that there are no worthwhile motel or eating facilities in the towns of Pine Ridge, Rosebud, or St. Francis. That in itself is a clue to how bad conditions are on the reservations today. Pine Ridge has one restaurant, St. Francis has none, and Rosebud opened a new one in 1976.

You will need to stay in the predominantly White towns some twenty to forty miles away from the usual Sun Dance sites. Some of them have two or three good motels and passable restaurants. The nearest cities are a hundred miles or so distant, much too far for a daily journey back and forth. The Antelope Motel in Mission, South Dakota, is where I lodge when I am at Rosebud and not staying with Indian friends, and I recommend both it and the management. Mission also has a fine supermarket. The golf club has a good but seldom-open restaurant, and a mobile-home restaurant downtown has good food and a friendly atmosphere.

Another small town near the reservation has several good motels, but the management of one, whose name I would dearly love to mention here, had, in 1975 at least, an absolutely poisonous attitude toward Indians. When Frank and Kate Fools Crow, Dallas Chief Eagle, and I stayed there for a few days in June, 1975, the owner made it very clear that he detested Indians and that he had only permitted them to stay there as a favor to me. Unfortunately, I learned this only as we were about to leave or we would have moved out forthwith. The owner even bragged that he was part of a vigilante group which had been formed to protect White property against such menaces as AIM. They were, he boasted, more than well enough armed to accomplish that. I sensed his principal disappointment in life was that the group was hindered by the law from going on the offensive.

Oh, not everyone is like that. Many are just the opposite. A Martin attorney named Fredric Cozad was extremely kind and gracious when we went to have a paper drawn up acknowledging the gift to me of Fools Crow's famous ceremonial pipe. And the head ranger at Bear Butte came all the way up the mountain to meet Frank when we were there. But you will find an impressive amount of White hostility toward Indians in general in the reservation areas. Some of it is justified, in that activist Indian groups have caused them great anguish and done considerable physical damage to property.

This does not, however, excuse blanket reactions toward all Indians, and especially toward people like Dallas Chief Eagle, a perfectly fine and actively churched man who does all he can to mediate differences, and the venerable Fools Crow, who hasn't a mean bone in his body. I have never heard him say a cruel word about or seen him do a hurtful thing to anyone.

The other side of the coin has to do with situations you might encounter among some of the Sioux themselves. Earlier I mentioned that there were three kinds of people on the reservations: the Traditionalists, the Liberal party, and the AIM faction.

Conditions being what they are and indeed have been for nearly a century, friction is constant today. Traditionalists are profoundly spiritual people who abhor violence. They will welcome and assist you, and you need not worry about them in any way. The Liberal political People at Pine Ridge are not a menace to Whites, but in 1976 they lost their power to the Traditionalists and the AIM faction, and might well continue their violent acts in an effort to regain their position. Traditionalist and AIM people charge that their activities include beatings, burning homes, threats, harassment with guns, and even murder. AIM's activities in response are well known. Besides this, the volatile atmosphere has spread to youth who, although attached to no group at all, become drugged or drunk and then indulge in senseless beatings of innocent people. Automobiles have been halted at roadblocks at night, and Indian men and women have been assaulted for no cause. Whites escape only because they are seldom out there. Sometimes when BIA policemen attempt to quiet people down or make arrests they are savagely beaten, too; however, the policemen are often accused of beating people in return.

Pine Ridge, with a population of less than 13,500, has averaged two unsolved murders a month over the past year. I have read that it has the highest crime rate in the country. Rosebud stands at only half that, with an average of one murder a month. On both reservations, girls are raped, homes with even as few possessions as these men and women have are regularly vandalized, and Indian friends will caution you to be exceedingly careful about where you go and how long you stay.

I was at Fools Crow's home near Kyle in June, 1975, when two FBI men were shot and killed by a group identified as young Sioux. That raised police and Government activity to a fever pitch and was attended by publicity for several weeks.

But the killings, rapes, and beatings of Indians which I have been describing go unrecorded, unsolved and unnoticed by the outside world. The authorities and the media seem to worry very little about what is happening among the Indians themselves. It is only when Whites are killed or desperate people seize Wounded Knee or a BIA building in Washington that anyone pays attention.

And why should this not be so? Who wishes to learn why the Indians are beset with civil strife? After all, they number less than one-half of 1 percent of the total United States population, and they have been neatly pushed off into such remote areas that only a few

Prayer before the day begins.

outsiders pass by to see them unemployed, starving, diseased, suffering through freezing winters, and frustrated.

Who is disturbed by the atmosphere of anxiety that has settled like a dense black cloud over Pine Ridge and Rosebud? Does it really matter in the great scheme of things that the well-behaved Sioux people can seldom venture far from home without a loaded rifle in the car? Is it of any consequence that Indian homes, poor as most are, are being vandalized, especially when so much of this same thing is going on everywhere?

Do go to the Sun Dances. Go, even though the otherwise splendid atmosphere may be tinged by the possibility of trouble by AIM or someone else. It is still more than worth it, and it remains true that White spectators who attend regularly do so with relative ease, believing that in the daytime it is probable that nothing unpleasant will take place.

But go there with understanding, respect, and reasonable caution, and do not wander alone about the immediate area or the reservation. My close Indian friends see to it that I am seldom left by myself for long when I am there, and at the slightest provocation they sit or walk beside me to make certain that everyone knows I am their friend. In just the space of one year, from 1974 to 1975, I could not help but notice how much more concerned they had become for my safety. Things are getting worse. And while my friends tried not to alarm me unduly, words of caution were issued as they felt they were needed. "Perhaps," they said, "we should go with you when you go there." Or, "Don't stay long in that place. Take care of what you wish to do and leave."

Next year, when the snow has melted and the spring plants break through the earth, Fools Crow will probably serve as Intercessor for another Sun Dance. If hope for the Sioux people he so dearly loves and serves is not there, in the Mystery Circle, where is it to be found?

At about the same time, only two hours' drive away at Rosebud, another Intercessor will probably be doing the same thing for the same reasons.

If I am fortunate, Arthur and I will be driving together across the South Dakota prairies toward a rendezvous with them and with Dallas Chief Eagle. Arthur will be looking at the golden wheat and the blue sky and saying, "Beautiful, isn't it?" And I will be agreeing. Perhaps we will meet you there. If so, leave your camera in the car, see it all with the reverence and the understanding that the Sun Dance deserves, and I promise that you will not ever again have a religious experience quite like it!

FOOTNOTES

Chapter I

1. Grinnel, *The Cheyenne Indians*, p. 213.
2. Utley, *The Last Days of the Sioux Nation*, p. 33.
3. Lowie, *Indians of the Plains*, p. 197.
4. Utley, *The Last Days of the Sioux Nation*, p. 33. See also Paige, *Songs of the Teton Sioux*, p. 120.
5. McLaughlin, *My Friend the Indian*, pp. 8-9.
6. Hodge, *Handbook of American Indians North of Mexico*, p. 651.
7. Utley, *The Last Days of the Sioux Nation*, p. 22.
8. Fools Crow verifies this, and other support is cited.
9. Standing Bear, *My People the Sioux*, p. 113.
10. Ibid., p. 113.
11. Hamilton, *The Sioux of the Rosebud*, pp. 155-157.
12. Paige, *Songs of the Teton Sioux*, p. 102.
13. Ibid., p. 214.
14. Mails, *The People Called Apache*, p. 429.
15. Densmore, *Teton Sioux Music*, p. 86, has Red Bird saying the same thing.
16. Nurge, *The Modern Sioux*, p. 287.

Chapter II

1. Buechel, *Lakota-English Dictionary*, p. 502, p. 526.
2. Terrell, *American Indian Almanac*, p. 268.
3. This is a consensus of opinion among students of the Sun Dance.
4. Black Elk and Brown, *The Sacred Pipe*, pp. 67-100.
5. Dorsey/Bushotter, *A Study of Siouan Cults*.
6. Densmore, pp. 84-151.
7. I find no different opinion among the Christian/Traditionalist Indians. See also Steiger, *Medicine Power*, p. 155, and Steiner, *The New Indians*, p. 107.
8. Rapid City *Journal*, Rapid City, S.D., July 31, 1975.
9. Shorris, *The Death of the Great Spirit*, pp. 137-154.
10. Brown, *Voices of Earth and Sky*, p. 139; pp. 200-209.
11. Mails, *Fools Crow*, to be published in 1978 by Doubleday and Co., Inc.
12. Standing Bear, p. 122.
13. Anderson, *The Sioux of the Rosebud*, p. 56.

Chapter III

1. Recommended reading for comprehensive descriptions of the Plains Indian culture: Lowie, *Indians of the Plains*; Hassrick, *The Sioux*; Mails, *Mystic Warriors of the Plains*; and Mails, *Dog Soldiers*.
2. The historical data is drawn from a number of sources, all of which are listed in the bibliography.
3. Nurge, p. 215.

Chapter V

1. Neihardt, *Black Elk Speaks*, p. 210.

Chapter X

1. Black Elk and Brown, p. 76.
2. Neihardt, pp. 204-205.
3. Dorsey/Bushotter, pp. 458-459.
4. Densmore, pp. 123-124.

Chapter XI

1. Dorsey/Bushotter, p. 459.
2. Densmore, p. 127.
3. Ibid,, p. 102.
4. Ibid., p. 122.

Chapter XII

1. Dorsey/Bushotter, p. 454.
2. Mails, *The Mystic Warriors of the Plains*, p. 19.
3. Miss Fletcher states that "the tent set apart for the consecrating ceremonies, which take place after sunset of the first day, was pitched within the line of tents, on the site formerly assigned to one of the sacred tents."
4. The author heard about this medicine in 1873 from a Ponca chief, one of the leaders of a dancing society. It is a bulbous root, which grows near the place where the sun pole is planted.
5. Dorsey/Bushotter, pp. 454-455.

Chapter XIII

1. Since the rawhide image they intended to use had been damaged, a new man was made of cardboard and painted red for the 1975 dance.
2. Dorsey/Bushotter, pp. 453-458.
3. Densmore, pp. 106-122.

Chapter XIV

1. Densmore, p. 126.
2. Ibid., p. 126.
3. Mails, *The Mystic Warriors of the Plains*, pp. 311-317. See also Black Elk and Brown, p. 29.
4. Densmore, p. 125.
5. Standing Bear, p. 120.
6. Densmore, pp. 103-104.
7. Dorsey/Bushotter, p. 459.
8. Densmore, pp. 124-129.

Chapter XV

1. Neihardt, p. 203.
2. Dorsey/Bushotter, pp. 465-467.
3. Densmore, pp. 132-138.
4. Dorsey/Bushotter, p. 483.
5. Densmore, pp. 150-151.

Chapter XVI

1. Densmore, pp. 78-83.
2. James A. Hanson, *Museum of the Fur Trade Quarterly*, Vol. 1, No. 3, 1965.

Chapter XVIII

1. Black Elk and Brown, p. XII.

Bibliography

Anderson, John A., Hamilton, H. W., and Hamilton, J. T., *The Sioux of the Rosebud,* University of Oklahoma Press, Norman, 1971.

Black Elk and Brown, Joseph Epes, *The Sacred Pipe,* University of Oklahoma Press, Norman, 1953.

Blish, Helen, *A Pictographic History of the Oglala Sioux,* University of Nebraska Press, Lincoln, 1967.

Brown, Vinson, *Voices of Earth and Sky,* Stackpole Books, Harrisburg, Pa., 1974.

Buechel, Rev. Eugene, S. J. and Manhart, Rev. Paul, S. J., editors, *A Dictionary of the Teton Dakota Sioux Language,* University of South Dakota and Red Cloud Indian School, Inc., Pine Ridge, South Dakota, 1975.

_____. *A Grammar of Lakota,* St. Francis Mission, St. Francis, South Dakota, 1939.

Catlin, George, *North American Indians,* Leary, Stuart and Company, Philadelphia, 1913.

Chief Eagle, Dallas, *Winter Count,* Johnson Publishing Company, Boulder, Colorado, 1967.

Curtis, Edward S., *The North American Indian,* Vol. III; 20 vols., The University Press, Cambridge, Mass., 1907-30.

Deloria, Vine, Jr., *God is Red,* Grosset and Dunlap, New York, 1973.

_____. *The Indian Affair,* Friendship Press, New York, 1974.

Denig, Edwin Thompson, *Five Indian Tribes of the Upper Missouri,* University of Oklahoma Press, Norman, 1961.

Densmore, Frances, *Teton Sioux Music,* Bureau of American Ethnology, Bulletin 61, Washington, D.C., 1918.

DeVoto, Bernard, editor, *The Journals of Lewis and Clark,* Houghton Mifflin Company, Boston, 1953.

Dodge, Col. Richard Irving, *33 Years Among Our Wild Indians,* Archer House, Inc., New York, 1959.

Dorsey, George A., *The Arapaho Sun Dance; the Ceremony of the Offerings Lodge,* Field Columbian Museum Publication 75, Vol. IV, Chicago, 1903.

_____. *The Cheyenne, Ceremonial Organization,* Field Columbian Museum Publication 99, Vol. IX, No. 1, Chicago, 1905.

Dorsey, James O., and George Bushotter, *A Study of Siouan Cults,* 11th Annual Report of the Bureau of American Ethnology, 1888-89, Washington, D.C., 1894.

Erdoes, Richard, *The Sun Dance People,* Alfred A. Knopf, New York, 1972.

Ewers, John C., *The Horse in Blackfoot Culture,* Smithsonian Institution Bureau of American Ethnology, Bulletin 159, Washington, D.C., 1955.

Gilmore, Melvin R., *Prarie Smoke,* Columbia University Press, New York, 1929.

Grinnell, George Bird, *The Cheyenne Indians,* Vol. II, Bison Books, University of Nebraska Press, Lincoln, 1972. First Editon by Yale University Press, New Haven, 1923.

Hans, Fred M., *The Great Sioux Nation,* Ross and Haines, Inc., Minneapolis, 1964.

Hassrick, Royal B., *The Sioux—Life and Customs of a Warrior Society,* University of Oklahoma Press, Norman, 1964.

Hodge, Frederick W., *Handbook of American Indians North of Mexico,* Smithsonian Institution, BAE, 1910, Bulletin 30, Part 2, Washington, D.C., 1910.

Hofmann, Charles, *American Indians Sing,* The John Day Company, New York, 1967.

Hyde, George E., *Red Cloud's Folk: A History of the Oglala Sioux Indians,* University of Oklahoma Press, Norman, 1937.

_____. *A Sioux Chronicle,* University of Oklahoma Press, Norman, 1956.

_____. *Spotted Tail's Folk: A History of the Brule Sioux,* University of Oklahoma Press, Norman, 1961.

Jorgensen, Joseph G., *The Sun Dance Religion,* University of Chicago Press, Chicago, 1972.

Lame Deer, John Fire, and Erdoes, Richard, *Lame Deer, Seeker of Visions,* Simon and Schuster, New York, 1972.

Lowie, Robert H., *Indians of the Plains,* McGraw-Hill Book Company, Inc., New York, 1954.

Mails, Thomas E., *The Mystic Warriors of the Plains,* Doubleday and Company, Inc., Garden City, New York, 1972.

_____. *Dog Soldiers, Bear Men and Buffalo Women,* Prentice-Hall, Inc., Englewood Cliffs, New Jersey, 1973.

_____. *The People Called Apache,* Prentice-Hall Inc., Englewood Cliffs, New Jersey, 1974.

Maine, Floyd Shuster, *Lone Eagle, The White Sioux,* The University of New Mexico Press, Albuquerque, 1956.

McLaughlin, James, *My Friend the Indian,* Houghton Mifflin Company, Boston and New York, 1910.

Neihardt, John G., *Black Elk Speaks,* William Morrow, New York, 1932.

Nurge, Ethel, *The Modern Sioux, Social Systems and Reservation Cultures,* University of Nebraska Press, Lincoln, 1970.

Paige, Harry W., *Songs of the Teton Sioux,* Westernlore Press, Los Angeles, 1970.

Powers, William K., *Indians of the Northern Plains,* G. P. Putnam's Sons, New York, 1969.

Robinson, Doane, *A History of the Dakota or Sioux Indians,* Ross and Haines, Inc., Minneapolis, 1958.

Ruby, Robert H., *The Oglala Sioux,* Vantage Press, Inc., New York, 1955.

Schulenberg, Raymond F., *Indians of North Dakota,* North Dakota History, Vol. 23, No. 3 and 4, July-October, 1956.

Shorris, Earl, *The Death of the Great Spirit,* Simon and Schuster, New York, 1971.

Sinte Gleska College Center, Rosebud, South Dakota, *Lakota Language,* published by North Plains Press, Aberdeen, South Dakota, 1973.

Smith, J. L., *A Short History of the Sacred Calf Pipe of the Teton Dakota,* Museum News, University of South Dakota, Vol. 28, Nos. 7-8, July-August, 1967.

Standing Bear, *My People the Sioux,* Houghton Mifflin Company, The Riverside Press, Cambridge, Mass., 1928.

Steiger, Brad, *Medicine Power,* Doubleday and Company, Inc., Garden City, New York, 1974.

_____. *Medicine Talk,* Doubleday and Company, Inc., Garden City, New York, 1975.

Steiner, Stan, *The New Indians,* Harper and Row, New York, 1968.

Terrell, John Upton, *American Indian Almanac,* The World Publishing Co., New York and Cleveland, 1971.

_____. *Sioux Trail,* McGraw-Hill Book Company, Inc., New York, 1974.

Utley, Robert M., *The Last Days of the Sioux Nation,* Yale University Press, New Haven, 1963.

Walker, J. R., *The Sun Dance and Other Ceremonies of the Oglala Divison of the Teton Dakota,* Anthropological Papers of the American Museum of Natural History, 16, Pt. 2, New York, 1917.

Wissler, Clark, *Societies and Ceremonial Organizations of the Oglala Division of the Teton Dakota,* Anthropological Papers of the American Museum of Natural History, 11, Pt. 2, New York, 1916.

_____. *North American Indians of the Plains,* American Museum of Natural History, New York, 1934.

The sign at the fairground entrance proclaims the Sun Dance of 1975, and gives its dates: July 3, 4, 5 and 6. Courtesy of Greg Pietz.

Pictorial Record of the Rosebud Sioux Sundances of 1974 and 1975

The Sacred Tree used for the 1975 Sun Dance in its natural setting. It is the tree closest to the center of the photograph.

The top of the Sacred Tree was not straight, bending considerably to one side. Research shows that Sacred Trees used in the past were seldom straight.

Eagle Feather gathering cottonwood for the sweatlodge fireplace.

Titus Smith and his father, Delbert, rest and visit during the cutting.

The cottonwood for the sweatlodge fireplace is cut with a manual saw. No ceremony is observed.

Delbert Smith does most of the work in a beautiful setting.

Titus Smith in 1975. At age 12 he had already been pierced twice in the Sun Dance.

Evelyn Staub watches with apprehension as the large trees are felled.

The size of the firewood trees collected is most impressive,

and Jerry Dragg carries astonishing loads.

All of the trees are loaded on a pickup truck,

and then transported to the sweatlodge area at the Rosebud Fairground.

The 1974 Sacred Tree has been cut into sections, and saved to be burned in the first sweatlodge fire of 1975. Some of the pledgers' ropes and some offerings are still attached to it.

The Four Generations sweatlodge fireplace, with the cottonwood piled on the north side, and a pile of willow bark strips peeled from the sweatlodge willows on the south.

242

Eagle Feather's camp for 1975, with the pole framework of the "cooler" up in front of the tent.

Hazel Schweigman moving her camping equipment into the camp. Most of the pledgers arrive two or more days before the Sun Dance begins.
Courtesy of Greg Pietz.

The finished cooler, covered with pine boughs, and ready to provide shade for eating and working.

A view of Holy Lodge Hill from the south. Eagle Feather vision quested here over a period of seven straight years.

One of the herbs used for the Sun Dance healing ceremonies was gathered at the base of the hill.

A close-up view of the sandstone formation at the top of Holy Lodge Hill.

Eagle Feather locates the healing root.

The small part of the healing plant which is visible above the ground. Only an expert medicine man would know it by sight.

Under Eagle Feather's diligent supervision, Delbert begins digging in the soft, sandy soil.

The excavating is done with utmost care, for the root must not be damaged before it is removed.

As the root and its bulb begin to appear, the dirt close to it is removed by hand.

Frequent pauses are made as Eagle Feather evaluates the progress.

The root as it appears when it is finally out of the ground. It will be cut into small pieces, and placed in patients' mouths during the healing ceremonies.

The careful excavation of the Slim Root, also to be administered to patients during the healing ceremonies.

The Slim Root as it appears when it has been removed from the ground.

The area on the Rosebud Reservation where the Slim Root is found.

Another view of the same area. The Little White River runs through the cut in the background.

Eagle Feather and Delbert cut cherry branches to make the pipe rack for the Sun Dance Altar.

Everyone joins in to collect sage. The site is very near Holy Lodge Hill, on the south side. Most of the people who help have special roles to play in the Sun Dance.

The gatherers look for long plants, and the sage is pulled up, roots and all.

The collecting goes on for some time, since a considerable quantity for many purposes will be required.

The sage is assembled into large bunches,

and Eagle Feather cuts off the roots.

The various activities which take place are used as training sessions for the young; as schools for future Sun Dance pledgers.

The sage is brought to the camp, and the adults begin to fashion the head wreaths, wristbands and ankle bands which will be worn by the pledgers.

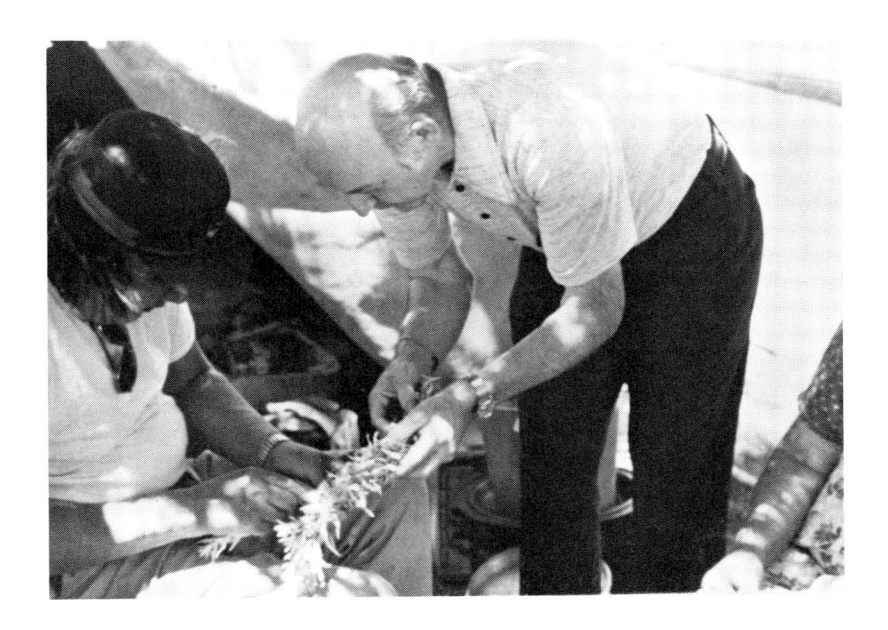

The work goes best with two people working together. By helping, one gets a close look at the plaiting method.

Orrie Farrell is still learning, and struggles some as he works on his head wreath. In another year or two he will be an expert.

Eagle Feather holds a head wreath together while Evelyn Staub wraps it with string to make it secure.

A nearly completed head wreath. The two sticks in the foreground are flag sticks waiting to be painted.

Evelyn Staub tries one sage wreath on for size as she fashions another.

A close-up view of the sage plaiting method. It must be bent slightly as the branches are interwoven to assure that the finished product will be round.

While the wreaths are being made, a new effigy of a man is made of cardboard to replace the damaged one of rawhide used in 1974.

The outside fireplace for the sweatlodge, called "Old Man Four Generations," viewed from the west end and showing its four horns.

View from the east end, showing the neck of Old Man Four Generations, and some of the white rocks to be heated for the sweatlodge.

The large rocks to be heated, and the cottonwood for the fireplace. The Preparations Tipi is in the background.

Jerry Dragg placing in 1975 the seven rocks which will make up the face of Old Man Four Generations.

The seven rocks in place. The fireplace wood is stacked over the rocks.

The method of stacking the cottonwood in the fireplace. It makes a roaring fire!

The sweatlodge framework and the Old Man Four Generations fireplace arrangement for the 1975 Sun Dance.

A close-up of the willow framework, which is lashed together with strips of willow bark. A comparison with Jerry Dragg illustrates the small size of the sweatlodge.

The rock cradle altar for the sweatlodge itself. Its chute to slide the rocks in is on the left, or west, side.

256

The canvas covering of the sweatlodge. It is weighted down with ropes tied to logs and rocks to keep the wind from blowing it off.

Eagle Feather's metal trunk, containing his medicine items, is placed on top of the sweatlodge. Exposed is the skin of his principal spirit helper, the badger. Here he clears his pipe stem and prepares it for use.

The pipe, tobacco pouch and braided sweetgrass are placed on the mole hill, a small mound of dirt located midway between the sweatlodge and Old Man Four Generations.

When the sweatlodge is ready, purification ceremonies are held in it each evening until the Sun Dance proper begins. In 1975, Eagle Feather and Mary Dragg gather sage for the ceremony near the shade cooler, from which food will be served to the pledgers and the visitors.

The sweatlodge participant enters on his hands and knees, saying as he does so, "all my relatives."

The sweetgrass used to purify the lodge itself, and then each rock as it is passed in, is lighted from ashes taken from Old Man Four Generations.

The Custodian passes the rocks in one at a time. In the old days a wooden fork was used. Today he uses a shovel.

At the entrance he pauses while the helper touches the rock with the stem of the pipe. Then the Custodian drops it in the Rock Cradle.

The door is closed, all light is sealed out, and the ceremony begins. Soon prayers and an eerie chanting are heard as the pledgers petition Wakan-Tanka and Grandfather for a successful Sun Dance.

The sweatlodge door is opened and closed three times. When it is opened the fourth time, the ceremony is finished. The water bucket sits near the doorway.

Prayer continues even when the door is open, and the Custodian prays with those who are in the lodge. Women take part in the sweatlodge ceremonies, and women can serve as custodians.

When the ceremony is done, the participants emerge, dry themselves off with towels and get dressed. They talk about the ceremony, and how good they feel after experiencing the intense heat.

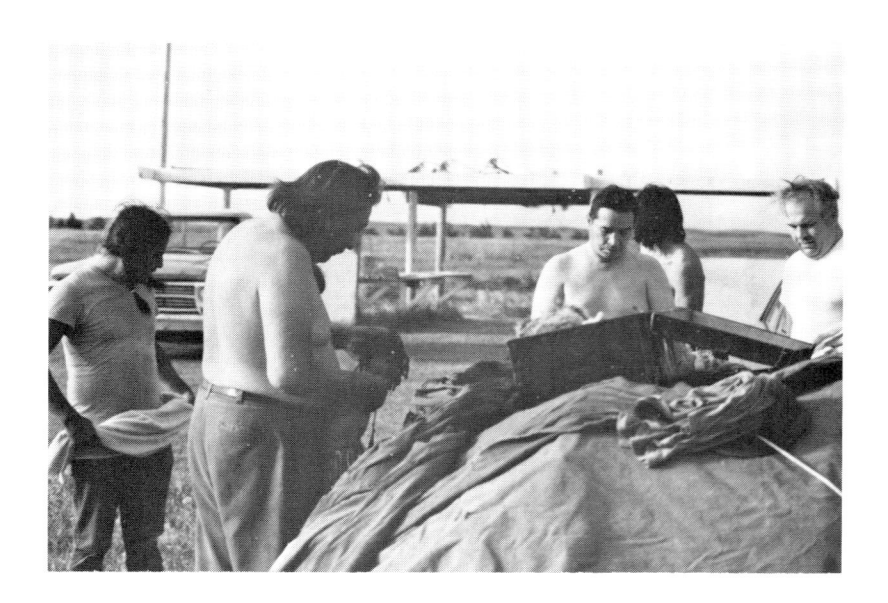

Under Eagle Feather's direction, helpers attempted to put up the Preparations Tipi for 1975. First they erected three central poles.

Then Eagle Feather wrapped the three poles where they intersected to secure them in place.

After this, the other poles were laid on the first three.

The canvas covering was lashed to a pole and then raised into place.

But it didn't fit, billowing out like a huge sail in the wind. Everything was taken down, and remained that way when darkness fell.

But early in the morning on the first day of the dance, the Preparations Tipi was up and ready. Someone who knew how had erected it during the night. Courtesy of Gregg Pietz.

The Preparations Tipi and the sweatlodge used in 1974.

The entrance of the Tipi of 1974. The Sun Dance buffalo skull, with a pipe resting on the bridge of its nose, sits just inside the entrance.

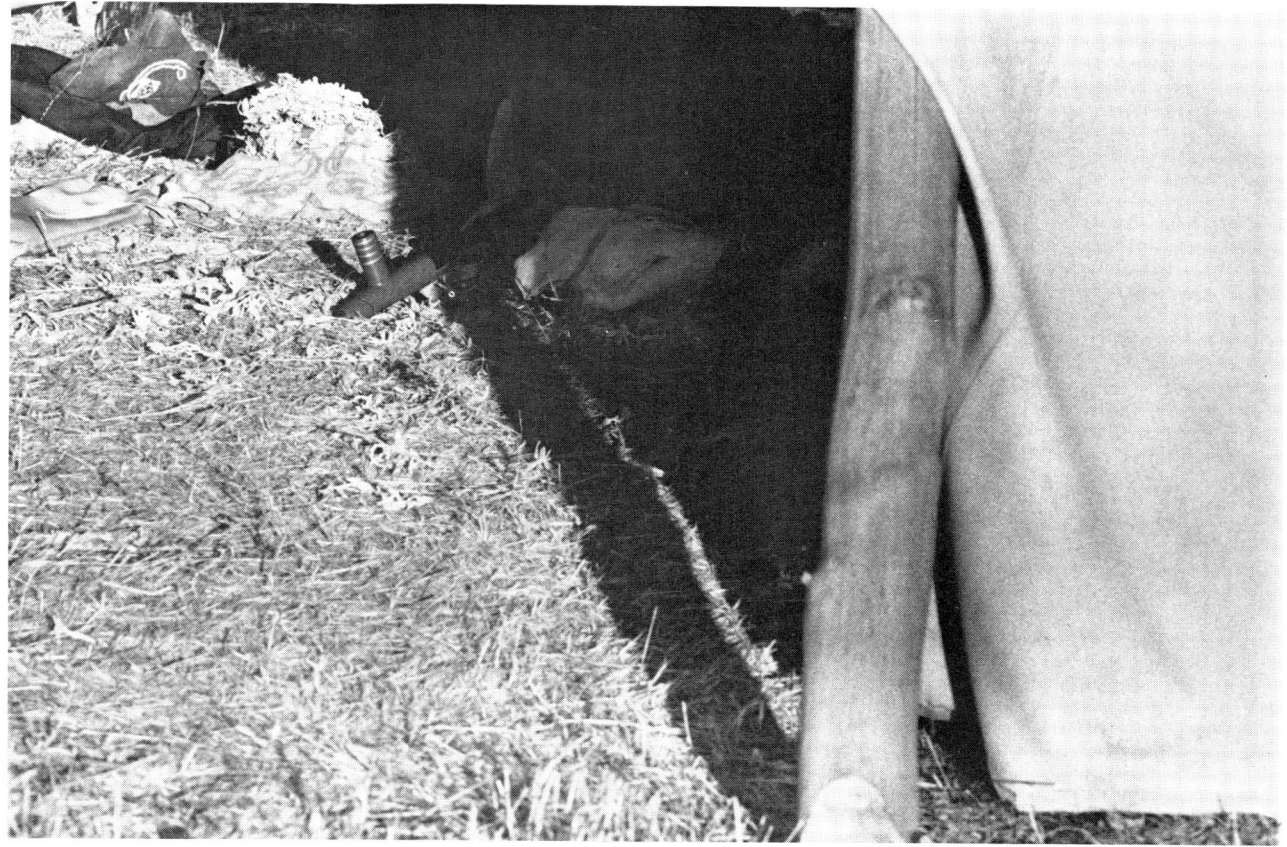

The day before the Sun Dance of 1975 was to begin, a large group of participants gathered at the site of the Sacred Tree. Before it could be cut, another cottonwood had to be gotten out of the way.

Eagle Feather, the Intercessor, blessed the Tree with an eagle-wing fan.

Then another medicine man prayed at the Tree with his sacred pipe.

While Eagle Feather mixed paint, the four girls who were chosen to chop the Tree assembled on its west side.

A round spot of red paint was applied to the palm of each hand.

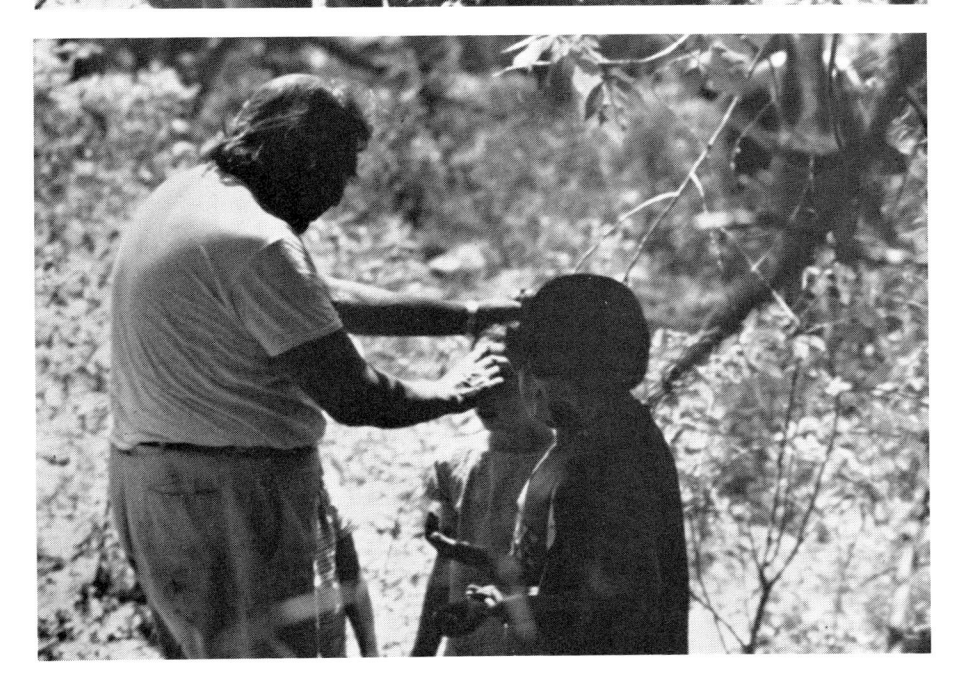

And a round spot of red paint was applied to each girl's forehead.

Eagle Feather prayed to the Sacred Tree with his pipe.

A third medicine man smoked and purified the Tree with burning sweetgrass.

Eagle Feather laid his hand on the Tree, and prayed to Grandfather with the pipe.

Then the four girls in turn each chopped the Tree once, the first chop being made on the east side, the second on the south,

the third chop was made on the west, and the final blow was struck on the north side of the Tree.

Then Joe Staub and Delbert Smith, using long handled axes, began to cut the Tree down.

A medicine man and Delbert finished the job.

Once the Tree was down, it took eight men to carry it to the truck.

It was loaded aboard butt first, with the butt extending far out in front of the truck cab.

The Tree was then transported to the Rosebud Fairground—to within fifty yards of the Mystery Circle entrance—and unloaded.

While care was employed in unloading the Tree, it was allowed to touch the ground at the butt. The rest of the Tree was held up, so that only a few of the leaves brushed the ground.

The Tree was then carried toward the east entrance of the Mystery Circle in four moves of equal length. Each time the bearers halted, the medicine man prayed and made the cry of a coyote.

With the medicine man, Gilbert Yellow Hawk, leading the way, the Tree was carried into the Mystery Circle.

The Tree was then deposited on the ground, with the butt of the Tree resting on the east rim of the previously excavated hole.

A short prayer for the Tree and for the success of the Sun Dance was said.

Joyce Crane, one of the girls who chopped the Tree, brought the four colored banners which would be tied to the top of the Tree.

Eagle Feather took the banners, and tied them to the top of the Tree.

A bundle of cherry branches was tied crossways at a mid-point on the Tree.

A medicine man, using his finger as a brush, painted a red line from the butt of the Tree to the first fork of the lowest branches.

The red line symbolized the red path which the Sioux people walk upon.

The four cloth banners were tied to the uppermost branches.

The white cloth was on top, next came the yellow, then red, and on the bottom was the black.

Then the images of the man and the buffalo were tied to the Tree.

The raw hide buffalo image used in 1975. It was left in its natural state. No paint was applied.

The red cardboard image of the man used in 1975. In his right hand he held the sacred pipe, and in his left hand he held the hoop of the nation.

The Sun Dance pledgers' ropes for piercing were sorted and straightened out by the pledgers.

Then they were tied to the Tree at a point just below the cherry branches. The loose ends were either coiled and tied, or coiled and stuffed in a cloth bag.

Detail showing all of the pledgers' ropes as they were secured to the Tree. Courtesy of Greg Pietz.

In 1975, Eagle Feather went to his metal suitcase and obtained his pipe and the offerings which would be placed in the hole.

First the hole was purified by the smoke from burning sweetgrass. Then the offerings: sage, buffalo fat, dried meat and pemmican were placed in the hole.

Before each offering was placed in the hole, Eagle Feather held it out to the four directions, to Mother Earth, and to Grandfather.

Before each offering was put down, a medicine man, George Eagle Elk, smoked and purified the hole.

Eagle Feather drove a long steel spike into the ground at the butt of the Tree, and braced it with his foot as eight men lifted the Tree.

Six men pulled on the pledgers' ropes as other men pushed the Tree up higher.

278

Slowly, the heavy green cottonwood Tree came erect.

It dropped into the hole, and while the men held it straight with the ropes, dirt was packed around the base to secure it.

Then a rope was tied around the Tree trunk at a point six feet above the ground.

After this the women who would participate in the dance brought the prayer offering cloths to be tied to the Tree.

Eagle Feather and Jerry Dragg tied them on, and the Tree was ready for the Sun Dance to begin.

When the Tree was completed, a prayer ceremony was held to consecrate the ground of the Mystery Circle. The Sun Dance participants sat on the ground in a circle, and smoked the pipe.

It was late in the afternoon when the consecration ceremony was held, and the wind caused the banners to extend out like arms from the Tree. It was a beautiful and touching moment; exciting too!

The first view of the Sacred Tree as the sun began to rise on the first morning of the 1974 Sun Dance.

As visitors began to stir and move about, the pledgers were already in the sweatlodge, and medicine men tested the ropes and tied new offering cloths to the Tree.

The Sun Dance Mystery Circle as viewed from the east in 1974.

The east entrance to the Mystery Circle in 1974.

The Sacred Tree in 1974. The announcer's booth is in the background.

Dallas Chief Eagle walks by the announcer's booth and toward the Preparations Tipi early in the morning of the fourth day of the 1974 Sun Dance.

The yellow flags of the east in 1974.

The Altar Pipe Rack of 1974, with several strings of flesh offerings wrapped in white cloth attached. These offerings were taken at the time of the ground consecration.

The top of the Sacred Tree of 1974, showing the location of the images of the buffalo and the man.

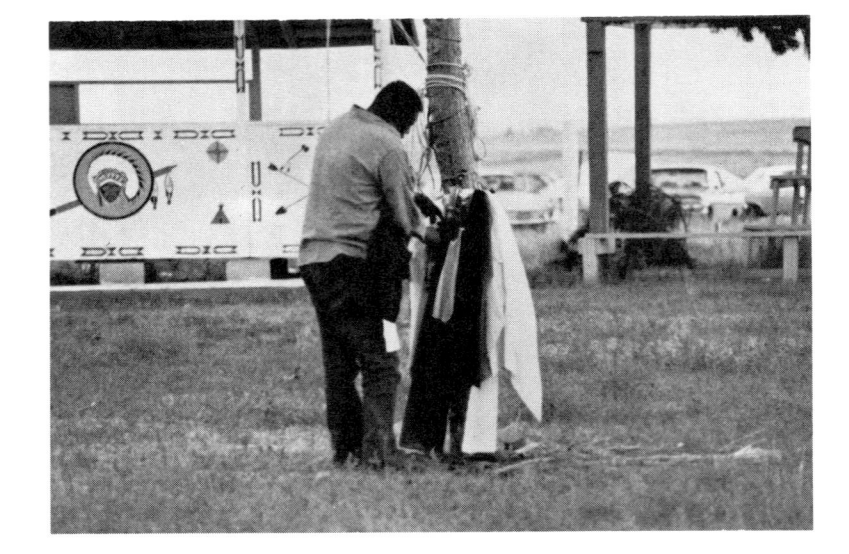

Tying additional cloth prayer offerings to the Tree on the fourth day of the Sun Dance in 1974.

The base of the Sacred Tree in 1974.

A close-up view, showing how the cloth offerings are tied, and how the pledgers' ropes are coiled to prevent the loose ends from dragging on the ground.

At the base of the 1974 Tree was a paper cup containing lard which would be used to grease the skewer sticks and the eagle claws used for piercing.

There was also an offering of tobacco, tied to a stick with a red cloth banner attached.

On the morning of the fourth day in 1974, medicine men added cloth offerings,

straightened out the pledgers' ropes, inspected them for flaws,

and stretched them out to determine the approximate position each male pledger would take when he was tied to the Tree.

Detail showing the ropes as they were attached to the Tree and stretched out. It is obvious that the pledgers could not circle the Tree while they are pierced without getting hopelessly entangled.

The sweatlodge door as it was opened for the fourth and last time on the morning of the fourth day. Two ceremonies were held to accommodate all of the pledgers.

The pledgers emerged from the steaming sweatlodge,

dried off, put on their socks, shoes and trousers, and proceeded to the Preparations Tipi.

There they put on their Sun Dance costumes—the skirt, the sage and the whistles, and when ready emerged from the Tipi.

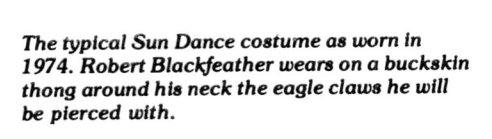

The typical Sun Dance costume as worn in 1974. Robert Blackfeather wears on a buckskin thong around his neck the eagle claws he will be pierced with.

Side view of the sage head wreath showing how the colored ribbons are attached.

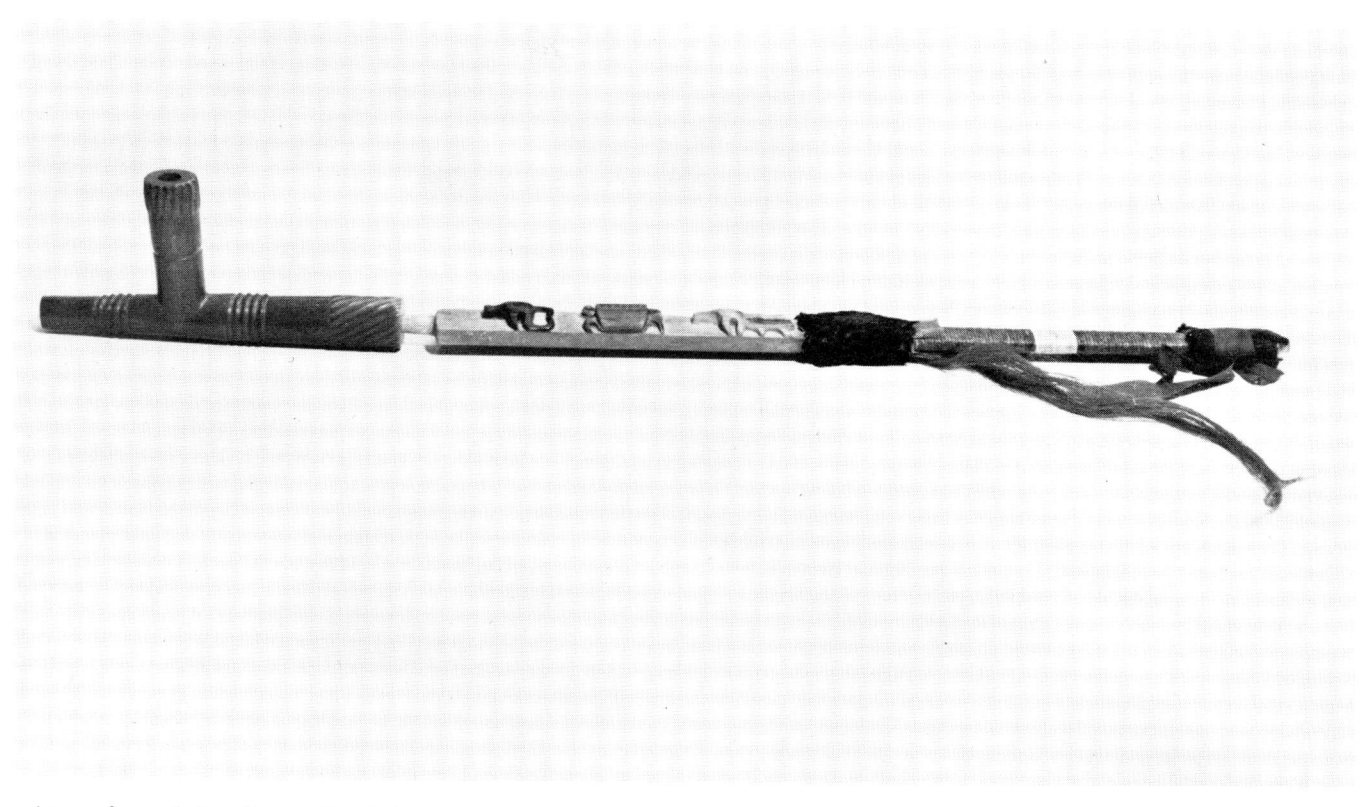

A type of sacred pipe often used by pledgers and Intercessors in both ancient and modern Sun Dances. The animal carvings on the stem represnt the four-legged creatures. Courtesy of the Gilcrease Institute, Tulsa, Oklahoma.

A type of eagle wing fan often used by medicine men in the Sun Dance. The handle is painted hide. Courtesy of the Gilcrease Institute, Tulsa, Oklahoma.

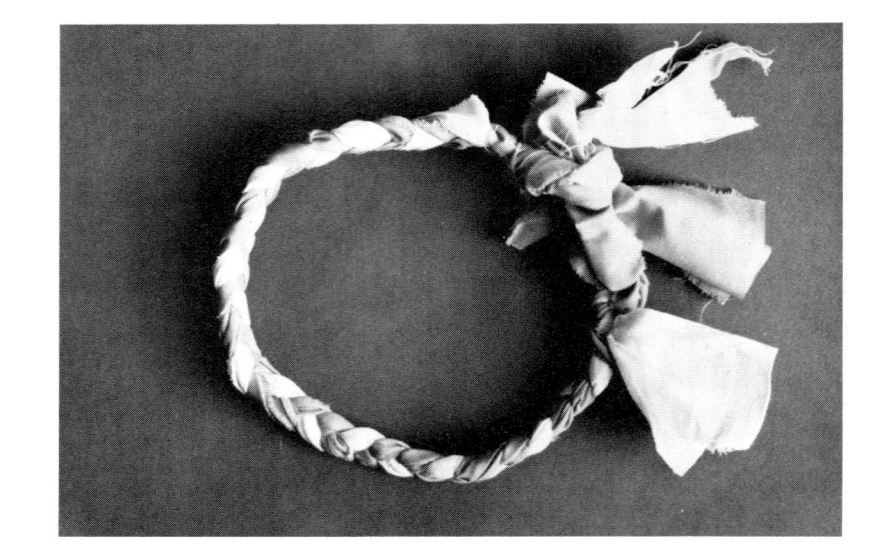

The braided cloth headband worn by Eagle Feather for the 1975 Sun Dance. It was yellow and red.

Sage wristbands worn by pledgers in 1974. The ankle bands are identical.

Sage headband worn by a pledger in 1974. The feathers are golden eagle.

Back view of sage headband worn in 1974.

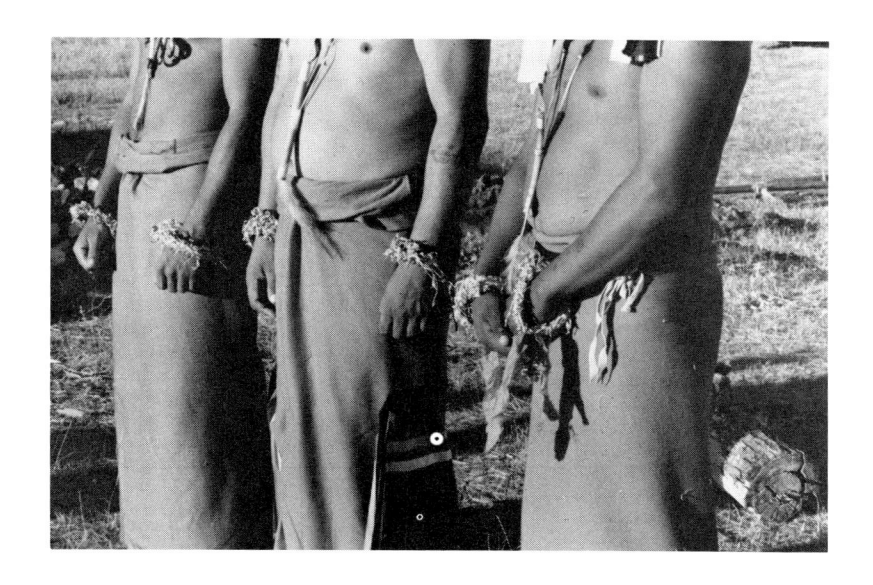

Sage wristbands worn by pledgers in 1974.

Eagle Feather painting a pledger in 1974. This arm paint has a fork at the top, indicating that the bearer is a medicine man who has had a vision of thunder beings.

Arm paint for 1974. There is no fork at the top.

The back paint for the fourth day in 1974—a circle with a dot in the center to represent the nation's hoop and the Tree. "The man carries the nation on his back."

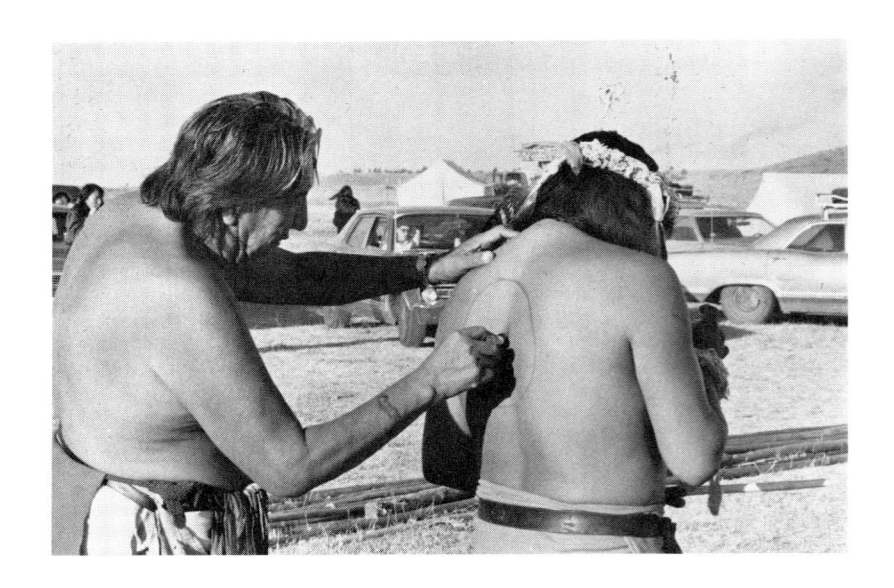

The instrument used for painting is a commercially made red marking pencil.

The women dressed in their own tents, and joined the men and Eagle Feather, now wearing his double-tailed bonnet, near the Preparations Tipi.

Each woman wore sage bands on her head, wrists and ankles, and carried a pipe.

Those women who wore upright feathers in their head wreaths would give flesh offerings during the Sun Dance.

Hazel Schweigman wearing her sage head wreath in 1975, and showing how the upright eagle feathers are inserted. Courtesy of Greg Pietz.

Orrie Farrell in 1975, wearing on his chest two red circles to indicate he will be pierced on both sides. Courtesy of Greg Pietz.

The singers assembling on their platform in front of the announcer's stand in 1974.

The singers seated on the south side of the Mystery Circle in 1975.

Eagle Feather and Medicine Man George Eagle Elk spread sage at the base of the Tree in 1974. A buffalo hide was laid over the sage for the pledgers to lie on as they were pierced.

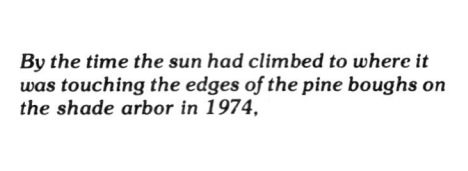

By the time the sun had climbed to where it was touching the edges of the pine boughs on the shade arbor in 1974,

Eagle Feather, the Intercessor, had come to get his pipe and pipe bag from his suitcase at the base of the Tree,

and returned to the preparations area where the assembled pledgers waited for him.

The small group of pledgers moving toward the Mystery Circle on the morning of the first day in 1975.

Another view of the same group. The Keeper of the Pipes has not arrived, and Eagle Feather himself carries the buffalo skull for the Altar.

He gave the pledgers a long lecture about the need to conduct themselves well and honorably during the dance in 1974.

He asked them to pray, and to seek with passion exceptional visions.

He reminded the pledgers of their great heritage as Sun Dancers, and of the importance of the dance to the Sioux and to all people.

Finally, he reminded them of their vows, and of how the vows must be kept.

Then the pledgers turned toward the east and the Mystery Circle, with the men in front,

and the women behind.

With Eagle Feather and the Keeper of the Pipes leading the way,

the pledgers moved toward the Mystery Circle.

Eagle Feather leading the way on the fourth morning in 1974.

The line paused four times on the way to the Mystery Circle, and each time Eagle Feather prayed.

The third stop was made just outside the east entrance to the Mystery Circle.

Upon entering the Circle, Eagle Feather, George Eagle Elk and the Keeper of the Pipes, Floyd Comes A Flying, proceeded to the black flags at the west and made the Altar.

The Altar in 1974, showing the black flags, the pipe rack, and the buffalo skull. The pipes of the Intercessor and his assistants rest on the skull.

The partial buffalo skull and the sage used for the Altar in 1975.

For some reason not explained, in 1975 the Intercessor and medicine man's pipes were placed on the ground under the pipe rack, while the pledgers' pipes were rested on the buffalo skull.

In 1974, the pledgers stood in a line and faced the Altar as it was made up.

Then, at a signal from Eagle Feather, the music started and the Sun Dance began.

306

The pledgers danced in place and blew shrill blasts on their whistles as the medicine man brushed their backs with his eagle wing fan and blessed them.

A front view of the women pledgers at the west as the dance began.

The sun was still low and the shadows were long as the pledgers raised their arms and sent their first prayer up to Grandfather.

As the pledgers, led by two medicine men, left the west and moved toward the north, they circled around the Altar.

As they moved from one direction to the next the men always went first.

George Eagle Elk blessing the pledgers with his eagle wing fan in 1975. The blessing is done many times during the dance to give the pledgers the power and vision of the eagle.

Eagle Feather leading the line of pledgers in 1974. He does not touch the other man, but holds onto the sage wristband, which has an extension for this purpose.

A back view of the moving line as it proceeds to the south.

An end view of the line facing the north in 1974. Courtesty of Arthur Mahoney.

Another view of the same line dancing in place.

A front view of the male pledgers in 1974.

The male pledgers at the south in 1975.

Once the line had reached the south, Eagle Feather prayed with the pipe while the Keeper got ready to receive it.

Then he presented the pipe to the first pledger.

312

When the pipe is given to the pledger,

he brings it forward to the Keeper of the Pipes,

who prays to the six directions before he receives it.

Lorenzo Hodgekiss presents the pipe in 1975 to Lame Deer, who serves as Keeper.

The pipe is offered four times, while unspoken questions are asked and answered between the two men.

Then the Keeper accepts the pipe and the pledgers rest.

Robert Blackfeather presented his pipe in a very dramatic manner in 1975.

He was going to pierce in a special and daring way, and this gave special emphasis to the presentation.

After several chanted prayers for Robert, Lame Deer accepted the pipe.

At the end of each round, when the line reaches the south, a pipe is presented.

The women present pipes in the same way as the men. Here, Hazel Schweigman presents her pipe to Floyd Comes A Flying.

The old timers know how to bring the pipe forward to the Keeper with a splendid gliding motion that is enchanting to see.

The pledgers resting in 1974. The men and the women sit a short distance apart.

The pledgers resting in 1975. Here they meditate and discuss their visions, insights, and the progress of the dance.

If a healing ceremony is to be held during the next round, the pledger brings the pipe forward on his knees. Sometimes this method is used before a flesh offering ceremony.

The Keeper also kneels as the pledger reaches the flags.

Then he and the Intercessor pray together for Grandfather's aid for those who are to be healed.

318

The Keeper kneels again and addresses the pledger in prayer.

Then he stands and touches the pipe,

but he refuses to accept it as a sign that the healing ceremony must first take place.

Those in the audience who have special healing needs are invited to come forward first. In 1974, this woman was prayed for and then took the pipe to the Sacred Tree, where she prayed for a considerable period of time.

The special prayer service for the mother of Delbert Lone Walker, wearing the white blouse, in 1974.

It was an emotional moment. She was expected to live only a few weeks, but as a result of the ceremony she lived almost a year.

Her parents, Mr. and Mrs. Floyd Comes A Flying, participated in the ceremony.

And the pipe was taken to the Sacred Tree, where prayer continued.

On the fourth day in 1975, a spirit keeping ceremony was held for the deceased mother of Delbert Lone Walker. A medicine man smoked the spirit bundle with sweetgrass.

and then gave it to the girl's father, who handed it to the Keeper of the Spirit.

She took the bundle to the Sacred Tree, and prayed there with it for the duration of the Sun dance.

On one occasion, little Delbert was brought to the Tree to receive the blessing and sympathy of the Spirit Keeper.

After the special healings in 1975, all those who had special problems came to the flags at the east and formed a line.

While the pledgers formed another line facing the people, Eagle Feather blessed the people with his eagle wing fan.

Then the pledgers passed down the line of people, laid their hands on their heads and shoulders, and prayed for them.

Even the children joined the line to receive an infusion of power from the pledgers.

The sincerity and devoutness of the pledgers

is matched by the people. They believe in what they are doing, and their faith is rewarded by Grandfather.

The medicine men pray for the people too.

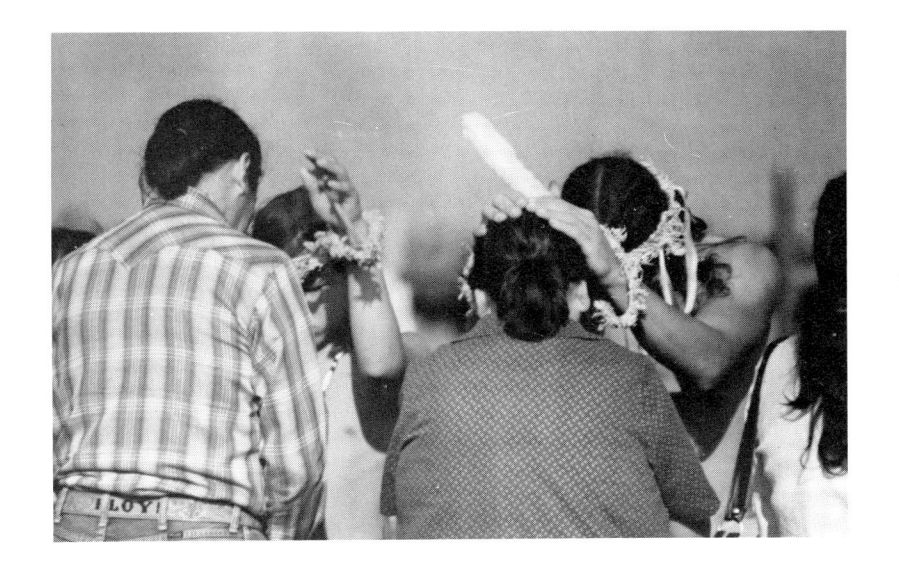

No one hurries, they take as much time as is necessary to do the healing ceremony well.

The men are followed by the women. Every pledger prays for every person.

Some of the women touched the people on the head with their sacred pipe as they prayed.

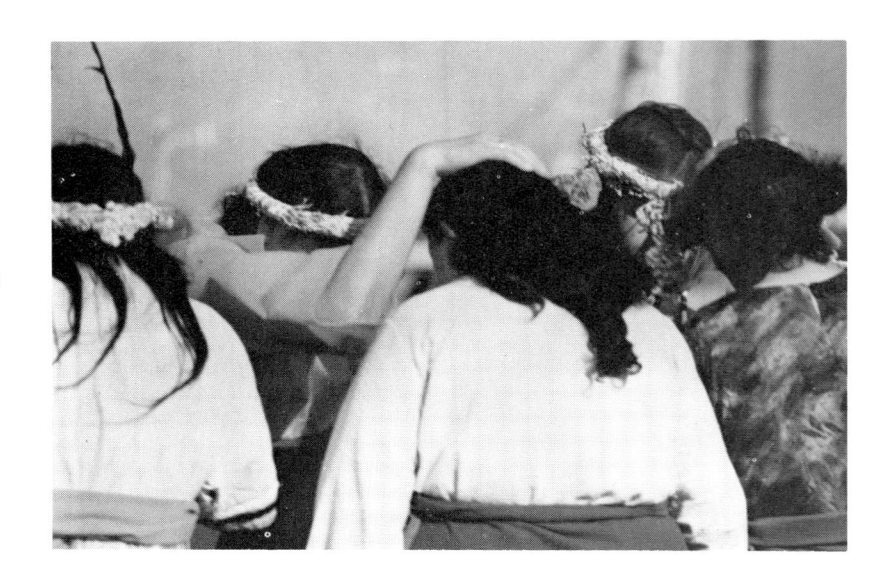

When the Keeper of the Spirit prays, she places her right hand on the person's head,

and with her left hand, holds the spirit bundle against the patient.

As each pledger finished the line, he took his place in a line of pledgers facing the people.

When the pledgers were done in 1975, George Eagle Elk passed down the line of people and blessed them with his eagle wing fan. After him came Eagle Feather,

who placed a small piece of healing roots in each person's mouth.

After the rest period, the dance resumes. This picture shows the full line of pledgers facing the Sacred Tree from the west in 1974.

When the pledgers face the Tree from the west, as soon as the dancing begins the women take positions on the south end of the line. When the line moves to the north the men lead off, and the women follow.

The pledgers facing the Tree from the north. The Altar is in the foreground between the black flags.

At the Intercessor's command, the pledgers raise their arms to the Sacred Tree and seek visions from it.

A back view of the pledgers facing the Tree from the east.

At each direction the pledgers raise their arms, blow on their whistles, pray, and seek visions from the Tree.

Eagle Feather prepares to move the pledgers from one direction to another in 1974.

A typical view of the pledgers as they dance in place and blow their whistles.

While the pledgers are dancing, the Intercessor often interrupts his own dancing to go to the flags to pray.

A view of the Sacred Tree, and Eagle Feather blessing the pledgers in 1975.

Eagle Feather leads Gilbert Yellow Hawk in 1975.

George Eagle Elk leads Reuben Fire Thunder after he has been pierced in 1975.

The women pledgers follow the men as the line moves to the east in 1974.

The pledgers at the south in 1975. One pledger carries a wooden hoop, and another an otterskin wrapped hoop.

A view of the pledgers in 1975 as they invoked the help of the Sun, and sought visions in it.

A view of the pledgers in 1974 as they invoked the help of Grandfather, and sought visions from Him.

Eagle Feather blessing the pledgers in 1975 by touching them on the shoulders with his eagle wing fan.

The pledgers in 1975 as they are turned and led from the west toward the north.

336

A back view of the women pledgers in 1975.

The same women as they raise their hands to pray to and seek visions from the Tree.

Left to right: Orrie Farrell, Lorenzo Hodgekiss, and Jerry Dragg in 1975. Orrie and Jerry wear bright blue skirts, and Lorenzo's skirt is a deep red. Courtesy of Greg Pietz.

Back view of their 1975 costumes. Some fashion shawls into skirts, and ribbons are often used for decoration.

Left to right: Robert Blackfeather, Reuben Fire Thunder, Hazel Schweigman, and Evelyn Staub in 1975.

Another view of the blessing which takes place continually as the pledgers dance. This is infusion of power from Grandfather's messenger, the eagle, to give them the strength needed to complete the dance and the wisdom to see into the future.

Flesh offering ceremonies are held on each of the four days. Here, Eagle Feather contemplates the pain associated with it as he heads toward the Tree to begin the ceremony in 1975. Courtesty of Greg Pietz.

The pledgers who have made vows to give flesh offerings line up at the Tree to do so.

The medicine men take the lead,

then come the male pledgers,

and the female pledgers follow.

The skin is lifted with a sharp stick,

cut off with a razor blade or knife, held up to the directions and prayed for, then wrapped in a piece of cloth and tied on a long string.

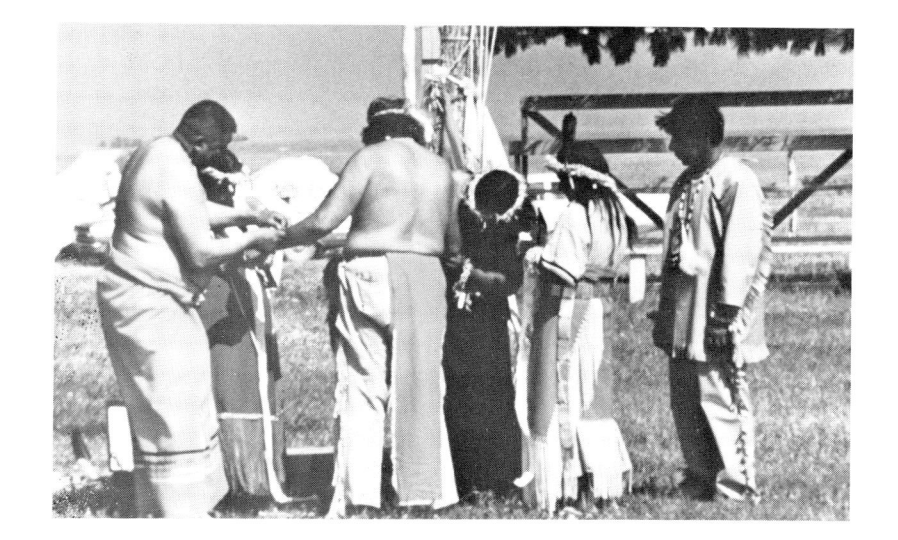

Eagle Feather has had as many as one hundred flesh offerings taken from each arm.

His arms are worked on simultaneously,

and even the other pledgers are amazed at how well he stands the pain.

His offerings are tied on the same string as the others. The string is then wrapped around the Tree, just above where the offering cloths are tied.

Eagle Feather after the flesh offerings in 1975. Most of the blood has been wiped from his arms with sage. Note that the offerings run from his shoulder to his wrist. Courtesy of Greg Pietz.

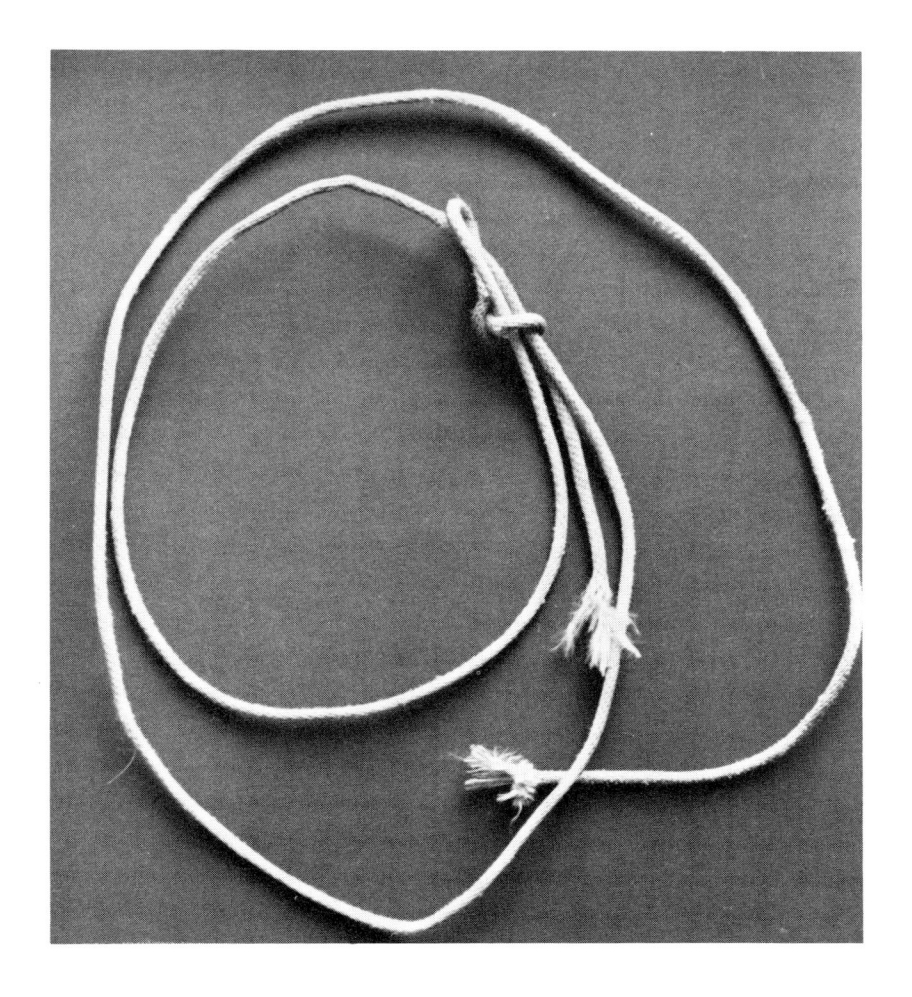

The typical commercial rope used by pledgers who pierce in Sun Dances today. Old timers, such as Eagle Feather, insist on using rawhide thongs cut from a buffalo hide.

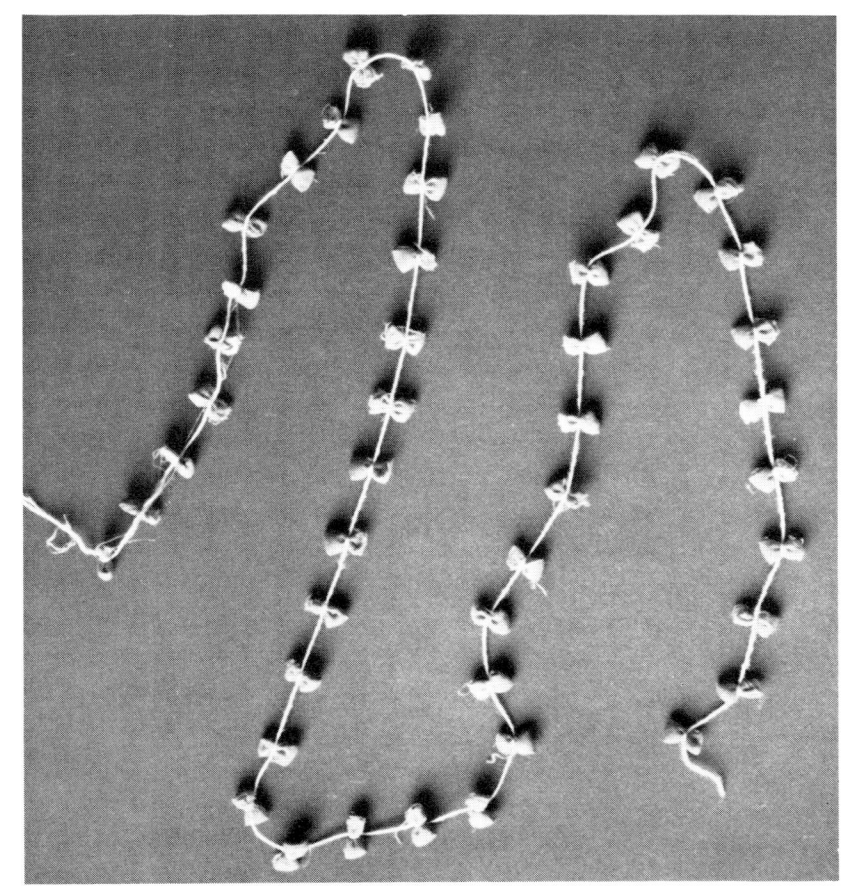

A typical string of flesh offerings. Each piece of flesh is wrapped in a piece of cloth—usually red or white.

Individual piercings may take place on one or more of the first three days of the Sun Dance. Reuben Fire Thunder was pierced on the second day of the dance in 1975.

He lay on his back on the buffalo robe and sage bed at the base of the Sacred Tree while Eagle Feather pierced him on both sides. His head was toward the north.

Evelyn Staub, the Mother of the Year, comforted Reuben as he was pierced, and wiped away the blood with sage and a white cloth.

Then with Reuben still biting on his head wreath to stem the pain, the ropes were attached to the skewers.

Reuben was helped to his feet, and he backed away from the tree together with the other pledgers. Four times they went forward and touched the Tree.

After the fourth time Reuben was blessed by both Eagle Feather and George Eagle Elk.

Then he raised his hands and prayed,

348

and while the spectators watched intently, the pulling back on the rope began.

The piercing was deep, and the flesh did not give way easily.

Finally, with a mighty lunge backwards, he broke free.

Eagle Feather rubbed dirt on the wounds and congratulated him.

The depth of the wounds can be measured by the amount of blood that flows from the wound.

Evelyn Staub wiped the wounds with sage,

and Reuben was led over to the flags at the east to be congratulated by the people.

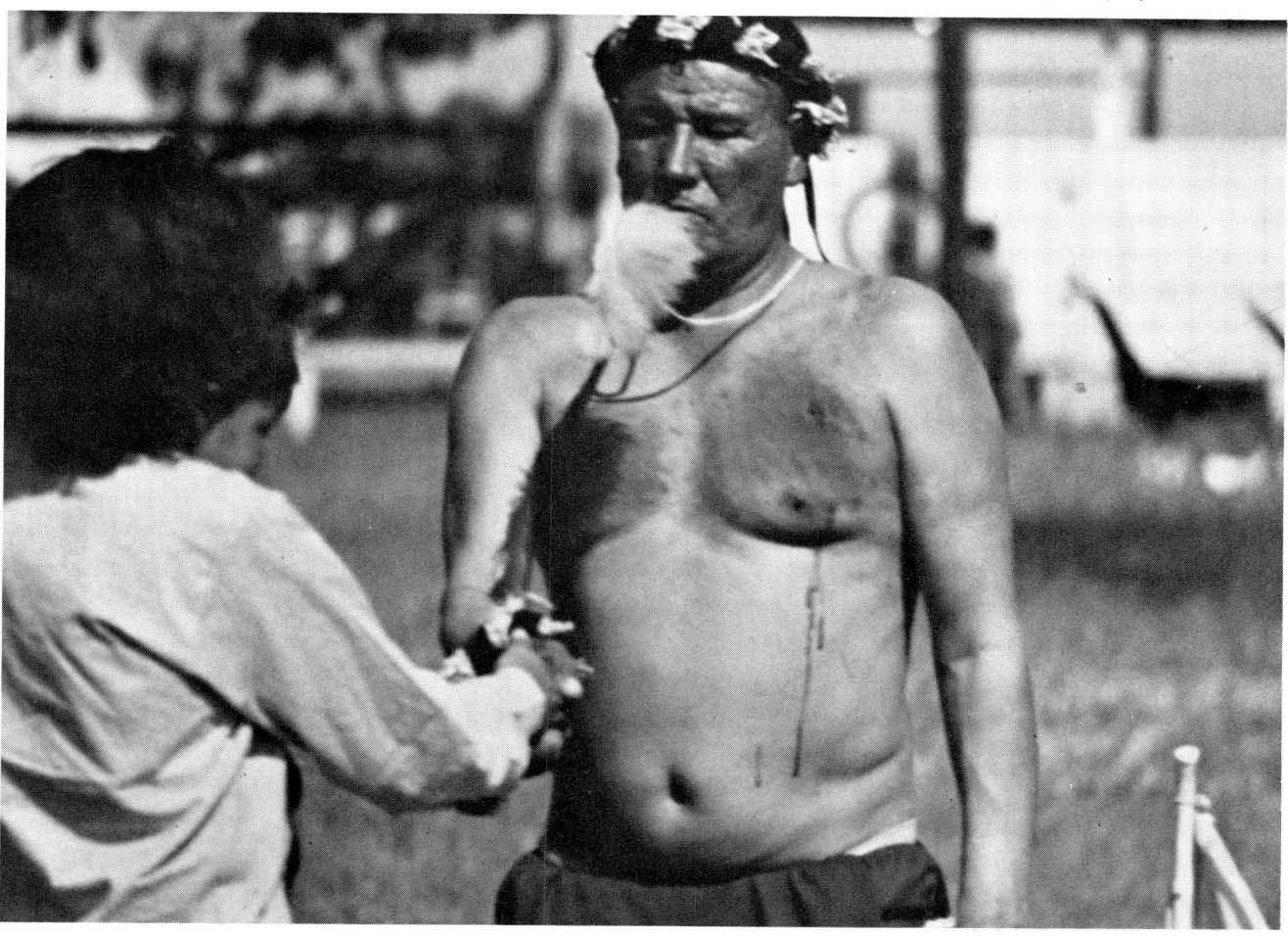

On some of the rounds, the pledgers are divided into four groups. This is a view of the division in 1974.

The division of the pledgers in 1975.

On command from the Intercessor, the divided groups go forward four times and touch the Tree, simultaneously backing away after each touch. This is the touching act in 1975.

The pledgers touching the Tree and drawing power from it in 1974.

Going forward to touch the Tree in 1975.

Touching the Tree in 1975. Each pledger lays one hand on the Tree and holds it there for perhaps thirty seconds.

The actions and moods of the Intercessor are interesting to watch as the Sun Dance progresses. Here he prays at the south with the pipe in 1974.

Other times he turns his palms up in supplication and prays to Grandfather, to the sun, and to the Tree.

His prayers are dramatic, impressive, devout and audible. Sometimes they are given in Sioux, and sometimes in English.

Here Eagle Feather prays to the sun with the pipe.

Now and then he is lost in contemplation, as he considers the progress of the Sun Dance.

Afternoons and evenings the social dancing takes place. The Sioux call them "wacipis," the whites call them "powwows." Contestants dance for prizes, and wear numbers on their arms for identification. The photographs included here are from the Mission, South Dakota, wacipi in 1974.

The modern fancy dancing is vigorous and impressive. The contemporary costumes are beautifully crafted, and exciting to see.

The men wear feather bustles on their backs, and porcupine-quill roaches on their heads. Bell straps are worn on the legs, and angora wool leggings extend from calf to ankle.

Traditional dances and costumes are gaining in popularity today. The dance steps are more measured and the costumes more simple than those of the fancy dancer shown here.

The singers for the social dances. There are usually several different groups who take turns accompanying the dancers.

Every part of the costume has a special meaning: the bustle is made of eagle, hawk, and owl feathers, and represents the cycles and unity of everything—its spikes symbolize vertical channels between the dancer and Grandfather.

The children join in the dancing, and parents take great pleasure in fashioning little costumes which are exactly like those of the adults.

The women dance in an inner circle, and the men form a larger circle around them, "to protect the women as men have always done in Sioux society."

The roach worn on the head is a carry-over from the old soldier societies. The two eagle feathers of the roach represent two men returning from a hunt. As they spin, the men are telling each other about their exploits.

This dancer is Charles Ross, a student of traditional Sioux ways, who at this time was superintendent of schools at the Lower Brule Reservation.

On July 14, 1974, the assembled Sioux at the wacipi at Mission, South Dakota, did me the great honor of asking me to lead, together with Ellis Head, the grand opening parade. At this time I was given an honor song and the name WA-O-KI-YE, which means "One who helps."

The social dancing goes on well into the night, and the crowd of spectators grows steadily, sometimes numbering several thousand.

Several hundred dancers will participate, but this one at Mission ended early on the night of the third day of the Sun Dance because of tornado warnings. Clouds did cover the sky, and the wind blew. . . .

but the sky was clear the next morning, and preparations for the final day of the Sun Dance got underway with the stretching and uncoiling of the pledgers' ropes.

When the time came for the piercing, the rope of each pledger was stretched out to its full length and attached to a wooden stake. Here, George Eagle Elk marks his with a white breath feather.

The Intercessor decided where each pledger would stand to begin the dance after he was pierced.

He stretched out the ropes to their full length.

Then Titus and another young man pulled them absolutely taut and staked them down.

Each rope was marked by its owner. This one had an eagle tail feather attached.

Eagle Feather supervised everything, including the staking down of the ropes.

When all of the ropes were ready in 1974, the pledgers formed a line facing the west.

Then they turned toward the Tree, and the piercing began.

The medicine men assisting Eagle Feather with the Sun Dance were pierced first. Here, Eagle Feather leads three of them toward the Sacred Tree.

Before the piercing, the medicine men, Eagle Feather and Titus went forward and touched the Tree.

They backed away, and with a shout from Eagle Feather went forward four times.

George Eagle Elk was the first medicine man to be pierced. Eagle Feather took his wristband and led him toward the Tree.

First he laid his hands on the Tree and prayed fervently.

After this he lay down on the buffalo robe with his head toward the north. He bit down hard on a bunch of sage, and Gilbert Yellow Hawk rubbed his chest to numb it.

Then the parallel slits were cut on his right side,

and while Eagle Feather made certain it was done correctly, the wooden skewer stick was inserted.

After this, the skewer stick was placed in George Eagle Elk's right side, and the rope was attached.

372

Then he was helped to his feet,

and led by Eagle Feather and Titus around the Tree and to his place.

George Eagle Elk was eighty years old, and the skin of his chest stretched out six inches or more as he began to pull back.

He alternately pulled back and rested, but the sticks held fast.

As time went on, the spectators grew anxious and restless.

A concerned Eagle Feather came out to encourage and comfort him.

Finally, he spun away from the Tree and broke loose.

Eagle Feather put his arm around him, and together with Titus congratulated him and comforted him.

The next man to be pierced in 1974 was another old timer named Albert Stands. He too danced forward to the Tree and back four times.

Then he was pierced by Yellow Hawk and raised to his feet.

After going forward to touch the Tree four times with Eagle Feather, Yellow Hawk and Titus, he pulled back on the rope until he broke free.

Gilbert Yellow Hawk was the last of the three medicine men to be pierced. Eagle Feather did the piercing as Titus watched.

When the rope was attached, Yellow Hawk was helped to his feet and led to his pulling place by Eagle Feather and Titus, who also kept the rope from tangling.

After he pulled free, Eagle Feather brushed and blessed him with his eagle feather fan.

When the medicine men were done, the rest of the male pledgers prepared to pierce.

First they went forward and back four times to touch the Tree.

Then each pledger went to his place,

and was pierced by Eagle Feather in turn.

When all were pierced and the ropes were attached, the men stood in their places,

then went forward again four times to touch the Tree and pray.

When this was done, they all began to pull on their ropes.

One by one they pulled free, some in an instant, others taking a few minutes.

Finally, only one, Robert Blackfeather, was still attached. He was pierced much deeper than the rest.

While the other pledgers reached for the heavens and prayed for him, Robert pulled steadily back on the rope.

Soon, everyone was pulling mentally with him, and some in the audience gasped as he struggled to get free.

Finally the flesh gave way, and he was congratulated and comforted by Eagle Feather. No one applauded. The great moment was greeted by respectful silence.

In 1975, the Mother of the Year sat by the pledgers to comfort them. She wiped their brow with a cloth, and their blood away with sage.

Some of the men bit down on their pipes as they were pierced, and others bit down on loose sage or their sage head wreaths.

The distribution of some of the pledgers on the fourth day in 1975.

Relatives and friends were asked to come forward and stand by the pledgers as they pulled back in 1975.

Jerry Dragg was pierced very deeply in 1975, as was Orrie Farrell. Both had a difficult time tearing loose from the rope. Courtesy of Greg Pietz.

Here the stretched skin stands out plainly as Jerry pulls back. Courtesy of Greg Pietz.

At last he lunges backward, the skin tears, and he is free. The wounds are large and deep.

In 1975, Robert Blackfeather underwent an unusual piercing. His eagle claws were attached at a mid-point on his rope as he stood on Gilbert Yellow Hawk's back.

Two ropes were arranged to make a path, and his relatives were asked to come forward to encourage and comfort him.

When the eagle claws were tested and found to be secure,

everyone stepped back, Gilbert Yellow Hawk moved swiftly from underneath him, and Robert dropped like a heavy weight, and hung swinging back and forth like a huge pendulum.

The audience gasped as he swung. Nothing like it had been seen, in public at least, at Rosebud for a century. The rope did not tear loose, so they lowered him to the ground and cut him free.

Evelyn Staub wiped his wounds with a cloth.

Robert was then helped to his feet and led around the Mystery Circle by Lame Deer and Eagle Feather. It was a great piercing and a great sacrifice for the people.

The wounds of Orrie Farrell after his piercing in 1975. Courtesy of Greg Pietz.

The Sun Dance concludes with pledgers and spectators assembling at the west side of the Mystery Circle,

and then proceeding in four equal moves across the Mystery Circle to the east. When they arrive there, everyone shakes hands, and the Sun Dance is over.